# Literary Texts and the Historian

Our knowledge of Greek history rests largely on literary texts – not merely historians (especially Herodotus, Thucydides and Xenophon), but also tragedies, comedies, speeches, biographies and philosophical works. These texts are among the most skilled and highly wrought productions of a brilliant rhetorical culture. How is the historian to use them?

This book takes a series of extended test-cases, and discusses how we should and should not try to exploit the texts. In some instances, we can investigate 'what really happened', and the ways in which the texts manipulate, remould, or colour it according to their own rhetorical strategies. In others, the most illuminating aspect may be those strategies themselves, and what they tell us about the culture – how it figured questions of sex and gender, politics, citizenship and the city, the law and the courts, how wars happen. *Literary Texts and the Greek Historian* concentrates on Athens in the second half of the fifth century, when many of the principal genres came together, but it includes some examples from earlier (Aeschylus' *Oresteia*) and later periods (including Aristotle's *Politics*).

*Literary Texts and the Greek Historian* examines possible responses to these texts and suggests new ways in which literary criticism can illuminate the society from which these texts sprang.

**Christopher Pelling** is Fellow in Classics at University College, Oxford. He has written extensively on Greek biography and historiography and edited *Greek Tragedy and the Historian* (1997).

# Approaching the Ancient World

Series editor: Richard Stoneman

The sources for the study of the Greek and Roman world are diffuse, diverse, and often complex, and special training is needed in order to use them to the best advantage in constructing a historical picture.

The books in this series provide an introduction to the problems and methods involved in the study of ancient history. The topics covered will range from the use of literary sources for Greek history and for Roman history, through numismatics, epigraphy, and dirt archaeology, to the use of legal evidence and of art and artefacts in chronology. There will also be books on statistical and comparative method, and on feminist approaches.

# Literary Texts and the Greek Historian

Christopher Pelling

London and New York

First published 2000
by Routledge
11 New Fetter Lane, London EC4P 4EE

Simultaneously published in the USA and Canada
by Routledge
29 West 35th Street, New York, NY 10001

*Routledge is an imprint of the Taylor & Francis Group*

Typeset in Baskerville by
Prepress Projects, Perth, Scotland
Printed and bound in Great Britain by
TJ International Ltd, Padstow, Cornwall

*British Library Cataloguing in Publication Data*
A catalogue record for this book is available
from the British Library

*Library of Congress Cataloging in Publication Data*
Pelling, C. B. R.
    Literary texts and the Greek historian / Christopher Pelling.
    p.   cm. –
    Includes bibliographical references and index.
    1. Greek literature–History and criticism. 2. Literature and
history–Greece–History. 3. History, Ancient–Historiography. 4.
Historiography–Greece–History. 5. Greece–Historiography.
    I. Title.
    PA3009.P45   1999
    880.9'0109358–dc21    99-33324
    CIP

ISBN 0415–07350–2 (hbk)
ISBN 0415–07351–0 (pbk)

# Contents

# Preface

Funding bodies used to be more relaxed, and when I became a graduate student I was admitted to research on 'Greek literature and/or Roman history'. That capacious definition more or less captures how I have spent my academic time ever since. The institutional divisions of my university mean that most of my teaching is in 'literature', mainly Greek. My first research work was on Plutarch's Roman *Lives*, 'Greek literature and/or Roman history' *par excellence*; the editors of volume 10 of the *Cambridge Ancient History* allowed me to try my hand at writing history myself (an experience no-one who presumes to write on narrative should lack) – Roman history, once again. Until now, Greek history has been an interest, certainly, but not something on which I have troubled the world. That has had advantages and disadvantages for this book. I have felt few temptations to digress and impart large views on how Greek history worked; and the book's strategy of starting from literary texts and working out towards what really happened is one which came naturally. On the other hand, I address large areas of which, until recently, I was fairly innocent; nor have I had the benefit of the continual rethinking and stimulus that comes with years of talking with able and interested students. I have done my best, and friends have helped to save me from the worst consequences of my inexperience. But this does remain an outsider's book, for good, or ill, or both.

Quite evidently, this is a vast subject. Two principles have been cardinal. First, I have narrowed the focus drastically. A fairer title would be 'Some literary texts and the historian of late fifth-century Athens'. I have chosen that focus because so many of the literary genres then come together and illuminate one another. I allow myself the odd foray backwards, to *Eumenides* of 458 BC, and forwards, to

*Against Neaera* and Aristotle's *Politics*; but only the odd one. Naturally, this has its downside. It means that Athenocentricity, the curse of Greek history, is embedded in the whole project; but then a work starting from literature was always going to suffer from that. It has also meant leaving out whole genres which I should have liked to include: epic; choral lyric; the Hippocratic corpus, not much of which is identifiably Athenian; the novel. It has also meant leaving out Herodotus, or almost. But something had to go, and I hope the sharpening of focus will compensate.

Secondly, even within that field I have been highly selective. I have normally preferred to take quite extended examples and discuss the methodological issues, rather than covering more ground more cursorily. I have often quoted passages at length: all translations are my own. This sampling approach has allowed me to address some quite detailed questions of historical truth.

Truth: there it is, the T-word, so often shied from that it seems desperately unsophisticated to mention it. But some things really happened back then, some ways of describing them are better than others, and we can do something to find out which. The jurors who listened to speeches were there to judge, not whose performance was the most glittering, but what really happened and whose fault it was. They had to try to get behind the rhetoric, and so do we. The choice between rival versions need not be simply a matter of aesthetic taste; it is not like deciding which would have been the better ending to *Casablanca*. There are methods we can apply to sources, not unlike those we apply in real life to try to detect the truth about things we care about. By all means let us play with the joys of textual openness and revel in multiple readings and perspectives; if we are careful, we can find those historically illuminating too, in their own way. But those who died at Salamis or Syracuse were not killed by a text, and we owe it to them to try to find out what happened.

The selection of passages and themes will not satisfy everyone. Certainly, it does not satisfy me. The chapter on gender is long, but could easily have been longer. It would have been good to talk about the conceptualisation of slaves, too, of barbarians, of other Greeks, of age, of town and country, of leisure, of learning, and particularly of gods: the list is endless. The strategy of beginning from texts has frequently meant accepting something of those texts' agenda: true, the Thucydidean chapters make some attempt to move the debate towards questions of conceptualisation – but it is still about war and politics, and a lot is about men. There is not much 'reading against the grain' to put our own questions to distant material. Perhaps there should have been; but even cross-grained reading needs to take account of the rhetorical strategies and manipulations of the text, and we identify these better if we start from sharing the author's own concerns. If we fail to make even a provisional attempt to engage with even an alien viewpoint, we will most certainly go wrong. And this is only meant to be a start.

It would have been possible, too, to frame the book more theoretically: possible for another writer, even in some ways possible for this one. I hope it does not require an excess of goodwill to see that contemporary theoretical work on (particularly) performance, narratology, reader-response, reception, and New Historicism has had some impact, though experts will rightly feel that the impact could have been greater; so will feminist writers on gender. If I have not started from theory, that is not because I believe any criticism to be theory-free, and certainly not because I regard the texts as speaking for themselves if only one applies good honest critical common sense. The reason is again one of space, and awareness of my limitations. Doubtless the book can be criticised for insinuating a particular set of reading strategies, and especially a questionable stance on contentious issues of reader-response. (*Can* real readers be inferred from implied readers in the ways I here explore? I think so, though there are often difficulties in practice – but I have not argued it here, except in so far as a series of worked examples can itself be a contribution to theory.) Anyway, I have preferred that Scylla of reticence to the Charybdis of passing off criticism as more sophisticated, and more driven by a particular theory, than it really is.

Versions of Chapters 3, 7–8, and 9 were delivered in Reading, Schenectady, Chapel Hill, Oxford, Bergen, and Lund: my thanks to all those audiences for valuable and sympathetic discussion. Many friends have been most helpful. Richard Rutherford, Christiane Sourvinou-Inwood, Lynette Mitchell, and Judith Mossman have read nearly everything, and been generous with comments and suggestions which I have silently appropriated. Particular chapters have been read and improved by Philip Stadter, Michael Flower, George Cawkwell, Kevin Crotty, and Tim Rood. Remarks made in seminars, tutorials, cars, bars, and over the electronic ether have been borrowed from Don Fowler, Edith Hall, Miranda Bevan, David Mumford, and Carolyn Dewald. Conversation with Francesca Albini, Rhiannon Ash, Franco Basso, Chris Burnand, Katherine Clarke, Michael Comber,

Tim Duff, David Gribble, Jasper Griffin, Simon Hornblower, Lisa Kallet, Chris Kraus, John Moles, Teresa Morgan, Robin Osborne, Robert Parker, Fran Titchener, Tony Woodman, and years ago Colin Macleod has left marks, often on areas distant from the ones they thought we were talking about. I was fortunate too in my teachers of Greek history: first my headmaster Clifford Diamond, a cultured historian who liked to teach immediately after lunch, when he would orate with inspiring brio and generous imagination; then Russell Meiggs taught me in his last year as a tutorial fellow and Oswyn Murray in his first. All three were examples to an impressionable youngster of how exciting the subject could be made.

The greatest debt is the usual one: to Margaret, to Sally (who gave invaluable help with the beginning of Chapter 7), and to Charlie.

Christopher Pelling
Oxford, April 1999

# Chapter 1

# A culture of rhetoric

## Audiences and genres

A statement in a literary text tells us what could be said, and what it
made sense to say, to a particular audience and in a particular context,
setting, and genre. It may or may not be true, or have some relation
to the truth; we do what we can to discover how true it is. But true,
false, or something in between, it is *always* a piece of rhetoric.

For 'rhetoric' is not limited to 'oratory', the literary genre of
speech-making. Rhetoric is the craft of persuasion. Often an author
tries to persuade the audience of a fact or facts – 'persuasion *that*'
something is or was the case. One instance is narrative, where an
author selects and presents material in such a way as to persuade
the audience that these were the facts, that they happened like this
and in this sequence, and that this is the right way of looking at
them: that Corcyra and Potidaea, in that order and with those details,
were the important antecedents of the Peloponnesian War; that they
are best viewed in a context of bad feeling between mother-city and
colony, international suspicion between the major powers, fear of
being outmanoeuvred unless pre-emptive steps are taken, and so
on. But such 'persuasion *that*' is already blurring into 'persuasion *to*'
feel something: to adopt a particular attitude to a state of affairs.
Oratory, and often historiography too, regularly inspires a range of
such responses: they may include something as simple as approval
or disapproval of an individual or a city, or perhaps a more complex
mode of empathy, admiration, shock, despair, or perplexity. And such
persuasion can also generate persuasion not just to feel, but also to
act. If I am persuaded that Athens is admirable, I may also be
persuaded to go out and fight and die for that inspirational ideal.

Drama, it is clear, is also 'rhetorical' in this sense, not merely in
the rhetoric with which figures within the plays address and influence

one another, but also in the wider impact which a play has on its audience, stimulating feelings and reflection in particular directions. Any attempt to disentangle the intellectual and the emotional elements in such a response is likely to fail: persuasion *that* something is true – possibly that Pericles brought on the war, possibly that the Athenians had little choice; possibly that Jason swore oaths to Medea, possibly that Medea is terrifyingly non-human – inspires persuasion *to* feel about the issue in a certain way; just as important, different emotional responses generate alertness to different facts – if I loathe a particular politician or dramatic character, I will be quick to notice and remember his or her mistakes.

So rhetoric spans the genres; speeches, histories, tragedies, comedies – all seek to affect their audience in particular ways, and to affect them through *performance*: these texts are scripts. This is very much an oral culture. However literate a popular audience may have been, written material still excited suspicion, and the spoken word was the natural, open way of conducting much of one's life.[1] Even historians will probably have had oral performance in mind as at least their primary mode of communication: they would very likely give readings themselves to a contemporary audience, and they might expect even posterity to hear their texts more often than read them silently.[2] It takes at least two to make a performance, a speaker and an audience, and performance is duly a two-way thing. That is true in several senses. First, audiences have ways of providing feedback. Speeches might be heckled or catcalled, and it is not clear that drama was treated with any more respect;[3] and anyway any actor or playwright knows when even a restrained audience's attention has been lost. Secondly, audiences as well as speakers bring something to the activity. Persuasion does not work in a vacuum: it works on an audience with certain knowledge, assumptions, and values, and interacts with these to produce a particular response. Much of our task as historians is to proceed from the literary text and infer what we can about the other ingredients in that performance, the presumptions which the author must have been making about the audience and the ways in which he must have hoped his persuasion would work.

Here, though, the differences among genres are as important as the similarities. Authors and audiences were peculiarly sensitive to genre. We shall even find substantial differences in audience expectation between tragedy and comedy, even though the plays were performed in the same festival to the same audience. We shall see, for instance, how in comedy references to political life were more specific and topical, whereas tragedy was 'political' in a more timeless, reflective sense (Chapters 7–10). Such generic expectations evidently affect the way a text illuminates its society and its time. We might well wish to tie a comedy like *Knights* closely to its immediate political setting, stressing for instance the bellicose optimism after Athens' success at Pylos;[1] if we find themes of contemporary relevance in Euripides' *Andromache* (faithless Spartans) or *Trojan Women* (the sufferings of war) or *Suppliant Women* or *Orestes* (the strengths and frailties of democracy), we shall be more inclined to see these as a response to the underlying facts of wartime life, and not search for any immediate stimulus in specific recent events.

Generic expectation can go very deep. Let us take two examples – vast examples, which can only be introduced here in a simplified way – where we see a gulf between the expectations of oratory and those of drama, especially tragedy. First, the gods. Parker (1997) has stressed the fundamental difference between the gods of tragedy and those of oratory, gods 'cruel' and 'kind'. In Attic oratory, speakers are obliged to count on the support of the gods through thick and thin: these gods will not allow their favourite state to be destroyed. We seem to be moving in a different world from tragedy, with those dark, unfathomable divine creatures whose goodwill is so precarious.

Secondly, the city itself and its democratic ideology. Much of the best recent work on Athenian ideology has begun from oratory, especially the books of Ober (1989) and Loraux (1986a); Loraux in particular brilliantly explores the Athenian *Epitaphioi*, the Funeral Speeches delivered in celebration of the war-dead. Such speeches say relatively little about the dead themselves; they praise Athens and its democracy, and everything is covered in a patriotic gleam which makes the suffering and death seem worthwhile. Tragedy is different. There too suffering is sometimes worthwhile; 'learning through suffering' is one watchword of the *Oresteia* (*Agam.* 177), which itself ends with an optimistic vision of Athens (Chapter 9). But the application of this watchword to the trilogy itself is anything but straightforward, and tragedy after tragedy leaves us dissatisfied with simple answers about war and death. Democracy too is sometimes idealised in tragedy, but often not; we shall find several plays where speakers say harsh words, and seem justified, about demagogues and the ease with which they take in an assembly (Chapter 9).

Comedy presents a different picture again; demagogues can be savaged, but there is a certain affection for old Demos itself, the

People, put upon and exploited rather than incurably feckless. There is no real idealisation of democratic free speech, and there is much emphasis on Athenian mistakes – but still a more oratory-like confidence that, whatever Athens may do wrong, it will all come out right in the end: 'For they say that blundering is the mark of this city, but the gods take your mistakes and make them turn out all right' (*Clouds* 587–9).

Faced with such conflicting views, we should not be so crude as to ask 'which did they *really* think?', or 'which is real life, and which is artistic licence?' Collective views are not so simple: 'they' thought *all* these things, in different contexts and at different times, despite any apparent incompatibility. That is partly because different individuals must have thought in different ways, but even the same individuals regularly think and feel in ways which resist simple formulation. After all, these are complicated issues. If we ask ourselves 'what we really think about democracy', we would find it hard to say whether we think it is all a sham and that politicians are all sleazebags, or that it is still the only system we would feel comfortable with and that its deficiencies are only skin-deep. Probably we think both, and it depends on who we are talking to, or on the stage the evening has reached.

If we think of other examples – how we construct gender, for instance – we again say and think different things at different times. We have all heard apparently civilised men, and maybe even some apparently civilised women, crack jokes at the expense of the other sex, or laugh uproariously at comedies which do the same; and we have learned to be suspicious of the familiar claim that somehow those remarks don't count, that it's just good fun and why can't these people take a joke. It is not that such humour falsifies what we 'really' think about gender; it is one aspect, but the same people would respond differently if they were talking in or listening to a late-night intellectual thought programme. If the Athenian male audience constructed females differently in the tragic theatre (disconcertingly rational despite their marginalised status, mistresses of words, threatening), the comic theatre (drunken, randy, rational but only intermittently), and the law-courts (sweet, homeloving put-upon things or appalling harridans), such variation may not be very different (Chapter 10). All this is what 'they' would think, even if they would not think it all at once.

So differences among texts and genres are not an irritation, something one has to penetrate to get at the real-life views and assumptions underneath. These *are* the real-life views and assumptions; this is what there is; this is how audiences would think, or could be brought to think, in particular settings. The more they were brought to think in those ways, the more those original generic expectations would be reinforced. And every one of those settings – law-court, assembly, tragic theatre, comic theatre, historiographic reading – is part of real life.

## Rhetorical narrative

This broad sense of 'rhetorical' is valuable, reminding us of the features which all forms of verbal persuasion share. But it is understandable that 'rhetoric' should often be used in a narrower sense, limited to the literary genre of oratory: for oratory is rhetoric in its clearest form, in a sense its defining form. That is particularly true of this culture, for the more formal styles of speech were central to the Athenians' view of their own civic identity. Xenophon's Ischomachus (admittedly a caricature; see pp. 236–45) prepares for legal battles by rehearsing and role-playing the different oratorical genres, forensic, epideictic, and symbouleutic, with the help of his wife, slaves, and friends (*Oec.* 11.23–5); Aristophanes' Strepsiades, when shown a world-map, cannot believe that what he sees is Athens because he cannot see any law-courts (*Clouds* 207–9, cf. *Peace* 505 as well as *Wasps*); Thucydides' Cleon derides his audience for being 'spectators of the sophists', carried away by the flashiness of the display and ignoring the substance of the issues, all the while providing a flamboyant example of precisely the rhetorical virtuosity which he is warning against (Thuc. 3.37). Thucydides' Athenian readers would find that a thought-provoking but familiar image of themselves, both as connoisseurs of oratory and as uneasily aware of its delusive power. To speak to Athenians was to communicate with an experienced and knowing audience, one which knew the rules of the listening game: or at least one which liked to think of itself as such, and it is the essence of rhetoric to accommodate one's argument to an audience's psychology and perception of themselves. This is indeed a culture of rhetoric.

This rhetorical culture has plusses and minuses for the historian. The plus comes when we wish to use literary texts as a way into collective perceptions and attitudes, in the ways we have already grazed. It is then a positive advantage that Athenian authors, especially the orators, are so skilled at gearing their work to what the audience will want to hear. We can presume that their arguments and strategies were unlikely, or less likely than any alternatives, to alienate audience sympathies; or at least we can presume that *they* presumed this, and they knew their audience better than we do. This is a theme to which we shall return in the final section of this chapter, and throughout the book.

The minus comes when we try to disentangle the history of events, what really happened. In such cases we are often dependent on narrative sources, typically in historiography but sometimes in oratory and even in drama (though the narrative there is filtered in particularly complex ways, as we shall see with Aristophanes' *Acharnians* in Chapter 8). The art of narrative is a basic skill for a speaker: that is recognised in contemporary legal theory, where the subtlety with which lawyers frame their story-telling has become a hot scholarly topic.[5] It is noticeable, for instance, how juries are readier to believe stories which fit patterns familiar from fiction, normally these days from *LA Law*-type television.[6] That is worth remembering when we consider intertextual issues in narrative. If Thucydides presents his Sicilian narrative in ways which are reminiscent of Herodotus – a climactic sea-battle, where confined space enables a David to see off a Goliath; a military engagement which settles a war, even though there is a book or more to come – that may suggest a cyclic quality of history, an idea very important to Thucydides;[7] but it also makes Thucydides' narrative more persuasive to a receptive, knowledgeable audience. All this happened before, classically and paradigmatically: that makes it the more convincing, as well as thought-provoking, that it should be happening again now.

In real speech-narratives, ancient and modern, we also see how adeptly orators bend events to leave a particular impression of the characters involved, how they gloss over embarrassing details, how they distract attention from the weaker parts of their case and emphasise those where they come out best. When Athenian tragedy explores rhetoric itself – and it does, just as tragedy explores most features which are basic to Athenian identity – it is striking how often speakers, especially disingenuous ones, are given narratives.[8] If you are going to be convincing, you need a story to tell. In Sophocles' *Electra* Orestes' tutor wins credibility with his elaborate narrative of Orestes' death in a chariot race; the narrative also affects the listening Clytemnestra in the way he wants, as she hears of the death of the son she has never known, a death of which she could be proud.

In Euripides' *Trojan Women* Helen and Hecuba, with great rhetorical verve, give incompatible accounts of how Helen behaved, whether it was her fault, whether she tried to escape or not; just as nearly a century later Demosthenes and Aeschines give very different versions of what happened on an embassy which they shared. In each case we are left not knowing which of two internally consistent but incompatible pictures to believe.

In tragedy we can leave that as part of the play's point, one way in which its exploration of rhetoric works. (And in the *Trojan Women* part of that point is that it does not matter even to the audience within the play, Menelaus and the Trojan women: right or wrong, and whatever Menelaus decides, Helen will live on.) With real life it matters differently: if we take history seriously, it is our job to get as close as possible to the 'facts' which the orator has been at such pains to mould. Of course we should not work with a picture of innocent, clear-as-day facts which exist independently of any such moulding. No fact is wholly interpretation-free. To claim that 'the Athenians killed Socrates' is to select that fact, from all the other things that happened on that day in 399 BC, and claim that this is one which mattered; and one could discuss whether 'killed' puts things too starkly, and so on. Put two facts together – 'Socrates was teacher of Critias and Alcibiades, and the Athenians put him to death', or 'Socrates asked awkward questions, and the Athenians put him to death' – and we have an embryonic narrative, one which carries an implicit interpretation. Still, that does not mean that every fact or every sequence is as interpretation-laden as every other; 'did the Athenians put Socrates to death?' can be given a much more yes-or-no, less hedged-around answer than 'was Athenian society based on slave-labour?' or 'was Pericles' power autocratic?'; 'Socrates drank hemlock and died' is much less tendentious in its causal implications than 'the Athenians recalled Alcibiades and lost catastrophically in Sicily'. For it is a dereliction of historical duty to assume that every version is as true and every interpretation is as good as any other. In this book we shall look at several oratorical narratives, especially that of Andocides' *On the Mysteries* in the next chapter, and see how far we can get at the 'facts', which methods work and which do not. An alertness to the speaker's rhetorical subtleties is here indispensable, as it helps to guide our suspicions of the version he gives. These are cases where we do try to penetrate the rhetoric, and to get at a reality which it may conceal or distort.

What about Herodotus, Thucydides, and Xenophon, with their

similar skill at narrative manipulation? Historians cast their narratives 'rhetorically', in both the broader and the narrower sense of the term. In the broader sense, they wished to persuade their audiences of the interest of their material and the validity of their emphases. They also learnt from oratory, or at least found oratory reinforcing lessons they had anyway learnt from the epic; and these lessons included the capacity to impose order on the recalcitrant messiness of facts, and to tell their story in such a way as to suggest particular interpretations or questions. So of course their narrative was rhetorical; it could not be anything else. It would indeed have been disrespectful to the past *not* to tell it with all the rhetorical skill they could muster.

We can usually tell a forensic or political orator's agenda. It is to get off, or to make sure his opponent does not get off; to praise or to blame; or to persuade the public to adopt a particular course of action. The identification of strategies which serve that agenda is often not too difficult. Can we talk of a historian's agenda, and investigate a historian's rhetorical strategies, in anything like the same way?

Yes and no. No, in the sense that the agenda of a Herodotus, a Thucydides, or a Xenophon are a good deal less crude. This genre is as sophisticated as the epic from which it sprang; when scholars suggest that a historian is simply aiming to present Themistocles or Pericles in a good or bad light, we should feel as suspicious as if they had said the *Iliad* was simply pro- or anti-Achilles, or the *Odyssey* pro- or anti-Odysseus. But yes, in the sense that the rhetorical skill of moulding narrative is still basic to whatever the historians *do* want to do. Greek historiography is fundamentally a narrative genre. If a modern historian has big ideas about the period – the strengths and weaknesses of Athenian democracy, the reasons for Athenian expansionism or Spartan victory – he or she will tell you, will intersperse the story-telling with passages of analysis. Greek historians do not do that, or only do it in such rare exceptions as Thucydides 2.65 on the death of Pericles or 3.82–3 on faction in wartime. Greek historians prefer to allow their big ideas to emerge *through* the narrative, to allow readers to infer the leading themes through recurrent patterning, selective emphasis, suggestive juxtaposition, and sometimes through the speeches of the characters themselves. 'Show, not Tell': that is the historian's craft.

The real presentational parallel is the modern novel, and it is unsurprising that modern narratological techniques, forged for analysing novelistic fiction, are proving so fruitful when applied to ancient historiographic texts. Novelists too have their big ideas about the ways humans interact, about the natures of the societies or circles they are describing, even about the cosmos as a whole; but, unless they happen to be Tolstoy, they do not usually stop and tell you about them. The reader is left to do some of the work, and to read things from and through the narrative. Of course, the novel parallel must not be pushed too far. We should certainly not take the further step and assume that the historian felt the same creative freedoms as the novelist to make it all up. The freedoms they took are something we need to investigate, and not beg the question by prejudging either that they wrote like contributors to the *Cambridge Ancient History* or that they wrote like Patrick O'Brian or Gore Vidal. But, whatever those freedoms, the historians can still be using their presentational subtleties to bring readers to a closer understanding of their themes. They orchestrated the narrative in such a way as to direct the receptive reader to put the best questions to the past and render it intelligible. Rhetorical narrative is a tool of *interpretation*.

So when we read Herodotus or Thucydides, we should be alert to the techniques which encourage us to read events in a certain way: not to discount them, for it matters that they saw events in a particular way, and it matters that they felt they could bring an audience, contemporary and/or future, to see them that way too; that has significance in its own right, and may enshrine behavioural assumptions which we will find most illuminating. But we may still choose to juggle the material in a different way and find our own patterns. It would be most odd if we did not.

## Attitude and occasion

Let us return to the plus, the way rhetorically skilful texts allow insight into the mentality of their audiences. There is nothing new in this procedure. Here too we can learn from Herodotus and Thucydides, who both knew very well how rhetoric can illuminate culture. Consider again Cleon's speech in Thucydides' Mytilenean debate (3.37–40), employing dazzling rhetoric to chide its audience for their taste for rhetorical dazzle. In his obituary of Pericles Thucydides had talked of those post-Periclean leaders who went on to play to the popular gallery, 'to allow affairs to be conducted according to the people's pleasure' (2.65.10). And yet Cleon is here telling the people off, not flattering them – or not flattering them *directly*. Still, is this reprimand not itself something that they like to hear, the facade of a strong leader who is not afraid to talk rough? So there is a wider sense, too, in which Cleon's rhetoric is playing to precisely the characteristic, that Athenian susceptibility to the skilful charmer, which he is purporting to criticise. That suggests a further comparison with Thucydides' Pericles, who had known how to chide the people authentically: 'his prestige had allowed him to answer them back with anger' (2.65.8). This is now Cleon's version of Pericles' leadership, yet surely a diminished version, one which spurs the people to indulge their immediate emotion rather than reflect calmly on the issues. Echoes of Pericles elsewhere in the speech[9] encourage the audience to reflect more on these differences in leadership style. 'The quarrel between Diodotos and Kleon is as much about how to conduct debate in the ekklesia as about the fate of Mytilene';[10] and it is the style of the debate which is so revealing, with its raucous insults and accusations, its concentration on self-interest rather than compassion, and even the strain it puts on language itself.[11]

Similarly, Herodotus had known how rhetoric can illuminate the style of the Persian court, or for that matter the more rumbustious manners of the freedom-loving Greeks. When Xerxes decides to invade Greece, he calls a council of his advisers 'in order to discover their opinions and himself set out his wishes' (7.8.1). It does not sound as if the advisers are expected to contribute much. The exuberant Mardonius immediately lards his speech with praise: of course Greece should be invaded, it will all be so easy (7.9). When the wise Artabanus airs his doubts, he has to do it in the most circumspect way (7.10). He speaks in proverbs and generalisations (the tallest trees and the biggest houses are the ones which are most vulnerable, good counsel is always desirable, haste is always dangerous), and avoids any criticism of the king. It is simply a good idea to hear the other side, so that the wisdom of one's own view can be all the clearer. His attack is saved for Mardonius, and it is very direct indeed. Yet all his diplomatic obliquity cannot deflect Xerxes' wrath. Only his status as Xerxes' uncle saves him as the king furiously derides his meanminded cowardice (7.11). Still, all is not over. Xerxes himself changes his mind later that night, and decides against invasion. When he reports his new view the counsellors prostrate themselves in relief (7.13.3), those same counsellors who had wordlessly accepted Xerxes' original decision at the first meeting. There is more to say about that sequence, and about the dream which persuades Xerxes that he has to invade after all;[12] but it will already be clear how the deference and nervousness of the court impedes the giving of good advice. No wonder kings so often go astray. This is a travesty of debate.

Yet speech can be travestied in more ways than one, and the Greek deliberations are no more direct. Themistocles cannot say openly what he really thinks to be the crucial argument for fighting at Salamis, the danger that the Greek forces will otherwise fragment (8.57.2, 58.2, 60.1); he resorts to a second-best argument which ironically captures the strategic truth, the military case for fighting in the narrows (8.60β). Yet that does not work either, and he has to resort to the threat of sailing away with the Athenian fleet unless the Council chooses his way (8.62) – another irony, for that obliquely captures the dangers of fragmentation which were his original concern. He finally shortcircuits the whole debate by sending his slave Sicinnus to trick Xerxes into attacking; and – yet another irony – he tricks him with a version of the truth, telling him of the Greek desires to flee (8.75). No-one is talking straight here either, even when they tell the truth; yet the styles of the travesty are expressively different, with terrified acquiescence the Persian keynote, wily articulate self-interest the Greek, and frank, constructive exploration of the issues nowhere at all.

So the style of the debates illuminates the two cultures. Notice, though, *how* rhetoric is telling. It is partly, but only partly, the way the historians use it for direct illumination of the internal audience's assumptions, what the speakers can and cannot say. Artabanus cannot say that Xerxes is wrong, Themistocles cannot say that the Greeks will fragment; Cleon's rebukes are geared to a public alert to both the delights and the dangers of rhetoric. We might be tempted to go further, and build something on the line taken by Cleon's adversary Diodotus, appealing as he does to prudential self-interest rather than the traditional Athenian sense of pity: what a hard, unfeeling audience – we might think. Yet this example itself gives us pause: for why is the debate happening at all? It is because the Athenians had felt that their initial decision to execute the Mytileneans had been 'cruel and excessive' (3.36.4). That suggests a measure of compassion. Then Cleon had argued against feelings of 'pity' in his audience (3.37.2, 40.2), which points the same way. There might be several reasons why 'Diodotus' does not play to pity,[13] but one of them is likely to be the rhetorical advantages of countering Cleon on his own terms: the debate, as Thucydides presents it, has developed in such a way as to require this harder line of approach. That already suggests that the arguments cannot always be used in a straightforward way to reveal the audience's pre-existing emotions.[14] The dynamics of Thucydides' debate are too complex.

It is indeed these dynamics, more than the underlying audience attitudes, which Herodotus and Thucydides make so revealing. The texture of the society is suggested by the way debate itself functions; by the roles the participants adopt, the hectoring chider Cleon, the silently acquiescent Persian grandees, the sycophantic Mardonius, the crafty Themistocles who shortcircuits the whole discussion; by the issues which surface and those which do not; even by the styles of speech, Artabanus' circumlocutory images, Cleon's flashy antitheses. When we turn to our own task as historians, we may find something similar, and the dynamics of rhetorical performance can be most expressive.[15]

Still, we can do something of the first sort as well, and reconstruct pre-existing audience attitudes from the speakers' strategies. When we look at Andocides' *On the Mysteries* we shall find some illumination in what the speaker can say – appealing to a code of loyalty to one's comrades and friends, for instance; and what he cannot – no suggestion that the people's panic was irrational in 415, and no play with the explosively contentious figure of Alcibiades (Chapter 2).

But complications swiftly loom. We have already seen some ways in which mass psychology is complex, with different attitudes prevailing in different settings. And, of course, not everyone in a mass may feel the same way. We will find some speeches, Lysias' *On the Murder of Eratosthenes* for instance, where the speaker had to cater for jurors with varying attitudes. The result is an argument which accommodates several different moral constituencies at once, and there is no way of determining which was dominant on the jury (Chapter 10); Lysias may not have been able to predict that himself. We shall find similar problems when we try to infer audience attitudes from tragedy. Euripides' *Medea* can be thought-provoking, and also work well as a play, for people with very different attitudes towards assertive women (Chapter 10); his *Suppliant Women* and *Orestes* might appeal to a spectator who was extremely cynical about democracy as well as one who applauded it, and could discomfit and satisfy both people to more or less the same extent (Chapter 9).

Yet a mass is more than an accumulation of individuals, all of them thinking their own way. Crowds will be crowds; people in crowds show attitudes and behavioural patterns which are at odds with those of the individuals which constitute them, but are what the occasion demands. The civilised lawyer becomes a baying loudmouth when he watches a football game; the polite flower-arranging lady joins the angry heckling at the party conference and calls for the lash and the noose, then nods approvingly at the sermon about compassion in church the next morning – and with total sincerity both times. And a future social historian would find this crowd dynamic – how people come to think and feel differently in a mass – very illuminating indeed.

Athenian fifth- and fourth-century assemblies and juries could also behave differently as a crowd; in particular, they often seem to be addressed as if they are of higher social and financial status than most of them really were, and have the appropriate prejudices to this higher standing.[16] In the fourth century they are sometimes addressed as if they were regular payers of the war-tax, for instance, whereas the vast majority of them were not; Lysias can address a popular audience and look back to the time when 'your houses were big', and so were the state-finances (28.3); and Demosthenes is superciliously condescending to decorators, clerks, and schoolmasters (19.237, 19.281), and presumably expects that this will not alienate his audience. Should we therefore assume that here too Athenians put on a different, more middle-class attitude as they went into court or assembly, just as they put on a problematising turn of mind as they went to a tragedy, or expected to think in more vulgar and sexist ways at a comedy?

Probably we should; but we should be careful how we put it. There are at least three further points we should make. First, there is once again the general issue. If they adopted a particular mindset for a particular context, aligning themselves with their social and financial betters, we should not think of them as acting 'out of character': this is *part of* their character.

Secondly, any such 'alignment' between audience and speakers need not be total. Litigants in the courts were typically of the wealthiest classes, those whose property was worth disputing; their court-disputes were in a sense a continuation of the traditional élite struggles for honour,[17] and the audience could naturally locate themselves as the honourers and the adjudicators, the counterparts of spectators at the games, not necessarily as *equals* in every sense. The regular speakers in the assembly again belonged to the richer, leisured classes, and often did not conceal it: the people probably welcomed that too, acknowledging the independence and the freedom from temptation that riches gave.[18] (Poor football-supporters today often welcome the immense wealth that their team-managers acquire

because 'they can walk away' at any time, and do not need to be at
the beck and call of even wealthier chairmen.) So speakers, especially
in the assembly, do not have to be *just* 'like us' listeners, and may for
instance pride themselves on an education and leisure which their
listeners lack: hence, perhaps, Demosthenes' superciliousness. But
like the football-managers they still need to persuade us that they
are on the same side, people one can respond to and get along with,
and there are various subtle ways in which they show their respect
for their listeners. The setting itself helped, with the need for élite
members to plead for the masses' goodwill, not take it for granted:
Demosthenes, it was said, defended his laboured preparation as a
sign of his democratic nature, for it showed his respect for a popular
audience who needed to be persuaded, not dragooned (Plut. *Dem.* 8).
Some of the passages implying the audience's 'higher social status'
are to be seen as another of these on-the-same-side techniques,
bringing the audience closer to the speaker but not necessarily
implying an identical status.

Thirdly, we need to be clearer about the way they create this effect.
Many of these passages are of the form of Demosthenes' *First Olynthiac*
(1) 6. He calls upon his audience 'to be stirred up and to apply
yourselves to the war more than ever, contributing money eagerly
and going out yourselves and not leaving anything undone'; there
are several similar passages in the *Second Olynthiac* (2), 13, 24, 27,
and 31. Such language need not mean that everyone need pay money
any more than that every citizen need go out; a modern orator could
invite the audience to think of their husbands, wives, and children
without implying that all had children, still less that all had both
husbands and wives. Later in the first speech, it is true, Demosthenes
speaks of the need for 'everyone to contribute a lot if a lot is needed,
or a little if a little' (20), but even this can without strain mean
'everyone *relevant*'; later still (28) he breaks it down so that war in
the north will mean the well-off (*euporoi*) spending a part of their
fortunes, those in the prime of life going out to fight, and the
politicians looking to careful scrutiny of their records. But such listing
is still an important part of the on-the-same-side strategy: we will
all be doing our bit. The ploy came particularly easily because of the
characteristic Greek taste for polar antithesis. There are just two
sides, it is us against them, idealised democratic harmony against
the disaffection under the tyrant. In the same way Lysias' 'big houses'
come in a speech where he is mobilising resentment against men
who 'have made their own houses big' at the state's expense (28.13):

he too is building a global 'us', good democrats who have fallen on hard times, against an unpatriotic and exploitative 'them', so insensitive to the straitened circumstances of today.

So in the *Olynthiacs* Demosthenes is not exactly addressing the assembly as if they are all rich enough to pay taxes, but he is certainly assuming that all classes *can* be assimilated together, are 'on the same side', and that the language will not so grate with the poorer classes that they will feel alienated. This sort of upwards assimilation is not universal, and sometimes the audience are encouraged to identify themselves with the poorer rather than the richer: in *Against Meidias* (21) Demosthenes mobilises popular resentment at the excesses of the filthily rich and arrogant. Still, the assimilation goes upward much more often than downward, towards the richer, more established, and more well-born.

That is partly the speakers' flattery, rather as Aristophanes talks of his audience as clever and discriminating (*dexioi*, *sophoi*), extending to the whole crowd a description which they would like to be true.[19] But there is more to it than that. The assembly and jury experience is itself a privilege, marking the listener out as a member of the élite of citizenship: it is not something that metics (non-citizen resident aliens) or slaves could do. That is one reason why citizens were paid for attendance, on the juries in the fifth century and at the assembly by the first years of the fourth (and one reason why the oligarchs of 411 abolished all state-pay except for those on campaign): of course the money mattered, but the eligibility for such money was itself a demarcation of citizen status. It is understandable that even the poorer citizens should, during this distinctively élite experience, have aligned themselves with the grander, the nobler, and the richer in any polarity.

For us, as for Herodotus and Thucydides, the delineation of audience attitude is therefore not possible without also considering the dynamics of the occasion. The question is not so much *what* the audience thought, but *how* they thought: what sort of mentality might operate in this particular social context, as the speaker sought to build some (qualified) degree of identification of audience with himself, and the audience was ready to play along, welcoming the on-the-same-side complicity which their shared citizen-status offered. That complicity would be reinforced by the perception that it *worked*, that decisions were reached in the assembly which everyone accepted, that courts imposed verdicts which controlled (even if they could not terminate) illegality and disorder. Both sides are role-playing here, but the role-playing is itself a great help as we try to grasp the way this society functioned.

One last point. With Herodotus' Artabanus and Thucydides' Cleon, we noticed that their styles and their imagery constituted one interpretative register. For us, too, style can matter, and suggest points about how the audience would think. Take imagery. Three favourite images of the Athenian *polis* or of politicians are, first, that of the 'ship of state', tossed by so many storms; secondly, that of disease, with a state that is healthy or sick; thirdly, that of athletics, with the state as a whole contending with others in battle, or more usually individual heroes struggling for a prize. The suggestions of these motifs are worth unpacking. A ship is tossed by storms, which come from outside; passengers on board are often afraid, often a cumbrance; it requires a captain or a helmsman to guide them to safety, though a captain is no use without a crew. A diseased body, especially in Greek thought, is normally diseased from within, with some internal balance thrown into disarray (even if it is some external disruption which triggers that disorder); a body is an organism which will inevitably grow and decay and die; yet here too a doctor is required, and a good doctor can make all the difference. An athlete contends for honour, but not everyone can win; one man's glory is another's humiliation, and glory and humiliation alike depend on an audience to watch and applaud – though also, perhaps, on a posterity who will hear and remember, for true glory is eternal. All these images capture something vital about the way Athenians constructed their own state. It is a democracy, certainly, but it is a democracy which needs helmsmen, doctors, great men who contend: otherwise the ship will be wrecked and the body will die. There is a fierce belief in *isotes* (equality or fairness), just as different forces within a body must be in proper tension with one another, just as rowers need to pull together, just as athletes need to start equal; but egalitarianism needs to co-exist, somehow, with a state which generates those great men to steer, heal, and win. These implied assumptions capture features – and indeed potential fissures too, for the co-existence is never easy – within the Athenians' self-image. They 'capture' partly because that is the way Athenians might readily think *anyway*, so that the images sat comfortably on pre-existing predispositions; and partly because familiar imagistic patterns *constitute* perceptions, themselves predisposing a society to accept the assumptions which the images encode.[20]

So texts tell us what could be said. They help us to reconstruct real-life events; one question we need to put to any narrative is 'how true is this?', and a sensitivity to that narrative's rhetoric is indispensable. To some extent, texts can also help us to understand an audience's assumptions; here the question is 'what needs to be true about the audience for it to make sense for an author to put it in that way?' In both cases we are using texts as a pointer to something outside themselves, to events that happened even if the text had never mentioned them, and to audience assumptions that pre-exist the text which appeals to them. But there is also a sense in which a text illuminates the dynamics of its own occasion, 'how' rather than 'what' the audience would think in a particular context. A speech is part of a trial or a debate; a script is part of a play; and it is the only part we have. Here we are not trying to infer something wholly independent of the text itself, we are rather inferring what we can of a whole experience from the part which survives. Here, most particularly, texts are the historian's best friend.

# Chapter 2

# Rhetoric and history (415 BC)

## Thucydides on the Herms and mysteries

It is summer 415.[1] Momentously, the Athenian assembly has just taken its decision to sail to Sicily, and the city is busy with preparations. Thucydides continues (6.27):

> One night most of the stone Herms in Athens had their faces mutilated. (These are a local feature, with their familiar square-cut figures, and there are many of them both in private porches and in temples.) Nobody knew who had done it; great rewards were offered by the state for information which would help the search, and they passed a further decree offering immunity to anyone, citizen, alien, or slave, who could give information concerning any other impiety. They took the affair more seriously than one might expect: it was taken as an omen for the expedition, and people thought that it sprang from a revolutionary conspiracy to overthrow the democracy.
>
> Information came from some metics and servants. It did not concern the Herms, but there was talk of certain earlier mutilations of statues, the work of young men during some drunken revels; and there were also reports of some insulting [lit. 'hybristic'] performances of the mysteries in private houses. Here Alcibiades was one of the people they accused. Alcibiades' bitterest personal enemies immediately seized on this. He stood in the way of their own ambitions to establish a firm leadership of the people, and they thought this their opportunity to be rid of him and get first place for themselves: so they exaggerated it all, and went around shouting that the mysteries and the mutilation of the Herms were a matter of revolutionary ambitions to destroy the democracy, and that Alcibiades was

involved in everything. Their evidence was his general undemocratic and transgressive style of behaviour...

– a theme which Thucydides has already stressed in a summary of his own at 6.15, where he emphasised the resentment which this transgressiveness[2] inspired.

Alcibiades himself pressed for any prosecution to take place before he sailed to Sicily, but his enemies were too shrewd: they knew that the expedition largely depended on Alcibiades – for instance, there were troops from Argos and Mantinea who were only sailing because of their personal ties with the man – and the people would never allow it to be compromised. So his enemies bided their time, aiming to let him go and recall him when the time was right. The expedition sailed (6.29).

With the fleet away, Alcibiades' enemies lost no time, and a few months later[3] one of the state galleys arrived in Sicily to arrest Alcibiades

> and certain others of the soldiers who had been denounced along with him of impiety in the mysteries affair, and also some accused of the mutilation of the Herms. For, after the expedition had set sail, the Athenians had not relaxed their investigation into the facts about the mysteries and the Herms; and they did not check the informants closely, but seized on everything as a ground for suspicion. So, putting their trust in scoundrels, they arrested and imprisoned people who were thoroughly good citizens. They thought it more important to examine the matter thoroughly and get at the truth than to allow any citizen, however good he appeared, to escape investigation on the grounds of the low character of the informant. For the people had heard how harsh the tyranny of Peisistratus and his sons had become in its final stages: what is more, they knew that it had not been the Athenians and Harmodius which had destroyed it, but the Spartans. So the people were always fearful and suspicious of everything.
>
> (6.53)

There is then a long digression setting out the truth, as Thucydides sees it, about the end of the Peisistratid tyranny nearly a century before.

This was what was in the mind of the Athenian people; they reminded themselves of the surviving tradition about the Peisistratids, and were relentless in their suspicions of those accused of the mysteries affair. Everything seemed to them to be a matter of oligarchic and tyrannical plotting. Their anger had already led to the imprisonment of many well-respected people; nor was there any respite, but every day they grew fiercer, and more and more people were arrested.

At this point one of the prisoners, who was thought to be one of the guiltiest, was persuaded by a fellow-prisoner to give information, whether true or false – for some conclude one thing, some the other, and nobody, then or later, has established clarity on the perpetrators of the deed. The fellow-prisoner persuaded him that it was better, even if he had not actually done it, to save himself by procuring immunity: that would also release the city from this prevailing mood of suspicion; it was better – so the argument went – to gain safety by means of a confession under promise of immunity than to deny it and be put on trial. So the first prisoner denounced himself and others for the mutilation of the Herms.

The Athenian *demos* was delighted to get at the truth, or what they thought to be the truth. Before they had felt outraged at the thought that they might not identify those plotting against the mass of the people. Now they released the informer straight away, along with those whom he had not accused; as for those he had named, they put them on trial and killed those whom they had in custody, and condemned to death those who had fled and put a price on their heads. In all this it is uncertain if the victims were punished unjustly, but it is utterly clear that the rest of the city benefitted greatly, things being as they were.

Alcibiades' personal enemies, who had been attacking him before he sailed, now pressed the matter, and the Athenians took a serious view. Now that they thought they had got at the truth about the Herms, they were all the more convinced that the affair of the mysteries (the charge against Alcibiades) had sprung in the same way from a conspiracy against the people, and that he was behind it. For it so happened that a Spartan force, not a large one, had advanced to the Isthmus of Corinth at the time when they were so agitated concerning these things: these Spartans were engaged on some business with the Boeotians. The Athenians formed the view that this force was Alcibiades' doing, and nothing to do with the Boeotians – and that, if they had not got in first and arrested the accused men, the city would have been betrayed. There was indeed one night when they slept in the city Theseion under arms. Around the same time Alcibiades' guest-friends in Argos were suspected of plotting a conspiracy against the democracy, and consequently the Argive hostages in the islands were at that time handed over to the Argive people for execution. Suspicion had crowded in on Alcibiades from every side. So, wishing to bring him to trial and to kill him, they sent the Salaminia [the state galley] to arrest him and the others who had been denounced.

(6.60.1–61.3)

Alcibiades was too wily. He was indeed arrested, but he and his fellow-captives managed to escape in Southern Italy during a stop on the homeward voyage. Not long afterwards he appeared at Sparta, and a new phase of his career began.

We know the identity of this 'prisoner' whom Thucydides mentions but does not name,[4] and who gave such crucial evidence: it was Andocides, who gives his own account of these affairs in his speech *On the Mysteries*, delivered fifteen years later in 400 or, less likely, 399.[5]

I have quoted Thucydides so extensively to give a narrative framework into which Andocides' evidence can be fitted and against which it can be gauged, and this will be this chapter's major concern. But we should not regard Thucydides as providing some unquestionable criterion, the whole truth and nothing but the truth. Thucydides himself was in exile by this time. No-one, he claims, ever really knew the truth about the culprits, and he would have found it more difficult than most. Just as importantly, no historical narrator can escape the responsibility of interpretation. To narrate is to discriminate, to choose some events and actions as relevant and to eliminate others. If Thucydides fails to name Andocides, if he has little to say about the religious element in the popular fears, if he does not mention élite *hetaireiai* and drinking-clubs – in each case, this was Thucydides' discrimination, the choice of a particularly intelligent observer, which we should respect as no more and no less than that.

The main significance for Thucydides is the way in which the scare eliminated Alcibiades from the Athenian leadership. That is partly because the main thrust of his narrative is now concerned with Sicily, and Alcibiades' removal was the most obvious way in which the Herms and mysteries affected that campaign; but there is a wider point as well. One crucial Thucydidean theme, we have already seen (pp. 9–10), is the way in which the relationship between leader and *demos* changed after Pericles; how private ambitions, jealousies, excesses came to intrude upon the conduct of the war. Now we find a new charismatic leader, Alcibiades, but one with a very different style from Pericles'; and at 6.15 Thucydides had elaborated his analysis of the way Alcibiades' transgressiveness provoked others into resentment and opposition. Pericles' Athens had been an exquisite blend of democracy and tyranny. It 'was becoming in name a democracy, in fact one-man rule' (2.65.9), and combined a fierce democratic ideology at home (the Funeral Speech of 2.35–46) with an acknowledgement of the tyrannical aspects of its empire (2.63.2). But a Pericles was needed to preserve so uneasy a balance. After his death, other leaders were 'more on a level with one another' (2.65.10); now, with Alcibiades, it was *suspicion* of tyrannical ambitions which dominated. Acquiescence in any elements of one-man rule had died with Pericles.

It is not surprising, then, that Thucydides puts so much stress on the resentments of Alcibiades' enemies, and on the transgressiveness which gave them their chance (6.28.2): that had been his emphasis at 6.15. Nor that he stresses that suspicions began with the Herms and spread to the mysteries, and twice in a similar rhythm, once when the scare began (6.28.1) and once at the time of the revelations (6.61.1): in each case the *demos* is being manipulated by Alcibiades' enemies. Nor that the *demos* emerges as so irresponsible; irresponsible people need strong leadership, and this is what is now lacking. Nor that suspicions of tyranny are everywhere. The tyrannicide 'digression' is most artful here, reflecting many themes of the surrounding narrative:[6] not merely in its surface relevance of explaining how hundred-year-old memories could still preoccupy the Athenians, but also in providing a paradigmatic instance where private excesses, lusts, and jealousies had a disastrous impact on public life, creating an atmosphere of irrationality, suspicion, and vindictiveness. With Hipparchus and Hippias, erotic rivalries led to death and to exile in an enemy land: the elimination of a vital figure triggered first a decline in leadership style, then constitutional revolution, and the crisis could only be resolved by the intervention of a hostile state. Something very similar is now to happen again.

These Thucydidean interests are relevant to a further point.

Thucydides makes very little of the religious dimension of the crisis. The mutilation 'seemed an omen for the expedition', that is all: his emphasis falls instead on those fears of an oligarchic or tyrannical revolution. Other versions convey much more of the feeling of religious dread, for instance that of Plutarch[7] – and we shall see (Chapter 3) that Plutarch deserves respect.

It is indeed easy to write a different story about these events, one which presents the *demos* as responsible and rational. To dishonour a god was a dangerous thing. And this was not just any god:[8] this was Hermes the god of travellers, whose goodwill was so important for so great a journey as the Athenians now planned; Hermes the master of deceit, who if he chose could repay this deceit so effectively in kind; Hermes the god of mediation, the go-between to the other gods;[9] Hermes who presided over so many other transitions, including (as Hermes Psychopompos) the final transition to the underworld. That could so easily be the fate that now awaited the journeyers to Sicily, if the god was as offended as it was reasonable to think – and it could be represented as dangerous to share a ship with one who had annoyed the gods.[10] To search for those responsible was no frantic witch-hunt: it was a duty to the city and to the citizens sailing into the unknown.

Nor was the extension of the inquiry to the mysteries a random step. The Eleusinian mysteries were central to Athenian *polis* religion: to attack the gods was to attack the city and its democracy, and one cannot divorce 'political' and 'religious' dimensions.[11] Demeter and Persephone, the deities worshipped in those mysteries, were powers whose goodwill was again essential; and especially so, if that possibility of the final transition to the underworld did come into play. (It was not coincidental that the rehabilitated Alcibiades made such a show of celebrating the mysteries eight years later, on his return in 407.[12] He needed to signify his reconciliation with the deities he had allegedly outraged.) And Sicily was where Persephone had been abducted; Sicily was still the site of much of her important cult. To many Athenians, too, Sicily would have suggested above all 'grain': that grain which was fundamental to the identity of Demeter.[13] If Demeter and Persephone too were offended, the Athenian hopes dwindled further. Nor, finally, was it irresponsible to put more weight on catching and punishing than on allowing the innocent to escape. We are in a world where 'justice', *dike*, is more concerned with retribution than with fairness; where such outrages required a scapegoat, and the wellbeing of the city as a whole could turn on the suffering of the unfortunate individual.[14]

But that is not the story Thucydides chooses to write. We can, if we like, put that down to a mental quirk of Thucydides himself, impatiently rationalist and impatient of what he saw as irrationality in others: there are other passages where religious elements receive short shrift.[15] Thucydides' dismissiveness here also goes closely with his presentation of the *demos* and its leaders, depicting the scares as irrational and the *demos* as irresponsible. What is clear is that he is *using* this material, moulding it in line with his own interpretative themes.

The moulding goes further. Narrative generally starts at the beginning and goes on to the end; generally – but not always, especially when narrative dislocation can make a point clearer.[16] Take that detail that 'a Spartan force, not a large one, had advanced to the Isthmus of Corinth at the time when they were so agitated concerning these things: these Spartans were engaged on some business with the Boeotians. The Athenians formed the view that this force was Alcibiades' doing. … There was indeed one night when they slept in the city Theseion under arms' (6.61.2: above, pp. 20–1). Thucydides gives this item late in the sequence, after Andocides' denunciation has ended the Herms inquiry and attention has switched to the mysteries. Critics usually infer that this 'Spartan expedition' and 'night under arms' genuinely belong at that late stage.[17] There is then a problem in reconciling this with Andocides' indication that the 'night under arms' belongs earlier, at the time when the Herms inquiry was in full swing, the revelations of Diocleides had just been made, and Andocides had not yet been released; he connects all this with fears of a 'Boeotian' force on the frontiers (*Myst.* 45: below, p. 29). The usual inference is that Andocides is falsifying the sequence to overstate the terrified atmosphere of the time. It was he, after all, who brought this terror to an end.

Andocides' notice causes difficulties of its own.[18] But in fact Thucydides is not necessarily putting this Spartan episode so late. The narrative has by now cleared up the Herms affair; as Thucydides stresses, it was the mysteries charge of which Alcibiades was accused. Thucydides now explains all the points which have stacked up against him. One is the hostility of his enemies; but we also need to know what made the *demos* so convinced that the affair of the mysteries, like that of the Herms, embodied some dreadful conspiracy. One factor was this Spartan expedition, another was the anti-democrat movement in Argos: thus '[s]uspicion had crowded in on Alcibiades from every side' (6.61.4: above, p. 21). Notice the pluperfect tense. There is no conflict here with the timing given by Andocides.

So far this is simply a matter of narrative smoothness, collecting together all the points creating this atmosphere of suspicion; but there is an interpretative point too. What was this Spartan expedition about? Thucydides is vague: 'some business with the Boeotians'; and he hurries on to his main point, what it was *not* about – it was nothing to do with Alcibiades, he implies, though the Athenians thought that it was. This is made to look like another panicky premature conclusion. Yet could any Spartan expedition *not* be aimed at Athens, at a time like this? Perhaps it was a Peloponnesian attempt to exploit the crisis, even if only to add to the scaremongering. Perhaps there was even some Peloponnesian involvement in the original outrage itself. There may be some truth in another version absent from Thucydides, the notion that the mutilation was inspired by the Corinthians: that view surfaces in Plutarch (*Alc.* 17), and seems to come from the knowledgeable fourth-century writer Philochorus.[19] That makes some sense: the Corinthians might well want to take some action in defence of their daughter-city Syracuse. Such a display might hamper the expedition in any of several ways even if it did not prevent it completely: by delaying it, by lowering morale, not to mention the way it eventually did hamper it – by removing Alcibiades from the leadership. Equally, the very plausibility of this version may explain why it might be fabricated, then or later. We cannot know.

Whatever the truth of that, here too Thucydides has clearly been at work, and the way he has textured this item goes closely with his interpretation of the whole affair. He passes over the expedition in the context where it chronologically belongs, and treats it at a point where he can emphasise the false and extravagant rumour (Alcibiades behind it) rather than the sober and scaring truth (the Spartans on the move). Once again, the *demos* emerges as less responsible and more panicky. There is no need to find this procedure of Thucydides sinister. Doubtless he genuinely thought the most significant aspect was the light cast on the relationship between the *demos* and its leaders, and in that case this was the most appropriate point to use the item. He may even have been right. But that is only one possible emphasis, doubtless a highly intelligent one, among many.

## Andocides

Andocides secured immunity from prosecution by his evidence on the Herms. However, he naturally became extremely unpopular; and soon afterwards the decree of Isotimides, barring from the Athenian temples and agora all who had admitted impiety, may well have been aimed specifically at him. This exclusion from the focal points of civic identity effectively turned him into a non-citizen, and he spent some years in exile.

He managed to return to Athens by 405, but it was not until the amnesty of 403 that he resumed his citizenship. His troubles were not yet at an end. In 400 or 399[20] he was prosecuted for violating the decree of Isotimides by attending the Eleusinian mysteries; a secondary charge was that he had placed a suppliant-branch on the altar of the Eleusinion. On both counts we again notice the strong religious dimension. His speech *On the Mysteries* was delivered at his trial. The prosecution demanded the death penalty.[21]

As usual in ancient oratory, he had to push several lines at once. He naturally (and perhaps plausibly)[22] claimed that the 403 amnesty invalidated the decree of Isotimides, so that there was nothing that his attendance at the mysteries would violate. But that was not enough. He could also not afford to admit any impiety in 415, and he had to do something to counter the unpopularity his denunciation had incurred. In particular, the prosecution claimed that he had denounced his own father Leogoras, and this transgression of family duties, if believed, would have been fatal.

The rhetoric of a man arguing for his life can evidently not be taken on trust. True, he is talking to an audience of Athenians, including many old enough to have been engaged observers fifteen years before. There were limits to what he could claim. But fifteen years is a long time, and niceties of detail would be blurred in the best of memories. We need to be on our guard, and particularly need to notice exactly what evidence Andocides cites for each of his claims. For many of them he adduces witnesses, which makes them look impressive to us – though even there we need to notice exactly what he is asking his witnesses to confirm, and it is often something rather specific. But in this culture personal associations and enmities went deep, and witnesses would often regard it as their duty to throw their weight behind their friend or against their enemy. Hence, no doubt, the many fourth-century cases where different eyewitnesses give totally incompatible versions of the same events.[23] That is interesting in terms of trial dynamics, if we have to see witnesses as supporters, choosing to be visible in the litigatory feuding; but it is certainly a problem when we try to get at the truth. After the 1963 Profumo scandal, the good-time girl Mandy Rice Davies was reminded in court that some distinguished personage had denied her embarrassing story; she reasonably replied that he would, wouldn't he? Many of our witnesses too were so personally committed that *of course* they would say what they said, and Ms Davies should be firmly in the historian's mind.

Early in the speech Andocides goes through various mysteries denunciations: first that of Pythonicus, then Teucrus, then Agariste, then Lydus. He strongly implies that this was the full list:

> These, then, were the denunciations concerning the mysteries, four in number: and, as for those who fled into exile after each denunciation, I have read out their names, and the witnesses have given their evidence.
>
> (25)

But Andocides has not in fact 'read out their names' (or had them read) in each case. He did this in the first case (Pythonicus), and also called a witness; he also had the names read in the second case (Teucrus). But in the third case (Agariste), he simply listed the names without citing any document or witness. In the fourth case (Lydus) – particularly important because it was Lydus who had denounced Andocides' father Leogoras – he again did not read the names. He did call two witnesses, for what that is worth, but the point of their testimony seems only that it was Lydus, not Andocides himself, who launched this denunciation (18–19, e.g. 'they should know whose fault it was that their kinsmen went into exile…'); Andocides claims to have stood by his father throughout. This is not testimony, then, to confirm who exactly was on Lydus' list, only that it was Lydus' list and not Andocides' own.

It is natural to suspect some sleight of hand here, though it is another question what exactly Andocides has to hide: more on this in a moment. There may be a further slipperiness too. As we saw, Andocides implies that there were only these four denunciations. Yet Plutarch cites a fifth, that of Thessalus, with names which do not precisely overlap any of the first four (*Alc.* 19, 22); and Plutarch seems to be following a documentary source, probably Craterus' collection of Athenian decrees.[24] Once again, does Andocides have something to hide here? It is unsurprising that scholars have concluded that Andocides' own name figured on Lydus' list, or that he was involved in the Thessalus denunciation:[25] though this may not be the only possible inference.[26]

Whatever suspicions we may have, they should not destroy the value which this evidence retains. The documentary underpinning of the first two denunciations renders them secure; and the denunciations of Agariste and Lydus are presumably not wholly fabricated, even if we are less sure exactly what they contained. Andocides challenges anyone who knew of any trial-appearance or denunciation of his to speak out now (23, 26): that is confidence not merely that most people would remember little, but that no-one would remember anything of this sort. There is something here to believe, despite our suspicions of the rest.

One other sort of witness is particularly suspect: the 'witness' of the jury themselves, seen on those times when they are appealed to in terms such as 'you all know' or 'you all remember'. A speaker drew attention to this trick nearly a hundred years later: 'The man is a voluble shameless scoundrel, so much so that, when he does not have any witnesses for a claim, he will say "you all know this", gentlemen of the jury – that trick used by everyone who has nothing good to say on his side.'[27] We might call this the 'truth universally acknowledged' ploy. Jane Austen's universally acknowledged truth – that a single man in possession of a good fortune must be in want of a wife – was no such thing: it gently mocked the wishful thinking of a particular class of observer. Andocides' counterpart is more sinister, and the wishful thinking may be his own. Take the claim that 'you all know' what my father said in a case marginal to the main inquiry, but still fifteen years ago (22); or the invitation to 'remind yourselves' who it was that Andocides then accused (69), for (he claims) there were only four who were exiled because of his testimony, and all the others he named had already been denounced by others. True, he here again brings on witnesses: but these were men who owed their freedom to his testimony (so they would say this, wouldn't they?), and they were attesting this simple fact that they were not on Andocides' list, not the identity of those whom he did name and who therefore had to flee. This 'truth universally acknowledged' ploy is only possible because these were indeed public events, so that 'you remember' or 'remind yourselves' is not a nonsensical suggestion. But it is hardly a realistic one, and one's nose should twitch. If Andocides had better evidence for his allegations here, he would have cited it.

The ploy is interesting not only for the conviction it may give to a dubious claim, but also for a wider point in the dynamics of the trial. Such an invitation to 'remind yourselves' encourages the fiction that the jurors are knowledgeable people who have carried the burden of the state for years; now they can demonstrate their harmony with one another and the defendant by confirmatory word and gesture. And the ploy was reasonably safe, for no-one was going to parade his ignorance by shouting out that he did not know any such thing. We keep our ignorance to ourselves.[28]

The most striking 'truth universally acknowledged' ploy comes at the critical point of Andocides' narrative (37–45). When the Herms panic was at its height, evidence was suddenly given by one Diocleides. This man reported that, on the night of the outrage, he happened to have woken while it was still dark, and in a world without clocks he had mistaken the time. Now he was awake, he decided to set out early on a journey. When passing through the city, he had seen – for it was a moonlit night – a gathering of some 300 men, standing around in groups of fifteen or twenty men, and had recognised most of them. When he later heard about the mutilation, he realised that these must have been the culprits. Diocleides had been attracted (he said) by the state reward of eleven minas, but first he had approached a certain Euphemus, one of those he claimed to have seen. 'He had no desire,' he claimed to have said, 'to take money from the state rather than from us [i.e. Andocides, Euphemus, and their friends], if in that way he could be our friend' (40).

Euphemus – so Diocleides' story went on – had invited him to Leogoras' house 'to join him in meeting Andocides and the others who are necessary'; Diocleides claimed to have been offered at this meeting 'two talents of silver' – that is, the equivalent of twelve minas – instead of the state reward of eleven minas, and it was agreed that, 'if we obtain what we want, he should be one of us, and that we should exchange pledges with him' (41). Diocleides had agreed; but the promised two talents did not materialise, and so Diocleides gave his evidence after all in the *boule*, naming forty-two men. It caused a sensation; the panic was all the greater because 'the Boeotians, hearing what had happened, were under arms on the borders' (45) – presumably the same incident as that mentioned by Thucydides (above, pp. 24–5), for here too there is a sudden call to arms, the *boule* spending the night on the Acropolis and the prytaneis in the Tholos. It was then that the imprisoned Andocides gave his evidence. The next day Diocleides was called back, and exposed as a liar: he confessed that he had been put up to it by Alcibiades of Phegus (not the famous Alcibiades, but almost certainly his cousin)[29] and Amiantus from Aegina (65).

The story is dramatic, and its circumstantial detail would have lent it cogency. But the main evidence cited for the whole tale rests, once again, with the memories of the jurors themselves:

> I beg you, gentlemen, to pay careful attention and remind one another of the truth, if I tell it, and act as each other's instructors: for these words were uttered among you, and you are my witnesses.
>
> (37)

Yet this is very odd. These proceedings took place in the *boule*, and part at least was in secret.[30] Andocides later acknowledges that only some of his hearers would have been there:

> First, gentlemen, those of you who were there should remind yourselves and instruct the others of these things.
>
> (46)

And then he does call the presiding officers, the prytaneis, and cite them as his witnesses (ibid.). But we have no way of knowing how much of the story was put to these witnesses, and the prosecution would not regularly cross-examine to probe further.[31] The crucial point remains the appeal to the jurors' own memories.

This is demographic nonsense. The *boule* in 415 would consist of 500 over-thirties. In normal circumstances fifteen years of ageing would kill off perhaps 55 per cent of these;[32] in 415–400 wartime losses would make the figure substantially larger. Let us say 150–75 were left. On the best estimates of the Athenian citizen population in 400, these might represent 0.5–0.7 per cent of the citizen body, or 0.75–1 per cent of those eligible for jury-service (again those over thirty). If Andocides' jury numbered 500 or 501[33] there might on this basis be only four or five who could 'remind one another and instruct the others' in this way. Even if we admit some slanting of the figures, with the rich or those living locally over-represented,[34] we are still probably talking only single figures. True, Andocides is not the only one to try this trick. At Demosthenes' trial in 323, Deinarchus (or rather the orator whose speech he wrote) calls in very similar terms upon the memories of any of the 300 trierarchs of

340/39 (1.42); but he at least asks 'Are there some men in the court who were among the Three Hundred...?', and that formulation makes it clearer that the numbers will be very small. And how much could they remember, at Andocides' trial or Demosthenes', and how many of their fellow-jurors would hear them or believe them? The ploy is aided by a convention that any jury, like the *boule*, 'was' – or at least represented – the state, and any one jury could therefore be regarded as continuous with any previous jury or assembly.[35] The notion of a single stream of 'citizens', embodied sequentially in one group after another, is ideologically suited to the Athenian mindset, and the ploy would therefore seem less transparent than it does to us. But Andocides is straining this convention to the limit. Our nose by now should be very twitchy indeed.

Finally, we should note the elements in Andocides' case which are most rhetorically indispensable, and be particularly alert to their evidential support. He faces a dilemma. It would be disastrous to admit impiety: true, some jurors might accept the argument that even the confessedly sacrilegious were covered by the amnesty of 403, and Andocides therefore argues that point strongly (71–89) – but he cannot rely on that alone. It would also be disastrous to admit that he denounced men whom he knew to be innocent. Yet how could he know who was guilty if he had not been guilty himself? At 61–3 he gives the answer:

> For these reasons [the argument that the moral balance favoured denouncing a few men to secure the lives of more] I told the *boule* that I knew who was guilty, and I revealed the facts. I told them that Euphiletus had proposed the scheme [of mutilating the Herms] during one of our drinking-sessions, but I opposed it, and that I was the one who prevented it from happening on that occasion. Later I was in Cynosarges, mounted one of my ponies, and had a fall: I broke my collar-bone and cracked my skull. I was carried home on a stretcher. Euphiletus discovered the state I was in. He told them that I had been persuaded to join them in their plan, that I had promised to play a part in it by mutilating the Herm by the Phorbanteion. This was untrue: and for that reason the Herm you all see, the one by the ancestral home of my family erected by the Aegeis tribe, was the only one in Athens not mutilated. This was because Euphiletus had told them that I would do it. When they discovered that I knew about the deed but had not done it, they were furious. The next day

> Meletus and Euphiletus visited me and said: 'It has happened,
> Andocides: we have done it. If you are willing to do nothing and
> keep silent, we will stay your friends. If not, you will find us
> warmer enemies than any friends you have made on our account.'

So there we have it: a circumstantial account of how Andocides
could know all about the culprits without having been one himself.
But the evidence? He claims he handed over a slave for torture to
confirm his injury (64), and that the *boule* and the commissioners of
inquiry checked and discovered that he was telling the truth (65):
that was when they summoned Diocleides and he admitted his lies.
But we have the speech of one of his prosecutors (*Against Andocides*,
i.e. [Lysias] 6), and that alleges that Andocides failed to produce a
slave for questioning (21–4). That account itself has difficulties,[36]
but Andocides seems to acknowledge that there was some fuss over
the non-production of slaves for torture.[37] In fact, such torture-
challenges were hardly ever accepted – indeed, we know of no case
at all where torture of a witness, as opposed to a suspected culprit,
materialised.[38] Perhaps Andocides at first offered the boy, not
expecting the offer to be taken up; after all, he was accepting
immunity, and his guilt was no longer relevant. If this was one of the
rare occasions when a challenge was accepted, some backtracking
would be the regular next move.[39] But, however we explain it, some
scepticism about this injury of Andocides is called for.
   The same applies to his account of his meeting with Euphiletus.
No-one else was present, and Euphiletus was presumably dead by
400, or at least in exile: otherwise he would surely be the star witness
on one side or the other. Andocides could claim what he wanted. Nor
is the single unmutilated Herm as convincing as Andocides pretends.
Plutarch used it in quite the opposite direction: the non-mutilation
of this 'Herm of Andocides', as it was later known, was the factor
which created most suspicion against Andocides himself (*Alc.* 21).
Plutarch does not explain why, but it is not hard to suggest reasons.
Perhaps Andocides was sparing a Herm for which he felt particular
affection or dread (this was probably Plutarch's line of thought).
Perhaps it was a double bluff, and he was prudently preparing his
own defence, thinking that if later accused he could argue in precisely
the way he does.
   Whatever his guilt or innocence, he had the further problem of
avoiding the suggestion that he had accused innocent men, or even
men who might otherwise have escaped. Here his language is most
delicate.

I thought over the wrongdoers, the people who had committed the crime: and I realised that some of them had already been executed on Teucrus' testimony, that others had fled into exile and had already been condemned to death, and that there were four guilty men left whom Teucrus had not denounced: Panaetius, Chaeredemus, Diacritus, and Lysistratus. It was reasonable to expect that they would appear to be in the group denounced by Diocleides, as friends of those who had already been killed. And these four were not yet safe, but my own kinsmen were clearly going to die if no-one told the Athenians what had really happened. It seemed to me better to drive these four men out of their country justly – men who are alive today, have returned, and are in possession of their property – than to let the others die unjustly.

(52–3)

Note the emphasis: these were the 'wrongdoers', 'the people who had committed the crime', the 'guilty men'; they suffered 'justly': he had told the Athenians 'what had really happened'. A few sentences later they are again 'the men who sinned' or 'the wrongdoers' (55 and 59). And Andocides knew it, for he was telling the Athenians 'what he had heard from Euphiletus' (62). More than this: they were not merely guilty, they were also likely to have been denounced by Diocleides, for they were friends of those who had already been killed – Andocides' language implies that he did not yet know the full list of those whom Diocleides had named. He is denouncing not merely men who were guilty, but even men who, to his best guesswork, were already likely to have been exposed. Once again, we may feel suspicions that all should be so neat, and so convenient for Andocides. Thucydides (6.60.4: above, p. 20) and for what it is worth[40] Plutarch (*Alc.* 21) are clear that some were exiled and some were killed because of Andocides' revelations.

Analysis of the rhetoric only takes us so far. It is easier to be clear that there is something surreptitious going on than to determine exactly what Andocides has to hide. Take, for instance, that circumstantial detail of the revelations of Diocleides, and the insistence that 'you all remember' events which only a handful could have witnessed. Now, Diocleides was executed afterwards (*Myst.* 66), and so the *boule* must have decided that his evidence was false: or rather that enough of it was false to justify execution, for it need not follow that every detail was discredited. It may well be that Diocleides had seen something, and that the true part of his evidence damningly incriminated Andocides himself: certainly, Andocides' rhetorical twists and turns suggest that something remained embarrassing. But if so, there is no way of telling what the damning points were. It may have been only the blackmail attempt and the agreement to pay Diocleides off: that was embarrassing enough. Or Diocleides may simply have claimed believably to have seen Andocides in mutilating action on that night; or have explained why that 'Herm of Andocides' remained untouched. We cannot know.

Here we face one classic methodological danger. Everyone is familiar with the type of detective story where the evidence is bewildering, till in the last chapter the detective summons to the library those most involved – all of them probably by now suspects – and gives a brilliant reconstruction of what really happened. We applaud the brilliance, and immediately see that, if the reconstruction is right, then the evidence would look exactly the way it does. In deference to the greatest exponent, let us call this a 'Poirot'. The great detective himself would call this his 'deduction' from the evidence, the prize performance of his little grey cells. In fact it is rather *in*duction: the detective proposes a story, then infers from that story what the evidence should look like if it were true, then points out that this maps perfectly on to the evidence that there is.[41] If the mortally ill judge faked his own death, did the killings, then finally killed himself, then indeed the evidence would have fallen out exactly the way it does.

The fallacy is that the detective needs to show, not just that this story could explain the evidence, but that this is the only story that could: that there was no other possible faked suicide among the ten deaths, or that some but not all of the travellers on the Orient Express might have been involved in the killing, and so on. If a logical causal chain goes forward from the reconstructed crime to the evidence, it need not follow that we can follow that chain backwards from the evidence to the crime: for any number of alternative chains might explain precisely the same evidence. No wonder that the brilliance of the detective is invariably followed by the breakdown of the criminal, for without the confession we would not, or at least should not, be wholly convinced.

We are all amateur detectives at heart, and historical puzzles are irresistible. Scholarly discussions are full of these methodological 'Poirots', and they come from the sharpest critics.

Take, for instance, Andocides' failure to quote any documentary evidence for the Lydus document (above, p. 27). MacDowell, in the standard commentary on the speech, concluded that Andocides' name stood on Lydus' list (1962: 167–71). This may be one possibility: but it is only one – in fact, a simple form of 'Poirot', giving *an* explanation, but not necessarily *the* explanation, for the way which Andocides' rhetoric looks. We cannot even be sure that any record of the Lydus denunciation existed in 400: records existed for Pythonicus (13) and Teucrus (15, 35), but this may be because it was they, not Lydus, who eventually received the state reward (28).[42] And even if there is something concealed here, it need not be the inclusion of Andocides' own name on Lydus' list. Andocides has to defend himself both on the impiety charge and against the accusation that he denounced his father: perhaps it is the father-denunciation which was the embarrassing part of the Lydus affair. True, this was Lydus' denunciation, not Andocides' own (18; above, p. 27) – but it remains possible that Andocides offered some sort of testimony in support of Lydus' charges, just as Andromachus provided the crucial support for the earlier denunciation by Pythonicus (11–13). But that is merely another possibility, one further 'Poirot' to add to MacDowell's.

Other 'Poirots' abound: the suggestion for instance that the unmutilated Herm reflected an agreement of Euphiletus to let Andocides off with just one to mutilate, a gesture to establish solidarity, but that Andocides was too sick even to do that (MacDowell 1962: 174), or that Andocides agreed but backed out at the last minute, remembering his own claimed descent from Hermes (Furley 1996: 64). But no incident is so productive of questionable reconstructions as the story of Diocleides, especially the claim that he identified the culprits by moonlight.

Plutarch (*Alc.* 20) and Diodorus (13.2.4) here seem to add another detail. The night was the last of the month, they say, and there was no moon: that came out in questioning, and exposed the man as a liar. Neither author names Diocleides. Diodorus adds that Alcibiades was among those denounced. It is odd that a man with his life at stake would make so elementary a blunder as to forget that it was a moonless night. MacDowell (1962: 188) here produces a particularly elegant 'Poirot'. His Diocleides is taken by surprise by the unexpected question, 'how could you see well enough to recognise them?', does not think quickly enough to say 'by the lights they were carrying', and, flustered, replies 'by the moon': then he breaks down when the mistake is exposed. One still wonders why Andocides did not mention this exposure if the story was current by his day: it is in his interest to represent Diocleides' testimony as wholly insubstantial, and this would have been the *coup de grâce*.

Yet other scholars' suggestions are no more convincing. Dover (*HCT* iv: 274–6) suggests that there were two similar night-time incidents, and that the Plutarch/Diodorus story originally referred to the mysteries profanation, not to the Herms: hence Diodorus' inclusion of Alcibiades. At some point in the tradition it was displaced to the better-known Herms incident. Like all good 'Poirots', Dover's reconstruction is perfectly possible: the evidence would in that case look exactly as it does. But what makes it more likely than the alternative explanation: that there was only one incident; that there was no 'moonless night' element by the time of Andocides; that this dramatic story was an elaboration at a later stage of the tradition (it was a natural way of elaborating any tale which had an informer denouncing people he had seen by moonlight, then exposed dramatically as a liar); and that Diodorus or his source included Alcibiades because he was the most notorious figure, and tended to be involved in any embellishment?[43] That would explain the evidence just as well.

Finally, a broader point. It is tempting to assume that, if we find Andocides' arguments unconvincing, we should infer that he is guilty. MacDowell (1962: 168) stated this as a firm principle: this is a skilled orator pleading for his life: if his arguments are not sufficient to establish innocence, then, MacDowell argues, we should conclude him guilty. But if we probe any forensic speech in Greek or Latin, we almost always find similar rhetorical subterfuges: yet, statistically, some of these cases must surely have been better than their opponents'.[44] Even innocent people usually have things that would damage their case and which they prefer to hide. Say Andocides did not formally denounce his father but did give damaging evidence; say he did not commit any mutilation himself, but was enthusiastic in promoting the suggestion; say he was not denounced by Lydus over the mysteries, but there were sufficient awkward episodes to suggest an unconventional attitude towards the gods. Say any of those things, provided we remember that none of them is proven. Andocides might then be innocent, but there would still be many things, too many, which he could not possibly acknowledge.

The most familiar modern parallel might be political rather than law-court speeches: after all, we well-behaved classicists and historians tend to be more familiar with fictional legal cases than real ones (or at least we were before O.J. Simpson). It is depressingly usual to find politicians' speeches on both sides shallow and question-begging, transparently inadequate to the complexities of the issues, putting every matter in black-and-white terms of heroes (us) and villains (them), perpetually nervous of making any concession which the opposition might twist. The adversarial system has enshrined the practice of overarguing all the time. The same was true of the Greek court. Even the innocent had to overargue there, just as even the better side in politics has to overargue today.

## Reconstructing mentalities

All this is dispiriting to the historian. Some things, it is true, can be extracted from the speech. We can believe in the sequence of denunciations, especially those supported by documents; and it is hard to believe that Diocleides' revelations, his exposure as a liar, and his execution could simply be made up in 400. Even fifteen years on, memories would be too good for that. But when we probe the rhetorical niceties and try to reconstruct the truth behind them, we find ourselves enveloped by the smokescreen which Andocides, innocent or guilty, has so assiduously laid.

There is another way, and it was already mapped out in Chapter 1. We can switch our attention from 415 to 400; we can use the speech to illustrate the mentality of the speaker and audience of the day; we can stop regarding the rhetoric and the trial-dynamics as annoying barriers to the facts, and view them instead as historically interesting in their own right.[45] Most of those accused in 415, like Andocides himself, were clearly well-born and wealthy, and many belonged to avant-garde intellectual circles.[46] Securing and keeping the goodwill of a popular jury was not straightforward. How can Andocides argue his case, and hope to win? What does he not even need to argue or to explain, because it can be taken for granted? What, in particular, does he *not* say, despite possible relevance, because it would be counterproductive in this sort of trial-setting and before this sort of jury?

Take, for instance, some of the vignettes we have already treated: that picture of Euphiletus 'proposing the scheme [of mutilating the Herms] during one of our drinking-sessions', with Andocides opposing it; then after his injury 'Euphiletus discovered the state I was in. He told them that I had been persuaded to join them in their plan, that I had promised to play a part in it by mutilating the Herm by the Phorbanteion. ... When they discovered that I knew about the deed but had not done it, they were furious.' Then the two men came round: if he was silent, they would stay his friends; if not, they would be warmer enemies than any friends he might have made on their account (63). It was an offer he could not refuse.

As we saw, there is no way of knowing how true this all was. The important point is that it was plausible, the view Andocides' audience would have of a drinking-club. They may be wrong: such drinking-clubs were the haunt of élite *hetaireiai* (groups of 'comrades'),[47] and a popular audience might have as vague an idea of what really went on there as most of us have of the inside of a London club or a Hollywood dinner-party.[48] But the perception is itself an item of historical interest. This is an audience whom Andocides expected to believe in a political gesture springing from a symposium, and in a succession of symposia where the same scheme was aired and planned; in one man, Euphiletus, who was clearly the dominating spirit, but also in a gathering of people who needed to be informed and persuaded; and in a close-knit body who would feel outraged if an individual member broke ranks.

Or take that story of Diocleides' attempt, or alleged attempt, to get Andocides' friends and kinsmen to buy his silence. Perhaps Andocides expected his audience to feel something of the outrage a modern reader feels at such 'blackmail': or perhaps an Athenian audience would be less shocked, more ready to admire a cunning manipulation of events as the way an Odysseus or a Themistocles would have behaved. Either way, the telling details come at the end, with the account of Diocleides' meeting with Andocides' circle (above, p. 29). Remember that readiness of Diocleides to accept their money 'if in that way he could be our friend' (40), the consequent offer of money, and the promise that 'if we obtain what we want, he should be one of us' (41). Again, we cannot be certain that all this is true: Andocides himself implies that it is not, for he presents Diocleides' evidence as a pack of lies. It is still a picture which is presumed to be plausible: it is presented as a version which was believed at the time. We should find very interesting this picture of trying to insinuate oneself into a politically active circle of 'friends' – and, even more so, that ominous phrase (variously taken by commentators)[49] 'if we obtain what we want', suggesting that the Herms mutilation was the prelude to something more ambitious. For the rhetoric to work, the jurors must think this the sort of thing which might have been true.

Then there is Diocleides' final confession that he was lying, and had been put up to it by Alcibiades of Phegus and Amiantus from Aegina (65; above, p. 30). The two men fled, Andocides tells us, and that is presumably true. It need not follow that they were guilty:[50] anyone denounced would have to be crazy rather than innocent to stay. What does follow is that people might believe it, that in 415 and 400 audiences could believe that one élite group could seek to exploit the panic by denouncing particular opponents. In this case, the name 'Alcibiades' – even though this is only a cousin – would probably suggest to an audience that the great Alcibiades' partisans were in the thick of these vindictive exchanges.

A little later Andocides is building a rhetorical climax:

> I should justly be pitied by everyone for my ill luck, but should receive the highest credit for what happened – I, who opposed Euphiletus when he introduced this pledge of faith which was the most faithless imaginable, and who opposed him and abused him as he deserved; and when they did what was wrong I helped them to conceal it, even after Teucrus' denunciation had led to the deaths of some and the exile of others, until the point when we were imprisoned because of Diocleides and were about to be killed.
>
> (67)

This 'pledge of faith which was the most faithless imaginable' is introduced casually, as needing no explanation. It picks up Andocides' earlier description of Euphiletus' mutilation proposal (61; above, p. 31), and must reflect the way the audience would have understood that passage. That helps to illuminate something that might bemuse us, though the original observers would clearly have taken it as read. This 'pledge' mentality is something we can parallel from Thucydides. In 411 there was an oligarchic conspiracy in Samos. The plotters killed the Athenian demagogue Hyperbolus, 'giving a pledge to one another', and later joined in sundry other joint enterprises before attacking the people (8.73.2). Earlier, Thucydides counted as one of the symptoms of catastrophic civic faction (*stasis*) the tendency to 'validate their mutual pledges in terms not so much of divine law and custom as of common transgression of laws and customs' (3.82.6) – a typically dense phrase, but one which points to 'pledges' as no longer depending on belief in the gods by which they swore, but on the shared (and very secular) ostentatious disregard of traditional behaviour.

These plotting groups depended on mutual solidarity, yet could not trust one another without some strong bond. The sharing of a terrible secret, the knowledge that any one participant had a hold over any other by their complicity, offered that trust that no-one could afford to drop out. Andocides clearly takes that mentality for granted in his audience: so indeed does Thucydides in the narrative of the Herms incident itself, for this makes clear why people could take the mutilation as a matter of revolutionary plotting (6.27.3, 60.1, 61.1), something which he felt no need to explain. That does not mean that this was all there was to it: a 'pledge' could be an action worth carrying through for its own sake, as Hyperbolus' antagonists surely thought his murder a good in itself.[51] Here too the mutilators may have had other, perhaps Sicilian, aims in view as well. But the text of Andocides is certainly illuminating here. It is the very casualness of his remark that reveals how embedded the 'pledge' was in the society.

Notice too how Andocides continues. He is proud to have concealed the outrage of his *hetairoi* for so long, and to have kept the secret until forced by his own danger to reveal it. This crime had produced widespread panic; there had been many deaths already; the whole state was endangered. And yet Andocides here has no compunction in confessing his placing of his *hetairoi* ahead of the state as a whole; just as earlier he assumes, and expects his audience to assume, that it would be agonising to choose between *hetairoi* on the one hand, family and city on the other (51).[52] We must be careful here what we conclude; it need not follow, as we saw in Chapter 1, that every juror would have felt the same way himself all the time. But at least *in this distinctively citizen-élite experience* of sitting on a jury, it is a code of values to which Andocides can appeal without wrecking his chances of sympathy. Athenian democracy, we increasingly realise, did not always set itself against the élite ideologies of its aristocratic past. There are ways in which it appropriated élite ideals: a democratic citizen might feel the same bonds for his comrades that an old-style symposiast might have felt for his. The comradeship might certainly extend to more of one's fellow-citizens, but the values and duties of comradeship remained familiar and cogent.

We should also give significance to what Andocides does not say, lines of argument which might logically strengthen his case but which his audience might find repugnant. He does not claim, for instance, that the profanations of the mysteries never happened (indeed, the audience all 'know' that they did, 30 – the 'truth universally acknowledged' once again); nor that the gods would not mind (instead he assumes that the gods would be most affronted by the various impieties his prosecutors alleged, and hence he must be innocent to remain unscathed)[53]; nor that the *demos* was panicking or over-reacting, the emphasis which is so clear in Thucydides. Andocides may or may not have thought the same; but it was not something which he could claim, for that would have been to doubt the wisdom of the Athenian *demos*.

Nor – a related point – does he deny that either the mutilation or the profanation was part of an oligarchic plot. That again would be to doubt the wisdom of the *demos*, who were so convinced of this at the time. But he does have to tread very carefully. His own oligarchic connections were doubtless well-known to the jury: naturally he does not dwell on them, but he cannot deny them, and at one point he even seems to seek to win sympathy by suggesting that the city is a dangerous place for people like him.[54] But to stress the oligarchic line would be to risk associating himself too closely and clearly with the culprits. Thus the nearest he comes to admitting the 'oligarchic conspiracy' interpretation is in the pledge passage at 67, where he is emphasising how he opposed his cronies. Elsewhere the clearest hint comes at 36:

> ... Peisander and Charicles, men who were on the commission of inquiry and seemed at that time to be very well-disposed to the *demos*, claimed that what had happened was not the work of just a few men, but was aimed at the overthrow of the democracy; and that the inquiry should not be stopped but should continue. The atmosphere at the time was such that, when the herald summoned the council and took down the emblem for a meeting, that was the signal both for the council to gather in the council-house and for everyone else to flee from the agora, each one of them fearing immediate arrest.

'[M]en ... who seemed *at that time* to be very well-disposed to the *demos*': the qualification is not accidental, for within a few years Peisander had emerged as one of the most unrelenting oligarchs. By 400 this was not a name to evoke trusting memories in the Athenian mind: yet Andocides has ensured that the suggestion of a revolutionary plot should be associated with Peisander, just as it is associated with that nervous, panicky atmosphere which he here so deftly paints. Even though he cannot claim that it was not an oligarchic plot, we can see some nimble footwork to play down those associations. That too is historically significant, of the mood of 400 if not of 415. The *demos* cannot be told clearly that they were wrong, but their confidence in their past wisdom may now be shaken – sufficiently shaken for Andocides to plant some intimations that the suspicions were the work of untrustworthy men in a panicky mood.

Andocides, then, uses names carefully, here the name of Peisander. We should also note a name which is surprisingly rare in the speech: Alcibiades. He is stressed strongly at the beginning, as a central figure in that first denunciation of Pythonicus (11–14, 16). After that he is neglected, and we are a world away from the Alcibiades-centred narrative of Thucydides. Andocides could, for instance, have argued that he himself had nothing to do with anything, for it was all the doing of the friends of Alcibiades, and 'I hated him as you do'; or he could have argued that the panic was so disastrous to the city that they even exiled Alcibiades, and 'I, like him, was an innocent victim, and the city suffered'; or he could have argued that 'you forgave Alcibiades for his later services, why not forgive me?' But he does none of these things. Alcibiades was too bound up with the fall of the city. His greatness and his weakness so perfectly mirrored those of Athens herself, her flair, her enterprise, her unpredictability. No wonder he was such a sensitive subject, with speakers for years after his death still deeply concerned to defend or attack this charismatic focus of Athens' last days:[55] and no wonder Andocides found him too delicate a figure to introduce. Whether he praised him or blamed him, there were too many toes to tread on.

Our focus has shifted from 415 to 400, to dwell on the sensitivities of a prickly audience rather than the motives of the mutilators or profaners. Still, we should not separate the two inquiries too starkly. It matters what was believable. If a 400 audience could believe in a world where the symposium was the focus for political conspiracy, if the notion of a bold transgressive 'pledge' was so familiar, if it was so easy in either 415 or 400 to believe that a Diocleides was set up by a group to eliminate their antagonists – these are glimpses of a distinctive political atmosphere and milieu. Even if false, these vignettes illuminate a world where something like them might be true, and that can be our starting-point for any guesswork about what really was true.

Not that we are likely to get very far, at least if we focus on the motives of the culprits. Thucydides certainly found the whole matter impenetrable (6.60.2). But there is the further question why the mutilation, whoever its perpetrators and whatever its motives, should have provoked such shattering consequences. For there had been earlier mutilations of statues (6.28.1), presumably holy ones;[56] the alleged profanations had been earlier too, and it was only the mutilation that made them an item of such concern. One reason for the reaction was the number of the mutilations, doubtless much greater than those other casual mutilations before: no one symposium or *hetaireia* could achieve so much, someone must have organised it, and sinister, transgressive organisation is so much more terrifying than sinister transgression itself. But we need not doubt that others swiftly tried to exploit the mood, and not all had the same motives. Alcibiades' enemies would try to exploit the mood against him: whether he was innocent or not, Alcibiades' transgressiveness was all too believable. Those who suspected oligarchic plotting would exploit the mood too: *hetaireiai* typically aided their members to gain supremacy within the democracy rather than to subvert it, but some, perhaps most, could turn oligarchic if the time was ripe (Peisander and the events of 411 show as much; Thuc. 8.54.4): that again was all too believable. Those suspicious of élite symposia would find it very easy to think that they were up to something: all too believable. Those opposed to the Sicilian adventure would seize on the dangers of hostile gods: all too believable.[57] Believability is what counts. The reaction is a question of mentality, not fact: and it is mentality, not fact – even if it is the mentality of fifteen years later – that Andocides' rhetoric reveals to us so well.

# Chapter 3

# How far would they go? Plutarch on Nicias and Alcibiades

## Plutarch

We have already seen ways in which Thucydides shapes his narrative: selection, emphasis, articulation, temporal dislocation come together to impose a particular reading of events. But how far would an author go in shaping detail to construct a persuasive narrative? 'The ability of the ancients to invent and their capacity to believe are persistently underestimated,' said Finley (1985: 9): what ways are there to arrive at a more accurate estimate?

One way is to start late and work back. We can trace the techniques of some of the later authors with more certainty, for we can sometimes compare them with their own source-material – for instance, when they are working with Thucydides' or Xenophon's material – and see the freedoms they take. This chapter will take Plutarch, especially his *Nicias* and *Alcibiades*, as a test-case. There are dangers too in this working back. We cannot be sure that Herodotus, Thucydides, or Xenophon would have assumed the same freedoms as one another (for there were no clear generic 'rules'[1]), still less as a writer five hundred years later; and Plutarch is anyway writing *Lives* rather than historiography.[2] Equally, we cannot be sure that they would *not*, and we may make fewer errors if we at least start by assuming that Thucydides' narrative mindset and techniques were closer to those of Plutarch than to those of a modern historian. Nor is this useful simply as an approach to the classical writers. Very often we are dependent on Plutarch for important material, and we need some guidelines on how far he can be trusted.

The *Parallel Lives* were written in the first decades of the second century AD. These are indeed *Parallel* Lives:[3] a Greek and a Roman are viewed together, with (normally) a brief epilogue pointing out the areas in which each was the stronger. Comparison is far more important than is often realised, and the themes of one *Life* are often affected, even directed, by those of its pair. *Pericles and Fabius* emphasises the two heroes' capacity to control themselves and their states, but Pericles' initial unnatural demagogy is mirrored, in an 'hour-glass structure', by a final period of equally unnatural demagogy in *Fabius*;[4] *Cimon* begins with Cimon's domestic excesses and ends with enthusiasm for his achievement, then its pair *Lucullus* symmetrically moves from warfare into a slothful, if civilised, old age. *Coriolanus and Alcibiades* explores how these two men of such different temperaments interacted with their difficult *demoi*. That pair reverses the normal pattern and treats the Roman first, then the Greek: Plutarch has his reasons for that, we shall see.

Plutarch has read extremely widely, especially in the literature of classical Athens. For *Nicias* and for *Alcibiades*, for instance, he can exploit – doubtless largely from memory – Euripides, Plato, Theophrastus, Aristophanes and other comic poets (and perhaps their later commentators too), fifth- and fourth-century rhetoric, Craterus' collection of Athenian decrees, as well as the standard historians Xenophon, Ephorus, and Theopompus, and for Sicily Philistus and Timaeus. In particular, he knows Thucydides' text intimately, and he alludes to it in a way which presupposes that his audience know it too.[5] He will not, he says at the beginning of *Nicias*, compete artistically against Thucydides, especially in the Sicilian narrative, for there the historian 'was at his most emotional, vivid, and varied'. Naturally he cannot avoid the material altogether, for the Sicilian disaster so tellingly showed what Nicias was like. But where he can he will

> try to collect material that is not well-known but scattered among other authors, or found on ancient dedications and decrees. Nor is this an accumulation of useless erudition: I am conveying material which is helpful for grasping the man's nature and character.
>
> (*Nic.* 1.5)

The interest in exploring the man's character is typical. At the beginning of *Alexander* he explains that he is writing biography, not history, and that a small matter, a word or a jest, can often reveal more about a person's nature than battles where thousands die. But in *Nicias* we also notice that determination to discover new facts; and there is indeed a good deal of this material which was 'scattered among other authors, or found on ancient dedications and decrees', and he is more concerned with that than to wring every last fact out of Thucydides.[6]

The desire to supplement Thucydides is visible elsewhere. At *Alc.* 20–1, for instance, he gives an unusual amount of detail, especially names, concerning Andocides' imprisonment, and at *Per.* 29–33 there is a marvellous nest of stories concerning the outbreak of the war;[7] in each case he is filling out cases where Thucydides was reticent. In the last third of *Alcibiades* (and *Lysander* and *Agesilaus* are similar) he similarly supplements Xenophon with material from elsewhere, especially for exploits which show Alcibiades at his most bold, resourceful, or cunning: the way he enticed the enemy out of Cyzicus, for instance, or the confident bluff which won over Selymbria, or the ruse which took Byzantium (28, 30, 31). Most of this material is anecdotal, though some will come from historiographic sources (these last cases are close enough to Diodorus to suggest that both draw on the same historiographic tradition). This supplementation of the mainstream sources makes Plutarch particularly useful to us. True, we will be suspicious of the historical accuracy of the anecdotes,[8] much more suspicious than Plutarch: we will find several cases when he draws uncomfortably large inferences from, say, joking remarks in comedy. But even the anecdotes can go some way to illustrating what was said about Alcibiades, or at least the *sort* of thing which was said.[9] For Plutarch, Alcibiades was someone people always talked about and never agreed on. And that is a point which Plutarch surely got right.

Plutarch was writing for a varied audience, including Philhellene Romans of great political power and Greeks so unfamiliar with Rome that they needed basic Roman institutions explained. The one thing Plutarch assumed was a readiness to enter imaginatively into the ethical issues which his *Lives* raised. For Plutarch is a moralist. He hopes that his writings, when properly read, will improve his audience's ethical behaviour and understanding. But he does not reduce his heroes to one-dimensional embodiments of virtues and vice: far from it, for even the most respected figures – Aristides, Pericles, the two Catos, Brutus – present difficult questions of ethical assessment. Should Aristides have so neglected his patrimony? Should Pericles have thrown himself so wholeheartedly into that early period of demagogy? Should the elder Cato have treated his slaves so inhumanely? And even the more 'negative' pairs, *Demetrius–Antony* and *Coriolanus–Alcibiades*, explore, not merely denounce, their subjects' behaviour. If Plutarch simply despised a figure, he found him uninteresting: thus there is no pair *Cleon and Clodius*. The figures he selects, like those of tragedy, face dilemmas and invite evaluation, and the application of a moral code to particular cases can be unstraightforward and disquieting. That is the imaginative world we are expected to enter, and share the moral exploration of his heroes' actions.

Take, for instance, *Nicias*, the *Life* in which the debt to Thucydides is clearest. The *Life* confronts problems of leadership. How should a public man combine religion with realism? How should he deal with a *demos* like that of Athens? The moralism is complex. Nicias is certainly not a role model: his preoccupation is to preserve his own reputation, and his treatment of the *demos* is typified by nervous unease, a theme which Plutarch takes from Thucydides but develops in a more thoroughgoing way. Yet it is hard to withhold all sympathy from Nicias, especially in his hopeless predicament in Sicily. It is in this second part of the *Life* that we can trace Plutarch's rewriting of Thucydides most closely, and it makes this ethical focus clear.

## Rewriting Nicias

Something like two-thirds of the Sicilian campaign itself is clearly drawn from Thucydides' narrative, but Plutarch's own retouchings are pervasive. He adds his verdict on Nicias' generalship: it was one thing to oppose the expedition in Athens, but he should not have wrecked it by his apathy, always gazing wistfully home from his ship (14.1–2). In other *Lives* we see Plutarch reconstructing the reactions of onlookers:[10] no surprise here, then, to find 'the terror of the Syracusans and the incredulity of the Greeks' at the circumvallation (17.2), or 'everyone' criticising Nicias for his strategy (16.9), both non-Thucydidean touches. But not everything is negative. The praise for Nicias' swiftness when he turns to action is again Plutarch's own (15.3–4), and he is again warmly approving a little later: 'Nicias was himself present at most of the actions, forcing his ailing body on' (18.1), then 'struggled out of his sickbed' to supervise the defence – a picturesque inference from Thucydides 6.101–2, but one of which Plutarch was certainly capable. His Nicias becomes a familiar figure, the cautious general who can still be effective when he finally stirs. At *Aratus* 10 he discusses the type elaborately: it is sufficiently a hallmark of Plutarch to confirm that it is he himself, not any intermediate source, who is rewriting here, just as at *Arat.* 10 he rewrites Polybius to produce this favourite figure.[11]

What, then, of his moving description of Nicias' final hours? There are many touches, italicised below, which seem to go well beyond Thucydides' account (7.75–6).

> There were many terrible sights in the camp, *but the most pitiful of all was Nicias himself.* Ravaged by sickness, *he was reduced against all dignity* to the most meagre of food and the slightest of bodily provisions, *at a time when he needed so much more because of his disease. Yet despite his weakness he carried on performing and enduring more than many of the healthy. It was clear to all that it was not for himself that he bore the toil, nor because he was clinging to life; it was for the sake of his men that he refused to give up hope.* Others were forced by their terror and suffering into tears and lamentation, but *if Nicias was ever driven to this it was clearly because he was measuring the disgrace and dishonour of the expedition's outcome against the greatness and glory of what he had hoped to achieve. Nor was it only the sight of the man that was so moving. They also recalled his words and advice when he had warned against the expedition, and that made it even clearer how undeserved were his sufferings.* They were dispirited too when *they thought of the hopes they might place in Heaven, reflecting how this pious man, who had performed so many religious duties with such great splendour, was faring no better than the lowest and humblest of his army.*
>
> (*Nic.* 26.4–6)

No shortage of italics there. Yet surprisingly much *could* still be inspired by Thucydides' original, given Plutarch's predilection for reconstructing observers' reactions. Thucydides too had dwelt on the men's agonised reflections, and in his case it is the men themselves who measure their sufferings against their original hopes (75.2, 6–7): elsewhere too we find Plutarch transferring thoughts and actions from others to Nicias,[12] and he is probably doing the same here. Thucydides had emphasised the pitiful state of the camp, in a very visual register (75); the lamentations can certainly come from him. And even in Thucydides Nicias had been active, making his desperate speech of encouragement (77); he was effective too in drawing up his army (78.1). Yet Thucydides had also emphasised the disease, making Nicias himself refer to it at 77.2, when he points out that he is weaker than his men. It was not difficult for Plutarch to infer that 'he achieved and endured more than many of the healthy', nor to guess how they admired him for his resilience. Thucydides' Nicias had spoken of 'the hopes from Heaven' and his own past religious dutifulness (77.2, 4): Plutarch could guess how his men would respond to that too. And Thucydides had commented on the horror of Nicias' fate: 'most unworthy of all the Greeks of my time to fall into such misfortune, when all his behaviour had been directed towards virtue' (7.86.5). Plutarch could transfer that reflection too to Nicias' men, and in this *Life*, with its stress on Nicias' religious observation, the shift from Thucydides' 'virtue' into 'piety' was natural.

We cannot be quite certain about this. Plutarch may have had a second source to combine with Thucydides: he had such a source a little later, for the final scenes of surrender and slaughter. But if he did, it is surprising that he draws so little of substance from it, and that all the rewriting could be an intelligent reconstruction from Thucydides. Intelligent reconstruction is Plutarch's strength; focalising through concerned spectators is his hallmark. Here too it is very probable that his imagination is heavily at work, highlighting the features which are most ethically interesting about Nicias' nobility at the end. And if this produces a closing cadence which is more generous than much of the preceding narrative, that too is typical of the *Lives*.[13]

## Duplication with a difference: the ostracism of Hyperbolus

Plutarch often described the same events in two or more *Lives*. This also shows 'how far he would go', for we find incompatible versions even in *Lives* which must have been composed at more or less the same time.[14] Thus in *Alcibiades* the story of Hyperbolus' ostracism (?416 or 415) is put before the trick on the Peloponnesian ambassadors and the Mantinea campaign of 418 (13–15); in *Nicias* it is the other way round (10–11). The ostracism story is itself told differently in the two *Lives*. In each it centres on a trick whereby the supporters of Nicias and Alcibiades combine to make Hyperbolus the unexpected loser; but more space is given to a fourth possible victim Phaeax in *Alcibiades*, while *Nicias* polarises events around Alcibiades and Nicias alone, and Phaeax is mentioned only in an afterword, 'I am not unaware of Theophrastus' version that it was Phaeax, not Nicias, who contended against Alcibiades...' (*Nic.* 11.10). There is also a third mention at *Aristides* 7: there the point is that ostracism had always befallen men of distinction (the same point is made at *Alc.* 13.9 and *Nic.* 11.6–8), and understandably Nicias and Alcibiades are stressed there, not the less distinguished Phaeax.

The differences between *Nicias* and *Alcibiades* are not casual: the ordering suits the needs of each *Life*. At this point of *Alcibiades* we are concerned with Alcibiades' first political steps, and the pranks of his youth are transposing into a public dimension: first the ostracism, a flamboyant outsmarting of prominent Athenians which is more continuous with his earlier brashness; then we move on to the international stage with the ambassadors and Mantinea, entering the diplomatic and military register which will dominate the rest of the *Life*. In *Nicias* we have been on that public stage for some time. The first movement of the *Life* had ended with the 'Peace of Nicias' (9): now we see, first, the collapse of that peace (the ambassadors and Mantinea), then the collapse of Nicias' own career, for the ostracism is linked closely to the Sicilian disaster which follows:

> Fortune is a hard thing to judge, it baffles calculation. If Nicias had risked casting the dice of the ostracism against Alcibiades, either he would have won, driven out the other man, and guided the city in safety, or he would have lost and left before his final misfortunes, preserving his reputation for outstanding generalship.
>
> (*Nic.* 11.9)

That reflection is less trivial than it may seem, for the *Life* repeatedly, and tragically, shows Nicias behaving in ways which fall back disastrously on himself. Thus his involuntary strengthening of Cleon's authority creates the political conditions he is unable to manage (8), and in the Sicilian debate it is his ostentatious caution that makes the Athenians so confident that, with such a man in charge, it could not go wrong (12.5).

That emphasis helps to explain the different detail. In *Nicias* it is both Nicias and Alcibiades (or at least their supporters – the phrase used is ambiguous) who are scheming against Hyperbolus, while in *Alcibiades* it is Alcibiades alone: it is important in *Nicias* that Nicias' actions should turn against himself. As for Phaeax, the 'if either Nicias or Alcibiades had lost…' reflection in *Nicias* would have been ruined if Phaeax had intruded too heavily, for his ostracism would evidently not have saved Nicias from Sicily. In *Alcibiades* the focus rests more on Alcibiades' relationship with the *demos*, and this extra character is a positive advantage: the *Life* recurrently highlights different styles of leadership, and here the incompetent rhetoric of Phaeax (13.2–3) contrasts effectively with Alcibiades' eloquence

(10.3–4), just as Hyperbolus' contempt for public acclaim (*doxa*, 13.5) contrasts with Alcibiades' love of honour and acclaim (*philodoxia*, 6.4 etc.).

What we must *not* do here is assume that we have two distinct accounts, with each *Life* following different source-material.[15] Plutarch's own adaptation can account for the divergences.

It so happens that Plutarch is a principal source for this ostracism; Thucydides, for his own reasons,[16] passed it over. And the use of Plutarch as a source is evidently here a tricky business. As it chances, comparison of the two *Lives* makes the freedom he takes with Phaeax demonstrable; there may be other Plutarchan touches which can only be suspected. What for instance of the notice, in *Alcibiades* but not in *Nicias*, that Hyperbolus initiated the ostracism vote? Some build a good deal on this;[17] but this picture of the biter (Hyperbolus) bit is suspiciously appropriate in a *Life* where many rivals underestimate Alcibiades' cunning, yet later Alcibiades himself is outplayed at his own game (below, p. 57). What of that view of ostracism as a preserve of the distinguished, so that the *demos* abandoned it once it was used on low-grade men like Hyperbolus? Plutarch probably has no better grounds for this than the fragment of the comic poet Plato which he quotes in both *Nicias* and *Alcibiades* – Hyperbolus deserved ostracism but ostracism did not deserve Hyperbolus, it was wasted on the likes of him. That was a good comic line, but it is scant foundation for building an interpretation: there are better ways of explaining both the institution and its abandonment.[18] What too of Plutarch's treatment of Hyperbolus as a scoundrel, and his lack of interest in his political programme? That again fits the comic fragment and it echoes Thucydides' dismissive judgement (8.73.3, quoted at *Alc.* 13.3); it also fits the interest in leadership styles. But it may fail to capture the reasons for holding an ostracism or the motives leading a voter to choose his victim.[19]

What, too, of the picture of politics? All three versions present a world in which politicians can deliver their supporters' votes, even in a case where it is *negative* preferences which is in point – and we should not expect all enthusiasts for Alcibiades to be of one mind on whether Hyperbolus, Nicias, or Phaeax was the most repellent. In *Nicias* he suggests that this could be set up 'secretly' (11.5), despite the large number of voters involved. Plutarch talks about the principals 'bringing their factions (*staseis*) together' (*Nic.* 11.5, *Alc.* 13.7), a notably vague phrase. Is he assuming large numbers of voters committed to a leading individual? If so, would this be on the basis of personal preference or of some lasting moral obligation? Or does he mean smaller groups of supporters who might hand out ready-made ostraka, and sing one man's praises and denounce another's vices? Are these *hetaireiai* or sympotic groups of the sort we found in the Herms and mysteries scare (also in 415)? Or are these 'factions' minor politicians, the hangers-on who attached themselves to a great man? Did Plutarch himself know what he meant? This is not an aspect of Athenian politics which interested him (below, p. 58): if he is combining sources, it would not be surprising if some nuances disappeared.

It is unfortunate that this passage has played a large part in the best discussions of Athenian politics,[20] given our total inability, and perhaps Plutarch's too, to be certain what is really implied.

## Alcibiades: dissent and decline

There are times when the differences between the two *Lives* go further. Take their treatment of the Athenian *demos*.[21] In *Nicias*, the *demos* are a grim, taunting presence: in the ostracism the emphasis falls on their hostility to both Nicias and Alcibiades. In *Alcibiades* we have a subtler picture, with the people fascinated by Alcibiades and sharing much of his temper and style. They too are ambitious and volatile, and understandably find his manner engaging: they are delighted when his pet quail escapes on his first public appearance, and bustle around helping him to catch it (*Alc.* 10.1–2). *Demos* and demagogue suit one another, and we can believe him when he tells the Spartan ambassadors that the *demos* is 'proud and ambitious, eager for great deeds' (14.8): a mirror-image, in fact, of Alcibiades himself (17.2).

Plutarch cares enough about this picture to reinterpret Thucydides himself. At 6.3 he refers to Thucydides' summary:

> The general people were frightened both by the massive unconventionality of his physical life and habits, and by the massive spirit with which he carried through everything he did; they consequently became his enemies, thinking that he was aspiring to tyranny. He managed public events excellently, but on a private level everyone became disgruntled with his manner as a person; thus they entrusted affairs to others – and before long brought the city down.
>
> (Thuc. 6.15.4)

We have seen how fundamental this passage is to Thucydides' vision of Athenian politics.[22] Alcibiades' private excesses are coming to compromise the city's welfare, and the 'private' register is infectious. Thus for Thucydides 'everybody' is disgruntled 'on a private level', and the city is the loser.

Plutarch found that picture unsatisfactorily blunt. His Alcibiades has always been a man about whom people talked, and disagreed. Here too he gives a more discriminating picture than Thucydides. In Chapter 16 he characterises the ambivalent, divided, but largely affectionate reaction of the *demos*. It is now the 'highly regarded' who 'feel disgust' and fear his 'unconventional behaviour' as 'tyrannical and outrageous'. The echo of Thucydides is clear; but also its transformation, for Plutarch limits this reaction to the 'highly regarded'. The popular attitude is summed up by the line of Aristophanes, 'it yearns for him, it hates him, it wants to have him' (16.2, quoting *Frogs* 1425): they were indulgent to his excesses – though *the older generation* were unhappy with them as (again) 'tyrannical and unconventional'. Then there was Archestratus' remark that Greece had room for only one Alcibiades, and the misanthrope Timon's genial greeting of this man who was going to cause the Athenians such pain. 'So unclearly defined was opinion (*doxa*) concerning him because of the inconsistencies of his nature.' Reputation or opinion (*doxa*) is important, as it always is for this 'lover of *doxa*' Alcibiades; but it is also hard to pin down.

This new emphasis is not irresponsible. Some of those cross-divisions of the *demos* rest on other remarks of Thucydides himself: in particular, Plutarch builds on the hints of a generation gap in the debate at Athens, where Thucydides' Nicias tries to win over the older generation and Alcibiades counters him (6.13.1, 18.6, 24.3).[23] There is a sense, too, in which Plutarch's own biographical reconstruction would have seemed to him good evidence for this reinterpretation. Given all the shifts in Alcibiades' career and all the dissent about him, could public reaction really have been so uniform as Thucydides says? No surprise that Plutarch wondered: we should wonder too.

The reinterpretation also serves some broader themes of the *Life*. This *demos* is again like Alcibiades himself, and the people's veering and divided reactions mirror Alcibiades' own veering and inconsistent qualities. That is one reason why so many of the *Life*'s reversals seem peculiarly neat. When Alcibiades returns from his first exile, it is to confront a *demos* (this time the one in Samos) eager to turn against their fellow-citizens and play into Spartan hands – all rather as he had once done himself. But now he shows constancy and leadership in arguing them out of it (26). Treachery is now afoot in Athens herself, while he is the patriot; the tables are turned; but they can be turned so neatly because city and leader are so like one another. The people respond in kind once again. On his return they greet Alcibiades with unanimous jubilation – more unanimous than in his main source Xenophon (*Hell*. 1.4.13–17) and in Diodorus (13.68.4–6), both of whom stress the range of reactions. Plutarch had earlier revised Thucydides to make the response more multifarious; here he revises Xenophon to make it more uniform. For by now it is the swiftness *and completeness* of the popular veerings which are of interest. Their enthusiasm is now as complete as their later disillusion (36.4) – and as their subsequent regret for that disillusion (38).

We can applaud some of Plutarch's rewriting for its insight as well as for its skill. When he treats Alcibiades' showmanship in celebrating the mysteries in 407, verbal echoes mark the reverse of that earlier mysteries outrage. That is not merely piquant, it is acute: Alcibiades surely *was* making a display of his patriotic piety, so traduced by his enemies of 415.[24] Plutarch may even be righter than Xenophon in his depiction of the unanimity in 407: Xenophon too has his agenda, and these clashing popular reactions here prepare the themes of leadership and responsibility before a changeable *demos* which dominate the trials of the Arginusae generals (*Hell*. 1.7) and of Theramenes (*Hell*. 2.3).

The mistake would be to think that Plutarch necessarily had authority for any of this. He may be right in refining Thucydides' picture of universal disgust; but if so, it is not because he has better sources. He uses his *Frogs* quotation and his anecdotes deftly enough, but does not ask whether their material is sufficient to pit against Thucydides' authority; in a different mood he could have exploited the same anecdotes in Thucydides' support. It is more because he knows fifth-century culture, and has come to know his Alcibiades, well enough to have a refined historical 'feel': in much the same way, he has sufficient feel to substitute a more religious register for Thucydides' political emphasis in treating the Herms and mysteries.[25] The same goes for Plutarch's reinterpretation of the popular mood on Alcibiades' recall. It may be a good guess, but a guess is what it is.

'If any one was destroyed by his own reputation (*doxa*), that man, it seems, was Alcibiades' (35.2): this man who had always been such a lover of honour and reputation himself, *philotimos* and *philodoxos*.

That view is not new to Plutarch; Nepos said something similar (Nep. *Alc.* 7). But Plutarch develops the insight in several ways. One is the explicit sense stressed in 35, the way in which the fame of Alcibiades' successes created expectations which, in the hard light of strategic reality, he could not fulfil. It will be a similar reputation, and the hopes it continued to inspire in the shattered city, which will eventually seal his death (38). But his darker reputation proves destructive too. In the second half of the *Life* we hear little of any further excesses, at least in Athens (though his affair with the Spartan queen showed that he was still the same old Alcibiades, 23.6). Any complicity in the Herms and mysteries affairs is left uncertain. What matters is that people thought he might be involved, and that when his enemies sought to implicate him the mud stuck (20.5).

Later too his enemies find him an easy target. In his absence his subordinate Antiochus loses to Lysander off Notium (35). Thrasybulus son of Thrason promptly accuses Alcibiades of

> luxuriating away his office and entrusting command to his cronies, men who owed their influence to being his close drinking friends and his partners in sailor gossip, so that he could make money sailing around, debauching away, getting drunk, frolicking with the Abydan and Ionian courtesans, with the enemy anchored just a little way away.
>
> (36.2)

The charge is false, as Plutarch's narrative has brought out. But the truth did not matter; Alcibiades' reputation did, and again the mud stuck. 'The Athenians believed it' (36.4), and Alcibiades was exiled once more. The brilliant achievements and the private excesses produced two forms of 'reputation' which proved equally destructive.

So this is a great man trapped by his past. That again is a distinctive Plutarchan figure, and we should have no doubt that it is he, not any predecessor, who has transformed the material to produce this picture. We see similar treatments, and can similarly detect Plutarch manipulating his material,[26] with Antony, undone by the public image which lent plausibility to false charges (especially *Ant.* 59. 1); with Caesar, trapped by the friends, army, and *demos* which brought him to power but then proved a catastrophic embarrassment (especially *Caes.* 51); and most significantly with Coriolanus, destroyed by the bitterness which his past actions had unleashed (*Cor.* 39). Reputation was the target of Alcibiades' ambition, and built his greatness. But it destroyed him in the end.

This is not a shallow view, but there are times when historians should be suspicious. At 35.3–5, Plutarch contrives a neat transition from his 'destroyed by his reputation' generalisation to the critical case of Antiochus and Notium. Alcibiades' successes generated the belief that he could do anything if he tried. Athens expected to hear that all Ionia had fallen, forgetting the crippling shortage of money: and Lysander was now offering four obols a day instead of three, while Alcibiades himself had to be 'niggardly in his funding' (35.5). So Alcibiades went off to Caria to collect money, and this is why he was away when Antiochus was so dangerously rash.

'Caria' was a typical place for money-collecting trips, especially ones which failed (Thuc. 2.69.1, 3.19; Xen. *Hell.* 1.4.8–9). But Plutarch's main source Xenophon says that Alcibiades had gone to Phocaea (*Hell.* 1.5.11); Diodorus (13.71.1) has Alcibiades go to Clazomenae, then on to Cyme. Nepos (*Alc.* 7.1) also mentions Cyme, and Diodorus and Nepos seem to reflect a tradition going back through Ephorus (of Cyme, hence the Cymocentricity?) to the so-called *Hellenica Oxyrhynchia*, which apparently mentions Clazomenae.[27]

Whatever we make of the Xenophon–Ephorus disagreement, we should not put any weight on Plutarch's version.[28] Plutarch himself follows Xenophon in his parallel version in *Lysander* (5.1), and we can see reasons why he should have altered Alcibiades' motive here. It deftly introduces Lysander and the danger he poses, and removes Alcibiades far away from the action for an unimpeachable reason. There is also a further reversal. 'Niggardly funding', the same phrase, had been Alcibiades' shrewd advice to Tissaphernes at 25.1, and his own policy is coming back to haunt him. On a generous view, the misrepresentation even conveys historical illumination: the funding clash with Lysander was more important than anything concerning Phocaea or Cyme, and the reader needs to know about it. But it would be a different matter to trust Plutarch on the motive for this particular journey.

Take, too, that attack of Thrasybulus son of Thrason. This man had a career of democratic leadership ahead of him, but no other source mentions him here. It would be going too far to suspect that Plutarch has made up his role: true, his name, so suggestive of shameless boldness (*thrasutes*), would have brought a welcome resonance – but still his namesake the famous Thrasybulus was active in the surrounding narrative, and had Plutarch wished to fabricate a role he would have picked someone less confusing. But it is *not* going too far to suspect that Plutarch has elaborated that role. Xenophon suggests that the criticisms may have been similar – the Athenians 'thought that Alcibiades had lost the ships through negligence and lack of self-control' (*Hell.* 1.5.16) – but is more low-key; Diodorus has quite different attacks, centring on the ravaging of Cyme and on Alcibiades' alleged tyrannical ambitions (13.73.6); Nepos too makes Cyme important (*Alc.* 7.2–3: more Ephoran Cymocentricity?). We know that Plutarch often reconstructs how observers reacted: he is surely doing the same here. So it is most injudicious of modern scholars to rehearse Thrasybulus' role and arguments without adding a health warning.[29]

There were further advantages in anchoring these attacks to a single person rather than vaguely 'the Athenians' (Xenophon) or 'the Cymaeans' and 'some of the soldiers who were at odds with him' (Diodorus). Another of Plutarch's techniques is to develop other characters in such a way as to offset his leading figure's traits. Alcibiades first outmatched figures of a different stamp from himself: the older man Nicias, the incompetent speaker Phaeax, the spurner of reputation Hyperbolus. But others now come closer to Alcibiades' style: Androcles and the other enemies who manipulate the *demos* in 415 (19); Andocides, well-connected, unscrupulous, eager to save himself (21); Tissaphernes, devious and multifaceted (24.5–6); Phrynichus, ready to commit treachery to further his political antagonisms (25.6–7); now this Thrasybulus, self-seeking and opportunist; at the end Critias, disillusioned with democracy, turning to Sparta, and giving shrewd advice – but this time the advice is that Alcibiades must die (38.5–6). Most of these are less effective than Alcibiades himself; but they produce so many eddies of political complication that even Alcibiades is helpless. This mirroring is again typically Plutarchan: we see the same features in his Lysander, initially the calculating courtier, eventually undone when others play the same games on him (*Lys.* 2.4, 4.1–6, 19.1–2) – especially when Agesilaus shows himself as ambitious as Lysander himself (23) and when Pharnabazus proves his match in deviousness (20).[30]

Nor must we forget comparison. Alcibiades is here a more complex equivalent of his pair Coriolanus. In *Coriolanus* too the hero tended to find others like himself, or inspire others to behave like himself: when he was noble on the battlefield, the commons responded in kind (10.4–6); when he treated them with rigidity and anger, he again met his match (e.g. 17.4, 18.2); and he ended among the Volsci, re-enacting his earlier history with a trial and a charge of tyranny, and undone by a man who was something of a mirror-image (39). But *Coriolanus* has a strong, linear narrative, and a few reverses, starkly traced. In *Alcibiades* we see a dazzling sequence of shifts, as the patterns kaleidoscopically rearrange. Alcibiades' treachery at Messene (22.1) and his shifts to Sparta (23.1–2) and Persia (37.7–8) are treated in almost casual, perfunctory language, so natural do they seem after so many breathtaking shifts: contrast Coriolanus' shift to the Volsci, a single massive gesture which reverses the tenor of a whole life (*Cor.* 21–3). All the more telling, then, that the pattern of *Coriolanus* still reasserts itself; Alcibiades, for all his flair, charm, and (important in this pair) education, can eventually handle a recalcitrant *demos* no better than his Roman equivalent. That makes it most appropriate that *Coriolanus* should come first; as so often in the *Lives*, we first see the simple pattern, then the complex variation. It is a large part of Alcibiades' tragedy that, no matter how different from Coriolanus, he eventually cannot avoid re-enacting his own flamboyant version of the self-destroying renegade's fate.

## Illuminating reception

There are other ways, too, in which Plutarch can help us to read the fifth century, and fifth- and fourth-century texts. Literary scholars have come to appreciate the importance of reception-criticism, and historians can learn something similar. How one culture reads the texts of another can illuminate both: here, both Plutarch's own day and the texts he is reading.

First, his own day. There are perhaps times when he applies interpretative schemes to the fifth century which are more appropriate to his own time: 'euergetism', for instance, the ostentatious civic benefactions distinctive of the Roman empire, may have influenced his portrayal of Pericles' building programme or of Cimon's lavish public entertainments.[31] But clear cases of this are rare. Many of Plutarch's loudest themes would be of little immediate relevance to his own day, when only a few of his audience would have great wars to fight, and fewer still would be dealing with demagogues, contumacious *demoi*, and aspiring tyrants, the stuff of so many of the *Lives*. It is better to see Plutarch as favouring those interpretative strands which seemed to him most timeless and recurrent,[32] for instance the conflict of 'the few' and 'the many', and leaving unexplored motifs which were peculiar to a particular time and place, Roman *equites*, for instance, or Greek élite symposia and *hetaireiai* – or those vague, unexplained 'factions' of the ostracism story.

This too must not be overstated. Plutarch *was* aware that cultures differed, in particular that Rome was more militaristic than Greece. But it remains important to him to assume that Greek and Roman figures can illuminatingly be compared, and that his readers can make the imaginative leap into the moral dilemmas faced by his characters and can appropriate, or at least weigh, the judgements others made on them. It is not surprising that he dwells more on what cultures shared than on what they did not. This taste of Plutarch's for timelessness, and the taste which he assumes in his audience, should itself play a part in mapping the intellectual history of Imperial Greece; it should also warn the historian of classical Athens that Plutarch's treatment will not always be attuned to the *particularities* of fifth-century society.

Secondly, the texts he is using. His rewritings constitute a critical response to the classical texts, and we have seen that his disagreements with Thucydides show an impressive historical sense. In other cases his response is implicit in his own narrative technique. He supplements Xenophon's account of the Ionian War with anecdotal material from elsewhere: such material suits his own style, but it is also a sharp insight into Xenophon's own manner. Xenophon is certainly interested in Alcibiades, and a narratological study of the early *Hellenica* would bring out how much impact Alcibiades has on events and how skilfully he reads them; but Xenophon's Alcibiades guides events through a masterful insight, not through tricksiness. It is interesting, though beyond the scope of this study, to wonder why. Again, if Plutarch's Alcibiades emblematises features of Athens, the thoroughness of the treatment may be new but the basic insight is not: for Plato, for the fourth-century orators, in some ways for Thucydides too,[33] Alcibiades became an interesting test-case precisely because he mirrored so many of the features which made Athens great and then destroyed her – flair, confidence, ambition, pride, lack of judgement. And Plutarch's view of Alcibiades as undone by his mirror-images again teases out an idea already in Thucydides, for at 8.50.5 Phrynichus' self-defence against Alcibiades' denunciation surely recalls Alcibiades himself: '…that it was unexceptionable for Phrynichus, already in mortal danger because of his opponents, to do this [i.e. betray his troops to the Spartans] and anything else rather than be destroyed himself by his bitterest enemies'.

So let us expect Plutarch to have insightful, as well as misguided, things to say. Once we treat him not merely as a 'source' but also as an intelligent and knowledgeable reader of events and texts, he can sensitise us to new reading strategies, and make us see how our own strategies do not have a monopoly on historical insight. It would not be surprising if some aspects of fifth-century culture were more perspicuous to a reader from an élite intellectual culture where the classical past was still a living tradition, which still understood Olympian religion, where a love of glory was unembarrassing, where leadership charisma was not always greeted by cynicism, and where serious moral evaluation was a sign of political sophistication rather than naïveté.

# Chapter 4

# Rhetoric and history II: Plataea (431–27 BC)

## The version of Apollodorus: [Demosthenes] 59

We have seen how far an orator (Andocides) and a biographer (Plutarch) would go in reshaping history. The story of Plataea takes us two steps further: first, more oratory, as we see how drastically a fourth-century speaker adapted the story to prove, and improve, his point; secondly, we can explore how Thucydides too exploited Plataea for his rather more profound purposes.

In 431 the Theban attack on Plataea began the fighting; in 429 the Spartan king Archidamus, after an attempt to come to terms, assaulted and then laid siege to the town; in 427 Plataea was destroyed. The two-year siege was unrelenting, with elaborate works and counterworks, and an exciting moment when two hundred Plataeans forced their escape. Thucydides gives the sequence some of his most gripping narrative (2.1–6, 2.71–8, 3.20–4, 3.52–68). It ended with a travesty of a trial, as Thucydides represents it, with the Spartans asking if each Plataean had done the Spartans and their allies any good. The Plataeans could only say no. The males were executed; the captured women were sold as slaves.

Plataea had been an ally of Athens for ninety-two years. Victory over Persia had been won there in 479; the allies had then sworn an oath to liberty, guaranteeing (so it seems) Plataean independence and binding the swearers to protect Plataean soil.[1] No wonder the town's destruction lived on in the Athenian memory, a scar in the popular historical consciousness, a perpetual reproach to Thebes and Sparta and an emblem of the horrors of war.[2]

Over eighty years later, between 343 and 340, the minor politician Apollodorus supported the prosecution of Neaera, the wife or concubine of his adversary Stephanus, on a charge of false citizenship.

The speech survives as [Demosthenes] 59. It includes a lengthy treatment of Plataea (94–103): the point is to contrast the Plataeans with Neaera herself. The Plataeans had given everything as Greek patriots and loyal allies; Neaera was, in Apollodorus' presentation, a worthless courtesan, much-travelled and much-used. Athens had been magnanimous in granting the Plataeans citizenship, yet even so they had been measured in their award, taking care that their pity should not be abused. How dare Neaera pass herself off as an Athenian, laying claim to that citizenship which was so fiercely prized and so selectively granted?

Most unusually, the orator chooses to include an extended narrative of the Plataean siege, and verbal echoes show that he is following Thucydides closely[3] – so closely that he must have had a text of Thucydides open before him as he composed, or have known the Thucydidean account virtually by heart. This, then, is a particularly clear-cut test-case for tracing how far an orator will go, especially interesting because his account is at times utterly incompatible with Thucydides. Perhaps he is mixing Thucydides with another source;[4] if so, that source was not well-informed, and even a casual comparison with Thucydides should have made that clear. Or perhaps Apollodorus is simply adapting Thucydides' account. Either way, we can see how freely he abandoned Thucydides' account when it suited his rhetorical purposes.

Only a detailed commentary could bring out all the divergences; many of them are innocent enough, and simply represent abbreviation. For instance, Apollodorus makes the Plataeans turn against the Thebans the day after the initial attack (99); Thucydides had a more elaborate version of the Plataeans concerting during the night, digging through the walls of their houses to link up, then attacking before dawn (2.3.3–4). Others may be simple mistakes of Apollodorus: for instance, he makes the Theban ringleader Eurymachus a Boeotarch (99), while Thucydides specified that he was not (2.2.1, 3).[5] But many are more tendentious, and it will be convenient to begin with a list.

First, the attack of 431. Apollodorus makes King Archidamus of Sparta attack the city (98), exacting vengeance for the Plataeans' slight to the Spartan royal family, that is 'King' Pausanias, in 'prosecuting them before the Amphictyones'.[6] In fact, Thucydides made it clear that it was the Thebans who then attacked, and Sparta was brought in later. Apollodorus claims that the Plataean traitors who opened the gates in 431 were bribed (99); Thucydides made them eager to use this outside force to increase their own power (2.2.2). Apollodorus has the Thebans withdraw when they see the Athenians coming to the Plataeans' help (100); Thucydides' Thebans withdrew when the Plataeans threatened to kill the prisoners, whether or not they swore an oath to this effect (that was the Theban claim: 2.5.5–6), and the Athenians arrived only at a later stage (2.6.4).

Then the siege begins. Apollodorus has a full catalogue for the attacking force: a two-thirds muster of Peloponnesian allies, all the other Boeotians, then also Locrians, Phocians, Malians, Oetaeans, and Aenianians (101). The two-thirds Peloponnesian muster and the Boeotians, Locrians, and Phocians may come from Thucydides (2.9.2, 10.2), but if so they have changed context (Thucydides was referring to the general muster at the beginning of the war); the Malians, Oetaeans, and Aenianians have no Thucydidean authority at all. Then Apollodorus' Spartans offer the Plataeans the option of retaining their land, provided they abandon the Athenian alliance (102); Thucydides had a more elaborate Spartan invitation to neutrality, followed by an offer to allow the Plataeans to move elsewhere for the duration of the war (2.72). When the Plataeans think of a break-out, Apollodorus has them draw lots to choose who will go (103); Thucydides had the bolder half go, and the rest too frightened (3.20.2). It is also likely that Apollodorus exaggerates the length of the siege, talking of 'ten' years rather than 'two' (102), though the text here is usually emended.[7] At the end Apollodorus has Plataea taken by storm (103); Thucydides' story of surrender and trial (3.52–68) is dropped. Apollodorus' final emphasis rests on a group who fled to Athens 'when they saw the Spartans were coming against the city' (103), a group Thucydides does not mention.[8] In Apollodorus this group gives the transition to the 'decree of citizenship' granted to these Plataeans. Thus his account finishes on the item relevant to his argument, contrasting the Athenians' treatment of the Plataeans with the outrageous claims of Neaera herself (104–6). Thucydides has no mention of that final decree, and remarks in both the Plataeans' and the Thebans' speeches imply that the Plataeans already held Athenian citizenship in 427 (3.55.3, 63.2).[9]

Without quite diverging from Thucydides, Apollodorus also glosses over certain points. We hear nothing of the Thebans' choice during the 431 attack to stop the killing and offer terms (Thuc. 2.2.4); nothing of the Plataeans' initial agreement to those terms (2.3.1); nothing of the dispute over the alleged Plataean oath not to execute their prisoners (2.5). There is nothing, either, on the Athenian failure to help Plataea, a recurrent Thucydidean theme.

This list follows a regular pattern. The alterations highlight Plataean pluckiness (hence the drawing of lots rather than the panic; hence they do not surrender but are taken by storm); or at least the pluckiness of those loyal to Athens (the traitors of 431 are just bribed). They show Plataea as a loyal ally, with a history more systematically aligned with Athens:[10] thus they are attacked by Sparta, Athens' great enemy of the war, rather than by Thebes; thus they refuse the offer to retain everything if they give up the Athenian alliance. The changes of emphasis downplay the Athenian failure to come to Plataea's help; or they direct more attention to the Plataean fugitives' reception in Athens, and the Athenian response. In other words, they suit exactly the rhetorical needs of Apollodorus here, who has to highlight the Plataeans' claims upon Athens and the Athenians' judicious moral sense.

That takes us back to the question of sources. Has Apollodorus added these divergences from a second authority, or is he simply manipulating Thucydides himself? The notion of a second source is not quite impossible; Apollodorus conceivably had such a source for the preceding item (98), Plataea's prosecution of Sparta before the Amphictyones in the 470s.[11] Still, here it is hard to believe in such a source. Even the most circumstantial addition, the list of allies, is implausible: the Aenianians, Oetaeans, and Malians are most unlikely to have been Sparta's allies in 429.[12] These form a group further up the Spercheius valley, beyond Phocis and Locris to the west; they are the next peoples a traveller would pass through on a journey north-west from Plataea. It is easier to see this item as a fabrication to make Plataea even more thoroughly surrounded, Peloponnesians to the south, Boeotia all round, beyond them swathes of other peoples to the west: plucky little Plataea once again, and particularly bonded with Athens, the only people left to look to.

So we are left with the choice of (a) positing a source which offered precisely the variants which suited Apollodorus' purpose; or (b) assuming that Apollodorus introduced the variants himself. Even if (a) were the case, it helps us to see how far Apollodorus would go: with nearly every variant there can, and could, be little doubt that Thucydides offers the more reliable account – or, to put it at its most cautious, that if the variant versions were correct they cast such doubt over the whole of Thucydides' account (the trial, the identity of the 431 attackers, the dispute over the oaths) that there would be no reason to believe *any* of Thucydides' material, including the facts which Apollodorus follows so closely. If Apollodorus thought about it at all, he must have known he was following a version which had no chance of being true. But in fact it is much more likely that he introduced the falsifications himself. Someone did, in precisely the same rhetorical interest as Apollodorus here; it is uneconomical to posit an unknown predecessor to do his job for him.

The turnings of Thucydides offer us guidance on a further point, Apollodorus' treatment of the Plataean citizenship decree. He has the secretary read the decree: let us assume that the version in our text genuinely represents what was read out.[13] It prescribes that the Plataeans should be Athenian citizens 'from this day', and should share in all Athenian privileges, including religious ones, except for any hereditary priesthood or rite; they should not be eligible for election as archons, though their descendants would be. The Plataeans should be distributed among the demes and tribes; after this allocation, no further Plataeans should become Athenian except by specific decree of the *demos*.

> Look, Athenians, [Apollodorus continues] at how fairly and justly the speaker framed the decree on behalf of the Athenian people! He thought it right that the Plataean recipients should first of all be examined individually in the court to see if each is a Plataean and is one of our city's friends, in order to prevent many securing the citizenship on the basis of this claim; then, that those approved should have their names inscribed on a stone column, set up in the Acropolis by the temple of Athena, so that the grant should be preserved for later generations and it should be possible for any individual to establish whose kinsman he is. And he excludes anyone not examined at that point in the law-court from becoming an Athenian at a later date: this was to prevent many from gaining the citizenship by claiming to be Plataeans. Then he established matters for the Plataeans clearly in the decree, on behalf of both the city and the gods, that none of them should become one of the nine archons nor hold any priesthood, but their descendants might, provided they are born of a lawfully wedded wife of citizen stock.
>
> (104–6)

Notice the mismatch here between decree and Apollodorus' summary. Some points of that summary closely represent the decree's wording; other points, firmly embedded in the rest, do not. The decree does not mention the careful court-examination of individual Plataeans: something like that will take place in future, but the immediate grant seems a block one. Nor does it mention the inscription on stone; nor does it exclude Plataeans from all priesthoods, only hereditary ones. The decree's distinction between first-generation citizens and their children applies only to the archonship, not to anything religious.[14] Nor does the decree define these children so specifically as 'provided they are born of a lawfully wedded wife of citizen stock'.

These mismatches have puzzled historians. One approach is to emend the text of the decree to bring it into line with the speech; another is to stress that this version of the decree is an abbreviation of a longer document which Apollodorus will have known.[15] Both approaches are misguided. Apollodorus' glosses again fit precisely the needs of his case. He stresses the need for careful examination of each Plataean's credentials; it would be embarrassing for his case if so many were admitted without individual examination. The focus on the priesthood also fits, for he has just been reviling Stephanus and Neaera for allowing her daughter Phano to marry Theogenes the 'king archon' and conduct certain ritual duties (§§ 72–84). All the more reason, then, to stress also that the Plataeans' children should only become priests – any sort of priests, not just those delimited by birth – if they were established as born of a lawfully wedded woman of citizen stock: that is, from an antithesis of a Neaera.

We noticed Andocides claiming that his documentary evidence proved more than it did.[16] Is this not a similar case? Formal language is hard to take in. An audience would find it difficult, even immediately after hearing it, to recall that it was only some priesthoods, not all, from which Plataeans were excluded; or that the distinction between first- and second-generation citizens applied only to the archonship, not to a priesthood. Exactly like Andocides, Apollodorus is trying to persuade his audience that they have just heard something they have not. The only item which they might recognise as new is the provision about inscription on stone; yet the decree itself will also have been written on stone, and would naturally be followed – or, at least, Apollodorus could pretend that it was followed – by a list of those enrolled.[17] Perhaps Apollodorus accompanied his initial 'Look...' with a physical pointing to the secretary's copy of the decree, and the names (understood to be) attached. None of this is good evidence for what the decree in fact contained.

How far would he go? Evidently, a very long way, fabricating lists of allies and stormings of cities. Apollodorus could rely on his audience not knowing enough fifth-century history to correct his version.[18] It would be unusual for the distant past to play so crucial a role in a case; yet we should not assume that, in the hurly-burly of everyday trials, jurors necessarily knew any more of the facts which the orators described to them, whether those 'facts' concerned the social life of a particular household or the doings of a Thracian tribe, a Macedonian king, or a rival politician. It happens that we can here follow the manipulation in detail; in most of the other cases, we are reduced to guesswork on what really happened. But Apollodorus' case should remind us how thin is the basis on which that guesswork rests.

Nor, finally, should we regard Apollodorus' manipulation as merely distorting history. There is a sense in which this *is* history: it tells us what the Athenians wanted to hear, or what Apollodorus hoped they wanted to hear, about their past; it shows that this aspect of the Athenian self-image was powerful enough to justify so much material on Plataea, and so roundabout a rhetorical stratagem against Neaera; it points the way his audience liked to think about Athenian generosity to the plucky little ally – but also how this pride would not be compromised by the emphasis on their cautiousness in giving away their privileges. True, this is the Athenian self-image of the 340s, not the 420s; but we should not think that, if a representation is a falsification, it stops being interesting. History is often the history of representations, and most of them are false.

## Thucydides on Plataea

What about our first representation, that of Thucydides itself? So far we have been taking that text as our starting-point and seeing what Apollodorus did with it. But the real starting-point is not Thucydides, but whatever happened in Plataea between 431 and 427. Can we see what Thucydides did with that, how far *his* representation is a moulding as well as a mimesis?

That last formulation is apposite here, for Thucydides' narrative is more mimetic than usual. That is partly the vivid detail of the operations, put in very visual[19] terms: the counting of the bricks, the estimating of the distance and depth to the tunnel, the planning of the break-out, the wind, the rain, the dislodged tile, the shouting, the chaos, the false signals. Any devotee of prison-camp escape films feels immediately at home. We are made to hear, feel, and particularly see things as if we were there, it is as if the story tells itself; but it takes subtlety to create this effect of unmediated, direct access to what happened.

Here it is useful to think in terms of 'focalisation', telling the story from a particular viewpoint, giving the audience particular eyes to view the events. It may be Theban eyes, as with the 431 assault-force as they are bewildered by the unexpected Plataean fight-back (2.4): first the noise of the attack, the shouts of the women, the hail of stones and tiles, the rain: then the rushing through the streets until they come to the gate; but it is barred, a javelin-shaft taking the place of the pin. Some come to another gate: there is an axe, a woman gave it, no-one saw them, they hack through the bar, they escape, not many of them – that is the effect of the staccato word-order, and the perceptions crowd in just as they would have done on the original participants.[20] More often, it is Plataean eyes. Take the messages to and from Athens at 2.73. The Plataeans report Archidamus' offer to the Athenians, consult with them, then return and say ... – and this is where the Athenian reply is placed, as it is reported to Plataea rather than as it was first given to the envoys (2.73.3). The effect is to involve the reader all the more in the Plataean experience, to make us sense the events as if they were happening to us: just as the story of the break-out at 3.22–3 is told largely in the sequence of impressions that an individual escaper would have received.[21]

This feeling of unmediated access to the events can blind us to the authorial control which Thucydides is exercising. Yet it is Thucydides who gives the episode such prominence. It is he who decides that this will be the first act of the war, not the last of its preliminaries.[22] This suits his vision of the war's genesis: by then both Sparta and her allies (1.88, 125) and Athens (1.139–45) have decided that they must fight when the time comes, so that the only thing left to happen is the start of the fighting itself. That comes with Plataea.[23] But it also gives a programmatic start to the narrative.[24] This is not to be the old-fashioned open war of large-scale army movements, the sort which might appropriately be introduced by Archidamus' invasion: the dominant notes will be the furtive plotting, the local hatreds, the faction-ridden little town which cannot solve its squabbles without calling in the powerful neighbours, the frustrated planning, the stealth, the dagger in the back in the middle of the night. It is Thucydides too who gives the later stages such prominence, by deploying his vivid detail here rather than in other contexts, then by including the debate and perhaps – more likely here than in some other settings, given the difficulty he must have had in gaining accurate reports[25] – enhancing the argumentation of the speeches. And it is Thucydides who decides when pieces of information are made available: it is a feature of Greek narrative technique to hold back information until the author decides it is most relevant,[26] but that decision is itself an interpretative one. Thucydides does not tell us at 2.2–6 that the Theban attack was made at a sacred time of the month (*hieromenia*), but holds it back to the debate of Book 3 (56.2 and 65.1): that delay categorises the item as one relevant to the rhetoric of praise and blame (the point in Book 3), not one that affected the Theban decision to attack one way or the other – for instance, by making them think that the Plataeans might be off their guard[27] – still less one that might explain, as it might have done in Herodotus, why the Theban attempt failed.

It is hopeless to expect a simple answer 'why' Thucydides should give Plataea such prominence: literary composition is not so straightforward. But we can see ways in which the Plataean sequence meshes with his preoccupations. Plataea is a tale of human suffering, one of those evils which, as with the *Iliad*, gave the story its importance;[28] it is also a story of ingenuity and contrivance, with all those siege-works and all the intelligence expended on combating them. We can sense the same hand as stressed the perversion of progress, the human wit devoted to human destruction, in the *stasis*-chapters (3.82–3).[29] There are pathetic ironies too: all that ingenuity in the Spartan fortifications, yet eventually they succeed by using that most conventional of siege-weapons, the simple passing of time. All that ingenuity is expended to kill a mere two hundred or so mortals; about a fifth of the number of Mytileneans executed at 3.50.1, after the Athenians decided to be *lenient*. But war is like that: hatred brings a desire for destruction out of proportion to the real gains.

It is all because of the war; but the war starts from here. As with Corcyra in Book 1, it begins with a little town, riddled by faction: it is the traitors who call in the Thebans. Once again, too, it is local jealousies, exacerbated by feelings of perverted kinship, which stimulate the hatred – what we may call the 'hate thy neighbour' theme: Thebes hates Plataea in a way reminiscent of the hatreds and jealousies which link Corcyra, Epidamnus, and Corinth. Little people start big conflicts; but eventually the world is dominated by the bigger folk, and the role of the small fry is to suffer. It is no coincidence that the first great movement of the war now ends with the catastrophes of Plataea, which began the war, then of Corcyra, which began the preliminaries. The smaller states here have something in common with the women of the *Iliad*. In a world dominated there by males, the conflicts begin with women – with Helen, with Chryseis and Briseis; the conflicts end with women too, and the female voice of suffering articulates what the powerful do to the world they dominate.

Again, one major theme of the debate is free will.[30] Were the Plataeans free agents in what they have done in concert with the Athenians, whether for good in 480–79 or, as the Thebans and Spartans have it, since then for ill? Were the Thebans free agents themselves when they medised in the Persian Wars, or can they pin responsibility on the 'power-clique of a few men' who ruled at the time?[31] That emphasis on freedom and necessity picks up themes from the narrative, especially 2.71–8. The Plataeans were clearly then tempted by Archidamus' overtures but their dependence on Athens, where their families were effectively hostages, left them no choice. One is left with a sense of moral *aporia*: the more the problems of free will are aired, the more difficult it seems to blame anyone for anything; and it all makes so little difference anyway, for the Spartans have already made their decision. The Plataeans' pleading for their lives is indeed off the point, as their Theban adversaries complain (61.1).[32]

Plataea and Mytilene are both small and vulnerable allies, and their stories interlace. Thebes was anxious to 'get in their anticipatory strike' at Plataea before the war broke out openly (*prokatalambanein*, 2.2.3), just as both Athens and Mytilene were eager to get in an anticipatory hit at one another (*prokatalambanein* again, 3.2.3, 3.3.2). Mytilene too feels that she has only one course of action, in her case to revolt: Sparta encourages her, just as Athens encouraged Plataea to remain loyal; yet Athens now gives as little effective help[33] as Sparta gave to Mytilene. Deft techniques underline the point. Each of the Plataean sequences ends with Athens, busy and involved at 2.6, at least something of a presence at 2.78.3, a mere receptacle for the fugitives at 3.24.2, then at 3.68.5 'that was the end of Plataea's story[34] in the ninety-third year of the Athenian alliance'. The precision is pathetic,[35] and the diminuendo of Athenian involvement is felt; it is in keeping with this that Thucydides passes over the Athenian gift of citizenship to the Plataeans, whatever exactly that may have been.[36]

Is this diminuendo also a 'reproach' to Athens?[37] That is more difficult: it depends again on how much freedom the principals really have. Why is it that Athens does not get involved in Plataea, any more than Sparta in Mytilene? It is not moral deficiency, nor would Thucydides' attentive reader think that it was. Athens cannot *afford* to get involved with Plataea: the preferred, rational Periclean strategy was to trust to the sea and avoid extensive commitment on land; the necessities of war require that the little town goes to the wall. There may be sympathy for the hopeless plight of the underdog; it need not mean reproach for those with the power. The Athenians, ultimately, have no more choice about staying out of Plataea than the Plataeans have about holding on.

Whatever else historians make of Plataea, those themes have their own interest as part of the intellectual history of the fifth and early fourth century. This fascination with the paradoxes of free will and responsibility, and with the power or powerlessness of slippery rhetoric, reflects the conceptual preoccupations of the day. Gorgias' *Helen* plays with the various considerations which might free Helen of blame: perhaps it was Eros which constrained her, perhaps the gods, perhaps Paris, perhaps – most powerful of all – the persuasive power of rhetoric. That is a piece of playfulness, *paignion* (*Helen* 21), but an elusive one. Perhaps we should take it as a dazzling display of virtuosity, perhaps as a model for aspiring rhetorical students, perhaps as a semi-serious play with the problems of free will and with the capacity of rhetorical exculpation to generate disturbingly non-intuitive conclusions – and that is possibly also the way to look at the debate of Helen and Hecuba in Euripides' *Trojan Women*, very likely written with Gorgias in mind. Antiphon's *Tetralogies* also play with paradoxical issues of responsibility, and their texture is similarly elusive. However we view these works, they clearly belong in the same intellectual world as Thucydides' Plataea.

Thucydides' presentation also maps on to other features of the contemporary Athenian sensibility, particularly visible in tragedy: the emphasis on hatred for those nearest to one, on relentlessness, on revenge; the elusive and transitory nature of friendship and enmity; the paradoxes of reciprocity, with a clash of differing conceptions of the multifaceted concept *charis* (the 'gratitude' the Plataeans claim for their past, the 'favour' – with an eye to future recompense – which the Spartans bestow on the Thebans); the debates about past actions which are pointless, for the decisions are already fixed (Hippolytus and Theseus in *Hippolytus*, Helen and

Hecuba in the *Trojan Women*); the plight of the vulnerable in wartime (the *Trojan Women* again, the *Hecuba*, the *Heracleidae*, Aeschylus' and Euripides' *Suppliant Women*); yet also the predicament of the powerful. 'I am the slave of the mob,' says Agamemnon in Euripides' *Iphigeneia in Aulis* (450), and *Hecuba* also shows an Agamemnon who feels sympathy for Hecuba but fears his army too much to give her any help (850–63): 'There is no single mortal who is free!', Hecuba pointedly retorts.[38] Powerlessness is not confined to the weak and vanquished.

So the Plataean sequence is extremely rich in Thucydidean thematic. The space it occupies and the vividness of the narrative are not surprising. What is more difficult is to go further, as we did with Plutarch and Apollodorus, and work out what source-material he had and how far he went in recasting it. For the initial phases – the raid of 431, the negotiations with Archidamus, the fortifications, the break-out – he could have heard details from the Plataean fugitives at Athens. It is harder to see how he could have reliable information concerning the later stages: after all, most of his potential informants were dead. True, he might have met some of the Spartans later, during his exile, and perhaps even some of the Thebans. But his information for the earlier phases is likely to have been distinctly richer, with greater possibilities of controlling the version of one witness against another. Even there that need not preclude some 'moulding' of his own, but we cannot trace it in detail.

What we can do, however, is to draw some lessons for our own historical vision of these events.

## Lesson 1: right and wrong

First, Thucydides' own reading should help us guard against oversimplification of the issues. His presentation of the final debate highlights the moral problematic. We cannot deny sympathy to the Plataeans in so hopeless a predicament, we must feel both pity and fear, for such ruthlessness could so easily be our own lot: war is like that. Yet the weaknesses of their moral case are also felt: they did execute their own Theban prisoners, and are now being repaid in their own coin. A verbal echo reinforces the point. The Plataeans plead with the Spartans not to execute 'men who surrendered willingly and now hold out their hands [as suppliants] – for it is Greek custom (*nomos*) not to kill these' (3.58.2); the Thebans retort by recalling 'the men who were holding out their hands when you took them prisoner, and you promised us you would not kill them afterwards – then you put them to death contrary to *nomos*' (3.66.2, cf. 67.5). Any clear-cut moral verdict is as difficult as it is pointless and irrelevant.

That may give us a clue as to how to read the earlier sequence, where Archidamus offers neutrality, then temporary migration for the course of the war (2.71–4). Scholars have here been prone to one-sided judgements. Gomme, for instance, felt that Archidamus' offer was insincere[39] and exposed as such by Thucydides: this involved a misreading of Thucydides' language later at 3.68, where some doubt is cast on the Spartans' justification of their final execution of the prisoners, but it need not follow that the offer of 2.72 would not have been honoured.[40] The Plataeans took the proposals seriously enough to refer them to the Athenians, and Thucydides implies that it was only the Athenian refusal which led to their being turned down.

Badian (1993: 110–16) argues the other side, suggesting that Archidamus was in the moral right. Archidamus puts to the Plataeans that they are protected by the 479 oaths only 'if you now behave consistently with what you are saying: just as Pausanias granted you, be free and independent yourself and join in freeing all those others who shared those dangers then, who swore oaths with you, and who are now under Athenian rule' (2.72.1). Badian infers that the 479 oath not merely protected the Plataeans, but also bound them to the defence of other Greek states' liberty: otherwise the Plataeans would now have objected to Archidamus' interpretation, and Archidamus' own confident invocation of the gods at 2.74.2 would have amounted to a 'solemn curse' on his own army, something which his officers would not have accepted without protest. Hence the oath of 479 must have involved a more general guarantee of Greek freedom. In that case, the Spartans clearly have the better of the moral argument.

Yet Thucydides gives no indication of such a general guarantee: he says 'as Pausanias granted to you', not 'as you then swore', and his language as easily suggests a moral implication of Pausanias' 'grant' as a term of the oath itself. It is true that Archidamus' invocation of the gods cannot be written off as hypocritical rhetoric: that is a fair point against Gomme's cynical view. But all this demonstrates is that the Spartans found their moral argument plausible. Given their viewpoint, that is not surprising: if this was a crusade of liberation, then it *was* easy to see Plataea as abusing their historical privilege, granted in the name of freedom, in order to play the tyrant's game; it was easy too to regard neutrality as an adequate compromise. Given that viewpoint, too, they could expect the gods to see it the same way. This does not mean that Archidamus would not have invaded but for the moral argument; it does mean that, if he and his men thought right was on their side, he would naturally – and 'sincerely' – try to enlist the gods' help.

Archidamus and his men might find their moral argument decisive: it need not follow that the Plataeans would,[41] or that we should. But it need not follow that we reject it either, at least out of hand. What we should expect, in view of Thucydides' later treatment, is for the issue to seem morally *complex* – even if it is also ultimately irrelevant, for the reader will already sense that the Plataean predicament is to be decided by necessity rather than right or wrong. In the earlier sequence too Thucydides could have made the rights and wrongs unequivocal, had he himself thought them so. He could easily, for instance, have intimated that Archidamus' imprecations were hypocritical: Thucydides is dismissive enough about religious motives elsewhere,[42] and there has already been one occasion when he contrived to suggest that Archidamus was concealing his true thoughts.[43] It would have been possible, too, to represent the Spartans as not (or not yet) too concerned about religion: that is indeed the impression he gives in the retrospect at 7.18, where Sparta's religious conscience becomes most relevant some years later – but he does not say that here.[44] Too clear an authorial commitment to a hypocritical reading would have tilted the scales too much against Archidamus: Thucydides prefers to leave us with moral equilibrium.

This is a case where gauging Thucydides' reading of these events can help to mould our own. It can guard us against a simplistic view of Archidamus' 'insincerity'; it can also guard us against concluding that the terms of the oath must have been clear-cut if Archidamus could argue in this way. Thucydides highlights the possibility of conflicting moral interpretations; and there is no reason why we should ourselves insist on seeing things more simply.

## Lesson 2: Plataean citizenship

An interest in the authors' agenda can also help us at the one point where Apollodorus seems to give valuable non-Thucydidean information, the case of the citizenship decree.

As we saw, Apollodorus emphasises the vote of citizenship to the Plataean refugees (104–6); Thucydides does not mention this, but allows both Plataeans and Thebans to refer to a gift of citizenship which the Athenians have already made (3.55.3, 63.2). There is a growing scholarly consensus[45] that both Apollodorus and Thucydides capture something of the truth. If some form of honorary (or potential) citizenship had been granted earlier (perhaps in 479 rather than 519?),[46] such citizenship would have been available to any individuals who chose to come to Athens, but the arrival of a mass of citizens in 428/7 might necessitate a particular measure to distribute them around the demes and tribes. In that case, one can see why each author accentuated the element he did. Apollodorus would naturally play down the earlier decree: his point is that the Plataeans' peculiar grant was only earned after quite unusual loyalty and sufferings. Thucydides would equally play down the final grant: his stress at the end is on Athenian non-involvement and passivity.[47] One can also see why he includes[48] the mentions of the earlier grant in the speeches. This may *seem* to fit the Plataeans' case, for it accentuates the bond with Athens and the moral claim which the Athenians had over them, thus extenuating their services to Athens; but the closer Plataea aligns herself with Sparta's and Thebes' mortal enemy, the more certain her fate seems.[49] Equally, it points the claim which the Plataeans might seem to have for Athenian support: a fruitless claim, of course.

So the evidence would all fit if we were to follow that modern consensus; but, before we assent to it, we should remember the pitfalls of a 'Poirot'.[50] Is there not a danger that we may be agreeing too readily because we are arguing forward from an assumed picture and concluding that, if it were true, our evidence would fit? Might there not be other pictures which could equally explain the evidence? In particular, what the last paragraph represented as reasons for each author's *emphasis* might also be reasons for *fabrication* of details which fit the argument so well. How can we be sure that either Apollodorus or Thucydides has not simply made up a citizenship item to suit his taste, or at least be transmitting a version that a predecessor made up? In fact, that question can probably be answered: the consensus view is likely to be best. But the question does need to be asked.

First, Apollodorus. It is surely impossible to believe that he has himself made up his decree: if he had, he would have made a better job of it, and there would not have been all those mismatches. But that is not enough to demonstrate the historical authenticity which our consensus demands. The decree might for instance have been fabricated in the later 370s, when the Plataeans were arguing for a repeat of Athens' earlier generosity after their second destruction by Thebes in (probably) 374; or a genuine but undated fifth-century decree might have been linked to the events of 427 by Apollodorus or a predecessor, for there is no prescript to date the decree indisputably.[51] But Isocrates gives some support to the notion of a block-grant in 428/7 at *Panathenaicus* (12) 93–4; and, more importantly, the wording of the decree itself tells against forgery. Osborne points out that both the omission of phratries and the assignation to demes and tribes are features of mass enfranchisements rather than the more normal individual grants, and a fabricator would be unlikely to know that.[52] The decree's distinction between the present mass grant and the careful presentation of credentials for any subsequent grant is also suggestive. That points to a sudden arrival of a large number of individuals, and that suits 428/7.[53]

As for Thucydides, the difficulty is to make any literary sense of allowing the Plataeans and Thebans to make a *bogus* claim of pre-427 citizenship. We should not put the problem too naïvely. Osborne, for instance, concentrates on what the *Plataeans*' motives might be: he suggests that the Plataeans 'were led to exaggerate the closeness of their relationship with the Athenians in the hope of ameliorating their defence' (1983: 11). That, effectively, is to regard Thucydides' speech as a verbatim transcript: but this will not do. For one thing, there is likelihood that he had less good evidence for this speech than for others (above, p. 72). But a wider point of principle is more important. Even if a particular remark was made in the historical debate, we still need to ask questions about Thucydides *as well*. He would still need reasons for keeping this part of their speeches in the editing process rather than others, and for choosing whether to give us the relevant narrative material to confirm or expose a speaker's claims. We need to make sense of Thucydides' technique as well as the Plataeans'.[54]

That is not the only form of naïveté. Amit writes as if it were rather bad taste to suspect Thucydides of including false material: orators might manipulate the past to improve their argument, but 'Thucydides is above any such suspicion' (1973: 76). Yet Thucydides is certainly not 'above' representing orators who do precisely that: his speeches are full of false claims, not to mention flagrant misreadings and misrepresentations of events. The Plataeans claim in this very speech that they supported the Greek cause in the Persian

Wars 'alone of the Boeotians' (3.54.3, cf. 62.1), suppressing the role played by Thespiae (Hdt. 7.132.1, 202, 8.50.2). Still, that case is easier. Thucydides could rely on his audience knowing enough from Herodotus to identify the overargument,[55] and the exaggeration is anyway so routine that the audience is unlikely to regard it as very significant.[56] With the citizenship, any misrepresentation would be more pointed, and yet Thucydides would have *left it impossible for us to identify*. He would need to give us that information himself in the narrative.[57] We should be left to assume either that Thucydides was wrong (yet it is hard to believe that he did not know the truth: he would have been in Athens when, or at least shortly after, the Plataeans received a block-grant); or that he is himself moving the citizenship grant from 428/7 to earlier in order to allow the Plataeans their rhetorical *faux pas*. If Thucydides were prepared to fabricate such a bogus claim in the interest of a poignant but minor effect, we should expect to find him doing the same sort of thing elsewhere. And clear-cut similar cases will not be easy to find.

So this is not a 'Poirot' after all. Alternative explanations turn out to be less powerful for explaining the evidence we have, and we do better to remain with the modern consensus.

## Lesson 3: a matter of motives

Thucydides is not slow to assign motives to his characters. Too much modern debate about these motives centres on whether he might have had any 'evidence' from the agents themselves,[58] as if it would make a great difference whether (say) the Plataean traitors had actually told Thucydides that they wanted to advance their own power (2.2.2), or any Spartan had told him that 'almost all the Spartan actions concerning the Plataeans were done for the sake of the Thebans, for they thought them useful for the war which was then only just beginning' (3.68.4). What public figures say about their motives is rarely the whole story; when we assign motives ourselves, we do so on the basis of a complex of factors – what sort of people we are dealing with, what sort of explanation makes sense, how the world, or a particular sector or system of the world, works. It is an attempt to render an action intelligible, and we make that attempt against the background of our own interpretative assumptions. It belongs at the end of an analysis, not at the beginning; what the character provides by way of explanation is only one element in that process.

If we are sceptical of privileging an actor's own explanations, that is not, or not only, because we may doubt his or her sincerity. In extreme cases, we may accept that people's accounts of their motives are sincere but inaccurate, that people do not describe their motives rightly even to themselves. 'The West did not fight the Gulf War for freedom, whatever they said or thought, but for oil'; 'Conservatives are committed to free enterprise not because they think it works, but because it puts money in their pockets'; 'Labour does not care about relieving social inequality, but about keeping power'. Whether right or wrong, such claims are shorthand for what legal theorists call a 'but for' analysis: A would not have happened but for B. However sincere politicians were in their talk about freedom, in fact, when the crunch came, they would not have fought the Gulf War but for the oil; and so on. It is easy to see how such motive claims depend on preconceptions about the way the world works.

When Thucydides assigns motives, these again should be seen as embedded in his entire conceptualisation of events. He will have taken into account all sorts of factors – what people said at the time, for what that was worth and if he could discover it; what eventually happened, with doubtless some wisdom after the event in reconstructing into what was planned;[59] and his general picture of how the world worked. When his Plataean traitors introduce a powerful neighbour to maximise their own domestic power, that fits his general picture of how *stasis* works, particularly in wartime: that is how he introduces his powerful survey of *stasis* at 3.82.1: 'the whole Greek world (so to speak) was later disrupted, with their divisions leading the champions of the people in each place to bring in the Athenians and the oligarchic élite to bring in the Spartans'; his Thebans here present their own oligarchic masters in 480 as acting similarly, supporting the Persians in order to bolster their own internal position (3.62.4). Apollodorus, we saw, assumed that the traitors were simply bribed; Diodorus claims that they were Boeotian federalists (12.41.3): none of the three need have any evidence other than their own presumptions of what makes traitors tick. Equally, when Thucydides' Thebans are anxious to 'get in their anticipatory strike' against Plataea in peacetime, this reflects his view of how such relationships work, especially where local hatreds are in point: get in your retaliation first. That recurs in his analysis of *stasis* (3.82.4–5), and it recurs often in similar motive-assessments elsewhere, both Thucydides' own (1.57.6, 5.30.1, 5.57.1) and his speakers' (1.33.3, 1.36.3, 6.28.3, and Diodotus' recommendation for the future at 3.46.6).

On another occasion, he seems to have privileged his own motive-analysis over the one which the agents themselves would have given, rather on the lines of our 'Gulf War' case. This is at 3.22.2, where he says that the escaping Plataeans wore only a single sandal to give them a firmer footing in the mud. In fact, this 'monosandalism' has a religious dimension, a fear of offending the gods of the underworld,[60] and Thucydides, infinitely more familiar with the religious world of his day than we are, must have known that the fugitives themselves would have given this explanation. Characteristically unsympathetic to religion himself, he prefers the rationalist interpretation. Perhaps he is opting for a version which was already current in his own day: Euripides too made one of his characters give a similarly rationalistic view of monosandalism among the Aetolians, they do it 'in order to have their knee nimble'.[61] Or perhaps he is simply convinced that, whatever the religious dimension in the Plataeans' own minds, they would still not have done it 'but for' the mud. We can recognise the same Thucydides who insists that there were many flute-players in the Spartan army at Mantinea 'not for any religious reason, but to help them keep their line when attacking as they keep step with the rhythm...' (5.70). Whatever the Spartans said themselves, Thucydides knew better – or thought he did.

More substantial questions surround Thucydides' view of the Spartan motives: the notion that they did it all, or 'almost all',[62] for Thebes: that is, we infer, to gratify Theban hatred.[63] That reading of events was not clear to us at the beginning of this final sequence,[64] any more than it was to the Plataeans themselves as they surrendered: but the Theban dominance became clear to both us and them (3.53.4–54.1, 57.2, 58.1, 59.1, 59.4) once the Spartans asked their question, and it is now finally given the authority of Thucydides' own voice. One can again see how it fits his interpretative scheme. His principals are driven from below, and the pressure of their smaller allies leaves them no choice.

Any Thucydidean view demands respect, and it is utterly credible that the Spartans would not have been so implacable 'but for' the Thebans; but we might still prefer to emphasise different 'but for' considerations. For in the case of virtually every action, there is a vast series of 'but for' statements that are all true: that man would not have said such a crass thing but for ... the thing the other person had just said to him, his bad mood because Sheffield Wednesday had just lost, the two gins he had had that lunch-time, his natural insensitivity, his early role-modelling on egotistic tennis-players, etc.

What 'but for' we emphasise depends on the type of intelligibility which we find most helpful in a particular context, and Thucydides' context might not be ours.

Consider, for instance, the sequence two years earlier, when Archidamus had begun by offering the Plataeans more moderate proposals, first neutrality and then the possibility of temporary migration (2.72–3). As we saw, it is hard to regard those terms as simply disingenuous play-acting.[65] It is hard, too, to think that these terms would have been all the vindictive Thebans would want, even though they might well profit from them (as the Plataeans feared, 2.72.2).[66] At that time Archidamus put other considerations higher than the Thebans' lust for vengeance. If now in 427 the Spartans privileged the desires of the Thebans above everything, that is not then because it was an *unconditional* priority which would obtain in any circumstances: it must be because things have changed, and now there was nothing to prevent the Thebans from being given the blood they craved. (Nor is it a priority that Thucydides' Thebans themselves have much confidence in: they are fearful that the Spartans may be influenced by the Plataeans' arguments, 3.60.1.) Had his preconceptions been different, Thucydides might have given a different 'but for' explanation: that the Spartans would not now have gratified the Thebans but for their genuine belief in the arguments put forward by Archidamus at 2.74: that the Plataean refusal of neutrality cast them as enemies, and the Spartans could therefore punish them in good religious faith. In terms of Spartan mentality, that point is just as illuminating, but it is not the interpretative frame of mind Thucydides was in here.

What, after all, had the Spartans to fear from taking a more moderate line over Plataea? That the Thebans would go over to Athens? Of course not: the Theban hatred and fear of Athens ruled that out, at least in wartime. They had nowhere else to go. *If anything else important had come into play*, the Spartans need not have regarded the Theban interest as being so decisive (and that is consistent with Thucydides' language at 3.68.4): so Thucydides is assuming a particular view about, for instance, the strategic importance of Plataea – as it did not matter, they might as well gratify the Thebans. It is therefore no surprise that Thucydides never suggests that Plataea possessed any strategic importance at all. Yet this is highly questionable. Plataea had *potential* strategic significance.[67] Boeotia was the 'dancing-floor of Ares',[68] the natural theatre for warring nations to fight over the path from Northern Greece to the

Peloponnese; the so-called first Peloponnesian War had proved true to form, with all the real fighting in Boeotia. A few years later, Boeotia was to see the next large-scale mainland fighting of the war, at Delium. No Athenian base in Boeotia, particularly one so close to the main North–South road, was strategically irrelevant. Had Athens chosen, it might even have been able to use Plataea as a Decelea-in-reverse against Thebes, dominating the territory and serving as a base for forays and a haven for defectors, rather as the Spartans later themselves used Plataea against Thebes in the later 380s and early 370s.

Thucydides' failure to stress that point is not stupidity. As we shall see in the next chapter,[69] it is one of his firmest narrative principles to suppress points which have no consequences; and, given his view of the strategic realities, Plataea indeed had little role to play. Athens could not mount large-scale land campaigns in the style of the 450s, Athens would not follow a Decelea-in-reverse policy, control of the road was not going to be an issue. But we should be clear that this is a silence conditioned by his own interpretative choices.

We moderns write our history differently. We are used to the idea that the most interesting history is often the history which does not happen, in this case the war which might have been expected but turned out not to be fought. In a different war, Plataea might have been so militarily crucial that Sparta would have insisted on a garrison there themselves. Thucydides' technique of interpretative silence is not ours, and we need to make such points explicit. This may well be our own preferred 'but for': Sparta would not have been so ready to give in to Theban pressure but for the strategic pattern the war was following, and, importantly, the pattern they could now *see* it was following: to leave Plataea ungarrisoned, they must by now have been confident that Athens would not turn to a land-campaign if she could avoid it. It is not Thucydides' way to make that point explicit. But it is *consistent* with the point he makes, for it was a consequence of Plataea's unexpected strategic negligibility that the Spartans could afford to do what the Thebans wanted; and it is up to us if we choose to make that our emphasis.

# Chapter 5

# Explaining the war

## Explanatory narrative

> Right at the beginning of his inquiry into the causes of the war,
> he ought to have set out first the one which was true, and which
> he thought true. For not only is it a natural requirement to set
> out earlier things before later and true things before false, but
> the start of his narrative would have been far more powerful if it
> had been organised in that way.
>
> (Dionysius of Halicarnassus, *On Thucydides* 11)

Thucydides' first book shows signs of acute narrative strain. The
back-to-front structure, as Dionysius implies, is one aspect. After
the introductory 'Archaeology', Thucydides begins with the very
recent antecedents of the war, Corcyra, Potidaea, and the Spartan
debate (1.24–88); then he goes back to earlier events in the
Pentekontaetia, that is the 'Fifty-year period' after 478 (89–118);
then, just as we think the war is about to start, he returns to the very
beginning of the Pentekontaetia with the Pausanias–Themistocles
'digression' (128–38). Even within this framework his choice of
material has seemed to many wilful, random, or at best unfinished:
much more on the beginning of the Pentekontaetia than the end;
nothing on such important events as the Peace of Callias (assuming
there was one); no narrative of the troubles with Megara or Aegina,
even though he acknowledges that they figured large in the final
diplomatic exchanges (1.67.2–4, 139.1, 2.27.1); no clear statement
of the terms of the 446 Thirty Years' Peace, though several allegations
of its rupture again figured in the diplomacy; almost nothing on
Athenian interests and activity in Sicily or the Thraceward region or
the Black Sea; very little on the organisation of the Athenian empire

or the Peloponnesian League; nothing, until the end, on Athenian domestic politics, with even Pericles 'introduced' astoundingly late – but then twice (1.127.3, 139.4, after some casual mentions in the fighting at 111–16). Yet, despite all the selectivity, he seems uneasy about the result. Several times he appears to warn that there are important points to which his narrative and speeches have not done justice (1.23.6, 88, 118). It seems a strange way, and anything but a simple way, to tell the story.

Yet telling a story is never simple. Thucydides is concerned to render that story intelligible, to ensure 'that no-one ever has to ask the origins from which so great a war came upon the Greeks' (1.22.1). The presumption may seem breathtaking:[1] once he has made things clear, the inquiry will be laid to rest. In so doing, he employs various conceptual categories familiar from Herodotus. It is a tale of imperialist expansion; of confidence bred of success; of a great state which will go on to destroy itself, undermined by the very qualities which built its power; of resentful subjects waiting for their moment; of resistance fed by pride, by a taste for liberty, and above all by fear. But Herodotus left the relation between the strands subtle, shifting, and indecisive. Herodotus' readers are continually brought to ask why events happen – is it the gods, is it human overconfidence, is it something to do with the court, is freedom an inspiration or a fragmenting delusion, are Persians doomed to defeat by their natural softness? – but any provisional answers are refined by the next sequence of events. Herodotus' text is 'dialogic' (to use Bakhtin's categories[2]). Multiple viewpoints and interpretations co-exist in the text; and the interaction between text and reader is itself a two-way 'dialogue', with each continually putting questions to the other – and not every reader will end by arranging the different causal strands in the same pattern.

That is not Thucydides' way. Where Herodotus opens questions up, Thucydides' tendency is to close them down, to impose a single 'monologic' view imperiously on his readers. His causal questions have answers, and he cares that his audience should get them right. But that meant trying to make historical narrative do an extraordinary amount, not merely making a story intelligible but excluding variant explanations and false leads. No wonder the strain shows.

There is a tension here between the preoccupations of Thucydides' *age* and the expectations of his *genre*. The late fifth and early fourth century was typified by an interest in explaining things, in tracing what or who brought them about. Forensic oratory, as we have already seen, frequently sought to identify who was responsible for particular actions or eventualities, and works of Antiphon and Gorgias, like some tragedies, explored the paradoxes here at a more abstract level.[3] Philosophers played with physical explanations of the cosmos, or of particular features of the physical world (the flooding of the Nile, the birth of seas or mountains), or of the genesis of society. Doctors essayed ambitious aetiologies of particular diseases, and clearly had to combat other, to our mind less 'scientific', ways of explaining the same phenomena. These genres regularly show 'an argumentative, competitive, even combative quality, reflected not only in the rejection of rivals' views, but also in over-sanguine self-justification':[4] *they* are not the genres to allow others' views to remain uncorrected, or to leave the reader or hearer to decide. No forensic pleader will end by saying 'so I don't think I'm to blame, but of course you may well think differently'. And it would be a rare philosopher or scientist who would leave the choice of cosmological explanations to his audience. Those are the worlds where monology rules.

Doctors strike the same confident note; few people, after all, have ever admired their doctor for lacking assurance. The body is composed of wind, one will argue; of water, the next. The right way to treat shoulder-dislocations is like this, not like that. Nor are the doctors' causal arguments typically open-ended or ambiguous. Quite often the point is to exclude rival explanations by exposing their inadequacy. If epilepsy were really of divine origin as people say, why would it particularly strike phlegmatic types ([Hipp.] *On the Sacred Disease* 5)? If Scythian impotence was really god-sent, why should it strike the rich more than the poor ([Hipp.] *Airs, Waters, Places* 22)? Still, even the confident explainer need not always regard alternative explanations as mutually exclusive, and we also see a desire to co-ordinate explanations with one another. It was originally custom that was 'most responsible' for the long heads of the Macrocephali, as they used to mould infants' heads while they were still soft; later it became part of their genetic inheritance, and nature came to 'contribute' (*Airs, Waters, Places* 14). Such interrelations can lead to a league-table of causes, with one explanation seen as more important than another. Acute seasonal changes in climate are the greatest factor in creating differences in people's natures; next comes the land and its waters (*Airs, Waters, Places* 24). Wind is 'lord of all', the most important factor in various physiological processes; blood, food, water are 'jointly or secondarily responsible' (*On Breaths* 15).

Such frameworks can accommodate a multiplicity of causes, but Greek conceptualisation was always most comfortable with twos: as the early philosopher Alcmaeon put it, 'most things come in pairs' (DK[12] 24 A 3). Thus combinations of two explanations are particularly frequent. One favoured binary scheme combines an underlying disposition with an immediate triggering cause; the vocabulary is not always consistent, but the disposition tends to be described as the *aition* (perhaps 'what is responsible'), the trigger as the *prophasis* (perhaps 'the obvious explanation').[5] Hard digestive organs create a predisposition to pleurisy, but the abscesses themselves can be triggered by 'every type of immediate cause' (*prophasis*, *Airs, Waters, Places* 4). A body's internal imbalance predisposes to epilepsy, but a particular epileptic attack will be triggered by something more specific, a change in the weather, a sudden panic, an unexpected noise, a child's failure to catch its breath (*On the Sacred Disease*, especially 13). This taste for twos is so ingrained that we often see works simplifying complex causal pictures to present a slick binary opposition. *Airs, Waters, Places* has itself developed a more complex chain, with climate helping to generate this physical type, then also producing the cold water that combines with the dry bodily structure to create lacerations; *On the Sacred Disease* has stressed the way the brain creates the right predisposing bodily structure, and talks too of the role of heredity, of fluxes of phlegm and of bile, and of a good deal more. Thus both works seem to admit several different layers and types of explanations. But when each author comes to specify a particular causal interrelation, he finds it natural once again to deal with a simple binary polarity, an *aition* and a *prophasis*.

Many of these tendencies of the age – the combative commitment to one explanation and rejection of others, the desire to order explanations in some sort of hierarchy, the binary combination of predisposition and triggering cause – are highly reminiscent of Thucydides, as we shall see. But it was one thing to present such argument and analysis in the literary form of a medical or philosophical treatise, or to impugn alternative assignments of responsibility in a forensic speech. It was quite another to articulate such complex ideas within the genre of historiography. True, such a 'genre' was not firmly established, and there were no firm rules: we saw that earlier (p. 44). But, as we also saw in Chapter 1, the nearest approach to a rule was that this was a narrative genre, that it told a story (or at least the various parts of a story) sequentially. The mode of presentation was not analytic; writers preferred to show, not tell.

Take Herodotus. Fascinated by explanations, he ended his proem by promising to investigate 'other things and in particular the explanation (*aitie*) for the war of Greeks and barbarians'. That word, *aitie*, is linked to the verb *aitiaomai*, 'I blame'; the formulation therefore comes close to saying 'who was to blame', and that in itself easily becomes 'who started it'. That invites a narrative exposition, and this is the way the beginning of the narrative picks up the question: 'the learned among the Persians say that the Phoenicians were responsible (*aitious*) for the rift...' (Hdt. 1.1.1). Certainly, Herodotus is more complex than this. The 'who started it' approach is soon complemented by other trains of thought, and before long we are taking into account the gods, then also wider human patterns, mutability, the nature of tyranny, the contrast of East and West. But these other strands indeed 'complement' and never wholly displace the approach based on 'who started it' and who responded, how the tit-for-tat exchanges began and continued.

For it is in the nature of narrative that alternative ways of looking at events readily co-exist, and that explanations are cumulative rather than competing. That was already true in the *Iliad*: why do the Greeks win? Because they were in the moral right? Because they had the more formidable heroes? Because they were a war-machine taking on vulnerable domesticity? Because they had more, and greater, gods on their side? Because Odysseus thought up a cunning plan on a wet afternoon? It makes no sense to ask which of these is 'the' cause, or even the main cause. It does not even always make sense to ask how they interrelate with one another; in narrative as in life, we can easily accept that all the ways of looking at events have their own validity.

Such a welter of concomitant explanations was not unwelcome to Herodotus. He is perfectly capable of weighing one explanation against another – the Persians may pretend to be avenging Arcesilaus of Cyrene, but the real motive is conquering Libya (4.167.3)[6] – but such cases are rare. It is more typical that at one moment Mardonius is attacking Plataea out of stubbornness, the next because he is running out of food (9.41.4, 45.2); in one context Croesus' motive for fighting Cyrus is pre-emptive (1.46.1), in another it is his desire for land (1.73.1). Elsewhere he jumbles together all sorts of explanation for Cyrus' attack on the Massagetae (1.204) or Darius' on Athens (6.94). Herodotus could readily accept such a plurality, and invite his readers to weigh up all the different factors – and keep weighing, and rethinking, as they read on. But it was less congenial to Thucydides, with his more clear-cut picture of the interrelation of different causal strands. How was he to incorporate his more combative, more imperious, more monologic approach within the texture of such a narrative genre?

First, there was no need to eschew passages of analysis completely. Such passages are usually brief, but they provide the clearest league-tables of causal hierarchy. He typically expresses himself very carefully. The Sicilian expedition was 'not so much an error of judgement with respect to its target, it was more that the Athenians at home did not make the appropriate follow-up decisions...' (2.65.11). That 'not so much' is important: it can still be an error, and that had an effect; but it was a less important cause of the expedition's collapse than those later decisions (Thucydides presumably has the recall of Alcibiades in mind).[7] The allies which joined each side in Sicily did so 'no more because of justice or because of kinship than because of chance or expediency or external forces' (7.57.1): that is not excluding justice or kinship either, but making it clear that they stood no higher on the causal hierarchy than the other factors. The Athenians invaded the island in the first place 'desiring – this is the truest explanation – to rule it all, but at the same time wishing to aid, in a way that would look good, their own kinsmen and the allies which had joined them' (6.6.1). The 'truest explanation' carries most power, but they *did* wish at the same time to give aid to their own side; and that 'in a way which would look good' does not devalue that completely – at the very least, it suggests that the desire to look good is itself an additional, even if secondary, cause.

That final passage echoes – it is all beginning again, and in a similar way – the most famous causal statement of all, that relating to the whole war at 1.23.5–6:

As for why they broke the truce, I have first set out the grounds (*aitiai*) and the elements of rift between the two sides, so that no one need ever enquire about the origins of so great a war among the Greeks. I regard the truest explanation (*prophasis*), which was most unclear in what was said openly, as this: the Athenians, by becoming great and frightening the Spartans, forced them into making war. The openly expressed grounds on each side were as follows, on the basis of [or 'because of'] which they broke the treaty and began fighting.

This passage is easy to get wrong. It is *not* saying that there is only one 'true' cause: one explanation is tru*est*, carries most explanatory power, but that does not exclude the other explanations from being true too, just as in the echoing Book 6 passage the Athenians also 'wanted at the same time' to aid their allies. The word translated here 'grounds', *aitias*, is the same as Herodotus used in his proem, and here as there the element of 'blame' is felt: these are grievances, what each side complained about, what they 'said openly' at the time (contrasting with the truest explanation, which was 'most unclear in what was said openly' – which again need not mean *totally* unclear). But a grievance can still be a genuine explanation, and the language indeed suggests that this was the case here.[8] These complaints were not *just* noise-level, but it is these that explain 'why they broke the treaty' and 'the origin of the war'; it is on their basis, or because of them – the Greek preposition *aph'* suggests both – that they began fighting.

There is an analogy here with the sort of interrelation of causes which contemporary medical writers often favoured, positing a disposition, that bodily state which ensures that an epileptic attack will happen some time, and also a trigger, explaining why it happens now. (This is not a question of vocabulary – the doctors, we saw, tend to use *prophasis* of the immediate trigger, not the underlying disposition,[9] and *aition* of the underlying cause – but rather of the underlying conceptualising habit.) The 'truest explanation' makes it clear why there was a war waiting to happen; the 'grounds and elements of rift' explain why it happened in 431 rather than 435 or 427. It is even clear why the one explanation is 'truer', or at least more powerful, than the other: without the less true explanation (Corcyra and Potidaea), we would still have had a war at some time; without the truer one (Athenian expansion), we should not have had a war at all, for no-one was going to fight just over Corcyra or Potidaea.

The sense of unease is still clear. The truest explanation was 'most unclear in what was openly said': Thucydides fears that his readers, however attentive to what was said, might miss the point. The same flavour attends the passages where Thucydides, at crucial moments, recalls this earlier passage. When the Spartans decided for war in 432 they did so

> not so much because they were persuaded by their allies' words, but more because they feared that the Athenians might become

even more powerful: most of Greece, they saw, was already in their power.

(1.88)

Once again, 'not so much': that does not exclude persuasion, it simply suggests that it was not the most important point: that was rather their pre-existing fear of Athenian growth, something of which they needed no persuasion.

At 1.118 the point recurs: the Spartans had been slow to oppose the Athenians, 'before the time that the increase in Athenian power became clear, and the Athenians began to lay hands on their allies. They then decided it could be borne no longer...'. This last formulation itself confirms that the 'grounds' were important: it was Corcyra and Potidaea that marked the phase when the Athenians 'laid hands on' the Spartan allies. But the accent falls unmistakably on the growth of Athenian power; and the recurrent emphasis again evinces unease that his readers, left to the narrative alone, might be misled. Many have found this odd, and felt that the narrative had made the point clearly enough: but we will return to this in the context of the speeches, and explore precisely what was left 'unclear in what was openly said'.[10]

So narrative alone is not enough for Thucydides to make his points, and the brief analytical passages make things particularly clear; but narrative remained his primary medium, and he naturally did what he could to make his narrative suggest the points he found most vital.

One important technique here is *narrative delay*. This is not new to Thucydides: Homer, Herodotus, the tragedians all often hold back information or explanatory strands as long as possible. That can be seen on a small scale. Fraenkel[11] brilliantly analysed a story in Herodotus (1.110–12) to show how the critical details all come later than we might have expected. The cowherd was called to court and given a child to expose; now he was on his way home. *His wife happened to be pregnant* and gave birth while he was away. When he returned he told her what had happened: *there was weeping everywhere at court*, he said, *the child was regally dressed; on my way home I met someone who told me that it was the newly born prince*. The wife was captivated by the child's smile, and urged him to spare it, but he would not. *I've had a baby*, she then said, *and the baby died*.... Not the way we would tell it at all; but brilliantly told, and with delays everywhere. And the same is true on a larger scale. The tale of Odysseus' scar in the *Odyssey*, for instance, is delayed to the moment of Eurycleia's recognition (*Od.* 19.393–466); it is not the chorus early in *Agamemnon* who tell us of Thyestes' banquet, but Cassandra at 1092ff. and 1214ff.; Herodotus tells us most of later sixth-century Greek history not on any of the opportunities in Book 3, but as the focus reverts to Greece in Book 5. This is all partly holding things back as long as possible; more importantly, it is feeding us details when we need to know them most, when they explain most.

Thucydides operates a similar policy of Need to Know. We do not need to know much about the background to make sense of the Corcyra or Potidaea sequences: true, some points suggest an atmosphere of unusual tension, with a big war in the air (1.33, 36.1, 44.2, 58.1)[12] – but still these are the sorts of inter-state squabbles which were happening all the time. Matters are different when the Peloponnesians decide that they must fight, vast though they see the war will be (1.88). That is where the narrative ceases to be comprehensible in its own terms; that is where we need to know why the Spartans took it all so seriously, and so we are given the Pentekontaetia and the sketch of the rise in Athenian power. That is the point where we move from the 'grounds and elements of rift' to the 'truest cause', and the story of how Athens became so great and so alarming.[13]

What we still do not need to know – at least, in Thucydides' view – is anything on the in-fighting of Athenian politics. He represents uncompromising imperialism as a feature of the city as a whole, not just of Pericles or his friends. That Athenian intransigence can certainly be given some nuancing: the Corcyrean sequence paints a subtle picture of an assembly not especially keen for war, indeed anxious to avoid providing their enemies with an excuse to fight, but still expecting war to come and thoughtful about procuring the best balance of naval power when it does (especially 1.44.2, where they hope to let the Corcyrean and Corinthian fleets fight it out and remain *tertii gaudentes* – not a plan that either Corinth or Corcyra had put to them). But this is not presented as an internally divisive question. It is only mildly in the final exchanges, and more intensely when the war has begun, that internal divisions become important: so that is where Pericles is introduced, and where his heartening speeches are given space.

This provides one reason for the Pausanias–Themistocles 'digression', too. Themistocles' description emphasises many categories which link him to Pericles, the foresight, the intelligence, the strategic wisdom, the power to impress his wisdom on others (1.138); just as earlier he had resembled Pericles in his trademark policies of wall and navy.[14] Yet Athens proved unable to live with its great man and his insight, rather as it will find it difficult to keep step with Pericles once the war begins and to maintain his policy after his death, and just as it will later find it difficult to live with Alcibiades, who inherits much, and misses much else, of Pericles' style. At the same time, Pausanias also shares much with Themistocles. Earlier in the book the Corinthians presented us with their clear-cut discrimination of the Athenian and Spartan tempers – surely too clear-cut despite its underlying truth (1.70–1). The wise Archidamus immediately doubted whether people were really so different (1.84.4), and now we see that the Spartan Pausanias and the Athenian Themistocles have much in common, just as Pericles' own insight has much in common with that of Archidamus: for instance, Pericles and Archidamus read the likely strategic realities similarly, that the Athenians can withstand land-devastation thanks to their sea-power, 1.81.6 ~ 1.143.5, 2.62.1–3, but that war is a chancy business, 2.11.4 ~ 1.140.1.[15] The characteristics of states and statesmen are more complex and varied than we at first thought, and by now we need to know it.

The need-to-know policy can also explain the distribution of detail within the narrative itself, especially the narrative of the Pentekontaetia.[16] Had this been 'Pericles' war', a war brought on by his personal policies and supporters, we should have needed to know a good deal about the events of recent years, both political and military. In Thucydides' conception it was not: it was a war whose roots were much deeper, which originated in the 470s, just after the last great war – just as the Second World War has often seemed to have its roots in 1919, in the immediate aftermath of the First. It was in the 470s, with the building of the city and Piraeus walls and the assumption of Aegean hegemony, that Themistocles and Athens became committed to a policy of maritime expansion; it was in the 470s that the pattern of Athenian determination and Spartan suspicion began. This was not 'Pericles' war'; it was more 'Athens' war', though that too is an oversimplification. No wonder, then, that the richest detail of the Pentekontaetia falls where it does, right at the beginning, on Themistocles' ploy and its success; no wonder even that the Themistoclean chapters, here and in the 'digression' of 1.136–8, have something of the Herodotean about them. It was back then, in a world which seemed different, colourful, even legendary, that the lines began which thrust forward into the grim, tough present.

No wonder, either, that the end of the Pentekontaetia is so much sketchier. By 446, the war was waiting to happen; there is nothing left to explain, no narrative we need to know – except for that time when the war could easily have started, the Samian revolt of 440, and this is narrated in more detail than usual.[17] We do not yet need to know about the build-up of Athenian finances: that does not explain why the war was fought (for instance in enhancing Athenian determination or Spartan fears), for the determination and the fears were there anyway: it becomes relevant for the war itself, not its genesis, and so the material is presented in Pericles' speech at 2.13.[18] We need to know something of how Athens built its imperial power, so we are given something on their ruthless 'rule' over their 'subjects', and the switch to tribute rather than ships (especially 1.96, 99) – though not the transfer of the treasury from Delos to Athens, which was symbolically rather than substantially significant. But the subjects' own attitude to Athens is not yet relevant, and so we are told no more than we might naturally infer, that they were not wild enthusiasts: their feelings become relevant when they 'revolt', and therefore it is the Mytilenean sequence in Book 3 and the Melian dialogue in Book 5 which trace the texture of ruler–subject relations more intricately. On the other side, though, it is the other way round: the feelings of Sparta's allies matter now, rather more than they will once the war has started; and so their pressure on Sparta to take on the hated Athens is traced. This is where we need to know about them.

Not that all Sparta's allies are treated in the same depth. Corinth matters; at Sparta they threaten to look for 'some other alliance' unless the Spartans do something now (1.71.4) – presumably an alliance with Argos, the enigmatic sleeping giant of the Peloponnese. Sthenelaidas, blunt but perceptive, sees the point: he does not understand all those long speeches, but he does know they have good allies and must not let them go (even if, less perceptively, he thinks they mean 'let them go to the Athenians', 1.86.3). So the Corinthian strand is given narrative space: Corcyra and Potidaea are not merely 'grievances', they also explain why the war happened now. But what of Megara, complaining about her exclusion from the Attic market contrary to the terms of the Thirty Years' Peace of 446, or Aegina, complaining that her autonomy was being infringed contrary to the 446 terms? These complaints were part of the diplomatic noise-level, and are mentioned as such (1.67, 1.139); but that is all we need to know about them. Sparta would not have fought for Megara or Aegina if she had not been going to fight anyway; these do not even explain why the war was fought in 431 rather than 427. These are *just* grievances, and to give them greater narrative space could only mislead. We see how important it is that the *aitiai*, the 'grounds' Corcyra and Potidaea, as well as the truest *prophasis*, Spartan fears of Athenian expansion, carry explanatory power at 1.23.5 6; otherwise it would be difficult to see why those grievances get narrative space when Megara and Aegina do not.

All this is tidy; but is it too tidy? Take the gruesome description of 1.106, in mid-Pentekontaetia, where the surrounding narrative is pretty scrappy. The year is perhaps 458. A Corinthian detachment lost their way and became trapped in a deep hollow; the Athenians blocked their way with their hoplites, and used their light-armed troops to stone the Corinthians to death. This, Thucydides said, was a great suffering (*pathos*) to the Corinthians. So doubtless it was; and doubtless it matters that it was the Corinthians rather than anyone else, explaining something of that build-up of ill will; it may also foreshadow other terrifying scenes of slaughter, especially that at the Assinarus (7.84).[19] But one can understand why scholars have found it bewildering that 'one afternoon's horrible work'[20] should get space when the Peace of Callias is ignored and the battle of the Eurymedon gets only five lines; surely, they think, Thucydides should have rethought this – and surely he would have done, had only he finished his work.

Perhaps he would. This is a work on which Thucydides laboured over many years, and it is not surprising that there are a few signs that different passages were completed at different times;[21] not surprising either that the text is surely unfinished (8.109 is no place to close a finished work).[22] But our methodology must still be to begin by addressing the text as we have it, and provisionally expect it to make literary and interpretative sense. If it does not, then we may fall back on the 'unfinished' hypothesis, and need not be ashamed; but that can come only at the end of an argument, and should not be the first recourse.

In the Pentekontaetia scholars turn to that recourse far too quickly, and even here we might not have to adopt it. No-one is going to be misled by the inclusion of that single bloody afternoon; no-one will think that this was what the development of the empire was all about, or that this explained the outbreak of war in 431. The Peace of Callias, or for that matter the Megarian decree(s), would be different. Readers might well have thought that the Peace marked an important turning-point in the empire (many have indeed thought precisely that); readers might well have thought that the war was fought over Megara (the idea was in the air at the time, as we shall see). Silence was there a way of avoiding misconception, and these are *combative* silences. If we like, we can think of Thucydides as combating the views of other authors, damning them by silence.[23] If we prefer a view of Thucydides as serenely confident that only his work would survive, we can just think that any narrative of Peace or decrees could start the wrong train of thought. Posterity needed to be saved from that.

So the brief analytic passages, ordering causes in their hierarchy, were not enough for Thucydides. Narrative was crucial too, so crucial that he put narrative under strain. The result is anything but smooth, far from the blander expectations of a Dionysius of Halicarnassus.[24] And speeches, of course, mattered too: but they raise so many complex issues that they need to be treated in a separate chapter (Chapter 6).

## To blame and to explain

Tracking actions and events to their origins was, we have seen, a preoccupation of the age; defending one's own explanation against rival views was just as natural – at least in the genres where this was straightforward. It is clearest in rhetoric, and it is rhetoric, as we see most clearly in Antiphon and Gorgias, which particularly developed a facility and deftness in weighing responsibility. An orator's preoccupation is with blaming and excusing individuals: the first concern is to identify, not *what*, but *who* is responsible (the other chap) and who is not (me). That 'who' question need not exclude a 'what': the more one can offload responsibility on to other targets, personal or non-personal, the more one can escape responsibility for oneself, and Gorgias' self-excusing Helen looks to 'love' and 'discourse' as possible alternative villains of the piece. But it all comes down to 'who' in the end. For Helen, the crucial point is 'not me'.

Gorgias' Helen shows so much exculpatory expertise that it seems difficult to blame anyone for anything. Similar paradoxes were clear to Thucydides too: we see that particularly in the play with problems of free will in the Plataean debate, but that is not the only case where those who blame and those who excuse seem to be dealing in half-truths, seeking to cloak their own self-seeking in spurious moral garb, and assigning both blame and credit for actions over which the agents had little choice. And we are frequently brought to feel it makes little difference anyway. The Plataeans will be executed, the Melians will be reduced, the Sicilian cities will pick their more promising or less loathsome allies, whatever the moral rights and wrongs of each case.

'Blaming' is certainly in the air in Thucydides' first book, in particular the blame which the Peloponnesian allies throw at the Athenians and at a crucial moment (1.69.1) at the Spartans too. We might wonder whether Thucydides himself enters into this debate: despite all the complexities which he so readily finds in easy assignments of blame, does he still find one side more blameworthy than the other? It is becoming more fashionable to find him taking sides, organising his narrative in ways which favour Pericles and favour Athens, and some of the best recent Thucydidean scholars have put versions of that view (especially Rhodes 1987, Badian 1993 [first published in 1990], and Hornblower 1991 and 1994).[25] How far, too, does Thucydides find factors other than personal ones 'to blame' for what happens, as we saw with Gorgias' Helen and can often see with doctors' explanations of disease, identifying 'what' rather than 'who' is responsible for the war?

When defensive wars are fought against an aggressive imperialist nation, there is always an easy answer at hand. *Of course* it was the Persians' fault, invading free state after free state, and the Greeks were simply defending themselves; of course it was the Germans' fault, annexing the Saarland and Austria and Czechoslovakia and trying to do the same with Poland; of course it was Saddam's fault, moving into Kuwait; and of course it was the Athenians' fault too, becoming frighteningly great masters of Greeks who were now their 'slaves'. Or so it easily seems; and in each case, even when one has refined the terms into something more sophisticated, the conclusion may still be right. But when Herodotus treated the first of those sequences, it is noticeable how skilfully he deflects that 'of course'. One Persian king after another does indeed launch on a campaign of expansion, initially successfully but then catastrophically, and we are made aware that Greece looms as the final target; but it is notable how often Greeks are implicated in their own downfall, as one meddlesome Greek after another plays a crucial role in drawing the Persian aggressor against their homes: Aristagoras and Histiaeus in the Ionian Revolt, the agitating expelled Peisistratid Hippias, the exiled Spartan king Demaratus who helps put Xerxes on the throne (7.3), the interfering Thessalian Aleuadae (7.6.2). The pattern begins with Democedes of Croton, who cures Darius' queen Atossa of her breast-cancer and demands as his price that she incite her husband to attack Greece. After all, he wants to go home (3.132–4).

Blaming in Herodotus remains important, but in a different way, less a question of the author or reader blaming the Persians, more of the 'blamings' narrated in the text. We see how one disputing party's blame for another frequently masks something else, a desire for aggrandisement, an underlying hatred;[26] we especially see how local 'blamings', with one power or party in a city bitterly recriminating with another, create the conditions which stimulate the Persian aggression or ensure its success.[27] Nor is it easy to assign blame to individual kings: various factors – the attitude of the gods, the dynamics of the court – suggest that Xerxes in particular eventually had little choice but to invade, and his attempts to avoid it are doomed from the beginning.[28] So do we blame, not particular kings, but the whole Persian character, with the gods giving a justified punishment to a transgressive people? That is not easy either, for by the end of the work we are made uneasy about over-facile discrimination between Greeks and barbarians, and come to see, as we saw in the *Iliad*, that the two warring peoples are not so very different.[29] That initial 'of course the Persians are to blame' has come to seem simple-minded, and we are given more interesting questions to put to the narrative.

It is possible to take Thucydides the same way; and that is not uninteresting, given the recurrent suggestion (itself arguably made by Herodotus too) that Athens is the moral heir of Persia, the new 'enslaving' 'tyrant city', with states now 'atticising' as two generations earlier they had 'medised'.[30] Yet even that 'enslaving' is made more morally problematic than the unfriendly term would suggest: the allies are themselves 'to blame', *aitioi*, for conniving in an organisation that secured their weakness (1.99.3), and once again the easy condemnation of the aggressor is confounded – or at least complicated. In fact Thucydides' judgement is harsh, just as Herodotus was harsh on the meddling Greeks who drew in the Persians: here those Athenian allies had little alternative.[31] It is too simple to make this pro-Athenianism, for Thucydides did not need to use this uncompromising language of 'empire', 'slavery', and 'revolt' at all, nor did he need to be so categorical that the anti-Persian crusade of vengeance was simply a 'pretext' (1.96.1).[32] But it does have the effect of suggesting that any 'of course the Athenians were to blame' approach is too easy.

The same is true of the Corinthians' attack on the Spartans – '*you are to blame*', they say, for letting things get to such a pitch (1.69.1, cf. 71.5). Again the claim is harsh, and it is a lazy reader who swallows it without further ado; the Corinthians have their own agenda, and are needling their Spartan audience. But again it complicates and deflects the simple moral view. Just as in Herodotus, too, we may already also be wondering whether the two great national characters are really so different from one another. The Spartans would have behaved exactly the same way, or even worse – so the Athenians say (1.76.1, 77.6).[33] We do not automatically believe them: they are arguing their case. But we do not automatically disbelieve them either. We do not yet know – but even in this book we are given hints that all humans, whatever their nation, will fight for their own interests and their own power, and not be too concerned with morality. This is not a world of angels and villains, goodies and baddies.

The principal effect is to deflect the audience's attention from the moral issue altogether. It becomes a story of power, not of right or wrong. That was already plain in the interpretative categories analysed in the first section of this chapter: there we saw Thucydides suppressing material which does not matter, or using material where it matters most – and that inevitably imposes one particular view on what 'matters'. Thucydides could have set out the terms of the Thirty Years' Peace in the Pentekontaetia; instead he introduces them as they become relevant, usually in accounts of the pre-war diplomatic complaints or incorporated within speeches. That categorises their importance as a point of rhetoric rather than substance; they may or may not 'matter' in explaining people's emotions, just as Herodotus makes mutual 'blamings' have a historical effect; but it avoids making the terms of the Peace a crucial theme in interpreting the period – indeed, it avoids giving us the material by which we can decide which side stayed closer to its terms.[34] That, for Thucydides, is something else which we do not need to know. This too need not be philo-Athenian, as Badian (1993: 137–45) argued; one of the terms which is left obscure, and is similarly confined to speeches[35] and therefore categorised as a matter of rhetoric, is the Treaty's demand that states should submit to arbitration before fighting. Morally, the Athenians' case here was probably the stronger; the Spartans themselves later came to think so (7.18.4; see above, p. 74, and p. 265, n. 44). But in the narrative of Book 1 the notion is left as a sideshow. Both sides assume that the only way to proceed is to talk to each other and then to fight, and there is not even any puzzling on who any arbitrator might be. Perhaps the whole notion of arbitration is a farce, as Badian suggests:[36] that dismissive approach too is aired (by Sthenelaidas, 1.86.3), and we are not made to feel he is wrong. This is not the way to make the most of Athens' strongest moral card.

That sidestepping of the moral issue is also clear if we consider Thucydides' treatment of the Samian revolt in 440, something which Badian (1993: 138–40) and Hornblower (1991: 83–4 and 1994: 144–5) again find tellingly philo-Athenian. At that point the Spartans summoned a conference of the Peloponnesian League. The question was whether the League should intervene on the Samians' behalf, and Corinth spoke out against intervention. Yet that League debate over Samos is introduced only in the Corinthians' speech at 1.40–3, and we are given no full account when the narrative reaches that point at 1.115. Badian thinks the effect is to maximise Sparta's aggressiveness towards Athens (for at 1.40–3 we automatically assume, he thinks, that Sparta was keen on intervention), and to deflect attention from the autonomy issue: had the debate been included at 1.115, he argues that this would have figured heavily, for the question would be whether Athens was meddling unacceptably with an ally's autonomy.

Yet it is hard to think that Thucydides' concern is really to maximise Spartan and minimise Athenian aggression. As Badian himself says (1993: 139) Thucydides' own account at 1.115 makes it 'clearly a case of Athenian aggression': a different impression could easily have been given.[37] Nor does the Corcyrean debate make it so clear that Sparta herself wished to intervene in 440. Modern historians tend to assume that the congress would not have been summoned unless Sparta had already decided for war;[38] that may or may not be true (I myself doubt it), but the important point is that Thucydides himself does not make it plain. Nor does the subsequent narrative make the Spartan position clearer. We naturally compare (and Thucydides' text surely encourages us to compare) the events of 432, and there Sparta apparently had no commitment before summoning the allies to debate (1.67):[39] and in 432 the Corinthians certainly feel that they cannot count on Spartan bellicosity.

Nor is there anything insidious in introducing the Samian debate at 1.40–3. If anything, that gives it more prominence, rather than tucked away in the Pentekontaetia at 1.115 (and it is hard to think that any airing of the issues there could have taken more than a couple of lines); 1.40–3 is anyway where it belongs, at the point where it most effectively influences arguments and thoughts. This effect on the reader's thoughts is worth pursuing further. The Corinthians claim especial credit for opposing intervention because it was 'the sort of crisis when people, set on confronting their enemies, ignore everything except victory: they regard yesterday's enemy as today's friend, if he brings service, and previous friends as their new enemies, for even the closest of relationships take second place because of the contentions of the present' (1.41.2). Now they ask for the Athenians to show their gratitude, 'realising that this is a version of that crisis where a helper is most especially a friend, and an opponent an enemy' (1.43.2). The effect is to direct attention to the expediency which they expect to govern people's actions at particularly critical moments, then (1.41.2) as now (1.43.2). That undercuts the whole drift of their moral argument, and suggests that prudential considerations will naturally decide the issue; as so often in Thucydides, a moral argument turns out to be uncomfortable and self-defeating; and so again we see, on a deeper level, Thucydides' deflection of moral questions into a more pragmatic register.

Even the enigmatic treatment of the Spartan attitude plays a suggestive role. We cannot be *sure* that the Spartans were eager to fight in 440; but we cannot be sure that they were not, either, and we find them as difficult to gauge as their own allies always found them. The impression is anyway of a war which could easily have broken out in 440, of the hair-breadth which made the difference between the Peloponnesians' pulling back and their going ahead; and it is the possibility of League intervention which, now as then, made it so possible for inter-state squabbling to escalate into a major war. It is that concern of the Peloponnesians, too, which the Athenians have to take into account in measuring their interests now, for it is that which makes it so likely that a war will come anyway: the Corcyreans put to them that the 'Spartans are eager to fight because of their fear of you' (1.33.3, cf. 36.1), and the Athenians accept the conclusion (1.44.2). This is no bad way for Thucydides to insinuate the view of a war which has been waiting to happen for fifteen years, and might so easily have happened already; and a war now brought on by the major powers' reasonable conviction that it is bound to happen in any case. Nor is it a bad way to convince the reader that, everyday and understandable though such mother-city-and-colony squabbles may be, there is something unusual about this one, something which makes it particularly likely to escalate, something which we may not yet need to know in detail but may already find adumbrated. That something is the attentive concern of the major background powers, fearful of allowing their rivals to get away with anything that would make them more formidable. Thus the *aitiai* explain; the *prophasis* will explain more. And those are not points about right and wrong. They are about power.

So to regard Thucydides as a straightforward partisan of Athens makes him too simple a writer. It is better to see him as deflecting the moral question rather than suggesting one particular answer to it; of working in a Herodotean tradition and with a similar agenda. We should see him, too, as insinuating a 'what' rather than a 'who' answer to the responsibility question: eventually it is human nature which explains most, the self-defending and self-advancing aspects which all humans share and which underlie all the national divergences. It would be as absurd, or at least as fruitless, to blame that as it would be to blame any other natural phenomenon, a storm, a flood, or a plague.

The issue is not yet ended. We cannot make Thucydides a simple partisan, but can we make him a subtle one? To blame anything less personal, to shift responsibility into any different register, automatically reduces the personal culpability of an individual. Gorgias knew that, and made his Helen know that; Aeschylus' Clytemnestra knows that when she blames the ancestral curse (*Agam.* 1497–504); any modern advocate who turns a culprit into a victim – of the marital condition, of his or her mental state, of society as a whole – knows that too. Should we see it as a reflex of Athens' or Pericles' moral indefensibility that the debate is shifted into a different register? Thucydides' combative silences and tendentious placements can doubtless be seen as interpretative; but can it be coincidence that so many of those interpretations turn out to favour Athens, and more particularly Pericles? In Thucydides, this is no longer Pericles' war, and his personal motivation is unquestioned; Thucydides' Pericles also presents the Spartans' demands over Megara as a trial of will rather than a matter of substance, and here too the narrative emphasis and selectivity supports Pericles' view (below, pp. 104–6). Megara and Aegina may have been clearer breaches of the Thirty Years' Peace terms, especially its autonomy provisions, than Corcyra and Potidaea;[40] is it coincidence that the narrative balance plays them down? Given Thucydides' power-play perspective, we can see why he thought Corcyra and Potidaea mattered more; they affected Corinth, and Corinth could exercise an influence that Megara and Aegina could not; but is not that perspective itself over-friendly to Athens? Hornblower's question is a good way of putting the point (1994: 148): if impartial interpretation rather than patriotic bias was the answer, might we not expect some at least of the displacements and silences to favour the Spartans, not all (or almost all) to cover Athenian embarrassment?

In fact, we have already seen some interpretative tendencies which are less philo-Athenian, for instance the language of slavery, or the distraction of attention from the arbitration clause; later we shall see that the suppressed Megarian material may include a decree framed in 'reasonable and courteous language', which could have been highlighted as an act of moderation, and a Megarian murder of an Athenian herald.[41] But such cases are hardly enough to even the scale, and Hornblower's question remains a fair one.

Perhaps, though, it can be answered, and it is not so surprising that most of the narrative silences and mouldings go in Athens' favour. Most of the 'grievances' would be against Athens: that is always the way when a war is fought to stop an unapologetically aggressive and intrusive power ('of course the Athenians are to blame...'). To suppress or deflect *any* of them could be regarded as friendly to Athens. Had Thucydides passed swiftly over Corcyra and Potidaea and dwelt on Megara and Aegina, his critics could reasonably have made him philo-Athenian for concealing the substantial Athenian interference with their enemies' spheres of interest, and representing the Spartans as fighting over trivialities.

So Thucydides' wider explanations in terms of human nature do complicate any attempt simply to blame Pericles or blame Athens. It is another thing, though, to make the desire for such exculpation Thucydides' *motive* for his interpretative strategies. That is simply a piece of long-distance psychological reconstruction, and not a particularly plausible one. It is really a refined form of 'Poirot';[42] if that had been Thucydides' aim, then the evidence, or some of it – the way he shapes his narrative – might look the way it looks now; but this is not the only or the best explanation. We can think of it just as well in terms of a writer steeped in Herodotus; clear (as Herodotus was clear) that the complications of human behaviour belie simple blame and exculpation; but a writer concerned, as Herodotus was not, to impose a single interpretation on the reader, one that was right not because it favoured Athens, limited as that city was in time and space, but because it was truer to an underlying human nature.

Underlying – and eternal. Thucydides was writing, at least partly, for posterity: this is a 'possession for ever, more than a prize composition for immediate hearing' (1.22.4; note, though, that characteristic 'more than', and Thucydides leaves it open that his text can be both). Thucydides thought events, or something like them, would recur. He was writing for people who wished to understand (he does not say 'do anything about' or 'avoid') 'things which will be the same and similar in future generations, the human condition being what it is' (1.22.4). That does not mean that the recurrence will be exact; as in the case of the hardships which attacked faction-ridden cities, phenomena will be 'more intense and gentler and different in form depending on what changes of circumstance are present in each case' (3.82.2). But he did expect further cases of imperialistic democracies, fired by self-belief and carried away by a run of success, who would eventually prove so threatening that they ran into a successful alliance of stubborn adversaries; he did expect such states to take a bullying step too far, as in Sicily, and to risk self-destruction; and he was absolutely right. Think of Napoleon and Russia; think of Hitler and Russia; think of the United States and Vietnam. He was providing a key for his readers to understand such recurrent events; but reader-response is always a two-way thing, and he expected his readers also to feed in their knowledge of their own times as they responded to his narrative and interpretation. The closer the parallels to their own experience, the more convincing they would find his own reading of the Peloponnesian War.

But what would recur? The power-politics, certainly; perhaps the psychology of expansion and resistance: but the *morality*? That was likely to vary; and readers' moral response to the similar phenomena of their own experience was likely to vary still more. Some readers will have been annoyed by the mischievous comparison of the modern USA to Napoleon and Hitler in the last paragraph. Why? Because they find the morality of the issues so different. Others will have found the comparison totally fair. But the effect on both groups may anyway have been to blur the main point of comparison between past and present: the more one dwells on the issues of right and wrong, the more one's own prejudices distract from the political parallels which remain. (It was precisely to illustrate that point from my own readers' response that I slipped in that sentence.) Thucydides did not need any of that: no wonder he moved his emphasis away from the moral issue. It was the power-relationships which were his theme. That need not stop his readers asking questions about morality, whether Athens' or Sparta's morality or that of Napoleon, Hitler, Lyndon Johnson, or Richard Nixon; nor need it stop readers asking whether anything could be done to impede or aid the aggressive self-believing democracies of their own times. The narrative certainly often invites a strong *emotional* response; and, human nature being what it is, moral questioning follows particularly swiftly when emotions are roused (which is not to say that every reader gives the same answers). But the moral questions were not his theme. There, the readers were on their own.

## Megarian decrees

As always, such points tell us something about audience as well as author, or rather about the audience (present and future) which the author had in mind. The text plays to an audience which is ready to ask questions about power more than morals, at least in the dynamic of the reading process itself; and an audience which will not bridle at the presumption of so monologic and autocratic an authorial persona. Yet posterity turned out to be less deferential, less willing to confine themselves to what Thucydides had selected for them. Parsimonious need-to-know informants have a way of generating curious want-to-know responses, and Thucydides' later readers certainly wanted to know what exactly he had cared so much about suppressing. Thucydides had fought against the suggestion that this was 'Pericles' war'; yet those readers found enough hints in other literature of the time, especially Aristophanes, that others had claimed precisely that.

The Megarian decree, or decrees, provided a particularly fascinating puzzle. Aristophanes makes great play with this in *Acharnians* and to an extent in *Peace*: those passages would at least suggest that, when contemporaries thought of Pericles' role, Megara immediately sprang to mind. Orators too sometimes spoke in terms of 'going to war for Megara' (Andoc. 3.8, followed closely by Aeschines 2.175). It need not follow that this was 'the popular view' of the cause of the war.[43] Andocides has his own rhetorical agenda, emphasising that Athens repeatedly fought Sparta for other states, just as in the 450s she went to war for Aegina and in 418 for Argos (3.6, 3.9). Those claims, especially the first, are preposterous, and could not possibly reflect a 'popular view'; modern politicians, in bombastic mode, could similarly say that 'Britain went to war for Poland's sake in 1939', without implying that they or their audience thought this the real 'cause' of the Second World War. But the passages in comedy and oratory could still intrigue later writers, and Thucydides' lack of a Megarian narrative would seem a deafening silence. It is no surprise that they tried to fill the gaps. That already seems to be true of Ephorus in the fourth century;[44] later, it was certainly true of Plutarch, who was particularly fond of supplementing Thucydides[45] and knew fifth-century literature well enough to collect some tantalising clues.

The result is a particularly knotty puzzle for us too, and provides a test-case for analysing and combining material from different genres; a test-case, too, for tracing the implications of Thucydides' technique for our own reconstruction. Aristophanes' material, suggesting that the 'clonking of shields' all came from a ridiculously slight beginning over Megara, poses issues of its own, and we will return to that in Chapter 8. But before we can place Aristophanes' material we need to look at the historiographic tradition, and unravel what can and cannot be inferred.

Combatively silent though he was, Thucydides would leave no-one in doubt that a Megarian decree figured prominently in the diplomacy. When the Peloponnesian allies gathered at Sparta in 432, the Spartans invited allies to make any complaints they might have against the Athenians: among these the Megarians

> made clear a number of other grievances, and in particular complained that they were barred from the harbours in the Athenian empire and the Attic agora[46] contrary to the treaty.
>
> (Thuc. 1.67.4)

That 'treaty' must be the Thirty Years' Peace of 446. Then the final diplomatic manoeuvring begins, and the Spartans send a series of embassies to Athens. The first demanded that the Athenians 'drive out the curse', that is expel Pericles as a descendant of the sacrilegious Alcmaeonids (1.126–7). Then several embassies demand that Athens leave Potidaea, grant Aegina autonomy, and

> in particular, and most clearly stated, they said that if the Athenians repealed the Megarian decree there would not be war – the decree in which it was specified that they should not make any use of the harbours in the Athenian empire nor of the Attic agora. The Athenians rejected the other requests and also did not repeal the decree: they charged the Megarians with working the sacred and the undefined land and with receiving runaway slaves.
>
> (Thuc. 1.139.1–2)

The final Spartan embassy made only the general demand that the Athenians should grant the Greeks autonomy. To judge from the speech which Thucydides gives Pericles on that occasion, it was again taken by some that the repeal of the Megarian decree would be enough to placate Sparta. The speech gives us to understand that some were saying that this decree was a small matter to fight over (1.140.3); Pericles' suggested reply (1.144.2), accepted by the assembly (1.145.1), began by specifying that 'we will allow the Megarians use of agora and harbours if the Spartans make no expulsions (*xenelasiai*) either of us or of our allies, for neither the one thing nor the other is forbidden by the treaty...'. The reply makes other points too, concerning autonomy and arbitration; but the Megarian decree, it seems, was prominent in people's minds.

What can we infer from this? The absence of a detailed narrative suggests only that Thucydides did not think this explained much. Unlike Corcyra and Potidaea, this was a grievance and no more. We cannot conclude that the decree(s), or some of them, belong (say) early in the 430s, during the 'dead' period of the Pentekontaetia (i.e. the years towards the end which Thucydides passes over in silence); or in the months after the Sparta congress, once the Spartans had already decided on war; or in a quite different context.[47]

Other points are more secure. Thucydides' phrasing of 'the' decree – from him we should infer that there was only one – is precise, and closely similar on two occasions and echoed on a third (1.144.2): the Megarians are 'barred from the harbours of the Athenian empire and the Attic agora'. It need not follow that this was the only provision of 'the' decree, but it does seem that Thucydides thought this the main provision, the one which both the Megarians (1.67.2) and the Spartans (1.139.2) made the centre of their complaint. We may also infer that this decree, along with a 'fair number of other grievances', preceded the Spartan assembly in (?autumn) 432, though we cannot tell by how much;[48] and that the alleged Megarian 'working of the sacred and the undefined land' and reception of runaway slaves preceded the Athenian response to the second series of Spartan embassies in winter 432–1, though it did not necessarily precede 'the' decree itself (it is given as a reason for not repealing the decree, not for passing it).

Also significant is the Spartan insistence that if the Megarian decree were repealed there would be no war. That may well be diplomatic manoeuvring and 'insincere';[49] but it must be manoeuvring with a purpose. Presumably the purpose, at least in

Thucydides' presentation, cannot be to avoid war: the Spartans have already decided to fight (1.88). So they are banking on this request being refused, or at least – as Thucydides' Pericles goes on to claim – on some follow-up request being refused. It makes best sense if this propaganda ploy is aimed not at the whole Greek world (for if Athens would seem to be fighting for a small matter so might Sparta), nor at the Spartans' allies (for Corinth was crucial, and Corinth would not believe, or if she did believe would not be impressed by believing, that Sparta was fighting for Megara), but at Athenian public opinion, with the intention of splitting it and persuading some that this was indeed too small a matter to fight over. That is the implication of Thucydides' narrative,[50] and it coheres with the motive he earlier suggests for the first Spartan embassy, their hope that their demands would either lead to Pericles' exile or, more likely, generate a hostile public feeling that the war will be his fault (1.127.2). That picture is plausible enough;[51] and if accurate, it makes it easy to believe that Aristophanes' Dicaeopolis, suggesting that this *was* a small matter to have led to so much 'clonking of shields', was picking up a view that was already in the air.[52]

Plutarch's *Pericles* is much fuller in detail than Thucydides but even more difficult to use. One problem is the way in which Plutarch here organises his material, partly chronologically and partly thematically.[53] By Chapter 29 the chronological line has reached the origins of the war, and Plutarch begins with Corcyra; but the dominant question for the next few chapters becomes that of Pericles' responsibility for the war, and the various hostile claims made about this. Different approaches and possibilities are aired, and historical details are fed in along the way; but Plutarch has no brief to keep them in any chronological order. Towards the end of this section, for instance, once he has established Pericles' uncompromising opposition to the Spartans, he turns to discussing the Spartan reaction to this intransigence. He stresses their belief that they would find Athens more malleable if they could remove Pericles, and illustrates this first with their demand that the Athenians 'drive out the curse' (33.1–2: above, p. 104). That reflects Thucydides' account of the first Spartan embassy, and is clearly earlier than some material Plutarch has already used: for instance, the Spartans' later insistence on Megara and Pericles' opposition (29.8). In that case Thucydides' own account has prevented historians from being misled; but it shows how rash it would be to interpret Plutarch's sequence as chronological in other cases where we have no such Thucydidean control.

Let us go back to the beginning of this section. Chapter 29 takes us through the Corcyra affair, supplementing Thucydides with some extra material on Pericles' role. It was he, we are told, who persuaded the Athenians to intervene in Corcyra, and also he who was responsible for sending so small an initial force; as Plutarch represents it, this was to humiliate the commander Lacedaemonius, the son of Pericles' old adversary Cimon (29.1–2). Public opinion was here against Pericles – this introduces the theme of popular hostility towards him – and so it is again Pericles who is responsible for sending a stronger fleet to reinforce (29.3). All this may be true;[54] but one favourite Plutarch trick is to expand the role of his hero and transfer to him the actions of others, and another is to make his points by reconstructing the reactions of contemporary observers.[55] A good deal of this could be extravagant inference from the single item of Lacedaemonius' appointment (not necessarily attributed to Pericles himself by a source, any more than it is by Thuc. 1.45.2),[56] combined with Thucydides' indication that there was first a small and then a much bigger Athenian force: indeed, the whole item *might* be no more than imaginative inference from Thucydides' own account. If Plutarch persuaded himself that the moving spirit must have been Pericles, then the reconstruction both of his motive and of the public response could easily fill in the rest.

Plutarch's narrative then reverts more straightforwardly to Thucydides. The Corinthians protest in Sparta, and the Megarians back them up, complaining 'that they are barred and driven away from every[57] agora and every harbour under Athenian control, contrary to international justice and the oaths sworn by the Greeks' (29.4). That is doubtless no more than Plutarch's own rhetorically enhanced version of Thucydides' phrasing. We then have Thucydidean material on Aegina and (displaced from earlier in Thucydides) Potidaea (29.5–6); then, after a mention of Archidamus' conciliating speech (29.7 ~ Thuc. 1.80–5), Plutarch goes forward to the embassies of 1.139.

> It did not [or, less likely, 'does not'[58]] seem that the other grounds would have been sufficient to bring the war upon the Athenians, if they had been persuaded to repeal the Megarian decree and be reconciled with the Megarians. Therefore Pericles opposed this particularly vehemently and stirred up the people to stick to their contentious hostility with Megara, and was therefore alone held responsible[59] for the war.
>
> (Plut. *Per.* 29.7–8)

There is nothing there that is not in, or easily inspired by, Thucydides.

Chapter 30 builds a new train of thought on this question of Pericles 'held responsible'. An initial anecdote begins 'when an embassy from Sparta was in Athens concerning this...': it need not be the same embassy as the one to which Pericles has just been responding, but it is clearly one which follows 'the' decree (30.1). The narrative goes on:

> There was some underlying personal hostility of Pericles towards the Megarians, it seems, but he put forward the communal and open charge against them that they were annexing the sacred tract of land, and proposed a decree that the same herald should be sent to them and to the Spartans, accusing the Megarians. This decree of Pericles is couched in a tone of generous and civilised remonstrance. When, however, the herald sent on this mission, Anthemocritus, was killed and the Megarians were thought to be responsible, Charinus proposed a decree against them: that there should be a state of hostility without truce and without exchange of heralds, that any Megarian who set foot on Attic soil should be put to death, that when the generals took the ancestral oath they should add an oath that they would invade Megarian soil twice in every year, and that Anthemocritus should be buried by the Thriasian gates, which are now called the Dipylon. The Megarians[60] deny the killing of Anthemocritus, and turn the charge against Aspasia and Pericles: they quote the famous and hackneyed lines from the *Acharnians*...
>
> (Plut. *Per.* 30.2–4)

– and Plutarch goes on to quote *Ach.* 525–8 on Aspasia's two girls (below, pp. 142–3). His own view, he says, is that the 'origin' (presumably of the decree, and/or possibly of Pericles' hostility) is hard to detect, but everyone alike makes Pericles responsible for the refusal to repeal 'the decree', some praising him for his greatness of spirit, others blaming him for being so stubbornly anti-Spartan (31.1).

The charges against Pericles continue to be traced in the next two chapters, which advance various suggestions for that personal hostility: the 'worst charge of all' concerning Pheidias' imprisonment, then other explanations centring on personal attacks on him and his friends, Aspasia and Anaxagoras (these include material which goes back several years, 31–2). 'Those are the grounds [*aitiai* – once again, there is a suggestion also of grievances, even charges] which people give for his refusal to let the people give in to the Spartans. The truth is unclear.' (32.6).

We evidently cannot be certain that the material of Chapter 30 belongs chronologically later than that of Chapter 29; once the question of 'underlying hostility' has been introduced, Plutarch has moved out of linear sequence, seeking the origin of that hostility (Chapters 31–2) but first stating the ways in which Pericles justified it in public. Once that is established, it seems clear that Plutarch himself *identified* Charinus' hard-line decree with 'the' decree, the Thucydidean exclusion decree which he had treated in the previous chapter:[61] the formulation in 31.1, 'everyone agrees that Pericles was responsible for the failure to repeal *the decree*', clearly refers to the Charinus decree – but it also ring-compositionally echoes the language of 29.7–8 ('if the decree had been repealed ... Pericles opposed ... and alone was held responsible for the war...'), where it was the failure to repeal the Thucydidean 'agora and harbours' decree which was in point.

Was, however, Plutarch right to identify the two? It is very likely to be his own inference. His knowledge of the two decrees of Chapter 30, the first 'couched in a tone of generous and civilised remonstrance' and the second of Charinus, is probably drawn directly from Craterus' collection of decrees, and it is unclear how much commentary Craterus afforded.[62] In that case, the terms of the Charinus decree are probably accurate, though not necessarily complete and doubtless rephrased in Plutarch's own language; Plutarch's judgement on the generous and civilised tone of the first decree also commands respect. But the identification of the Charinus and Thucydidean decrees carries no weight; all we can infer is that Plutarch himself thought their terms similar enough to encourage the identification, a view which most modern scholars have found wholly impossible.[63]

Is the identification right? This is the point to which analysis of the texts can take us; from now on, the historian has to use her or his own judgement. We cannot assume that Plutarch, any more than Thucydides, aims to give the full provisions: even if Charinus' decree had specified the empire's harbours as well as Attic soil, Plutarch might naturally cut that out, feeling that he had already made that clause clear when introducing 'the' decree in the previous chapter. Also in favour of the identification is the difficulty scholars find in reconstructing a plausible sequence to accommodate three rather than two decrees. The 'generous and civilised remonstrance' most naturally[64] belongs at the beginning, Charinus' decree as the most extreme belongs at the end; yet if a separate Thucydidean exclusion decree has to belong in the middle, it interrupts the close chronological linkage we naturally assume between the generous and civilised decree and that of Charinus, providing as it does for the burial of Anthemocritus who had died on that first, generous and civilised, mission.

Still, a lot tells against that Plutarchan identification. One problem is the terms of the two decrees: how could a ban on Megarians entering Attica at all (Charinus) co-exist with a ban on their entering the Athenian agora (the Thucydidean decree)? Yet both wordings command respect, if one comes from Craterus and the other is guaranteed by Thucydides' repeated precision. And Thucydides' 'agora and harbours' formulation suggests a further problem. If Thucydides specified only one provision of a longer decree, it should at least be the provision which was most significant and most rhetorically effective: it must be the point which can figure most strikingly both in the Megarian appeal to Sparta (Thuc. 1.67) and in the Spartan demands to Athens (1.139). Opinions differ on how economically effective the 'agora and harbours' restriction could have been, or was intended to be;[65] but in any case would this seem more dramatic and drastic than the threat of immediate execution if any Megarian set foot on Attic soil, or the commitment to invade the Megarid twice a year? (If indeed this identification is right, one of the most interesting implications would be that Thucydides, a highly rational observer, could regard the agora and harbours restriction as more important than the threat to life – or at least as mattering more to the Megarians.) It is true that the agora and harbours may have had more impact on Megarian traders than, say, exclusion from Attic temples, and that if she had been so minded Sparta might have passed over twice-yearly invasions as insufficient to constitute an act of war;[66] but she was not so minded, she and Megara were both collecting grievances which were meant to sound convincing, and the other provisions of the Charinus decree surely offered irresistible rhetorical potential for complaint.

The arguments are finely balanced, with probability perhaps tilting against identification. The decrees' chronological sequence depends on the identification issue. If the Charinus and Thucydidean decrees are identical, the question solves itself: the 'generous and civilised remonstrance' comes first, then Anthemocritus gets killed, then the Charinus/Thucydidean decree is passed; these events will all be close to one another and all before the 432 Spartan congress, though we cannot tell how long before.[67] If the Charinus and Thucydidean decrees are different, it is more difficult. The Charinus decree will be later than the Thucydidean: it would make no sense to exclude from the agora after a more total exclusion from Attic soil. It will also be later than the Megarian protests in Thuc. 1.67 and the diplomatic exchanges in 1.139, otherwise the more extreme provisions would have formed part of the rhetoric, and would probably have affected the case enough for Thucydides to think them worth mentioning. The 'generous and civilised remonstrance' should belong shortly before the Charinus decree. The objection to this, as we saw, was that the softest decree more naturally belongs at the beginning of the whole sequence; but that objection need not be decisive. The herald there goes both to Megara and to Sparta, something which may in itself suggest a phase later than Thuc. 1.67, once Sparta is firmly embroiled.[68] If Athens' language is meant to impress international opinion, especially Spartan opinion, then it may well have been phrased with a careful display of reasonableness as well as firmness, even if the Thucydidean exclusion decree had already been passed: after all, the Athenian position was that the exclusion decree was not contrary to the terms of the Peace (1.144.2). The description of the decree's language is also surely Plutarch's own, and is a foil for the extreme terms of the Charinus decree which he goes on to quote. It need not have been as soft as all that. So there would be no problem in a sequence of exclusion decree before the Spartan congress in 432, then at uncertain dates in 432 and 431 the generous and civilised remonstrance and finally the Charinus decree.[69]

The most important questions about the exclusion decree remain. Was this purely a formal exclusion for religious reasons? Even if it was, did its provocative and humiliating character also have a political aim? Whatever its motive, would it have affected Megarian trade and economy? How, and how far, was such an exclusion expected to be practicable? All these issues have been much discussed, especially since de Ste Croix (1972), but I must resist the temptation to join in the debate here.[70] It raises fundamental questions of Greek religion and economics, and little is added by the disentangling of the specific source-material, my concern here.

The most entertaining literary evidence on Megara is that of Aristophanes' *Acharnians*: but that must wait for later.

# Chapter 6

# Thucydides' speeches

The last two chapters have made it clear how difficult it is to discuss Thucydides' narrative in isolation from his speeches. There are tough methodological questions here which we have glossed over. They need a chapter, even though a short one, to themselves.

The *aitiai*, Thucydides said, were 'openly expressed'; the truest *prophasis* was 'most unclear in what was said'. In the last chapter we noticed the recurrent unease, the fear that we might miss something crucial. Readers often find that strange: is not the growth of Athenian power utterly clear in the speeches? Was Thucydides over-nervous about his ability to make it clear?

What, though, precisely is this aspect which might be 'unclear'? We too often speak as if it is simply that growth of Athenian power. Thucydides says more than that: it is 'the Athenians, by (a) becoming great and (b) frightening the Spartans, (c) forced them into making war'. The growth of power is only one point of three:[1] and we might well feel that the Spartan 'fear' and the fact that they were 'forced' are both points that are genuinely 'most unclear in what was said'. The first is addressed in economic terms by the Corinthians at 1.120.2, the inland needs the coast if it is to get its goods; and more crucially in political terms at 1.71.4, they will seek another ally if the Spartans fail them now. But even the second makes little impact (wise Archidamus ignores it); the first is embedded in a speech of such chirpy overconfidence that it is unimpressive, and is anyway not the most central point either of the speech or of the Sparta–ally relationship. Modern writers would talk about the Spartans' internal problems with their helots and their consequent need for a surrounding protective cocoon, or perhaps about the way that states naturally strive to retain their international power. Neither point is alien to Thucydides' thought, but neither surfaces clearly in these speeches in Book 1.

Nor does the fact that they are 'forced'. The Greek word *anankazein* need not suggest an unconditional lack of alternatives, but then neither does the English 'force' or 'have to' ('her employer forces her to work on Sundays', 'I have to be back home for dinner'):[2] it simply conveys that any alternative is not ultimately a real or viable one. It still suggests an inevitability that the speakers and actors of Book 1 do not acknowledge. (There is *ananke* in the air, but not concerning the coming war, at least until it is imminent at 1.124.2 and 144.3. The *ananke* rather concerns earlier events, the pressure on Corcyra and Corinth to escalate their conflict, 1.28.3, 32.5, 40.3, and 49.7, and the Athenian assumption of hegemony in the 470s, 1.75.3, 76.1–2. An adequate narratological analysis would bring out how this is one of the subtle links suggested between those earlier sequences and the present,[3] but the speakers themselves are not presented as aware of those links.) In the 1.67–88 debate the Spartans speak as if it were at least possible to refuse; they could decide either way, and in fact eventually decide for a compromise of Sthenelaidas' view (we must fight...) and Archidamus' (...but not immediately). The Corinthians and Corcyreans address the Athenians as if they could choose to support either side, and the two-day agonising over the decision (1.44) suggests that the assembly could genuinely have gone either way. Both Spartans and Athenians are grimly aware that the war is likely to happen anyway, and this is an important ingredient in both decisions; but no speaker really gives the impression that their choice is inevitable, that they are forced to take the measures – if not this one, then one like it soon – which will bring on the war whose likelihood they reluctantly accept.[4]

So perhaps Thucydides' nervousness was not so excessive: these are vital points, but ones which his speakers pass over. Nor is it difficult, on a first glance, to see why. They do not speak about the helots because they need not: the audiences knew about that already. They do not speak about the inevitability because cannot: that was only going to become clear in retrospect.[5] But that is to think as if these were speakers in real life, or at least to imply that the speeches satisfy some conditions of verisimilitude. That is problematic: if we apply the same conditions of verisimilitude elsewhere, we swiftly find problems. It is always a dangerous game to write mental speeches for people in a different culture, with an audience we find hard to gauge; but still, can we really think that the Corinthian speakers at Sparta would give quite so much of their air-time to an elaborate comparison of the Athenian and Spartan characters, say almost nothing of Corcyra or Potidaea, and make so little, only a fifth of a sentence, of their threat to 'turn to another alliance' (1.71.4)? Greek diplomats admittedly went in for plain speaking;[6] still, is it credible that the Athenian speakers, intent – Thucydides assures us – on encouraging their audience to inaction, should not have bothered with saccharine assurances that 'we have no plans' to move against Sparta herself? If this is verisimilitude, the truth it mimics points to a strange world indeed.

Thucydides does tell us something of his method in the speeches (and it is striking that he does; he thinks that there is a problem, and fears his audience might not understand). It is important to set the passage in context. The 'Archaeology' (1.1–19), summarising the growth of power and explaining why Greek states were earlier in no position to fight a great war, has reached its end; Thucydides has just been commenting on the difficulty of getting at the truth, and claiming that his account is more reliable than any alternative.

> ... Admittedly, people always think the war they are fighting is the greatest ever, and once it is over they resume the habit of admiring those of old; but anyone who looks at the facts themselves will find it clear that this war was bigger than any of them.
>
> First, concerning what they said, either before the war or after its outbreak: it was difficult, both for me in the case of the speeches I heard myself and for my various informants, to remember the precise things that they said; but I have put things so as to capture how each speaker would most have seemed to me to say what he should about the issues at hand, keeping as close as possible to the general sense of what was really said. Secondly, the actions among the things that were done in the war: I have thought it right not to use just anyone as my informant for my account, nor to write it as it seemed to me, but to pursue things with as much precision as possible, in the case both of events at which I was present and of those of which I heard from others.
>
> (1.21.2–22.2)

(Translation is more than usually difficult, as we will see: this version is as non-committal as possible.)

'Looking at the facts themselves' is the handle on which this methodological disquisition is hung. The discriminating reader will examine both the analysis of earlier history and the account of the war, and compare the two. Considering 'what they said', like the 'actions' in the next sentence, will be a part of this 'looking at the facts themselves', and will enable readers to be more confident that they have grasped the facts; indeed, the awkward phrase 'the actions among the things that were done in the war' implies some sub-division among 'the things that were done in the war' – the facts – into 'what they said' and 'the actions'.[7] Speeches, quite clearly, are to be a crucial tool of historical investigation, both for Thucydides and for his readers; no wonder he agonised, and expected his readers to agonise, about their degree of historical accuracy.

No sentence in the Greek language can have been taken quite so variously as that on the speeches here. Some scholars think it clear that the guiding principle here is as much historical accuracy as possible, others think it points to a high degree of free composition; the only feature which most interpreters share is their confidence in their interpretation, and their utter bemusement that others should not see it the same way. Yet perhaps this variation in interpretation is not so surprising. For, despite the apparent carefulness of the phrasing, Thucydides' words are quite extraordinarily ambiguous, and could describe a range of different procedures.[8] Let us take the ambiguities in turn.

First, 'how each of them would most have seemed to me to say what he should about the issues at hand'. All orators have always tried to say 'what should be said', *ta deonta*, and it covers every aspect of their craft: finding the right policies to urge, the right arguments for urging them, the right ways of putting the arguments and arranging them, the right words to use. Thucydides cannot presumably here be saying that he gave his speakers the right policies to urge, otherwise we could not explain the existence of head-to-head debates, with both speakers urging diametrically opposite policies. But is he implying that he took the policies as a given, and found the best arguments? (Yet if he did, he often made a bad job of it: recent scholars, especially Macleod, have ruthlessly exposed the frequency with which the arguments are contradictory or self-unmasking. It is hard to think that Thucydides, of all people, was too unintelligent to notice.) Or took the arguments as given, and found the most elegant and pungent way of putting them? Or what?

Secondly, 'keeping as close as possible' to what was really said. What defines what is possible? Does he mean that *absolutely*, that he has kept as close as he could to what was said, that where he knew what was said he would always reproduce it?[9] Or does he mean 'as much as possible, *given that I am trying to do what I have just said*'? He has just made it clear that he will make his speakers say what seemed to him appropriate. If that 'appropriateness' is his main principle, does that become one of the criteria delimiting what is 'possible'? If a speaker had said something inappropriate and Thucydides knew it, would he exclude it as 'impossible' to include, given those principles for composition? If so, we might rather translate 'keeping *where possible* to what was really said'. In that case, it would be the same sort of 'as … as possible' as if one said 'I always did what seemed to me right for my country, but I did as much as possible [i.e. when my duty allowed it] to help my friends'. But that sentence would be unambiguous; Thucydides' phrasing is far harder to pin down, and it could mean either this or 'keeping as close as possible' absolutely. In fact we have as little idea of what he means as if a producer of a historical drama said 'I have tried to convey what seemed to me the spirit and essence of their conversations, keeping as close as possible to what they really said'; or indeed if a motorist said 'I kept on the tail of that car, but I stayed as close as I could to the speed limit'. That could convey any degree at all of respect for veracity in the first case, or the speed limit in the second.

Finally, 'the general sense'[10] of what was really said'. How general is general? Scholars have taken very different views. One influential and well-argued view takes it as meaning the sort of thing that can be summarised in a simple sentence:[11] you Melians are too weak to resist Athens on your own, can expect no help, and therefore should surrender. The equivalents in Book 1 might be 'we Spartans should not fight yet because we are unready'; or 'we Athenians should fight, because this demand is simply a test of our resolve'. Yet it seems odd to talk of 'keeping as close as possible' to such a line: one can keep it or drop it, but 'keep as close as possible' suggests something more elaborate from which one can take some parts and drop others, something to which one can approximate.[12] And there are some occasions where 'the general sense' would resist formulation into anything so simple anyway – Pericles' funeral speech, for instance.[13] Once again, this 'general sense' could be defined in any degree of detail, and the language itself does not help us.

So an extreme 'historical accuracy' interpreter – historical accurist, let us say – will translate something like this: 'It was hard … to remember the exact words of the speeches, but I have composed them in the way in which the speakers would have seemed to pick the most appropriate method of expression for their argument – though I have [always] kept as close as possible to the general sense of what was really said'. Meanwhile an extreme 'free composition' interpreter will shrug, and take it rather as 'It was hard ... to remember the precise lines taken by the speeches, but I have made the speakers argue their positions in the way which would seem to me most appropriate; in doing so I have kept closely, wherever possible, to the general line they really took'. But, of course, we cannot ask which translation is 'right', as if a Greek audience would have puzzled out which English equivalent would be better two and a half millennia later. Both are as right as one another: the Greek means either and both.

Is it not strange, though, that the phrasing should be so vague, especially on a matter so important? Thucydides' Greek is not easy, but it is seldom unclear; we are not, for instance, left in any serious doubt about his procedures about collecting and investigating the 'actions'. Surely the vagueness must be deliberate, and one wonders why. One strong possibility[14] is that he is providing an umbrella description which could cover a range of different procedures, and that he composed[15] more freely at some times than at others. Nor is that so surprising, given the very different types of source-material which he would have had for different speeches. Sometimes he would have heard the speeches himself (the Corcyrean debate, perhaps), or have a large number of reliable informants for an exchange which all knew would be critical (the Sicilian debate at the beginning of Book 6); sometimes he would have scarcely any informants at all, as they were nearly all dead (Plataean debate, Nicias' final speeches at Syracuse); sometimes he may have been welding together material from several different originals, as perhaps with Pericles' first[16] and second speeches, and most obviously when he has multiple speakers such as the two Plataeans at 3.52.5 or Gylippus and the Syracusan generals at 7.65. Whatever the speech, we can infer that he expected to be blending his own reconstructions with what he knew had been said; but the blend itself can be very variable, and it will be impossible to work out what that blend is in any particular case.

So the extreme historical accurist and the extreme free compositioner can both be right, or rightish, some of the time. Perhaps there are other ways too that historical accurist and free compositioner can be brought closer together. The free compositioner has to concede that Thucydides' original readers would not respond to the formulation in the same way as we do. What strikes us, accustomed to verbatim accuracy in at least some historical citations, is the suggestion that speeches might *only* be as accurate 'as possible'. The original audience, accustomed as they were to epic, Herodotus, and logographers, might rather be struck by *any* concern for accuracy, that Thucydides claimed *so much* as to keep as closely as possible to the real speeches. The free compositioner should also acknowledge that Thucydides did at least collect information on what was said ('my various informants'), just as he did on the actions ('those of which I heard from others'). He cared. If the last paragraph's explanation of the umbrella phrasing is accepted, then it also seems to follow that, when he had good information, he would behave differently from when he did not: if it was wholly free composition all the time, there would seem no need to prepare for such variation. It is also clear from the context that speeches were a vital way in to 'looking at the facts themselves': they serve historical knowledge and interpretation. That need not exclude all types of authorial fabrication, but it is hard, for instance, to square with this the view that he was constructing models of set-piece speeches (a strange view in any case, given the frequent logical knots in which the speakers tie themselves);[17] or that he was imagining how speakers would best have expressed their general political standpoints, divorced from particular circumstances[18] (yet there are several occasions where we can see speeches disingenuously concealing the speakers' real thoughts – Archidamus at 2.11, Nicias at 6.21–3 – precisely because the particular circumstances called for such lack of frankness); hard, too, to think that (say), when the Corinthians in 432 foresee the possibility of a fortified garrison-post in Attica on the style realised twenty years later at Decelea (1.122.1), such prescience is historically impossible. That surely would mislead, and give a false impression of the mentality with which both sides went to war. It is better to think that this possibility did figure in people's minds, but in 432 was still jostling with other, much less insightful forecasts.

The historical accurist has things to concede as well. The procedure with speeches is after all carefully contrasted with that of 'actions', with careful verbal antitheses:[19] one of these concerns the 'precision' attainable in each case.[20] Those critics who treat the speeches as having the same *sort of* reliability as the actions are on slippery ground.

Nor can one get away from Thucydides' part in this. It was up to him where to put speeches at all: no speeches for the opponents of

Pericles in Book 1, for instance (for Thucydides, was the opposition too unimportant to count?); no Athenian speeches in the Corcyrean debate (for him, it was not a question of internal divisions); but some speeches whose ironic significance only becomes clear in the light of later events – Hermocrates' pan-Sicilian slogans in 424, for instance, or Athenagoras' complacency in 415 (4.59–64, 6.36–40). Thucydides does not say that Cleon and Diodotus were the most influential speeches in the Mytilenean debate, only 'the most opposite' (3.49.1):[21] if others gave more space to considerations of compassion and humanity, it was Thucydides' choice to reproduce Diodotus' speech rather than the rest. Had unkind chance robbed us of the first half of Book 2, we should never have expected it to contain a Funeral Speech: that is a staggering departure from his normal practice. When we try to explain it, or any other speech we have, it is only the beginning of an explanation to say that they were really delivered: we also need to ask why Thucydides put them in, given the vast number he must have excluded.

One point deserves particular stress. It is also up to Thucydides to abbreviate.[22] Nearly all the speeches must have been longer in their original, real-life form; even in the cases where he has the fullest knowledge of what was said, it is up to Thucydides what to keep and what to drop. Of course he keeps what he finds most interesting to develop in each context, what he can use; and of course he regularly puts it in something like his own language.[23] Compare taking notes of a talk or a lecture. We all note down what we like or need; some bits will be omitted because we know it all already or think we do, some because they seem crazy or boring; half the notes on the final sheet of paper might represent no more than five minutes of the original talk, the bits which we think we can make our own.

Let us spend longer on this question of abbreviation, and see how this might work out in practice. Take the speech of the Corinthians at Sparta (1.68–71). Say that they did wax furious about Corcyra and Potidaea. There was no need for Thucydides to give that more than a line or so (1.68.4), because we know all about this already: forty-three chapters have seen to that. Say that they did drop larger hints about the prospect of an Argive alliance: the point was an important one, but it is hard to see that elaboration would have taken it much further ('nice chaps, the Argives…'). Thucydides could cut the wordiness, and emphasise the point by its placing: it is the climax of the exposition, and it sticks in the mind. Say that they did contrast the Athenians and Spartans, but only in a short part of their speech, perhaps indeed the length at which Thucydides records it. That he can use, that provides the crude ground-statement of national differences which he can later refine.[24] So that he keeps.

Then say the Athenians did adopt placatory language, assuring the Spartans they had no plans to attack them; that is not interesting, that is just rhetorical cotton wool. Better to indicate their intentions in a preamble ('…thinking that their words would turn the Spartans more to inaction than to war', 1.72.1), and give the valuable direct-speech space to more interesting things, revealing how the Athenians thought about their past,[25] about the factors which might direct a state to accept leadership of an alliance ('honour, fear, and benefit' – interestingly and revealingly, precisely the factors which now inspire the Spartans to lead *their* alliance into action), and about their lack of compromise now. We can be left in each case with arguments which were genuinely used, or at least with Thucydides' best guess at those which were used; but they are presented with a selectivity which might leave a misleading impression of the balance of the whole. And, in each case, the arguments he chooses are naturally those which focus on the 'truest explanation', especially those relevant to the Athenians' expansion and their formidable determination. They may have been a smaller part of the original, thus decidedly more 'unclear in what was [really] said openly' (1.23.6); but what there was, Thucydides will keep, precisely because its emphasis is so valuable. So we have found a further reason why the 'truest explanation' figures more heavily in the Thucydidean excerpts than that 'most unclear in what was said' had led us to expect.

Where does this leave the historian? We need not write off the content of the speeches completely, even as a record of what was really said. The language at 1.22.1–2 shows enough interest in finding that out and doing something to incorporate it, though the phrasing may also suggest that the historical substratum may in some cases be small, and we will find it very difficult to distinguish substratum from Thucydides' own reconstructive elaboration. At the same time, we must always be prepared to ask questions about Thucydides as well as about the speaker:[26] not merely why the speaker said it or might be thought to have said something like it, but also what made it interesting enough to Thucydides to survive the selective process and figure in his version. We might provisionally assume any individual part of a speech either to be what was really said, or to be appropriate enough for Thucydides to include it in his own reconstruction: hence our initial expectation of verisimilitude was not astray. Speakers would not, in life or in Thucydides, make points about Spartan internal tensions which they need not, or points about their absence of choice which they could not. But we cannot base any arguments on a speaker's silence,[27] especially when it is silence about an issue which Thucydides has already treated elsewhere; that silence can easily be the result of the abbreviation process. And we should not assume that the balance of a speech conveys an accurate impression of the balance of the original. This can leave us with a version which, if delivered in the form Thucydides gives, would have had a very different rhetorical impact from the speech really given.

To gauge that impact, we do better to look at the preambles, where Thucydides often summarises succinctly what a speech set out to achieve. Scholars are often puzzled when a preamble seems at odds with the speech which follows: the Athenian speech at Sparta has sometimes been taken as a prime example of that phenomenon.[28] It is better to take the preamble and speech as complementing one another, with the speech picking up selected highlights of the argument for dissection, but not necessarily keeping anything like the balance of the original. Direct speech is appropriate for some things, for intricate logical argument, for presenting (and implicitly unmasking) the thought-processes which underlie an action or the disingenuous rationalisations which purport to justify it: for Thucydides, with his interest in wartime mentality, that is vital. It is also appropriate for giving his characters a dramatic voice, with all the immediacy that direct speech gives; but for their speaking tones, we should have a much less vivid impression of the authoritative and great-spirited Pericles, the bullying Cleon, the insecure Nicias, the slippery Alcibiades. But many parts of the real-life speeches did not require such direct-speech elaboration in Thucydides' text. Thus Thucydides' version of the Athenians' speech has more defensiveness against particular charges (1.77) and less on Athens' present power than the formulation of 1.72.1 would lead us to expect ('...they did not intend to answer the charges that the cities brought against them ... they wanted to show the greatness of their city's power').[29] Still, what little was said on the charges was revealing about the way the Athenians thought about their empire, and was worth keeping in Thucydides' own version. So was the way the Athenians talk about 480 and 479, revealing as it was of the Athenians' pride and confidence in their greatness: it also gave some subtle, indirect indications of the Athenians' military might – but displaced to the events of the past. If the speakers also included some less subtle, more direct indications of their current strength (and a Spartan audience might not appreciate indirectness), Thucydides could naturally find them less interesting and less worthy of retention, feeling that the preamble had done enough to indicate their presence and their prominence.

Remember too the Mytilenean debate, where, we saw, Thucydides gives little room to arguments for pity.[30] Say there had been plenteous appeals to pity in the debate: there doubtless were. There too one can understand why Thucydides did not think they needed a full-dress speech in his own account. He had already made it clear in the setting that such considerations were at play, for the debate was only happening at all because the previous day's decision was coming to seem 'cruel and excessive'. Far better to pick the speeches that suggest wider points about the Athenians' increasing concern with expediency and their attitude towards the recalcitrant allies. Those Thucydides can use and make his own; a routine lament, conjuring pictures of slaughtered innocents and weeping widows and children, was not his sort of thing. But he has not misled us, for he has found other ways to make it clear that pity mattered; he will remind us of such sentiments again at its conclusion, when the ship of executioners is sailing slowly and unenthusiastically 'to its outlandish task' (3.49.4).[31] The speech itself is the central part of his technique, but speech and narrative setting inextricably combine into a wider, and much more suggestive, whole.

# Chapter 7

# 'You cannot be serious': approaching Aristophanes

## Comedy and society

An American observer, so the story goes, once expressed surprise at the way in which Margaret Thatcher dominated the British cabinet. He was advised to read P.G. Wodehouse on Bertie Wooster and his aunts. Comedy tells. And Dionysius of Syracuse, so another story went, once asked Plato to explain to him the nature of Athenian political life. Plato responded by sending him a work of Aristophanes.[1]

Even if the story is true, Plato doubtless had his own agenda: the play in question was *Clouds*, and the Athenians' hostility to Socrates is the point of the story.[2] But there is indeed a sense in which comedy brings us closer to some aspects of Athenian life than tragedy, with its heroic moulding, or rhetoric, with its bias towards the culture of the rich. Athenian comedy has its share of ordinary people from ordinary (or at least not too extraordinary[3]) backgrounds; and, even if the things they can do swiftly takes wing into fantasy, it at least begins from something like an everyday setting. It is natural to assume an audience engagement with a Dicaeopolis or a Peisetaerus which is not merely different from, but also greater than, with an Oedipus or an Agamemnon; and, if we are trying to recapture audience attitudes and prejudices, it is attractive to think that a sympathetic comic hero or chorus might be a firmer guide than the tragic equivalents, just as comedy's settings might be a firmer guide to the realities of everyday life. And there is something in this. Despite all the dangers of modern parallels, one can similarly see that an alien or a time-traveller might find modern situation comedies the most revealing media entrée into this strange society into which he or she had arrived.

Yet that parallel suggests the dangers as well as the attractions of this approach. A literally minded time-traveller might infer from late-1990s British comedies that a homosexual couple might excite amused acceptance, never indignation or incomprehension; that an old people's home never had anyone who was senile or sick; that a rich mother and her friend could live on champagne, rarely visit the office, and never lose their high-powered jobs; and that everyone used cordless phones.[4] Turning in bewilderment to American shows, the time-traveller would decide that everyone over the age of thirteen or fourteen either had a girlfriend/boyfriend or was a computer geek with a spotty tie, checked shirt, and tartan trousers;[5] that a sixteen-year-old band member could be married to his headmistress; and that New York twentysomethings with low incomes could afford plush apartments.

Nor can sympathetic comic characters serve as quite so helpful a guide to audience prejudices as we might have hoped. We often find sympathetic figures – especially, we might note with an eye to Aristophanes' Philocleon or Strepsiades, if they belong to an older generation – saying things which many of the audience would find quite dreadful in everyday life. Depending on your generation or nationality, think of Father Steptoe, Alf Garnett, Victor Meldrew, Abe Simpson, or Roseanne's mother. And comic attitudes can be specially dated or stereotyped when particular issues are in point, such as the representation of foreigners or of women. One should not apply the modern model blindly: there is no reason why the comic moulding should have taken precisely the same form in fifth-century Athens. But this can still open our eyes to the dangers, and some of the parallels are surprisingly close.

## Bewildering fantasy

Even once the time-traveller had sensed the need to correct for literary stylisation, there would still be the problem of judging exactly where realism ends and fantasy begins. That is not easy: for much of the humour so often rests on the way in which one blurs so undetectably into the other, how everyday happenings could so easily combine in such a way as to produce something which we persuade ourselves would not happen. Why should a list of legacies not have a few mistypings, and a mention of a 'cot' with a broken leg? But would the cow with the bandaged leg really get as far as turning up in the back garden? If not, why not? Why should a chef not get madly drunk just as guests were arriving for a Gourmet Evening? Would the owner not then think of getting a friendly restaurateur to provide a takeaway substitute meal? Why should it not all go wrong in the way that it does? It is precisely the logicality of it all that makes it difficult even for us to say exactly where things go over the edge of plausibility, where the real world would not function in the way the comedy presents it as functioning; and that is especially so because there is not a smooth continuous development, that even when the plot is no longer realistically credible there are numerous elements which blur back into real life.[6] If our time-travellers were trying to detect where the story represented things which could happen in our society and where it had taken wing, it would be odd if they could do better than we can.

Some of the problems we face in interpreting Aristophanes are not too different. It may be the plausibility of a detail. Would Hyperbolus really be talking about attacking Carthage in 424 (*Knights* 1303–4), or is that a fantastic elaboration of the crazy schemes he gets up to? A fine line divides plausible fantasy from fantastic plausibility;[7] the only useful thing to say is that it is close to that line.

Or it may be a question of a whole plot-sequence. Comedy, we are often told, is related to carnival, and it is fundamental to carnival to depict 'a world turned upside down' with the temporary and licensed reversal of the norms of everyday life: élite leadership is replaced by a transient 'Lord of Misrule', and so on.[8] The carnival parallel is only partly illuminating. The problem is not so much that the comic festival is an institutionalised part of civic ceremonial, and reinforces rather than challenges normative schemata:[9] for carnival as a whole is often institutionally authorised, and in ordered circumstances[10] even reinforces the norms it transiently challenges, by recognising both their normal status and the transience of the challenge. And it is not so much that class-structure is basic to carnival, whereas the egalitarian ideology of the *demos* remains unchallenged in comedy:[11] for in any carnival the world can only be turned upside down if one retains an axis on which to turn it, and one has opposite figures within the same framework. One can only have a Lord of Misrule by keeping a skeleton of lordship, just as one has comedy's inversions within a skeleton of democratic ideology – and that ideology certainly retains hierarchical frameworks which can be inverted in this way, gods, humans, and animals, males and females, citizens and slaves.

The problem is rather that carnival *begins from and assumes* a position of norm-reversal, whereas one form of comedy begins from a more everyday position (Dicaeopolis in the assembly, 'Nicias' and

'Demosthenes' fed up with the demagogue of the day) or one comically akin to the everyday (Philocleon addicted to the courts, Strepsiades worried about his debts), and moves into the world of the fantastic and the upside down (an individual peace, an even more vulgar and successful demagogic rival, a rejuvenated and lawless but unpunished Philocleon, a son miraculously educated overnight and a school burnt down). Admittedly, not all comedies are like that: consider *Birds* and *Frogs*. But often, as with our modern situation comedies, we are still left with the problem of identifying where the recognisably everyday ends and the unrecognisably unreal and fantastic begin.

One approach is not to bother about the distinction, or at least not to bother too much: and this is particularly fruitful if we are thinking about patterns of mentality and conceptualisation. All fantasy, it is increasingly realised,[12] is historically situated: not just in the sense that one cannot fantasise or dream about telephones or planes if one has never seen one, but much more substantially in terms of underlying thought-patterns and aspirations.[13] These may form part of the 'axis' around which any upside-down turnings take place; even where things are more complicated, they may well juggle aspects of familiar reality and re-sort them in intriguing and thought-provoking new patterns.

The inversions and fantasies of comedy, wherever precisely they leave the world of one-to-one reality, are thus themselves an item of historical interest. In *Birds* Peisetaerus and Euelpides, after making a fantastic escape from the real world, find in the clouds all the trademarks of Athens herself: a sycophant, a father-beater, an oracle-monger, a government inspector, and so on. That not merely illuminates the way in which, at least in this comic register, the audience might figure some aspects of their own Athenian identity; the mental scheme it reflects is also something we can trace in other genres and contexts, most strikingly in Thucydides' account of the Sicilian expedition, where the narrative subtly highlights – perhaps indeed exaggerates – both the initial step into the unknown and the familiar, Athenian quality of the democracy which the Athenians discover.[14] We should not (or at least not only) infer that *Birds* is a parable on the Sicilian expedition, despite the coincidence of date: *Birds* was put on in 414 and might certainly reflect a mood for far-flung adventure – but it would have been shaped in the second half of 415, when little news of the Syracusan enemy would have arrived. It is better to conclude that this scheme – try to escape, and discover only a version of home – was a category which was already part of the Athenian mental furniture, available for them as they sought to structure and make sense of the news when it came. Equally, if Peisetaerus ends by executing and even eating some subject birds on suspicion of conspiracy (*Birds* 1583–5, 1688–9),[15] that may in its avian register reflect an expectation, however resigned, of how any regime will support itself.[16] It need not be a direct *comment*, acid or otherwise, on Athenian democracy or on the fears of tyranny; but the casual assumption, even in fantasy, can still illuminate some expectations which the audience could apply to everyday power-politics. This approach can be taken much further, identifying schemata – perhaps those of age and youth, perhaps those of religious initiation – which can underlie the inverted fantasies precisely because they are categories applicable to all experience, upside down and right way up alike.[17]

That does not end our problems. It is no easy matter to decide what is 'axis' and what is 'inversion', especially as there may be some 'hybridisation',[18] with features of the axis confused or shifting to accommodate the inversion. A sausage-seller could evidently not really climb to political stardom overnight and rout the Paphlagonian; but what is the nearest conceivable real-life pattern on which the idea feeds? Might someone of much higher social status achieve success which was almost as sudden? Or would a slower rise be conceivable for someone of low status but not that low? Or neither? No-one could really make a private peace for the pleasure of a restored trade in Copaic eels; but might the assembly as a whole regard that as the natural way to think of peace's blessings? Or is this hedonistic register itself part of Dicaeopolis' selfish refusal to play the normal citizen's game? Would a worried father really approach a 'sophist' and ask him to take on a feckless son, or has *Clouds* already taken wing from the real world by then? We cannot avoid that problem of probing where familiar experience might end and where the inverted and fantastic might begin – even while acknowledging that it is the art of comedy to blur that line. Sometimes other evidence helps, as Thucydides helped us with *Birds*; but we are still often left with real difficulties.

Take the end of *Wasps*. The rejuvenated Philocleon is being educated into the ways of the symposium: his son invites him to imagine a symposium with various popular politicians, including Cleon himself (1219–64). If we may infer that real-life symposia included the likes of Cleon, that will be important for our construction of élite society: it would invite us to reconsider the lazy assumption that sympotic *hetaireiai* naturally had something oligarchic about them. But this is an *imagined* symposium, part of the world which Bdelycleon maps out for his father once he has seen the folly of his law-court-ridden life. Is it part of the imagined fantasy that Cleon and his demagogic friends should similarly have seen the error of their ways, and turned to a life of healthy bodily indulgence? Probably not; it is still probably better to assume that such a symposium is not so unrealistic, that even demagogues drank socially, and the symposium was the natural way of doing it; indeed, if the scene were expressively fantastic and unreal, we should have expected it to have been introduced rather less casually. But it is hard to be quite sure.

It is not simply modern critics who find it difficult. It is clear, for instance, that in later antiquity some Aristophanic jokes were taken very literally. As we saw,[19] Plutarch soberly tells us that the Megarians blamed Aspasia and Pericles for starting the trouble at the beginning of the war, 'quoting the lines from the *Acharnians* about Aspasia and her whores' (*Per.* 30.4). We shall spend some time on *Acharnians* 523–39 in the next chapter, but it is improbable that Plutarch (or those 'Megarian' sources[20]) had anything to go on beyond the play itself. Nor, doubtless, did Athenaeus (13.569f–570a), who introduces his quotation of the lines with a mention of Aspasia trafficking in 'masses of beautiful women' and 'all Greece filled with her whores': such topics tend to titillate the imagination into lubricious exaggeration. A little later in Plutarch's narrative, we have a story of the various scrapes Pericles' friend Pheidias fell into in the 430s (*Per.* 31). Here we do have more than Plutarch's own imagination: we can see variant versions of Pheidias' troubles taking shape as early as the fourth century, with Philochorus and Ephorus moulding different traditions;[21] and it looks as if there is some basis in fact, if Plutarch's details of Pheidias' prosecutor derive, as is likely, from a documentary source.[22] But, even if there was a genuine trial, it is another question whether this had anything to do with Pericles' motives for 'inflaming the war', which is how Plutarch presents it. Here there is no doubt that Ephorus has influenced Plutarch, and equally no doubt that Ephorus himself drew on the mention of Pheidias in Aristophanes' *Peace* (605–11) and took that passage very literally. That is another text which we will discuss in the next chapter (pp. 151–2), but it will be difficult to take it as literally as Ephorus clearly did. That charge looks like something new and unfamiliar when the *Peace* was performed in 421, and belongs in the realm of fantasy, not fact.

Theopompus, a fourth-century historian whose reputation stands
quite high, may be no more critical. He made a good deal of the bad
feeling and confrontation between 'the knights' and Cleon: that, we
are told, was a theme of his digression on the demagogues in Book
10 of his *Philippica*.[23] If this were true, this would be valuable evidence
for the knights as a coherent political body as early as the
Archidamian War.[24] But is it true? This may be no more than inference
from Aristophanes' *Knights*, where the knights are certainly opposed
to the Paphlagonian and the Paphlagonian has something of Cleon
about him, though thoroughly interwoven with elements of 'the
typical demagogue'. Theopompus also knew, or thought he knew, of
particular actions of Cleon aimed at the knights or the wealthy as a
social class, perhaps no more than his enthusiastic exaction of
*eisphora*[25] – something which, if historical, is enough to make sense of
Aristophanes' chorus of anti-Cleon knights (like a chorus of
academics or single mothers opposed to a cost-cutting Government,
or wealthy doctors opposed to a President bent on reforming health
insurance). It would still take faith to believe that this chorus really
reflected a coherent *political* force,[26] any more than Ameipsias' chorus
of philosophers in *Konnos* or Plato Comicus' chorus of 'sophists' in
*Sophistai*,[27] or indeed Monty Python's singing Australian philosophers,
need point to a body who regularly agree and act as a unit.
Philosophers rarely do.

Again, Theopompus seems to have told of Cleon being fined (or
at least having to repay) five talents for dishonouring the knights
(fr. 94): he took, Theopompus probably[28] said, five talents from the
islanders to persuade the Athenians to lighten their taxes (*eisphorai*),
and the knights opposed him and demanded the money back. That
clearly relates to a passage early in *Acharnians*, where Dicaeopolis is
listing the things he has recently enjoyed:

> Come on then, what pleasure have I had which was worthy of
> joyfulness. I know what sight warmed my heart: it was those five
> talents which Cleon spewed up. Oh, did I like that! I love the
> knights for that exploit: 'a worthy thing for Greece'.[29]

> (*Ach.* 5–8)

Was Cleon really forced to disgorge five talents? It again requires
faith to believe it.[30] Dicaeopolis' other pleasures and pains are
theatrical and musical: he was expecting Aeschylus, and it was a let-
down when a play by the frigid Theognis was put on instead (7–11) –

that was a real 'tragic' pain; then one singer, Moschus, gave him joy, another, Chaeris, did not. The natural reading[31] would make Cleon's trial a theatrical experience too, presumably in a comedy of the previous year (though not necessarily Aristophanes' own *Babylonians*[32]) – a comic pleasure to set against that 'tragic pain'. If that is so, Theopompus or his source will simply have got it wrong, taking it all too literally.

Admittedly, we are still left with Theopompus'[33] 'islanders' and their *eisphora* concerns. But here too we should not be too impressed. For one thing, there is no firm evidence for islanders paying *eisphora* at all.[34] For another, Cleon seems to have been particularly associated with *eisphora*, screwing as much as possible out of those who paid it.[35] For a third, the 'five talents' might seem to require an explanation – too big for a normal fine at a trial,[36] and why this rather than any other sum? Presumably because this was the 'bribe' he needed to repay – or so Theopompus could infer. For a fourth, the rest of *Acharnians* seems to present a clash between Cleon and Aristophanes over last year's comedy,[37] with Aristophanes priding himself on exposing irregularities in the relation of Athenian democracy with 'the cities' (633–42): so what was Cleon's role in those irregularities? Any competent embellisher, puzzling over the 'five talents', could easily come up with an answer very like that given by the story in Theopompus. Indeed, we need not even call it 'embellishment', but might prefer something blander like 'creative reconstruction', for the story has something in common with those elegant 'Poirots' which modern scholars craft to explain a particular combination of evidence. And there is no reason for us to believe a word of it.[38]

## Making comic sense

This is so far very negative, but sometimes we can make progress: more often, perhaps, in using the comedies to illuminate recurrent features of everyday life than specific happenings or events; and always, of course, doing what we can to combine comic indications with evidence from other sources. The crucial question is 'what do the audience need to know if the scene is to make sense?', both literal sense (so that it will not be distractingly bewildering) and comic sense (so that it will be funny).[39] That is closely related to a further, more difficult and subjective question, 'what needs to be the case for the comic poet to have written the scene like this?' And these are questions which we can sometimes go some way to answering. Take the moment later in Dicaeopolis' prologue when he complains that everyone is late for the assembly, then the prytaneis arrive, all pushing and shoving to get to the front (*Ach*. 17–42, esp. 24–6, 41–2). Some details of assembly life can certainly be illuminated here. Most obviously, the casual way in which Dicaeopolis talks of the crowd 'trying to get away from the vermilion rope' (22) only makes sense if this were a familiar feature, and the best modern commentator can reasonably combine this with other comic passages to infer what happened: 'this was used to herd people out of the Agora and towards the Pnyx when an Assembly meeting was about to begin (and perhaps also to clear the Pnyx after the meeting: *Eccl*. 378–9). Persons smeared by the red dye were liable to a fine (Plato com. fr. [82 K-A])'.[40] Similarly, some of the Herald's announcements later in this scene – 'Come forward, come forward, to within the purified area' (43–4), or 'silence, sit down' (123) – are outside the metre: such intrusiveness into the metrical scheme only makes sense if they, or something very like them, really were features of everyday life.[41]

What, though, about the picture of pushing and shoving prytaneis? Is this an exaggerated version of something which really happened in everyday life? Or is the joke rather that it is unthinkable, that real-life prytanis-behaviour was quietly dignified? That reading would make the joke something like the old Monty Python version of the royal party walking staidly down the race-course at Ascot, then suddenly speeded up to an excited racing commentary: 'and it's Princess Margaret coming up on the rails…'. In the prytaneis instance, we should probably prefer the exaggerated version of real life: the Princess Margaret alternative would make a reasonable joke in itself, but in that case the joke would surely wear thin some time before the end of Dicaeopolis' protracted indignation. If in fact the assembly and prytaneis were a model of demure behaviour, it is hard to think Aristophanes would have written the scene like this. And this is how the argument must run, not 'it's funnier if the prytaneis really did push and shove'. Aristophanes could not mould real life in such a way as to make his joke funnier; all he could do is decide what jokes to make, and where and how to make them.

'Real life or joke?' is often an inadequate way of stating the alternatives: comedy lives by exaggeration. In *Ecclesiazusae* the chorus of women say that they will need to get to the assembly early, now that it's so crowded: there were never such crowds when the pay was only an obol a day, but now it has been raised to three everyone comes (300–2) Theopompus. Some, for example Markle (1985: 274–5), assume from this that assembly-attendance had genuinely climbed; Dover (1974: 35 note 3) doubts it, pointing out that the plot requires the overcrowding, for the women need to pack the assembly and make sure there's no room for the men. It is hard to know. Part of the joke might even be that the women are so ill-informed that they are getting it all wrong; all that is *needed* for the joke to work is the assumption that an increase in pay might naturally increase attendance. Yet that is indeed so natural that we should surely assume that there had been *some* increased crowding, and the better bet is that, once again, the joke bites on something in real life. What does *not* follow is that the increase was remotely as great as the women here imply: an exaggeration of any perceptible increase, however small, is quite enough for the joke to work.[42] That leaves the historian with no idea of the scale of the real-life phenomenon behind the joke.

The problem of reality is relevant to a more important issue, important because it touches on the way comedy was taken by victims and audience: the question of Aristophanes' brushes with Cleon. There are several references to these in the plays, of which *Acharnians* offers the first and most difficult: we shall spend some time on this in the next chapter. There are later troubles too. In the parabasis[43] of *Wasps* Aristophanes prides himself on his boldness in that, as soon as he started putting on plays himself,[44] he took on the monster Cleon (*Wasps* 1028–34). Then, in the brief second parabasis, he comes back to Cleon again:

> There are some who said I'd made my peace, when Cleon set about me, and tried to terrify me, and abused me, and got under my skin; and then, when I was being flayed, outsiders laughed as they watched me howl so loudly. They didn't care for me – their only concern was to see if I'd let out some little joke as I was squeezed. I saw it, and I played a little trick; and now the stake has deceived the vine.
>
> (*Wasps* 1284–91)

That is, Cleon[45] thought he could trust me – but I've deceived him, and attacked him once more.

The easiest way of taking this is to assume that Cleon attacked Aristophanes a second time, after *Knights* and perhaps after *Clouds* too, and not necessarily in the courts;[46] that Aristophanes made some promise or concession; and that 'now' – that is, in *Wasps* itself – Aristophanes has double-crossed him, and come back to the attack once more. If that is true, that would be evidence that comedy could hurt. And it probably is true. One point is the obscurity and allusiveness of the reference here: it would only be comprehensible if the audience had some pre-existing knowledge which they could apply, for it would make an unrealistic demand on them to create a new fantastic structure from this language. The only question is what *sort* of pre-existing knowledge, whether it is of a real-life brush between Aristophanes and Cleon or of some earlier fantasy which was still remembered.

If there were only one reference to Cleon 'attacking' Aristophanes, then we might be able to explain it away as fantasy. The point could even be that it was so unthinkable that a politician could react in so humourless and undignified a way. It is the *recurrence* of the references which is so telling. Aristophanes knew better than to labour a fantasy, unless it was a particularly good one.[47] However whimsical the first time, the notion of an attack would only be something to keep going back to if it had some solid foundation in the spectators' extradramatic knowledge. His language in the *Acharnians*, as we shall see, makes best sense if it draws on something the audience already know about an extradramatic event, whatever precisely that may have been. The *Wasps* passage should be treated the same way.

So we do here have a suggestion that comedy's targets took the attacks seriously. That goes with some other indications: the remark of the contemporary pamphleteer known as the 'Old Oligarch', for instance, that the Athenians like to hear the rich and famous attacked in comedy, but not people of its own sort ([Xen.] *Ath. Pol.* 2.18: below, p. 158); or various indications, most admittedly of doubtful value, that comic attacks on individuals were outlawed or restricted at particular moments of national danger (and the further implication that most of the time they were not, and comedy enjoyed a peculiar licence for free speech).[48] This will be important for certain other conclusions which we might draw about comedy's purposes and impact. But such issues are best discussed in the context of a single example: we shall do that in the next chapter, with the specially vexed case of *Acharnians* and, in particular, Dicaeopolis' great speech.

## 'We are not amused': audience prejudices and audience sympathies

In the last section we were concerned with reconstructing audience knowledge, what they needed to know if the scenes were to make comic sense. There is also the far trickier question of reconstructing audience attitudes, preconceptions, and sympathies: what they need to *feel* if the comedy is to be funny – or, perhaps better put negatively, if it is to avoid an audience response that 'that's no laughing matter', 'we are not amused'.

Problems abound. One is familiar from Chapter 1: different occasions create their own expectations and have their own dynamic, and the audience may feel differently about issues simply because this is comedy. We should not be remotely surprised if people laughed uproariously and cruelly at Cleon's expense, then went off and elected him to the highest political office.[49] The British public did the same with *Spitting Image* and Margaret Thatcher; nor were jokes at Ronald Reagan's or Bill Clinton's expense rare at the height of their electoral success. Comedy is a part of life like any other, but ridicule in the theatre was only one of the range of appropriate reactions to prominent individuals, and does not exclude other reactions in the rest of one's life.[50] Nor should we be surprised if the audience of *Medea* or *Hippolytus* – or some of them – reflected with thoughtfulness and sympathy on a woman's lot, then a few hours later laughed at the same old dismissive comic jokes about women's irrationality and drunkenness and uncontrolled sexuality. Many men still act the same way.

But cosy 'it's just like Margaret Thatcher' or 'it's just like men today' statements are dangerous too. They may be useful eye-openers, and that is why this chapter uses modern parallels so heavily; but humour is surely the least trans-cultural phenomenon of all. (A British lecturer who tries too much dead-pan irony on some American audiences learns that rather quickly.) Take cruelty. *Acharnians* finds it uproarious that the Megarian should be so starving that he sells his own daughters (729–835); *Birds* extracts casual humour from the destruction of Melos (186). Even in wartime, it is hard to think a modern audience would find these laughing matters.[51] (Or at least a large audience: tasteless jokes about Somalian famine have not been unknown, but tend to be made among small groups who know each other well.) Violence to slaves, screwing the allies for all they are worth, routine rape at a festival: none of those count as 'no laughing matter' for Aristophanes' audience, and casual assumption of twentieth-century-like comic sensibilities would lead us astray.

Nor would a modern audience put on too different a set of political and moral prejudices just because they were going to the theatre (though they might if, say, going to church). Yet fifth-century theatre-going was a distinctively citizen experience: the audience is figured as the *demos*, even if perhaps half those present were non-citizens.[52] It may be that citizens already received a grant, the *theorikon*, to cover their entry-charge; if so, this was a further way of demarcating their privileged status.[53] When Athenians listened to assembly oratory, we noticed that the citizen experience encouraged more privileged, perhaps more snobbish audience attitudes;[54] in the theatre too we can sense that a distinctive viewpoint, this time presenting good-old-days attitudes with affectionate indulgence and deriding the vulgar or new, seems to have been a feature not merely of Aristophanes but of the other poets as well.[55] It is not that such nostalgia is inconsistent with the way the audience would feel outside the theatre: respect for birth, tradition, age are easy to trace elsewhere, and so is dismissiveness towards the demagogues' personal style.[56] It is just that these prejudices rather than any others are those which are most in focus here.

The difficulty of cross-cultural reading makes it difficult to gauge what really would grate with the fifth-century audience. Even modern viewers can accept some humour at the expense of values they hold dear. Late-nineties enthusiasts for New Labour can smile at the notion of Tony Blair planning to modernise sex (with appropriate downsizing); and it was a witty Conservative, Edwina Currie, who commented that her party was so committed to family values that many of her colleagues kept several families going at once. But there are limits. Ridiculing Hitler and Mussolini was all very well for a British and American audience in 1940 (Chaplin's *Great Dictator*); a comedy ridiculing Churchill and representing peace as desirable would not have seemed funny. Nor, today, would a piece representing Neo-Nazis as amiable buffoons, or the struggles of a disabled child as uproariously amusing.[57]

In Athens too we can assume there were limits. It did not seem nonsense for Cleon to attack[58] Aristophanes for 'making fun of the city and dishonouring the *demos*' (*Ach.* 631, cf. 503), not (he evidently claimed) a fit way for comedy to behave. Aristophanes refers to the mutilators of the Herms (*Lys.* 1094), but could he have presented a scene of Alcibiades parodying the mysteries? The Magistrate similarly silences Lysistrata when she begins to talk about the young dead ('don't speak of our miseries', *Lys.* 590), in a moving passage with few laughs. 'There were limits, even for Aristophanes: no essential levity touches the Maiden of the Acropolis or Demeter.'[59]

What we cannot assume is that a fifth-century Athenian audience – in a comedy, with that licensed freedom and that distinctive set of assumed attitudes – would place its limits in an equivalent place to our own. We shall see that in the next chapter, when we consider *Acharnians* and its representation of Dicaeopolis' private peace. It is indeed interesting that Aristophanes expected that not to alienate a wartime audience, when any equivalent in 1942 London would have been impossible – but does it follow that the audience would find peace-making so congenial in their life outside the comic theatre? Or only that they would laugh more readily at the outrageously unacceptable than we would? For the moment, let us take a difficult but less contentious example for investigating audience prejudice, and return to Aristophanes' *Wasps* of 422.

Any attack on the law-courts trod on delicate ideological grounds. It was regular for the jury to be addressed as if they 'were' the people, with references for instance to 'your decisions' in the assembly.[60] *Eumenides* too, as we shall see in Chapter 9, suggests how a charter for a judicial system could be made emblematic of an idealised Athenian democracy. Yet in *Wasps* that judicial system, or at least part of it, is held up to ridicule. What is more, Philocleon is weaned away from his obsession with the law-courts to a new life hobnobbing with the social élite at symposia. We discussed earlier whether the presence of Cleon and his cronies at such a symposium was historically plausible, but that symposium was anyway only imagined: Philocleon goes on to attend, and make a riotous mockery of, a genuine symposium as well. So the whole rhythm of the play represents a move away from the outdoor, open, egalitarian one-of-the-whole-people world of the courts to an indoor, closed, exclusive, us-but-not-them world of the symposia. A liminal half-way house is marked by Philocleon's private court at home – or rather not quite at home, still outdoors but only just, marked off by the household fence.[61]

One can understand why the play has been seen as 'valorising'[62] an élite tendency to shy away from the rough and tumble of real politics – the sort of tendency which Thucydides' Pericles treats with contempt and tars as the mark of the man who is useless (2.40.2). These are un-Athenian activities.[63] And, if that reading of the play were correct, the historian could certainly wonder what could be inferred about the sympathies of the audience. Aristophanes felt that this could all be put in this way before a popular audience in 422 without risking loss of popular support, and without fearing that it might cost him the prize.[64] Is this evidence, we would ask, for a popular disillusionment with their own democratic flagship, the judicial system itself?

But this is going too fast too soon. The most important point is that already raised: it is unclear how far this audience would accept humour at the expense of cherished values and institutions without offence. But there are particular problems too. First, we need more definition of those notions of 'criticising' or 'at the expense of' the judicial system. In the trial scene, the target is not so much the system as the way in which the demagogues abuse it, diverting the proceeds of empire into their own pockets and not letting the jury see enough of these rewards. In the Labes scene too 'Dog' (i.e. 'Kuon', with more than a hint of Cleon attacking the politician Laches) concentrates not so much on Labes' theft of the cheese, more on the way this 'biggest loner among eaters' has kept it all for himself (914–18, 923); the defending Bdelycleon replies in kind (965, 970–2). If there is 'criticism' there, it can be taken as criticism not of the judicial ideal, but of the way in which reality falls short of the ideal:[65] of the way the courts work, not of the way democracy envisages them as being. (In Chapter 9 we shall discuss how far it is possible to make similar moves in tragedy, particularly with *Eumenides* and *Orestes*.)

Not that all the audience need take, or feel, that 'criticism' in an identical way. Some might go along with Bdelycleon's arguments, or at least find it easy to transpose them into an acceptable 'serious' equivalent: those demagogues are indeed pocketing it all, and it should be ours. Others might find Bdelycleon's and Dog's arguments much less appealing, and see them more as a parody of commonplace demagogic exchanges, with unconstructive denunciations and populist appeals to the audience's self-interest.[66] In that case the 'criticism' might be less of the jury-courts than of the texture of political rhetoric, and indeed of the Athenian public for being taken in by such trite rubbish.[67] There are reasons, we shall see, for doubting whether this would be the dominant audience response; but there is no reason to deny that some would react in that way, or that this reaction can blend in varying mixes with the first ('yes, the level of debate is dreadfully low, but then all politicians are scoundrels anyway, so Bdelycleon might be on to something after all...'). We already sense the secret of many a successful comedy – that people of different prejudices and standpoints can all find something in it to appeal to them. That makes any attempt to infer a simple, uniform set of audience prejudices as fruitless as the assumption of a simple, uniform audience response.

The closing scenes, and the moves towards symposiastic excess, are similarly hard to gauge. Even though the jury-chorus by now regard Bdelycleon as the ideal son and Philocleon's move to self-indulgence as a beatific fulfilment, all the audience need not go along with that. Reactions to Bdelycleon and his wisdom earlier in the play may have been too varied; some may indeed think that democratic justice, for all its flaws, is better than this arrogant élite behaviour, flouting the laws in the confidence that the outraged can always be bought off.[68] And the final symposiasts are not sympathetic. They are snobbish and exclusive, with their brittle wit and their grimaces at Philocleon's broader vulgarity; some of the names might have an oligarchic flavour,[69] and one, Lysistratus, a certain Spartanness;[70] and Philocleon *wrecks* their symposium, even stealing their flute-girl when they were just ready for her *fellatio* – not a good way to make new friends. The old man has not changed his ways as much as all that.[71]

So is *Wasps* more like *Acharnians*, where (for most critics[72]) Dicaeopolis ultimately does what, on some level, we should all like to do: does Philocleon similarly climb into a symposiastic lifestyle which we should all like if we could get it? Or is it like *Clouds*, where Strepsiades probably wins (perhaps qualified, in one way or another) audience sympathy as he destroys the school: is the élite symposiast culture here as alien to the audience as Socrates' school there, at least in the set of attitudes which the audience have put on for the comic occasion? The tempting answer is that it is both, that once again different members of the audience can react in different ways and still find it funny. Many could identify with a desire to move into élite society, even if they did not find the present group of symposiasts exactly their cup of wine. But those who had no time at all for the élite need not 'valorise' this élite move at all. Those viewers could delight in vicarious identification not with the Philocleon who is a self-indulgent symposiast, but with the Philocleon who causes those snotty élitists so much discomfort. Aristophanes has contrived to characterise both Philocleon and the jurors in such a way that a range of different reactions are possible, all of them funny and satisfying in their own way.

Similar points could be made about other Aristophanic 'heroes' too, Peisetaerus, Euripides and the kinsman in *Thesmophoriazusae*, perhaps even Dicaeopolis and Strepsiades themselves. Is there something distinctive about comic characterisation which allows such a range not merely of response (for different responses are possible to Antigone and Medea) but of *sympathetic* response, something which avoids too great a challenge to an audience's sensibilities?[73]

One point is particularly relevant. These equivocally sympathetic characters are typically old men. We noticed earlier that age often allows appalling things to be said and done without sacrificing the sympathy of a comic audience.[74] We must again beware the snares of cross-cultural comparison, but various points about Athenian society suggest that this is likely to be no less, and probably more, true then than now: there was the accepted duty to repay one's nurturing debt to parents, and the respect for (even idealisation of) what the parents' generation achieved – that has its comic version with those crusty but admired old Marathon fighters. If this is so, then the comic figures may help to illuminate the audience's attitude to age itself; but it makes it far more difficult to gauge how far the audience would go along with the old men's views and actions.

This makes comedy no less interesting for the historian, even though distinctly more delicate to use. It remains interesting that such things could be said about the courts, even if we have to add 'in comedy, in a festival context': it need not follow that they could *always* be said so acceptably, but this remains one way in which the courts could be viewed. We can notice also the register in which the criticism moves, 'how' rather than 'what' the audience thought about it. If 'the courts are ridiculous' is the theme of the meal, the menu will include self-seeking speakers, vindictive jurors, low level of argument, mutual abuse and accusations of tyrannical ambitions, clichéd pathetic ploys and so on.

We can push this further, and reflect on the value of comedy within the city. In Chapter 1 we noticed that the greatest value of rhetoric to the historian was the study of the communication process itself, and what the dynamics of the occasion illuminated about the society. Comedy is admittedly one of the most delicate genres to explore in this way. We have seen how scenes can work differently with different viewers, how humour can work with more than a single dynamic. Where one viewer finds comedy reassuringly Athenian because (say) hierarchies are challenged, another reaches the same conclusion because they are reinforced. But, despite the range of response, some shared dynamic remains, at least in the sense that this is where awkward ideas are naturally *raised*. Comedy keeps that menu of reservations about the judicial system on the table. In some times and with some topics, comedy may be helpful to society by affording such anxieties a voice but also controlling them, by defining the special time and place as their normal limits. But we should not assume that anxieties were always so confined, and once in the air they may not be easy to reserve to the privileged occasion; and that aspect, the articulation of challenges rather than their control, may be the greater contribution to a reflective society.[75]

Nor are we simply trying to read comedy by itself. Once we combine it with other literature, we can see that such reservations were already more widespread: the motifs of our menu recur elsewhere, especially tragedy (Chapter 9). We can see other assumptions too elsewhere, for instance the notion that the empire is there to be exploited: that is traceable in the Old Oligarch, in Thucydides' speakers, in Xenophon playing with the idea that Athens can simply live off its revenues.[76] The Athenians are both a self-critical people and a ruthless one, and this is the form the self-criticism and the ruthlessness take in comedy.

Even in investigating prejudices, we can go further. It may indeed be that *some* of the audience will feel that the realities of the jury-system are impeccable, and more fool the jurors for being so susceptible to Bdelycleon; and that some will feel as much distaste for Philocleon's rapid susceptibility to the attractions of the élite symposium as relish for the embarrassment he causes his new drinking companions. It is more difficult to feel that this captures the *dominant* response. It runs too big a risk of satirising the ordinary people for being stupid, when they also embody the citizen *demos* whom the audience represent; just as important, it is too big an aesthetic danger to leave the audience without anyone they can sympathise with in the final scenes. Especially as *Wasps* follows the usual comic rhythm towards riotous bonhomie (a rhythm accentuated by the spectacular final dancing), it is hard to think that the play works well for a viewer who feels bitter with everyone. If that was what Aristophanes expected, there were better ways to end – with jurors who were not so won over, and with Bdelycleon being the discomfited one at the end, pelted, denounced, and stung as he deserved: that would have been a play more on the model of *Knights*. It is better to think that, amid the mix of different emotional responses in different minds (and indeed in the same mind, for who said emotional responses need to be simple?), Aristophanes expected the leading thought to be acceptance that the courts did have their ridiculous side, that a juror's obsession was unnatural, and that it was a far more normal human response to drink, and drink sympotically, where one can.

# Chapter 8

# Aristophanes' *Acharnians*
# (425 BC)

## Dicaeopolis and Telephus

Dicaeopolis is disgusted. He has turned up promptly at the assembly; no-one else is there. Eventually the prytaneis arrive, jostling as usual. But the assembly is as unsatisfactory as ever. An exotic Persian envoy is there; so are the ambassadors sent to Persia some twelve years ago, years spent drinking at the public expense. So too are some Thracian mercenaries, who enterprisingly steal Dicaeopolis' lunch. But what of peace? When someone speaks for that, the Archers immediately throw him out.

Enough is enough. Dicaeopolis now proposes to make his own private peace with Sparta. But he reckons without the chorus of fierce old Acharnians, gung-ho for the war, who hunt him down. He says he will convince them that the Spartans are not to blame for everything. The chorus are furious and flabbergasted. Only one thing can persuade them to listen: so he seizes a hostage, their 'child' – or rather a charcoal-basket, the mascot of the Acharnians' livelihood.

That is the first trick stolen from Euripides' *Telephus*, where Telephus grabbed the infant Orestes as a hostage to gain a hearing: more on that in a moment. But he will need more of the *Telephus* than this. In Euripides' play Telephus had also delivered a notorious speech defending the Trojans,[1] introducing it with an extravagant image of 'even if someone were to threaten my neck with an axe' (fr. 706 N[2]). Aristophanes now turns the image into visual reality, and the chopping-block is brought on. And one cannot possibly make a speech like that without the proper clothes, those rags which, in comedy, are the Euripidean trademark.

Dicaeopolis calls on Euripides himself to get them: Euripides is hard at work reclining on his couch, but eventually they work out which play is in Dicaeopolis' mind, and the rags are found.

Immediately he puts them on, Dicaeopolis' own tragic style becomes more pronounced (435–44). There was a sixties sketch where Dudley Moore was a blacked-up singer, crooning *Old Man River* to himself as he removed his make-up. He began in a cracked, deep bass voice; as more of the blacking came off, the voice grew higher and the vowels plummier. Eventually a Louis Armstrong had turned into a Noël Coward, just as Dicaeopolis becomes a Euripides here.

That is the setting for the speech which has been more scoured by historians than any other part of Aristophanes. It is full of the *Telephus*, and the borrowings extend to some phrases – doubtless the most notorious ones – as well as to the entire setting. The parts which most certainly have a Telephan original are italicised below,[2] but there may well be more.

> *Do not begrudge me this, you men in the audience: beggar I may be, but let me speak among you* Athenians about the city (~ *Telephus* fr. 703 N[2]): for this is trugody,[3] and trugody too knows what is just. And what I have to say is indeed just, though you'll find it shocking. Cleon won't attack me now for speaking ill of the city when strangers are present. For *we are on our own*. This is the Lenaea,[4] and the strangers are not here yet: the tribute has not arrived, nor the allies from the cities. No, *we're on our own*, all hulled – for I count the metics here as the bran of the citizens.[5]
>
> *Now I hate the Spartans deeply.* I only wish that Poseidon, the god of Taenarum, would give them a quaking, and bring down their houses on their heads. For I too have had my vines cut down. But *(we are all friends here, so I can speak) why do we blame all this on the Spartans?* For it was some individuals from among us – and I am not speaking about the city; remember this, that I do not mean the city – no, it was some wretched little individuals, false coins of people, worthless, badly franked, half-foreign, who would keep on with their denouncings: 'these woolly cloaks are Megarian'. Is that a cucumber they could see? Or a little hare? A piglet? Some garlic? Grains of salt? They're Megarian! And off they'd go the same day to be sold off.
>
> All right, that was just a little local difficulty. But then some drunken kids got up from their party-games,[6] went off to Megara, and stole the hooker Simaetha. The Megarians, all garlicked up in their anger, stole back two of Aspasia's hookers. And then that was the origin of the war for all the Greeks – from three bonkers. And then Pericles the Olympian thundered and

lightened in his wrath, and stirred up Greece. He made laws
worded like drinking-songs: the Megarians should have nowhere
to stay, 'not earth, not market, not sea, not land'. And then the
Megarians, gradually starving, asked the Spartans to ensure that
the bonkers-decree should be repealed. They asked us many
times, but we wouldn't do it. And then we moved from bonking
to clonking – of shields.

*Someone will say: 'The Spartans shouldn't have done that.' But tell me
then what they should have done.* Let's imagine a Spartan *had sailed
out in his bark,* found a puppy at Seriphus, declared it contraband
and sold it. *Would you have sat at home? Far from it.* There's no doubt
about it. You'd have launched three hundred ships just like that,
and the city would have been chockablock: the soldiers shoving
and shouting, the yelling about the ship-captains, the pay being
doled out, the gilding of good-luck Athenas, the groaning
colonnades, the food being measured out, the wine-skins, the
rowing-thongs, the people buying jars, the garlic, the olives, the
netfulls of onions, the crowns, the anchovies, the flute-girls, the
black eyes. The harbour would have been full of oars being
planed, the roar of calloused knobs, the oar-holes being bored,
the flutes, the commands, the whistles, the pipes. *That is what
you would have done. I know you would. And do we not think Telephus
would do the same? We must be senseless.*

(Ach. 497–556)

Half of the Acharnians are immediately persuaded; the other half
demur at first, but are won over after a swift appearance of the
militarist Lamachus, and his discomfiture at Dicaeopolis' hands.
Lamachus goes off to make his war – 'I shall fight against all the
Peloponnesians for ever' – while Dicaeopolis stays to enjoy his peace.
And, private though this peace may be and selfish though it appears
to us, the chorus are from now on firmly on his side. He is doing
what they would all like to be able to do.

It is not unusual for Aristophanes to make play with tragedy, and
he has plenty of 'paratragedy', that is (for there is no real point in
distinguishing the two) tragic parody.[7] The modern alertness to
intertextuality should protect us from too crude a view of what
'parody' entails: it is not simply a question of deflating a more
elevated original for laughs, but rather of providing a model which
can be in the audience's minds, and can add perspectives and
comparisons which enrich their response in various ways.

Whatever use Aristophanes makes of tragic models, his quarry is usually fairly *recent* tragedy. *Thesmophoriazusae*, for instance, put on in 411, makes much play with Euripides' *Andromeda* and *Helen*, both from the year before, and with *Palamedes* of 415. *Telephus* however dates from 438, and that makes it something of a special case; already by the time of *Acharnians* (425) it was thirteen years old, and after a flurry of minor references in other plays it is once again a major source of humour in *Thesmophoriazusae*, a full twenty-seven years after its first performance. There may be several reasons. One, doubtless, is that the play came relatively early in Euripides' career – his first victory was only three years earlier, in 441 – and did much to fix him in the public eye: rather as we find that great actors, however versatile their later repertoire, may still carry indelible public memories of early roles (Diana Rigg as Emma Peel, Sean Connery as James Bond, Derek Jacobi as Claudius). But a further reason will be the spectacular nature of some of its scenes. Those would be memorable in themselves, and would also have done much to establish the public (or at least comic) image of Euripides' style, with ragged kings, disguise and intrigue, and bold challenges to established tragic style and to established mythical conventions. Why, even the rights and wrongs of the Trojan War could be thoroughly rethought, something which may have seemed more breathtaking in 438 than a generation later.

The plot ran something like this.[8] The invading Greeks at first mistook Mysia for Troy, and attacked that country instead. Telephus was a Mysian prince, and was wounded by Achilles' spear; an oracle told him that what inflicted the wound must heal it. He made his way to a gathering of the Greeks at Argos as they prepared to relaunch their expedition, and won his way into Clytemnestra's confidence. His own big speech, the prototype of Dicaeopolis' version, was given in disguise to the assembled Greeks, urging them to see it from the Trojan point of view. But then the news broke that there was an intruder in the midst; and the hunt began. (Only a perfunctory version of the hunt is taken up in *Acharnians*: Dicaeopolis is carried away by his peaceful erotic fantasies as he celebrates his rural Dionysia, and he is too surprised to hide. A more vigorous hunt comes in *Thesmo*.) Then the young Orestes was seized as a hostage, probably on stage: the scene's fascination for Aristophanes' audience is easier to understand if the original was a spectacular *scene*, not simply a messenger-speech.[9] The ploy worked; but Telephus too conceded something, for the Greeks had received an oracle that they needed

Telephus' assistance to take Troy, and he now agreed to act as their guide. His wound was healed by filings from Achilles' spear. The notion of the sufferings to come, and inflicted on the very Trojans whom he had so vigorously defended, will have given a characteristically thought-provoking twist to the play's tail.

There is much here which would live in the popular memory, especially if the memory was regularly reprimed by comic pastiche – and we have no reason to suppose that Aristophanes was the only poet to find *Telephus* a rich source of pickings.[10] It is noticeable that – except for the hunt – it is the same scenes and themes which are taken in *Acharnians* and in *Thesmophoriazusae*: the disguise, the hostage (in *Thesmo.* it is one of the women's wine-skins), the virtuoso defence-speech. These scenes must have been notorious, and it is clear that Aristophanes could count on his audience's familiarity with them. It is clear, too, that this needs to be taken into account when we try to gauge what history, if any, we can extract from this highly Telephan speech.

The inferences which are usually drawn concern three aspects: first, the brush of Aristophanes (or, just as likely, his producer Callistratus)[11] with Cleon in the previous year; secondly, the Megarian decrees which preceded the outbreak of the Peloponnesian War; thirdly, the question whether this speech makes any serious contribution to the *Acharnians* as a 'peace play' – in other words, whether we can regard Aristophanes as taking a serious political stance on the rights and wrongs of the Peloponnesian War, and whether we can deduce anything about the audience and their feelings about the war.

## Cleon

'Cleon won't attack me now for speaking ill of the city when strangers are present...' These lines need to be taken with an earlier passage, just as Dicaeopolis is musing on the threats he has to face, and deciding that the best answer lies with the trip to Euripides:

> And I know what I myself suffered from Cleon because of last year's comedy. He dragged me into the council-chamber (*bouleuterion*), he attacked me, he tongued down thoroughly, he drenched me, with his torrent and washed me away, so that I very nearly died in a sewer of squabbles and filth. ...
>
> (377–82)

'Last year's comedy' must be *Babylonians*, which Aristophanes tells us more about in the parabasis (626–718). There it emerges that 'the producer' (*didaskalos*, 628), or 'the poet' or 'maker' (*poietes*, 633), was attacked by his enemies for 'making fun of the city and dishonouring the *demos*'; the parabasis retorts that he in fact did the city a great favour, stopping them being so susceptible to the flatteries of foreigners, and 'showing that the *demoi* in the cities enjoy democracy' (642) – or, with a presumably deliberate ambiguity, 'showing what sort of democracy the *demoi* in the cities really have', or even 'showing how they're ruled by our democracy here'. Now Cleon can do his worst against him. 'The good and the just will be on my side' (659–60): that seems to be yet another quotation from the *Telephus* (fr. 918 N$^2$).

Evidently, Dicaeopolis and Aristophanes/Callistratus have a lot in common: the parabasis leaves us in no doubt of this.[12] Just as *Babylonians* revealed the shallow flatteries of 'foreigners', so Dicaeopolis saw through the wheedling compliments of foreign kings reported in the first scene; just as *Babylonians* told what was just and was reviled for it, so Dicaeopolis delivers a speech which was 'just, though you'll find it shocking' (501); Dicaeopolis suffered from Cleon last year, Aristophanes/Callistratus suffered from his 'enemies' then, and bids Cleon do his worst now.

Who, then, is the 'I' or the 'me' in Dicaeopolis' words at 377, and again at 502, in the context of these brushes with Cleon? Most scholars have assumed that this means Aristophanes or Callistratus himself. In parabases we several times find the chorus using the first person to refer to the poet, serving as a sort of poet's mouthpiece; and there may be similar phenomena in lyric, where a chorus or soloist can sing of an 'I' who has often – not uncontroversially, but in most cases also not unreasonably[13] – been taken to be the lyric poet himself. There is no exact parallel for this extension from lyric or parabasis to an iambic scene; but, given the strong parallels between Dicaeopolis and poet/producer, one can understand why many find this interpretation so tempting. The next step is to infer that Aristophanes/Callistratus' experiences the previous year were as Dicaeopolis describes them here: that Aristophanes/Callistratus was not merely 'attacked by his enemies', as the parabasis tells us, but hauled by Cleon before the *bouleuterion* (379), and – whether we should think of formal prosecution or a less formal denunciation for treachery or un-Athenian behaviour – the charge was 'speaking ill of the city in front of the allies' (502–3). And that, normally with

Aristophanes rather than Callistratus, is the version which appears, often without argument, in standard biographical sketches of Aristophanes and works on Athenian law.[14]

But we should be cautious here. The poetic 'I' is a slippery and flexible thing, and reference to the 'poet' is by no means the only possible way it can be interpreted. The audience will take each case in its context, and may redefine, 'renegotiate', its conclusions as it goes on – especially when so elusive a thing as the poet's self-characterisation, his 'voice', is in point, something which in drama, with its profusion of different characters and fragmented voices, is always hard to pin down.[15] Another type of 'I', for instance, will be seen later in this same play, when the chorus make some play with the stingy *choregos* Antimachus: this man – or so they claim – was too mean to give 'me' the usual feast after the performance at last year's Lenaea (1152). The two passages doubtless link: things ended up badly for both hero and chorus last year, this year things are different for Dicaeopolis, and the chorus hope that they will be different for themselves too.[16] There the chorus are clearly speaking for last year's equivalent, who would not have been the same individuals.[17] It may be that the audience's first impression will be that Dicaeopolis is here speaking similarly for last year's leading figure, rather as a pantomime dame might start a story by saying 'the last time I was in town, …' without suggesting that the same actor, character, or even plot had been here last year.[18]

Even so, that need not preclude *some* degree of assimilation of Dicaeopolis to the poet and the producer, for we shall certainly see such assimilation by the time we reach the parabasis. Of course, the audience have not heard the parabasis yet: still, redefinition and renegotiation have their limits, and it would bewilder them if they have to rethink totally the implications they have drawn from the earlier passages ('oh, I see, *that's* what he must have meant, and I was quite wrong…').[19] It is much easier to think that the parabasis is taking further and deepening an assimilation which the audience already sense. As we saw in the last chapter (pp. 132–3), the continual harping, in several plays, on Cleon and his attacks makes best sense if there was some real danger of censorship, and if there were some real extradramatic attacks. The audience, Aristophanes must be assuming, know about these earlier attacks, and feed that knowledge into their understanding of these lines.

Yet it begs the question to assume that this assimilation must be total, that Dicaeopolis simply 'is', or 'speaks for', the poet or the producer here.[20] This wholly depends on the nature of the pre-existing knowledge which the audience are feeding in: our problem is to try to reconstruct that knowledge, and that is anything but easy. If it were true that the attacks were exactly along the lines which Dicaeopolis here describes, then the audience might indeed assume that the poetic 'I' here refers straightforwardly to the poet/producer himself, and that the identification is complete. But if they were not, if the attacks had simply been *the same sort of thing* as Dicaeopolis describes, then the audience will assume a different sort of relationship, a similarity rather than an identity of experience (and similarity rather than identity is what they will go on to infer from the parabasis). All we need to assume is something which will make the lines funny, and not too perplexing.

Suppose, for instance, that Cleon's attacks had been less formal, threats of prosecution, perhaps, or pressure to deny Callistratus a chorus for the following year, or an intimidating attack in a public speech. That is quite enough to make this passage funny. Cleon, we are given to understand, was so indiscriminate in his attacks that he even hauled people off the comic stage, and dragged a Dicaeopolis-like figure, still doubtless (in this comic fantasy) in costume and mask, to defend himself in the *bouleuterion*. No-one, clearly, was safe… And why the *bouleuterion*? It might be because that was the place where Aristophanes/Callistratus was similarly hounded, if indeed that was the case; but it might equally be that this was where denunciations typically took place,[21] where Cleon was felt to be particularly at home. In *Knights* (773–6) the Cleon-like Paphlagonian similarly begins his list of services to the people with the time when 'he was a member of the *boule*' – extortion from some victims, torturing and strangling others, not respecting anyone;[22] earlier in the same play the slave 'Demosthenes' warns the sausage-seller to sprint to the *bouleuterion*, for 'the Paphlagonian is going to dash in, bad-mouth us all, and scream his scream' (465–7, cf. 626–9). There was a time when one could imagine a comic fantasy of a Margaret Thatcher, smarting at a series of Euro-rebuffs, taking it out on a hapless Eurocrat by dragging him into the House of Commons and setting about him, with verbal dressing-down or with handbag. It need not follow that anything like this had happened or could ever happen, only that this was a Thatcher's, or a Cleon's, natural ring.

So we need not assume that in real life Aristophanes or Callistratus was hauled before the Council. What of the charge? Need it follow from 502–3 that Cleon attacked poet or producer 'for speaking ill of the city when strangers are present'?

Here the *Telephus* parody becomes important. It is safe to assume that this argument – 'we are all Greeks together here and there are no strangers present, so we can speak honestly' – featured in Telephus' defence, and right at the beginning:[23] and audiences remember beginnings and ends of speeches particularly clearly.[24] The irony in the original would be that the speaker is himself a 'stranger present' in disguise, Telephus.

Now, *if* Cleon had made the 'when strangers are present' argument, then of course the parallel would be particularly close, and the joke particularly funny. But here we are in danger of the 'Poirot' fallacy[25] of depicting a scenario which, *when we argue forward*, explains the evidence so neatly that we are in danger of assuming that *we can also argue backward* from the evidence to it, that it and only it explains the evidence. Suppose instead that Cleon had not: suppose he had limited himself to the general charge of 'making fun of the city and dishonouring the *demos*' (the phrase used in the parabasis, 631). The joke here remains a funny one, funny enough that we cannot argue that Aristophanes 'would not have done it this way' if the facts were as we are now supposing. The audience, or enough of them, remember the 'we are on our own now' line from *Telephus*, Dicaeopolis makes his defence as close as possible to the original, and for that he needs a set of 'strangers' who might have been here but are not. The allies will do nicely, those allies who would be present in greater numbers at the Dionysia than at the Lenaea. That is all we need to assume for the joke to work well.

This passage has often been exploited in a further direction. Some scholars have argued that Lenaea plays have a different texture from those produced at the Dionysia, with Lenaea plays concentrating on more domestic issues and Dionysia ones more concerned to put their city on display to the Greek world.[26] Those who sense such a difference naturally concentrate on the difference of audiences traced here. But, once again, caution is advised. True, the audiences must have been different, to a degree: this cannot be a nonsensical thing to say, though it is hard to think that the differences in audience composition could have been very big.[27] But it is the joke, the parodic context, which makes this a natural thing to say: Dicaeopolis needs to explain why the 'we are on our own' claim is truer of this festival than of the Dionysia. It is noticeable, too, that he *needs* to explain it, by spelling out that it is not yet time for the tribute-payments, and so the allies are not present. This would be lame if a difference in audience and in ideological texture were taken as read by the spectators.[28] It does not follow that this would have been an obvious point to make otherwise, still less that the small differences in audience composition regularly imposed a different style of humour or of plot.[29] While Leader of the Opposition, Neil Kinnock once mildly criticised the British Government when abroad, and Conservative backbenchers self-righteously attacked him for unpatriotic disloyalty. Had he been gifted with the average politician's sense of humour, he might well have begun his next speech in the Commons with a jokey suggestion that perhaps he might now be allowed to resume opposition, for it was not yet the tourist season and so the gallery was free of foreign visitors. (In fact, he was wittier than average, and did not.) In that case it would have been the background alone which gave point to the joke, as here it is the *Telephus*; and it would have been rash to infer from such a joke that the style of speeches was really different in the summer-time.

Not much is left of 'evidence' for the brush of Aristophanes/ Callistratus with Cleon in 426. We cannot assume that Cleon's charges were as Dicaeopolis implies, nor that poet or producer was brought before the *bouleuterion*, nor that there was anything formal at all: any such inference would imply a degree of one-to-one identification of character and poet/producer which begs the question. All the audience need assume, or know, is that the same *sorts of* thing happened to Aristophanes or Callistratus as Dicaeopolis claims happened to him, and that there had been some sort of attack by Cleon on poet or producer for attacking the city. There *may* have been more than this, and the parallels may have been closer; but we cannot be sure of it. In other words, those passages tell us nothing which we would not anyway be able to infer from the parabasis.

Scant though the inference may be, it is an important one. It still seems very likely that there was some real-life attack on Aristophanes/Callistratus, and – just as important – that this was notorious enough for the playwright to be certain that his audience (or at least enough of them) would know about it: for otherwise 377– 82 will pose a puzzle to the audience which is simply distracting,[30] and will make a joke which the audience will not get. That confirms that Cleon took comic attacks seriously, and that the audience took Cleon's response seriously too, seriously enough for the poet to count on its being in their minds a year later. This sort of comedy is not simply entertainment, entertaining though it is. It is important to politicians, and to *polis*. It is the nature of comedy itself and its popular reception, not the factual details of any prosecution, attack, or charge, which is genuinely illuminated by this passage.

## Megara: the comic version

In Chapter 5 we discussed the historiographic material on the Megarian decree. We saw that 'the' Megarian decree – the exclusion decree – specified that the Megarians should be excluded from the Attic agora and the harbours in the empire (a formulation which *Ach.* 533–4 wittily fuses with the language of a well-known drinking-song[31]); that there may have been a further decree, the 'Charinus decree' of Plut. *Per.* 30.3,[32] which threatened any Megarian found on Attic soil with the death penalty; and that in the diplomatic manoeuvrings at the beginning of the war the Spartans claimed that there would be no war if the Athenians repealed the Megarian decree, something which leaves it unsurprising if there were those saying that Athens had gone to war over a small matter (the view that 'Pericles' combats at Thuc. 1.140.4–5). Dicaeopolis' contrast of a trivial beginning and shattering consequences is likely to draw on a view which was already in the air – though people who said such things need not have concluded that Athens should swallow her pride and make peace.

The main issue here will be the question whether the Simaetha story – the drunken Athenian lads stealing the Megarian 'hooker' Simaetha, then Aspasia's two hookers stolen off to Megara in retaliation – is comic fantasy, or has some basis in fact.[33] Other issues will require discussion too: in particular, the line that the Megarians were 'gradually starving' as a result of the exclusion decree (535); and the question whether the 'little local difficulties' described at 515–23 point to an earlier decree, aimed at Megarian goods within Attica.

First, Simaetha and Aspasia's hookers. This is not Aristophanes' only comic treatment of the Megarian decree and the causes of the war: in *Peace*, celebrating the imminent end of hostilities in 421, the god Hermes gives an alternative account of how it all started.

*Hermes:*   Oh, you needy farmers, pay attention to my words,[34] if you want to find out how Peace was lost. The start of it all was Pheidias and his misfortunes. Then Pericles feared that he'd share the same fate: he was frightened of your natures and your snapping temper; so before anything nasty could happen to him, he set the city on fire, setting it off by that little spark of the Megarian decree. Then he fanned up such a big war that the smoke brought tears to the eyes of all the Greeks, over here

|  | and over there. Once the first vine reluctantly began to crackle and once the first winejar was hit and angrily kicked out at another jar, by then there was no-one who could stop it, and Peace began to disappear. |
| --- | --- |
| *Trygaeus:* | Good God, that's all news to me, and nobody had ever told me that she was linked to Pheidias. |
| *Chorus:* | News to me too. So that's why her face is so beautiful: she's a relation of his. What a lot we don't know! |
| *Hermes:* | Then all the cities you ruled realised you were cross and snarling at one another: so they started meddling in every way they could, because they were afraid of the tribute-payments. They bribed the Spartan bigwigs, and you know how lightfingered *they* are, and how they're always putting one over on strangers. So they threw out Peace disgracefully, and seized on War instead. Then their profits turned sour for the farmers; for we sent out triremes in retaliation, and they ate up the fig-sprays of people who didn't deserve it. |

(*Peace* 605–27)

That certainly confirms that the Megarian decree was especially associated with Pericles and the war's outbreak, for the decree need not have been included at all in this passage: there is nothing Megarian about Pericles' motivation here. Presumably it is there because the audience is familiar with the idea that this was how Pericles brought on the war.

Less familiar, though, was the connection of Pheidias and the outbreak of the war – at least to judge from the response of Trygaeus and the chorus ('that's all news to me' … 'news to me too').[35] We need not infer that there was anything in it, at least as far as Pericles' motivation is concerned. If some later writers, especially Diodorus (12.39.1–2, apparently following Ephorus) and Plutarch (*Pericles* 31), took such allegations seriously, that can simply be because they or their sources read Aristophanes too literally, another stark warning of how dangerous it is to regard comic material as 'confirmed' by later historians or biographers.[36] It still seems safe to infer that Pheidias did get into some trouble, and that it was notorious enough to be remembered;[37] for otherwise the audience would need some clearer explanation than 'Pheidias and his misfortunes'. That would simply be bemusing if there were no misfortunes at all. What is 'news' must simply be the connection of those troubles with Pericles and the war.

What of Simaetha and Aspasia in *Acharnians*? Can we infer that here too there would be some troubles or other?[38] That is less certain: again, we must remember the *Telephus* parody. True, there are no identifiable *Telephus* lines in this section, but then we should not expect any: whatever Telephus said, he would not have talked about a madame and a brothel.[39] But Telephus was still arguing that the Greeks were wrong to attack Troy. He could hardly have avoided mentioning Helen and suggesting it was all an over-reaction. It certainly looks as if the comic poet Cratinus developed the same point in a very similar context: in his *Dionysalexandros* he too introduced the notion of Pericles 'bringing the war upon the Athenians', though Cratinus did it 'powerfully through indirect means'; he too transposed it into a mythical context, casting Pericles as Dionysus and making him judge the beauty-contest as Paris in disguise; and he too evidently made much of Helen.[40] Indeed, the paradox that in this very male heroic world the men keep fighting over a woman – first Helen, then Briseis – was central to the story as early as the *Iliad*, as we see male pride taking the original conflict to such disastrous lengths.[41] That is familiar too in tragedy, which can also stress that the war was for a faithless, immoral, husband-deserting woman,[42] and *Telephus* would hardly have neglected the theme. Thus far the Simaetha and Aspasia sequence can easily be a vulgarised version of the Helen-theme, and there is no need to think it corresponds closely to anything in reality.

What, though, of the retaliatory tit-for-tat element which is so central to the Simaetha story? Here too there is no problem, and no reason to believe in any real-life talk of Simaetha or retaliatory abductions. For one thing, the retaliatory element may well itself have figured in *Telephus*: Telephus seems to have said that 'the Greeks had done no more than they had suffered' (fr. 711 N², cf. *Thesmo.* 518–19).[43] Or perhaps there was some intrusion from real life, but one which need not involve any real-life Simaetha. We know that a charge of 'receiving Athenian slaves' figured in the diplomatic manoeuvrings with Megara (Thuc. 1.139.2), something which could easily have involved 'well, you do the same...' exchanges; and Aristophanes may simply be combining this with the 'all for a woman' idea from *Telephus*.[44] Or it may simply be the requirements of the argument. Aristophanes requires a personal emphasis in the declaration of war ('I am not speaking about the city; remember this, that I do not mean the city': cf. below, pp. 157–8), and that points to Pericles: he requires the thesis that not all the moral points are on Athens' side, so he can't have Athens *simply* as the offended party; it is natural then to have the abduction of Aspasia's two Helens as retaliation for something the Athenians – but Athenian individuals – had already done.

At all events, the audience would not be bemused if there had been no Megarian abduction like this at all, if all they knew was that there were charges against Aspasia in the air at the beginning of the war,[45] doubtless including talk of her providing girls for Pericles, and that the *Telephus* original had developed the 'all for a woman' motif. Such a girl could only now be one of Aspasia's, and the rest would fit into place. We do not need anything real for the joke to work.

The *Telephus* parody therefore takes us a long way. But there is a further parodic complication too, for many have seen parody of Herodotus' opening chapters here as well. Herodotus is there quoting the version of knowledgeable Persians. He presents himself as impatient of such stories, and will shortly hurry down to the first man he knows started injustices against the Greeks, Croesus of Lydia (1.5.3). This Persian version does tie in the Helen story to a series of tit-for-tat abductions: first the Phoenicians took Io from Greece, then Greeks retaliated by taking Europa; the Greeks started the next phase by seizing Medea, and Paris, realising that he might get away with an abduction of his own, took Helen from Greece to Asia (1.1– 4). So, *if* Herodotus is in the minds of Aristophanes and his audience, we might have more tit-for-tat intertextuality, and the retaliatory motif would again come from the Trojan War rather than from real life in the 430s.

That 'if', however, is a big one. There is a problem of dates, for the text of Herodotus' histories suggests knowledge of events later than 425, and we might infer that it was in some sense 'published' after *Acharnians*.[46] That difficulty is not insuperable; we know very little about fifth-century 'publication', but other prose works – Gorgias', for instance – were performed orally before any formal or definitive 'publication', and there is no reason to infer that things were different with earlier versions of Herodotus. Later stories of his reading at Athens and Olympia may be true or false, but were at least plausible.[47] The bigger problem is the difficulty of thinking that Aristophanes could have expected his audience, or enough of them, to catch the parody.[48] He often includes some signals even with paratragedy, and even with plays which many of his audience would certainly remember and recognise;[49] such signals would be essential here. Dicaeopolis could perhaps have borrowed a book of Herodotus from Euripides' library, or he could have made some mention of Io or Europa or Medea: it would not have been difficult to do.

At the very least, any such parody would only make sense if the hints of Herodotus combined with a more general target, so that those vast numbers who missed the Herodotean allusion could still have something to bite on: and, if that is so, the general target would be more important than the specific pointer to Herodotus. Perhaps there is indeed such a general target for the parody: the way ordinary people explain wars. Notice all those 'and thens': 'And then that was the origin of the war for all the Greeks – from three bonkers. And then Pericles the Olympian thundered and lightened in his wrath … And then the Megarians, gradually starving, asked the Spartans to ensure that the bonkers-decree should be repealed. … And then we moved from bonking to clonking – of shields'. It is one retaliation after another, each escalating a little further; tit-for-tat gone mad.

The 'and then' schematising was doubtless familiar from the epic tradition,[50] transposed in the *Iliad* to reveal some deeper patterning underlying the mere sequentiality. Herodotus too responds to it, presenting us initially with a picture of 'and then' exchanges which are close to[51] retaliation, first with that sequence of mutual abductions (1.1–4) then with the introduction of Croesus as the 'first man to commit injustices against the Greeks' (1.5.3): this, the language intimates, will begin the see-sawing exchanges that eventually draw the Persians in. He also makes his story begin with a woman, not merely in the introductory abductions but with Candaules' memorable queen (1.8–12). Of course there is more than this to Herodotus' historical explanation;[52] but this is where it starts, with a simple and doubtless popular model of how a great war can start. Where Thucydides would suppress such a model, Herodotus takes it and builds upon it.

If that is so, then we should see not so much Aristophanes parodying Herodotus, but rather Herodotus and Aristophanes as *doing the same thing* here. Both are 'parodying' popular mentality – provided, once again, we do not take 'parody' too crudely as a sheer deflating technique, but rather as a provision of a model to build on and refer to. If Aristophanes was inspired by his own personal reading or hearing of Herodotus, then of course that would be an interesting piece of literary biography; but, given how few of the audience would have caught the hint, it would not tell us much about the way the play works. That pattern of popular historical explanation is what matters there, and this pattern then becomes one of the most historically interesting aspects of the scene.

'One of' the interesting aspects, but not the only one: historians would not be historians if they did not try to extract what other details they could. Take that notice that the Megarians were 'gradually starving' when they 'asked the Spartans to ensure that the bonkers-decree should be repealed' (535–7). It is hard to make sense of that unless starvation was regarded as a natural result of the exclusion decree, for there cannot have been anything like this in the *Telephus*. That is relevant to the religious interpretation of the decree championed by de Ste Croix (1972):[53] whatever the motivation (and the Athenian feeling of outrage surely did have a religious dimension), we may at least assume that hunger was *expected* to follow, for otherwise we need not have had 'hunger' as the transition here at all. Indignation at the humiliation would here have been enough to explain the Megarians' turning to Sparta, and unless the audience were used to associating decree and hunger they would be bemused indeed. In fact, it is a conceptual error to separate 'religious' and 'economic' too sharply. The Megarians will starve both because the indignant gods have been invoked against them, and because they cannot buy food: both are parts of the same campaign.

That is not to exclude some exaggeration: this is comedy, after all, and it is also a play with a unity. In particular, there is a strong thematic continuity between now and events later in the play, where the starving Megarians appear, followed by a sycophant who denounces their sale as contraband. 'It's the same old story,' laments the Megarian there (820–1): 'here it comes again, the source of all our troubles is back'.[54] This later starvation is doubtless because of the war itself (the sycophant cries 'these are enemy goods'); its pre-war antecedents may still be given more stress, and moulded to seem more closely similar, than would otherwise be natural. But the exaggeration must be exaggeration of something the audience would find immediately comprehensible. Otherwise it does not make enough sense.

Let us turn to that assumed 'earlier phase', before the exclusion decree, when it was merely individual Athenians who were responsible for the Megarian troubles. Dicaeopolis is certainly insistent that the problem lay with 'some individuals from among us – and I am not speaking about the city; remember this, that I do not mean the city…'; and these individuals would denounce goods as Megarian – 'these clothes are Megarian'. 'Is that a cucumber they could see? Or a little hare? A piglet? Some garlic? Grains of salt? They're Megarian! And off they'd go the same day to be sold off.'

Does it follow from this that there was no previous decree *of the city* about Megara, only the enthusiastic application by individuals of some general provision about contraband goods?[55] (In fact, we know next to nothing about any general import duties, but that does not mean that they did not exist.)

The reason for Dicaeopolis' 'not speaking about the city' emphasis is obviously last year's charge of 'speaking ill of the city': this, he underlines, is not a repetition of the offence. But we need not infer that the *polis* had taken no collective decision at all about Megara,[56] only that the emphasis of the attack falls on individual denouncers ('I'm not blaming the city, only the people who were over-enthusiastic...'). At first sight, that might still make it odd if there was a recent specific anti-Megarian decree, where it would sound strange to blame the enforcers rather than the city who decreed it. But there may also be a dig here at the assembly's tendency to blame everyone except themselves for their decisions and the consequences[57] (something that also worried Thucydides' Nicias, 7.48.3–4, cf. e.g. 1.140.1, 8.1). If so, that makes it more, not less, likely that there was some previous anti-Megarian decree, but that speaker and people are presented as conniving to blame those who carried it out rather than those who passed it.

We certainly need *something* specific about Megara in the background. Megara has not featured so far in Dicaeopolis' presentation, but the worthless individuals' denunciation begins 'these clothes are Megarian', and the audience must not find that strange. If it is more a question of a general customs law, we need some explanation why 'these clothes are Megarian' can fail to bemuse. Perhaps de Ste Croix is right, and 'Megarian' would be the most usual variety of contraband because Megara is so close. Or perhaps these particular goods are distinctively Megarian,[58] and so the denouncer's cry is the equivalent of 'That sausage is German! Those undies are French!' But this remains less likely: unless *all* Megarian cloaks and cucumbers were excluded, we should expect the cry to be 'those cloaks are *smuggled*', not just foreign. No-one need object to German sausages and French undies in themselves unless they are altogether prohibited. It is better to posit an earlier decree, passed some time around 446.[59]

The most interesting thing for the historian might be the importance, but also the ease, of disentangling attack on individuals from attacks on the *polis*: the second can remain unthinkable, but audience and speaker alike do not find it difficult to slither away from that unthinkable into blaming the hapless individuals. Compare Euelpides at the beginning of *Birds*, explaining the delicate issue of why he and Peisetaerus are so anxious to escape from Athens: 'we've nothing against the city itself', it's just the things that go on there (36ff.). That too is the suggestion of the Old Oligarch, who complains that 'the Athenians refuse to allow comic fun or abuse at the expense of the *demos*, to ensure that they themselves do not suffer criticism, but encourage it at the expense of individuals...' (2.18). He goes on to explain that '...this is because they know that the target of comic fun is not a member of the *demos* or the commons, but some rich or noble or powerful fellow; only a few of the poor and those on the people's side become comic targets, and only for over-meddling and trying to get a bigger share of things than the ordinary people, so the people are not sorry to see them too ridiculed'. Doubtless we should rephrase that in more ideologically nuanced terms, concentrating on the unattackability of the *polis* itself rather than any class within it; but it still grazes part of the truth.[60]

## 'Now, seriously, though...': a plea for peace?

So far our attention has focussed on the audience: what an audience needs to know in order for a joke to work, whether that knowledge turns on last year's brush with Cleon, on the plot of *Telephus*; or the claim, which we have seen reason to reject, that they need to know of a genuine Simaetha incident for Dicaeopolis' narrative to make sense. We have also dwelt on the audience's response in the dynamic of the occasion, the way in which particular attitudes might accompany theatre-going, and also the nature and importance of the challenge in this privileged setting to some fundamental civic values. The question of 'seriousness', at least as it is traditionally put, focusses more on the playwright, and the notoriously awkward issue of the playwright's intentions. Did Aristophanes intend *Acharnians* to make a 'serious' political point, and can we possibly know?

Two points should be made at the outset. First, it is a travesty of artistic creativity to believe that the only 'seriousness' one finds must centre on political message-broking. Of course Aristophanes will have taken his art and his comedy seriously. Many comic writers wax portentously about the value of comedy to the health of a society, without limiting that point to its potential for moral or political messages; that will be even truer in a culture where comedy is afforded an important role in a central civic festival. If we ask how Dicaeopolis' treatment of peace is to be taken, we are not investigating *whether* comedy was a serious art-form, but *how* its seriousness is to be figured.

Secondly, however politically serious (to use 'political' in our sense) Aristophanes may have been, that need not mean that he was serious at the expense of all else. In the *Acharnians* parabasis the chorus revel in the notion that the Athenians, with a poet like Aristophanes to help them, will 'win the war by a distance' (651); the later scenes of the play depict how effectively the Athenians are starving their enemies, especially the hated Thebans and Megarians. That is hardly a good way of urging the benefits of an early peace (for, given the sensibilities of audience and genre,[61] the sufferings of a Megarian or Theban were scarcely likely to excite audience *sympathy*: Athenian sympathy for a Megarian is as unlikely as a Liverpool supporter feeling sympathy for a relegated Evertonian, or – for most of our past – British sympathy for a suffering Frenchman). It brings out how well the war is going. But it need not follow that any 'plea for peace' was merely playful. It simply reflects the way in which Aristophanes, like most comedians, is happy to extract laughs and jollity wherever laughs and jollity are to be had; just as in *Clouds* he extracts humour from the old-fashioned, blustery 'Better Argument', but that does not mean that he approved of the 'Worse' counterpart. Contributions to political debate were not his only priority; it does not follow that they were no priority at all.

It is easy to be simplistic about the 'seriousness' question. Some write as if it is just a question of separating out the 'serious' from the 'funny': a line may be a joke, may advance the plot, may act as a cover for stage business, but otherwise there is a real chance it may carry a serious message – so claims MacDowell (1983): 144; it is passages which are neither integral to the plot nor funny in themselves which are most likely to represent the poet's own views, says de Ste Croix (1972): 234 (though he is admirably clear on the difficulty of identifying exactly what is and what is not a joke). But the examples taken show the weakness of this 'separating out' approach. MacDowell finds the Simaetha sequence sufficiently unfunny to need a basis in Aristophanic seriousness;[62] the *Telephus* parody has encouraged us to take a different view. De Ste Croix puts special weight on a speech in *Lysistrata* which is *completely serious in character and without a single jest*,[63] in which Lysistrata urges the Athenians and Spartans to accept that there have been faults on both sides, to give up their squabbles, and to begin fighting barbarians (1114–77): yet what makes the scene work is the way in which the sexually out-of-practice Spartans and Athenians are far more interested in the beautiful – and naked – female figure Reconciliation. Lysistrata's seriousness is accepted absent-mindedly: their thoughts are on lower things. 'My cock is killing me ... what a lovely arse – never seen a prettier pussy...'. The point might be that, with listeners in this frame of mind, one can get away with saying anything at all, even this outlandish stuff about faults on both sides; or it may be that they've heard it all so many times before. Whatever it is, it is clearly not what de Ste Croix claims. This would be the worst possible way for a preaching dramatist to couch a serious message.

In fact, comedy just does not work like that. We cannot discard the funny and build on what is left, but that does not mean there is no political impact at all. It is precisely the things that are funny – John Major's greyness, Harold Wilson's pipe and raincoat, Margaret Thatcher's handbag – which can be politically telling (and in a positive as well as negative way, as Wilson and Thatcher were alert enough to realise). The funny *is* the serious.

Dicaeopolis' speech is certainly funny: is it serious too?

Some have regarded the assumed identification of Dicaeopolis with Aristophanes as the clinching argument for the 'seriousness' of Dicaeopolis' speech:[64] we have seen reasons for doubting that inference. That 'identification' all depends on what the audience would know already, and we cannot confidently work back to reconstruct that knowledge. But perhaps a more sophisticated version of that argument, shifted from the poet's identity problems to the audience's reception, still has some purchase. For we have also seen that the parabasis offers some assimilation of Dicaeopolis to the producer or poet, with the comedies performing a service to the city equivalent to that claimed for Dicaeopolis.[65] It is hard to think that this would work if the audience had been *alienated* by what Dicaeopolis had said. True, the characters on stage had gone on to be convinced, and that in itself had generated an atmosphere of enthusiasm for Dicaeopolis: but if the audience were reacting in a different way from the characters, their dominant emotion would be at odds with the drift of the parabasis, and it is hard to see what could be gained by this.[66]

We equally cannot blandify the speech completely. The earlier parts of the play have prepared us for something special and something shocking, something which may offend, something which needs all the paraphernalia of tragedy in order to underpin.[67] And the paratragic distancing can also help: Dicaeopolis is presenting the views as so shocking that he could not have put them forward any other way. So far, this could still be like an Alf Garnett or a Father Steptoe, an engagingly outspoken character who says things that most would reject.

It still remains telling that, for all the cloaking and the qualifications, this could still be said without making it ridiculous for the poet/producer to claim in the parabasis that his trademark was speaking 'what is just' (645, 655, 661), and to feel that the assimilation to Dicaeopolis would not compromise that claim; to say it in a genre which was expected to treat contemporary affairs with some genuine bite; and to say it on an occasion when the audience were particularly conscious of their citizen identity. In one of the most provocative articles on this subject, Forrest (1963) commented on the contrast with the 'total wars' of our own century. No comedy could have suggested in 1916 that the British were partly to blame for the Great War, or in 1942 for the Second World War. Forrest himself concluded that this could not remotely be a plea for peace; it was harmless fantasy, in the style of the Ealing comedies *Passport to Pimlico* and especially (with its skit on militarism) *Whisky Galore*; Dicaeopolis and the audience long for a Copaic eel just as the young Forrest had once longed in wartime for a banana. This, he explained, would only become treacherous if one was prepared to make peace to get a banana. This is where Forrest's argument becomes difficult, for on the face of it that is exactly what Dicaeopolis is prepared to do. If the audience would really interpret Dicaeopolis' stance, and speech, as harmless fun, then we still need to explain why. Their twentieth-century equivalents would certainly not have done so: as we saw in the last chapter (p. 136), the modern parallel is here best taken as opening our eyes to the differences, not as a model for the similarities.

Yet at one level Forrest must surely be right. As we have seen, the audience cannot have taken the argument as so outrageous as to be alienating (the play won first prize), though they must also have regarded it as bold. So perhaps we should begin from the other end of the Forrest argument: that this *cannot* be taken as treachery, that in context this *must* in some senses be like longing for a banana – a more shocking equivalent of that, one that needs to be paratragically cloaked, but still one which is not alienating.

That need not imply that the audience – or even a substantial part of them – were genuinely keen to make peace, now, on any terms. Indeed, the speech might even rely for its acceptability on an audience who could accept that the rights and wrongs were pretty even, that the war's origins might even be trivial, but that nothing followed about making peace now: this is something that even those keen on the war could accept as well, or at least put up with hearing – in the comic festival, with comic licence, and accompanied by all the other provisos to which we have become accustomed.[68] They probably did not hear it just from Aristophanes; Cratinus' *Dionysalexandros*, whenever it is to be dated, seems to have burlesqued 'Pericles bringing on the war' in tones which hardly suggest enthusiasm.[69] But even if this was one of the ways in which the public would look on the war, it need not follow that it was the only or decisive way; and outside the comic theatre they might carry on fighting with the usual range of resigned, cynical, but businesslike soldier's emotions.[70]

If we had only *Acharnians* itself to go on, that would be as far as we could go; but if we feed in other material too, we may find reasons for supposing that peace-treating was not so unthinkable in 425 as in 1942, that the idea of 'total war' (Forrest) was different. This is a culture where recurrent war, frequently interrupted and frequently resumed, was a fact of life, and need not mean either that war was anything but 'total' while it lasted or that peace embodied a permanent abdication of one's aims and aspirations in fighting. There were in fact several peace-feelers from both sides in the ups-and-downs of the war: the Athenians had made one in 430 (Thuc. 2.59.2), at a time when they were demoralised by the plague;[71] there were others from Sparta a little after *Acharnians* in 425 (Thuc. 4.15–22, cf. 41.3–4, *Knights* 794–6, *Peace* 667). Some took these very seriously, and Thucydides himself presented the Athenians as irresponsibly greedy in refusing the offered terms. To think that peace and a Copaic eel might not be far away need not be so ridiculous; to think of making peace need not be treacherous, and – provided that it was adequately comically articulated – need not alienate irredeemably even those who disagreed.

As usual, we have found questions about the audience more illuminating than questions about the playwright's views: whatever Aristophanes himself thought about peace, the more illuminating point – illuminating because it reveals a collective and not an individual view – is that such things *could* be said, would not grate so much with the audience's pre-existing assumptions that they would alienate. But there is no need to lose the playwright from our gaze completely. The pre-existing assumptions cannot be too far away from those which the play or the character encourages, but it certainly does not follow that they were identical. The best propaganda works by exploiting ideas which the audience may already find acceptable (or at least not too alienating) but then by moulding, renuancing, extending them.[72] And there are lots of other pre-existing audience assumptions which Aristophanes might have fastened on but does not. No artist can avoid responsibility on grounds that he or she is simply telling the audience what they want to hear, or what they know already, or what Cratinus said a year or so ago. The reinforcement of one view rather than another must crystallise, must strengthen, must encourage thoughts in a particular direction. Aristophanes' fire, it has been well observed, is *selective*. Some themes, peace prime among them, keep coming back; just as some targets (Cleon and the demagogues) come into much more searching and recurrent focus than others who might offer just as much material – the superstitious, nervous Nicias, the outrageous and charismatic Alcibiades.[73] Those themes represent a choice, and that choice was Aristophanes' own. The plays tell us about both audience and playwright: the audience, whose preoccupations and prejudices may be challenged but only within limits, and the playwright, who selects the preoccupations and prejudices to exploit.

# Chapter 9

# Tragedy and ideology

## Tragedy, comedy, and topicality: Euripides' *Orestes*

Taplin (1986) explores the way in which tragedy and comedy tend to define themselves against one another. Tragedy is and does what comedy is not and does not do. That is particularly so when metatheatre is in point, the degree to which drama refers to audience, theatre, stage-mechanics, costume, or even to other theatrical artefacts by parody: we saw a good deal of that in *Acharnians*.[1] One of Taplin's other main areas concerns 'political' allusiveness. Tragedy is often in a deep sense 'political', exploring issues which are important to the citizen as citizen. But comedy is topical in a cruder sense: it includes characters bearing everyday names and refers to real figures or real types of figure – Socrates, Euripides, the Inspector, or the typical 'Xanthias'; it handles contemporary issues such as the war and demagogic politicians; and it does all this either directly or in ways which require a minimum of decoding (the Cleon-like Paphlagonian in *Knights*; 'Labes' and 'Kuon' in *Wasps*). Tragedy explores issues in a more timeless register: the nature of democracy rather than the deficiencies of Cleon; the sufferings of war (*Hecuba* and *Trojan Women*) rather than issues of Megara, Pericles, and what Simaetha's hookers did or did not do.

What Easterling calls 'heroic vagueness' is in keeping with this.[2] Tragedies can accommodate aspects with a contemporary tone, but any anachronism must not be too stark. It may be a matter of vocabulary. One can have assemblies and voting, but the language is of the more elevated *psephos* (the literal 'pebble') rather than the more technical *kheirotonia* (the abstract act of 'voting' itself).[3] Other contemporary institutions are hinted rather than precisely duplicated; language of *xenia* or *metoikia*, for instance, is not infrequent, but does not map exactly on to contemporary realities.[4] There are similar blurrings when the origins of institutions are in point. *Eumenides* provides the charter-myth for the Areopagus, but the trial procedures do not seem very specific to that court: they provide a prototype for *any* (at least, any Athenian or democratic) court to follow.[5] Even when tragedy comes closest to specific events, there is a similar vagueness. The battle of Delium (424 BC), when the Thebans refused to return the Athenian dead, is in the background of the similar episode in Euripides' *Suppliant Women*, but the details are not reproduced exactly in their mythical equivalent.[6] Real life still matters; but it must be seen through a blurring filter, appropriate to the timeless nature of the reflections it inspires.

This affects the way the historian should treat the material. Contrast, for instance, the assembly in *Acharnians* with the debate described in Euripides' *Orestes* of 408 BC (844–958). In *Acharnians* we can detect quite precise things about real assemblies: we may infer details of formal procedure, of how the prytaneis behaved (above, p. 131); we may even reconstruct the topical background to the jokes (for instance, those gibes at the ambassadors to Persia who drag out their luxuries as long as possible, *Ach.* 65–90). In *Orestes* we must be more cautious. Orestes and Electra are on trial for their lives, yet is this an assembly or a court? It first seems that it is the court established earlier for the judging of the claim of Danaus and his daughters for sanctuary (871–3);[7] once the narrative begins, the texture is more of an assembly, with heavy Athenian overtones.[8] Then at the end we have a hint of court-procedure again: at the point when alternative sentences would be proposed in a real-life court, Orestes puts forward an alternative penalty (suicide) to the stoning which his opponents have been urging (946–9).[9] Within the assembly itself, the procedures are again presented in blurred terms. The nearest we come to real procedure is the proclamation 'who wishes to speak?'; but even this is transmuted, so that we have a close equivalent of the Athenian formulation rather than the actual words (Τίς χρῄζει λέγειν; 885, rather than, as at *Ach.* 45, Τίς ἀγορεύειν βούλεται...).[10] Earlier 'it seemed good to Argos' to ban Electra and Orestes from human contact even before the trial (46): again a *half-echo* of Athenian procedures, for 'it seemed good to...' is the normal formula for a decision, but it is left vague what sort of body has taken it. Similarly, the assembly itself is not described in the natural Attic word, *ekklesia*, but with a close etymological equivalent, *ekkletos ochlos* (literally, a 'called-out crowd', 612).

Since antiquity it has been a favourite interpretative procedure to look for real-life models for the speakers: the loud-mouthed demagogue of 902–16 has often been seen as Cleophon, or the two-faced Talthybius as Theramenes (887–97), or Orestes himself as Antiphon.[11] Yet one-to-one allegory is alien to the blurred texture. We should rather concentrate on the *types* of speaker, the fawner on the great, the demagogue, the naïve moralist from the country who seldom attends; and we should see the assumptions about the way democratic debate works – how the more even-handed rhetoric of Talthybius and Diomedes is swept away in more extreme views; how even the 'moral' old-fashioned countryman presents only a travesty of the issues, ignoring the fact that this is matricide (917–30). Then there is the Menelaus figure at 682–716, who mouths canny clichés about the way to handle a crowd, then uses them as a timid excuse and does not even turn up at the assembly; and the Oeax figure of 432–4, using popular justice as a way to prosecute private vengeance. The role of Apollo, leaving Orestes no real choice[12] and yet now offering no help, is suppressed – yet the earlier parts of the play have encouraged us to regard this as a critical factor.[13] This is no way for a case to be aired, no way to achieve justice.

This does not make the play less illuminating, just *differently* illuminating. It is not a commentary on individuals, but it does shed light on the categories which come easily to the audience, those available for a Theramenes or a Cleophon to be constructed and judged. Of course the recent prominence of particular figures will have given force and relevance to the stereotypes; but categories they remain, not individuals. Of course too one cannot assume that audiences would think precisely in the same categories outside the theatre as here; but the contemporary flavouring itself suggests that the play is 'zooming' to fit more closely with the audience's everyday experience.[14]

Nor is it just the stereotypes of politicians, but those of political debate itself. It may be that the Argive people themselves are innocent, and it is their leaders who are at fault;[15] yet the failure of the debate to grapple with the real issues remains disquieting, and suggests reservations about the whole process. Yet this, in 408 BC, can be put to a democratic audience without fear of alienating them. That is a point to which we shall return.

*Orestes* is one of the most self-reflexive of Greek plays, frequently drawing attention to its place within a mythical and theatrical tradition. The most important intertextual references are to

Aeschylus' *Eumenides*, produced exactly fifty years before in 458. It is rewarding to see what the intertextuality contributes to particular passages,[16] but a wider point affects the whole play. The allusions remind us of the myth of which this is a part, and point the innovations; the democratic debate, the attempt to kill Helen, the hostage scene with Hermione would all strike the audience as bold and new. But as educated theatre-goers they also know that the innovation will only go so far. Orestes and Electra will not die here; nor, almost certainly, will Helen.[17] However many attempts there may be to impose a new pattern on events, we know that human ingenuity will fail: what will happen is what has always been fixed to happen, mythographically if not cosmically determined;[18] and that suggests its own conclusions about the limits on humans' freedom to decide their own destinies – a contemporary preoccupation which we have noticed before.[19]

There is a further resonance. In *Eumenides* too there were contemporary overtones; but that play ended with a more optimistic vision of democratic politics, with Athens as a site for reflection and persuasion rather than grim and vengeful violence. At the end of *Eumenides*, a torchlit procession celebrated the integration of the Furies in the state; at the end of *Orestes*, torches are waved as Electra, Orestes, and Pylades threaten to burn the palace if their demands are not met. As Euripides' audience recalled *Eumenides*, they might reflect on the way the civic vision had changed.

But how, precisely, had it changed? We too can find the contrast of the two plays suggestive. On the face of it, they suggest very different approaches to democratic ideology, with *Eumenides* commending those ideals of debate which *Orestes* destroys. Has the audience's commitment to the democratic ideal been so buffeted that now its weaknesses can be assumed, no longer even need to be contested? Or should we rather find the change in the political texture of tragedy, now more subversive and less acquiescent? Let us look more closely at *Eumenides*, and test whether its ideological content is quite so straightforward as we have so far claimed. That will also give us a further example to test the degree of topicality in tragedy, and the differences from comedy.

## Aeschylus' *Eumenides* (458 BC)

The *Oresteia* is unusually direct in its political allusiveness. *Eumenides* draws the audience's attention to two items of recent controversy, the reform of the Areopagus and the question of an Argive alliance. In 462/1 BC both had figured in the struggles between the supporters of Ephialtes and those of Cimon. For some years Cimon had dominated, with his policy of co-operation with Sparta; but he had been embarrassed by some clodhopping Spartan diplomacy in (probably) 462, when they had asked for help in dealing with their helot revolt, then sent the Athenian detachment home. Ephialtes had seized the moment, and turned Athens to the alternative policy of an alliance with Argos. He had also – perhaps at the same point, less likely earlier while Cimon was away in the Peloponnese[20] – introduced a series of democratic measures. The flagship reform was an attack on the powers of the Areopagus council, which consisted of ex-archons and had traditionally constituted a political élite.[21] That body had come to play a large, possibly even a dominant, role in the state; now Ephialtes and his associates tried to curtail its functions.

The role of the Areopagus both before and after the reforms is controversial,[22] but it appears that it had possessed a loose but potentially vast role as 'guardian of the laws'. Any citizen could make 'reports' (*eisangeliai*) about a serious crime or threat to the state, and the Areopagus could punish the accused (*Ath. Pol.* 8.4); it had probably also conducted the investigation (*euthunai*) into the performance of retiring magistrates. The Aristotelian *Ath. Pol.* (25.2) describes Ephialtes as removing its 'additional powers', *epitheta*, and 'restoring' them (or, less likely, 'giving them as was due') to other bodies, the Council of 500, assembly, and courts. It is easiest to see this as reflecting Ephialtes' own rhetoric, claiming that he was restoring the Areopagus to its original role and stripping away the later accretions. If this is right, one notices the rhetorical strategy of appealing to an 'ancestral custom' which needed to be restored, familiar in the fourth century and already (it seems) a political argument which was expected to have force.[23] In future the role of the Areopagus was to be more limited: it is hard to say what was included, but most important was the trying of certain homicide cases.[24]

The audience of *Eumenides* could hardly ignore these recent struggles, particularly as they hear Athena's charter-speech for the Areopagus court. The cases have been heard, and the vote is about to be cast. Now the goddess herself speaks.

People of Athens! Hear now the ordinance, you who are the judges of this first trial for the shedding of blood. In future too this will always remain the council of jurors for Aegeus' regiment. And this 'Areopagus', where the Amazons took position and pitched their tents when they came in arms, resentful of Theseus, and fortified this new high-walled city up against our own, and sacrificed to Ares here where the rock still carries the name, this 'hill of Ares': here the citizens' reverence [or 'reverence for the citizens'[25]] and their inborn [or 'inborn along with it'] fear will prevent them from committing injustice through day and night – provided that the citizens themselves do not make innovations in the laws. If you dirty clean waters with foul admixtures and with mud, you will never find it drinkable. I counsel the citizens to foster and revere neither anarchy nor tyranny, nor to expel all fear from the city: for what mortal is just, if he has no fear? If you are justly timid of such a reverend body, you will have a bulwark of the land and a salvation of the city such as no-one has, not in the Scythians, not in Pelops' domain. I establish this council to be untouched by gain, revered, swift in wrath, a waking guard for a sleeping people. That is the advice which I have laid forth, advice for my citizens and for the future. You must arise, take your votes, and judge the case in reverence of the oath. That is all.

(Aeschylus, *Eumenides* 681–710)

The Argive alliance also features prominently. Orestes promises that Athena will

without fighting obtain myself, and my land, and the Argive people as a loyal ally, justly, and for ever.

(289–91)

Then Apollo explains to Athena:

I have sent him to be a suppliant at your halls, so that he should be faithful for all time, and you, goddess, should gain him as your ally, and his posterity, and that this should remain for ever, that descendants should accept this as a binding covenant.

(669–73)

Once acquitted, Orestes finally expresses his jubilant thanks:

I will return home, having made this oath to this land and to

your regiment for the full reach of following time, that no leader
of my land should ever bring here a well-equipped force…

(762–6)

…and vows that even in his grave he shall aid those who faithfully
honour Athens, while persecuting those who break his promise.

Once the audience were primed to think back to 462/1, other
parallels might spring to mind. Ephialtes himself had had a hint of
the theatrical, just as the theatre now has a hint of Ephialtes. His
agitation had begun with his sitting in supplication at an altar (*Ath.
Pol.* 25.3). It ended with his being assassinated; his murderers were
never found.[26] A sequence which begins with a supplication, goes on
to shape the Areopagus court, and ends with the threat of violence:
*Eumenides* is of course not a precise parallel, but it juggles elements
of that political story into a new pattern. But the play ends in
reconciliation rather than slaughter, and the threat of bloodshed has
receded – at least for the moment.

The politics clearly matter. We could again use an analogy from
cinema, and say that the contemporary echoes 'zoom' the mythical
picture closer to the audience's extradramatic concerns.[27] How
similar, and how different, is the political allusiveness of *Eumenides*
to that of comedy, or to that of *Orestes*?

One point is clear. 462/1 is not 458. These are political issues which
had recently been live, but now had receded a little – even if they
might easily come back. True, we know little about this period, but it
would be odd if the same questions were still at the front of most
minds: events were moving quickly, with a host of Athenian
commitments. A famous inscription, ML 33 = Fornara 78, lists 177
members of the tribe Erechtheis 'who died in the war, in Cyprus, in
Egypt, in Phoenicia, at Halieis, at Aegina, at Megara, in the same
year': that dates perhaps precisely from 458, perhaps from a year or
two before. So if tragedy deals with news, it has (it seems) to be
pretty old news.

That ties in well with Aeschylus' *Persians* (472 BC), the other prime
example of a play with a contemporary theme. The momentous story
it treats was one of eight years earlier, and though more recent events
are also relevant   at 858–906, for instance, the Persian chorus fear
for their Ionian subject-states, which the audience would know had
by now been freed – those events give a contemporary *resonance*, no
more. There might also be a feeling of a Persian threat which may
come back, but it need not follow that this threat was any more

burning in 472 than for several years before or after.[28] That also fits what we have seen about heroic vagueness in *Orestes*; it will suit plays such as Euripides' *Heracleidae* and *Suppliant Women*, which we will look at later in this chapter. It matters that they were produced against the general background of the Peloponnesian War, but there is no sharp version of or comment on specific topical issues, and no particular alliance or rupture with Argos need be in point for *Heracleidae*. You can bring contemporary events into drama, but you cannot bring them too close.

What are the politics actually *doing* in the *Oresteia*? As with Aristophanes (above, pp. 158–63), the traditional approach has been to try to detect Aeschylus' own views. Thus de Ste Croix:[29]

> In the *Eumenides*, produced early in 458, Aeschylus goes right out of his way, and far beyond the demands of the plot, to stress the necessity of *a military alliance for ever* [his italics] between Athens and Argos – which could only involve perpetual hostility to Sparta ... The poet had no intention of being tactful about this burning political issue, and he went far beyond what was dramatically necessary.

De Ste Croix is emphasising the use of technical diplomatic language – not just vague talk of 'friendship', *philia*, but 'a full military alliance for ever'. That point is well taken: the language of contemporary diplomacy is a further 'zooming' aspect. But 'right out of his way', and 'far beyond the demands of the plot'? Much of this was answered by Macleod,[30] who emphasised the close integration of the 'political' themes into the trilogy. *Agamemnon* began by linking Argos with the city of Troy, with its wealth and corruption, and linking it in war; the text had subtly intimated the ways in which the truth about Troy and about Argos was connected (most strikingly in the choral ode 355–487). The trilogy ends by linking Argos in peace and alliance with Athens, guaranteeing the prosperity which the initial corrupt cities had so destroyed. The house of Atreus, once so perverted,[31] has now been set aright, and Orestes is now in a position to promise such an alliance: that is itself an index of the proper re-ordering of the *oikos*.

The treatment of the Areopagus is similarly integrated. Athena's founding-speech has been taken apart in the search for contemporary allusions and political advice;[32] within the play, it is more important that it echoes what the Furies sang only a little while before (517–

37) – the need for fear in society, for a middle path between anarchy and despotism, for respect for tradition.

> There is a place where fear that is good and overlooks the human mind must abide, firmly seated. It is good to be wise under suffering. For what man who has no fear in his heart[33] would feel the same reverence for justice, or what human city? Praise a life which is neither anarchic nor ruled by a tyrant. God had granted power always to the middle, but brings one thing to pass in one way, another in another. My advice fits that view. *Hubris* is truly the child of impiety; from health of heart springs the prosperity which is friend to all, the object of much prayer.

Nor is this the only suggestion of the Furies, for Athena's 'waking guard for a sleeping people' (706) also evokes their awakening at the beginning of *Eumenides*.

It matters that Athena and the Furies are now speaking the same language: that prepares for the final reconciliation of younger and older gods. But it matters too that their agreement centres on the Areopagus. In future the court will protect the principles which the Furies have so vehemently upheld. This is the institutionalisation of justice, the establishment of an ordered system for extracting penalty and imposing fear: the Furies' violent hunting may no longer be necessary. The court is to ensure that the Furies' principles are respected, and this is one aspect of the honour (*time*) which they are to receive, important as that is to Athena's successful 'persuasion' (*peitho*).[34] The local juxtaposition of the shrine and the court is suggestive: the court embodies the principles of the goddesses. The Areopagus and the Argive alliance both capture ways in which the future will be ordered differently from the past. 'Far beyond the demands of the plot?' Hardly!

What of Aeschylus' own views? We may well be able to infer enthusiasm for the Argive alliance;[35] at least, Orestes must be offering Athena something valuable, and there is nothing in the text to cast doubt on that value. It is harder to be sure of his position on the 462/1 Areopagus reforms.[36] If he supports the reduction in its powers, it is odd that the language is so fulsome in praise of the Areopagus as a council (*bouleuterion*, 684, 704), not just a court, and as the keystone of the democracy; if he is against the reforms, it is odd that that language centres on their role as a homicide court, the one function which they retained; and also that this anti-democratic stance should be combined with enthusiasm for the Argive alliance, the other democratic cause. Even when his language comes close to precision, it is strangely ambiguous. Athena looks forward to the reverence for the Areopagus which will safeguard justice, *provided that the citizens themselves do not make any innovations in the laws* (690–3): is that regret for the changes in the Areopagus' function in 462/1, or approval for a reform which stripped away the 'additional functions' (*epitheta*: cf. above, p. 168)? They are to be 'a waking guard for a sleeping people' (705–6), but does that refer to that role of 'guardian of the laws' which Ephialtes may have attacked, or to their continuing function as a homicide court, and the way in which that can emblematise the whole legal system? Both sides could take it as they wished.[37]

So Aeschylus is not anxious to press one particular partisan line; but the contemporary issues still matter. What is important is that they were contemporary and that they were issues. The roots of the trilogy go back into the past, to Troy; the implications thrust forward into the distant future; and both time-perspectives are vital. The hints of a contemporary local cavalry victory over Thebes similarly 'zoom' the relevance of Sophocles' *Oedipus at Colonus*:[38] there as here it all still matters.[39]

We have moved to questions of audience response rather than authorial stance: can we go further? Can we say with Gomme that 'Aeschylus reflects current feeling in Athens in *Eumenides*, 287ff. ...' in his enthusiasm for the Argive alliance,[40] or assume with Heath that the political material needs to be Panathenian rather than partisan, so the issues must have become non-controversial by 458 and we should therefore posit a 'new political consensus'?[41] If that were right, it would be most important for the historian. But such assumptions are dangerous. It is equally possible to find it central that these issues remained the stuff of controversy, even if they were not the hottest of the day. So much of *Eumenides* centres on how divisions can be dealt with; persuasion, *peitho*, is vital both in court and among the gods. The Athenian *polis* need not be a focus for self-congratulation on its harmony; the congratulation can rather focus on the way that it can deal with controversial issues, and has the institutions which allow it to process its divisions. This is a city where clashes can be resolved and decisions reached: and the clash and the controversy are as important as the resolution.

Within the play, the clash and the controversy are handled through the law-court. We notice again how the courts can be made such a keynote of *polis*-democracy, emblematising so much of what is different between Athens and Troy; and how homicide can in its turn be made emblematic of the whole legal process. Democracy is indeed, one way or another,[42] the rule of law – and the rule as exercised by the court, not by a king or even by a god: Athena eloquently finds the issue too difficult for one being, even a god, to decide.

Yet many have found this keynote court disturbingly shallow. Modern readers usually identify a key element as the duress which Orestes was under (just as we saw it to be central in Euripides' *Orestes*). Apollo's threats left him no choice, and we find it deeply 'unfair' – fairness being for us a crucial element in justice – that he should be left with no way out. But that figures only briefly in the trial, in Apollo's initial list of pleas (579–80, 'I am to blame for his mother's death').[43] Instead discussion focusses on the act itself: is it a greater thing to kill a man than a woman, a husband than a mother? Here too the issue seems more trivial than earlier. The link of mother and son was crucial in *Choephori*: had we not felt a strong mother–son bond to be natural, the Nurse scene would not have worked, inviting as it does the comparison of the Nurse's spontaneous grief with Clytemnestra's more enigmatic reaction (730–82, cf. 691–718); and, however we respond to Clytemnestra's baring of her breast to her son, it is an odd viewer who feels that the mother, whatever she has done, has no special claim at all (896–8). Now Apollo argues that the mother is no true parent of the child, acting only as a receptacle for the father's seed: a theory which can be paralleled in contemporary thought – Anaxagoras said something similar[44] – but which is likely to have seemed too sophistic to be plausible. True, we can tie this into the trilogy's rhythm: there is a 'progressive diminution'[45] of Clytemnestra, in *Choephori* she is not much of a parent and now she is no parent at all. But here, surely, the argument goes too far.

The same goes for Apollo's dismissal of Zeus' fettering of Cronos: a fetter is one thing, but bloodshed is different (*Eum.* 644–51). 'Blood demands blood' has been a deep insight: but this mythologised mudslinging[46] is hardly an adequate way of focussing it, and it is a style of argument which elsewhere typifies the over-clever speaker.[47] The jury are right to find the case so difficult, so that Athena's casting vote is needed. That vote too is problematic: the motherless Athena is 'wholly of [or 'for'] the father' (738). Once again, it is easy to relate this to an earlier theme, that of the man–woman Clytemnestra; this corrects, a god–goddess rather than a man–woman, a force for good instead of evil. But it is not a very *satisfactory* mode of correction, building on that most special of special cases, Athena's birth. Many readers and viewers have also felt uneasy at the role of threats and promises: the Furies' threats of blight, Orestes' promise of an Argive alliance if the Athenian jury decide his way.[48]

Nor are the strongest parts of each side's case aired here. The Furies earlier sang impressively of the need for fear as a cementing principle in society (517–48), impressively enough for Athena to echo it in her charter-speech (above, pp. 169, 171–2): but they themselves do not make the point here. Apollo earlier pressed the Furies for hounding Orestes but not Clytemnestra. Does not this devalue that most precious of institutions, marriage itself, he asked (213–24): a powerful point – but not made here.

Not all these points need be treated in the same way. It is misleading, for instance, to talk of 'bribes' and 'threats'. An Athenian court, unlike its modern equivalent in most western countries, thought of itself as acting on behalf of the state and the *demos*.[49] It was natural to take the state's interest into account; a promise of future benefits is not much different from the stress in real-life trials on the good the accused can do for the state if he is acquitted.[50]

If, too, we are surprised by the small attention given to duress, that may be because we are thinking too much of what is 'fair'. Greek *dike* was more concerned with punishment, with righting an imbalance caused to the natural order, than with reward. Even if the law-code allowed a plea of 'involuntary homicide' in such circumstances, it is not clear that a concerned jury would regard such duress as deciding the issue without more ado.[51] Here too a community might lay more weight on the danger of harbouring the polluted perpetrator of a crime, however great the extenuating circumstances: that makes it understandable that discussion centres on how hideous the crime was, not on the circumstances of the doer. Even in the more enlightened future, the chorus look forward to a time when

> wrongdoings from their predecessors bring a man into contact with these [the Furies], and silently destruction brings him down, cry loudly as he will, with its hostile anger.
>
> (932–7)

It is hard to avoid *some* implication that those 'wrongdoings from their predecessors' involve ancestral crimes, and that these will continue to bring victims into clashes with the Furies[52] – even if the clashes can then be resolved in a more ordered way. Whatever has been wrong with justice earlier in the trilogy, it need not be that individuals are trapped in hopeless situations through no fault of their own.

It is difficult, though, to explain away all those reservations. Most telling is the way in which they map on to reservations which we see in other genres about democracy and the courts. They are similar to the points made in a different register in the *agon* of *Wasps* (above, pp. 136–40): there too we heard of speakers' sophistic cleverness and rhetoric's tendency to conceal the deepest issues (here we recall not merely Bdelycleon, but also Thucydides' Cleon: above, pp. 5, 9–10), and the way in which a juror's self-interest can decide the issue. Some of the reservations are also close to those we saw emerging from Euripides' *Orestes*, where the negative view of the 'trial' remained strikingly uncontested. That suggests that *Eumenides*, even if it presents institutionalised justice positively, is also presenting it warts and all, not eliding but acknowledging the anxieties. This in turn suggests that contemporary concerns are relevant in a further way, with real life influencing the reception of the text. Despite the mythical setting, the debate will seem all too familiar, and the familiar criticisms of real-life trials will sensitise the audience to its deficiencies. This is a blueprint for how the future will really be, not for an idealised dream.

Nor is this the only occasion where the audience will find realities affecting their response. Take the glorious picture of a future where Athens will be the home of calm persuasion, with civil discord, *stasis*, far removed: both Athena (864) and the reconciled Furies (976–87) here utter similar hopes. Yet Ephialtes, in the audience minds as the author of those reforms, had been murdered only a few years earlier: that was the way that *Eumenides* did *not* map on to the real-life story (above, p. 170). Shortly after the play was performed, Athenian aristocrats would plan to open the gates to the Spartans 'hoping that they would overthrow the democracy' (Thuc. 1.107.4),[53] and such *stasis* was surely simmering already. Does that not complicate the picture of Athens as a home for persuasion and calm?

By now that initial contrast of *Eumenides* and Euripides' *Orestes* looks more blurred. The dominant tones of each play remain strikingly different, different enough for the audience of *Orestes* to find the contrast an important element in their response. Yet *Eumenides* itself has come to look more equivocal, and to show sensitivity to precisely those deficiencies of debate which *Orestes* so highlights. That raises larger issues about the way in which the trilogy encourages Athenian citizens to think, and assumes that Athenian citizens were prepared to think, about Athens herself: in a word, about ideology.

## What is ideology?

'Ideology' is a very slippery word. The twentieth century has suffered a good deal from 'ideologies', in one sense of the term: ideology as a state-imposed, domineering, straitjacketing system of thought, imposing questionable assumptions and principles – racial superiority, gender-stereotyping, communism, free marketeering – and refusing to brook criticism or exploration of those ideas. Even if we accept a different sense of 'ideology', accepting that non-dominant classes and movements can have ideologies too, we rarely mean it as a compliment when we speak of a programme or an argument as 'ideological': we usually imply that a conclusion has been reached on broad general principles rather than by a careful and open-minded examination of circumstances.[54] These negative associations can be misleading, as there is a sense in which *every* programme and argument is 'ideological', making assumptions about values which others – the conversational partner, the audience, the group – are taken to share; the previous sentence, for instance, makes the ideological assumption that careful and open-minded examination of circumstances is a good thing.

True, there is a danger of defining ideology so broadly that it drains the word of meaning. By ideology we normally mean something which focusses particularly on public and political roles. A very provisional fourfold definition can bridge most aspects: (a) it represents a scheme, a web, of *interconnected* values or tenets; (b) it is societal, probably societally constructed and certainly connected with societal roles; (c) it naturally generates action; it has an imperative, not just descriptive, element to it.[55] That is most normally true of one's own ideology: thus an imperialistic ideology inspires one to spread one's power, a freedom-loving ideology to spread at least one's word; but it can also be true when ideology is pejorative, the thing the other chap has – as Marx and Engels attacked entrenched interests in *The German Ideology*, as before them Napoleon attacked the 'ideologues', and as now some politicians, on both left and right, regard themselves as possessing common sense and their adversaries as the ideological bigots. In all three cases the categorising of 'ideology' was, and is, a call to responsive action. Finally, (d) it implies that the web of values are not just selected randomly but have some conceptual underpinning and argument; yet it is in the essence of ideological thought that one does not always go back to first principles to support a given stance, but takes the short-cut of referring to the ideology one is committed to. Some stress this lack of explicit critical reflection as basic to ideological thought: thus Finley (1982: 17) defined ideology as 'the matrix of attitudes and beliefs out of which people normally respond to the need to action, ... without a process of ratiocination leading them back to the attitudinal roots or justification of their response'. But here one must be careful. The fact that one can make short-cuts need not imply that one *never* questions basic tenets and first principles; and, as we see several times in this book, it is arguable that at Athens the element of questioning, in the right context and setting, is itself something ideologically authorised, part of what it is to be an Athenian citizen.[56]

'What it is to be a citizen': for ideology is articulable, even if not always articulated, as distinctive of a particular society or group, and here the citizen-audience is the relevant group. There is one important sense of ideology, associated with Althusser,[57] which deals in those elements of consciousness so deeply embedded in a society that its members are unable themselves to identify them, and only an outsider can give them adequate articulation; but there are other senses too, and it is typically the awareness of alternatives that strengthens a strong ideological consciousness – 'as Athenians' (or 'as Christians', 'as western liberals', 'as believers in the free market', 'as socialists', 'as feminists') 'we think *this*'.[58] That makes it natural that ideology should often be defined against something else, some (often caricatured) alternative way of doing things or looking at things; and this was particularly natural in Greek conceptualisation, with its taste for binary polarities, 'on the one hand's' and 'on the other hand's', 'us' and 'them'.[59]

It is easy to think of *polis*-ideology as a glorifying, unproblematic praise of the city, especially as contrasted with those rejected alternatives: and, if we concentrate on some genres, notably the great Funeral Speeches celebrating those who have given their lives for the city, we do find a comparatively straightforward view of the *polis* and the demands it makes on its individuals.[60] But we have already seen that people can think differently on different occasions. In tragedy citizens could think in a more reflective mode about some of the city's ideals. We can phrase that, if we like, as questioning and even subverting the city's ideology.[61] Or, better, we can see this questioning as itself ideologically authorised: one of the marks of the good citizen is to feel the problems which the *polis* raised, or at least to feel them in the right setting; and the tragic theatre was the right setting.[62]

*Eumenides* and *Orestes* offer a good starting-point. We have seen that disquieting features of the courts are presented in *Eumenides*, even as we also see the legal system as a move towards a better future; in *Orestes* the negative features of a popular court are impossible to doubt. It is doubtless correct to say that the audiences therefore 'explore', 'challenge', 'test', 'interrogate' the ideology of the democratic courts; but these can be slack terms, and it is worth discussing what questions the audience might ask, and what answers the questions' articulation might allow.

First, many of the reservations centre not on the ideal itself, but on how far real life falls short of it – a move we also made with the law-court burlesque in *Wasps* (above, pp. 136–40). In *Eumenides* an ideal picture of reconciliation is set against an awareness of a less satisfactory present; but that need not be subversive. If there is *stasis*, that is the fault of real life. The ideal of calm persuasion may not always be lived up to, but it can remain as an ideal. Ideology gives us a check-list of questions to put to real life; it need not mean that the audience sweep awareness of such problems under the carpet.

Secondly, even if there are unsatisfactory features which remind us of the trials of real life, that *need* not undermine the real progress embodied in the court-structure. Politics and law-courts often have to trivialise in the interest of giving clear-cut answers to complex cases. That need not mean that discussion is frivolous or negligible: shallow it may be in *Eumenides*, but it gives an answer, and probably the right answer; it was right, too, that the balance of the (trivialised) arguments should be felt to be close. There is interest in seeing how legal discussion is figured, the qualifications which can be accepted without destroying the value of the structure: or so, at least, many of the audience might have thought. On that reading *Eumenides* articulates an ideology which does not suppress the reservations, but *contains* them by acknowledging their force and presenting an ideal robust enough to survive the critique. Conflict will not cease in future; but it is healthier that it is conducted in this way.

So it is possible to see ideology as submitting the ideal to the test of real life and letting it survive. On that view, there is nothing subversive in the play, and the optimistic tones of the final procession can remain unscathed. That provides a tragic counterpart to the view that many might have taken of *Wasps* (above, p. 137), or *Knights*: not criticism of the democratic institutions as such, but an alertness to their weak spots and the ways that scoundrels exploit them. And that would surely be a *possible* reading, one which many viewers would feel comfortable with: it is hard to feel that many would leave the theatre feeling that the solution was no solution at all, that the judicial decision had been a travesty, that the text had undermined itself and that the friendly transformation of the Erinyes was only delusive.

In other plays too the audience would notice a mismatch between contemporary experience and the drama's ideals. *Heracleidae* celebrates Athenian compassion, conventionally prized as a national virtue;[63] the play looks forward to a future where Athens will reap the rewards through the gratitude of the children of Heracles and their descendants (note especially the strong words of Iolaus at 308–20). Yet she has just been defending those children against the hostile Eurystheus and his Argives. The future had evidently worked out all wrong, with the Spartans, the descendants of Heracles, as Athens' bitterest enemies and the Argives as their real or potential friends.[64] Eurystheus himself makes the point clear (1027–44), when he promises that his body, buried in Attica, will one day give aid to the Athenians when the Heraclids' descendants attack. But it is not Athens' fault that the future turned out so zany. The ideal of mercifulness is not deconstructed: any more than it is deconstructed in Euripides' *Medea* by being innocently extended to the child-slayer. There too the audience will recognise the mismatch between glorified Athens and the polluted figure to whom they are giving refuge: the chorus point the paradox (846–50). But again it is to Athens' credit that she can afford such refuge, even if it is going to be abused: compassion is not simply self-interest, and is still valuable even when gratitude turns sour. Reality, not the Athenian ideal, is defective.

Euripides' *Suppliant Women* gives a more elaborate case. Theseus gives a highly idealised picture of democracy, defending the mythical Athens against the sceptical Theban herald.

> There is no worse enemy to a city than a tyrant. In the first place, there are no common laws; one man rules, the law in his own possession; and that is no longer fair. With written laws, the weak man and the rich have the same standing in justice, and the weaker can give the fortunate as good as he gets when

he is abused; the lesser man beats the greater, if he has right on his side. *That* is freedom: 'Who has some idea that is good for the city, and wants to propose it in public?'[65] And the man who wants to speak wins glory, and the one who does not is silent. What is fairer for a city than that? ...

(Euripides, *Suppliant Women* 429–41)

That passage is often quoted as a straightforward presentation of Athenian 'ideology'. But it is also important *within the drama* that this view is played against other more realistic insights into the way a *polis* functions. Theseus himself talks of the three classes in a city, only the middle one of which is any use (238–45). The Theban herald points out how a democracy can be ruled by irresponsible town-dwellers, for honest countryfolk find it hard to participate (409–25); he also talks of the way in which a mob is initially swept off its feet by enthusiasm for a war, and only later sees how dreadful it is (481–5, cf. 232–7). Adrastus looks back to his people's unwise and greedy rejection of peace terms (739–41). All of those gibes will seem rather closer to home than the glib generalisations of Theseus' upbeat defence; we think of Thucydides' picture of the enthusiasm for fighting in 431, or of the *demos* as 'eager for more' and rejecting peace terms after Pylos.[66] But it is again *possible* for viewers to think that the criticisms do not undermine democracy, but simply point its deficiencies in action: once again, the reality rather than the ideal can be at fault.

So far that comfortable picture is surviving: we can see plays 'attacking' reality, not the Athenian ideal itself. So far, indeed, we could posit an audience inspired by the ideal to try to reverse all those unfortunate features of distorted contemporary reality. Yet that too is an over-cosy picture, and posits too simple and single a picture of audience response. Those who were unsympathetic to democratic debate or to the popular law-courts, or felt Athens was too merciful for its own good, would deploy precisely the same texture of argument as we see here: that is clear, at different intellectual levels, in the Old Oligarch, in Plato, even in Thucydides.[67] If democracy leads so certainly to such excesses in practice, there comes a point where the reality discredits the ideal. That is particularly so if the excesses are seen not as a freak or an unnatural perversion, but as a timeless feature of the institutions; and the presentation in tragedy, working as tragedy does in the timeless register, encourages an audience to see things in that way. If in *Eumenides* the less satisfactory features are there from the beginning, with the argument conducted by two gods particularly associated with wisdom (Athena and Apollo) and by the underworld force particularly linked with justice (the Erinyes), it is hard to dismiss the banality or misfirings of everyday law-court argument as a manageable, reversible, unfortunate deflection of an unimpeachable original reality.

We should not overstate this. *Most* of the audience, in most of their minds, would doubtless feel that the qualifications did not undermine the ideal; we can even see ways in which the playwrights manipulate their audience to ensure that the negative response should not be the dominant one. In Euripides' *Suppliant Women*, the negative views are all distanced in one way or another. The audience will be more likely to agree with the national hero Theseus than with the unreconstructed Theban who presents the negative insights; Theseus' own remarks about the 'three classes' are concerned in the first instance with Argos rather than with Athens. Still, those negative insights can still come close to home, 'zoom' on to current realities, and those who felt less enthusiastic for democracy would find plenty to support their view.

For the historian, that need not matter. It would always be a crude view to have every member of the audience responding to plays in precisely the same ways. What we can still infer is along the same lines as with *Wasps* (above, pp. 136–40): we can see some ways the 'problem of democracy' might be conceptualised, the agenda for any debate: that is, the nature of the reservations which might be felt, and the check-list of 'tests' which democratic ideology needs to overcome if it is to remain attractive. We can also infer that most, or at least enough, of the audience could stand hearing those reservations without finding their sympathies for the poet or his play alienated – or at least that the poet expected that they would, and he knew his audience better than we do: so the dominant interpretation, that of most of the audience, would not be to find the play's content *unacceptably* 'subversive' of the civic values to which they were most attached. The challenge to those values can still be real; but, in this tragic setting, it was one which they could take hearing.

It should follow, too, that the balance between positive and negative elements was close enough for most to find it interesting: and this can be the most historically telling element of all. One of the surest ways of investigating a person's – even one's own – moral sensibility is to ask what dilemmas he or she will find most poised, most difficult to decide: where would we find animal-experimentation tolerable, but only just, in the interest of medical research? Where would the Athenians have found it difficult to decide where the authority of state, or of its prized institutions, should no longer be acceptable? This oblique method for investigating moral sensibilities is one which we use too rarely. It is an approach where tragedy, dealing unlike rhetoric with the difficult test-cases, is uniquely able to help us.

This approach also brings plays like *Eumenides* and *Suppliant Women* closer to those plays which more clearly explore the ideology itself, not just the reality which the ideology exposes: *Philoctetes*, perhaps, or *Antigone*. (It is interesting that it is not the *enfant terrible* Euripides but Sophocles, often viewed as more conventionally minded, who provides the clearest cases.) In *Philoctetes* the young Neoptolemus is ordered by his commander to perform a task he finds morally unacceptable; *Antigone* presents a young woman who feels morally compelled to go against the decision imposed by the male head of her city and her family. In each case the audience will find themselves morally engaging with individuals who transgress ordinances which in normal circumstances would be straightforwardly binding. 'Engaging with', doubtless, rather than 'identifying with': it does not follow that the audience will all think that Neoptolemus and Antigone are right. But at least they will understand why the characters feel driven to act as they do.

Let us assume that the playwright has loaded the dice so that the audience will find the issues in some moral balance. In that case we *need* a Philoctetes who is more civilised than the community which has forsaken him; we *need* an Odysseus who is so dislikable; we *need* a Neoptolemus who is peculiarly susceptible to appeals to his father's nobility. The case needs to be that extreme to make it even contestable whether a young man should disobey orders – in front of an audience, we should remember, who have already been fighting a 'total war' (whatever that then meant: above, p. 162) for most of a twenty-two-year period, and have become used to tough military decisions. In *Antigone* we have the claims of family loyalty to her brother on the one side, but of obedience to the head of the family on the other; her conviction in the divine will (and Teiresias later confirms that the gods indeed disapproved of Creon's act) and the increasingly tyrannical behaviour of Creon on the one side, the fact she is a woman confronting a man and encroaching on the public sphere on the other. It need not follow that the audience think the same way at all points of the play; they will probably become more convinced as the play develops that Creon was wrong, though it need not follow that Antigone was right. At many points they should still have found the moral scales fairly even, the issues interesting and contestable. And that is more illuminating than the way the scales eventually come down.

## Orestes again: disillusionment or disorientation?

Against that background, let us return to Euripides' *Orestes*. That play's reservations about the democratic processes are not new: they are versions of what can be seen in *Eumenides* and Euripides' *Suppliant Women*, and in Aeschylus' *Suppliant Women* too.[68] But there is a difference. In the earlier plays there was always an alternative, more favourable way of looking at democracy, and one which (as we saw with Euripides' *Suppliant Women*) the poet manipulated his plot to favour. Now, in *Orestes*, there is no competing positive view. Any attempt to reassure seems lame: Apollo's final promise that he will put everything right between the city and Orestes (1664) – as if such rifts could be easily set aside;[69] any feeling that this is all Argos, and Athenian realities may be less awful – but the flavour is too Athenian for that.

A first bid at an explanation would be to remind ourselves that this is 408 BC. The audience has lived through the disaster in Sicily, the oligarchic revolutions and the democratic counter-revolution; they have become used to the bloody vengeance, the abuse of *philia*, the terrorist outrages which are refracted in the last part of the play. If they, together with the playwright, are disillusioned, that is no surprise. On that view, *Orestes* points a mood of pessimistic realism about the *polis*. This is a fragmented, directionless, ungoverned world.

On such readings the play becomes a 'denunciation' of grim contemporary reality,[70] and the audience react negatively to everybody: just as the participants in the debate are appalling, so also the young aristocrats will win no sympathy when they take Hermione hostage.[71] Critics here often quote Thucydides on *stasis* ('faction'):

> So the cities were riven by faction, and later developments brought even more advances in innovation (for people had knowledge of what had gone before) in the ingenuity of modes of attack and the outlandishness of acts of vengeance. People

came to apply words to things in ways which reversed
conventional expectations. Senseless boldness was called
courageous loyalty to one's comrades; cautious delay was called
specious cowardice; prudence was a cloak for unmanliness; total
intelligence became total lack of activity. ... A man who plotted
and succeeded was intelligent, a man who suspected it was even
cleverer; but the man who took thought first to ensure that he
had no need of such things, that man was thought destructive of
his band of comrades (*hetaireia*) and fearful of his enemies. ...
Indeed, kinship became a less close link than bonds of
comradeship (*hetairikon*) because of the latter's greater readiness
to mount deeds of daring without excuse. ... The man who
succeeded through deceit won a prize for intelligence... And it
was the citizens caught in the middle who were killed by both,
either because they did not participate in the conflict or simply
because the others grudged them their survival.

(Thuc. 3.82)

The parallels are close: Euripides' text too uses the language of
'intelligence' (*synesis*), chillingly (396, 492–3, 1180, 1522–4); the play's
recurrent stress on 'comradeship' exploits that language of *hetaireia*
(804–6, 1072, 1079) which was so prominent in the affair of the
mysteries,[72] and Euripides' characters like Thucydides' stress how
comradeship is a closer bond than blood.[73]

If we do accept this view of the play, we again find something of
historical importance, not merely the categories into which political
experience can be sorted (above, p. 166) but also the audience's
readiness (or so Euripides anticipated) to accept a play which presents
such a negative view of political reality.

There may well be something in that reading; but it leaves out
too much. It leaves out the readiness of an Athenian audience to
respond positively to self-protection and cunning;[74] it leaves out the
way the early scenes encourage us to engage with the brother and
sister; it leaves out the clarity in the text that they have had a raw
deal, outmanoeuvred in a travesty of a court by disreputable
opponents and faithless friends. It is better to assume that, however
untraditional a tragedy this may be, there were again elements here
which the audience would find too complex for immediate and one-
sided judgement. Let us adopt the same approach as before: to make
the issues interesting, Orestes and Electra *need* to have been treated
so badly, first by Apollo and then by the court; their case needs not
to have been heard; Menelaus needs to be such a faithless friend.[75]

It does not follow that we justify their violence. Here too there are ways in which Euripides tilts the scales, and the kidnapping of Hermione is presented in a way which must be alienating: she is so naïve, so trusting, so willing to help. Most important, Electra pretends that Hermione is being asked to supplicate her mother (1332), and supplication is too sacred an institution to be abused in this way. Language too helps: Orestes, Electra, and Pylades are increasingly figured in animal imagery,[76] pointing to that bestiality which Tyndareus had characterised as the enemy of civilised existence (524–5). But that does not exclude the audience from understanding, and to some extent sympathising with, the reasons why they should have been driven so far. The *Medea* (another play which *Orestes* pervasively recalls[77]) is a good parallel. Not all will feel sympathy with Medea to the same degree; even those most sympathetic will not all find their sympathies switching against Medea, or here against Orestes, Electra, and Pylades, at the same time. Nor is sympathy the same as identification; an audience can understand why people feel deeply without thinking that they would themselves react in the same way, and it almost defines the tragic figure that he or she does not draw back when others would. But in both plays there is at least initially a possibility of audience sympathy; and we can see the myth being moulded in order to produce it, just as we can see the balance being tilted the other way at the end.

On this reading contemporary events deepen the audience response in a different way. The audience's memories of those events, and of their own reactions to those events, will affect the way they respond to what they see on stage. Many will have been disillusioned by the pre-411 democracy and sympathised with some of the oligarchic moves; they may now recall their own earlier sympathies – and perhaps relive their own disillusion with the aristocrats' excesses which followed, murders like those of Androcles and others in 411 (Thuc. 8.65.2, 66.2). Many must have felt that the ingratitude and unreliability of the democracy did something to justify those who took extreme measures in self-protection, Alcibiades, Theramenes, or Phrynichus; they too will have felt more doubts as events went on. Many, though, would have had nothing but distaste for those aristocrats and their friendships, working so shamelessly against the interest of the people, and may have revelled in the recent trials of men like Antiphon and Archeptolemus and others, corrupt though those trials could be claimed to be.[78] They too might find something to think about here, finding the popular trial

uncomfortably familiar, and coming to understand how frustration
with a travesty of democracy can bring good people to breaking-point.
As sympathies had veered in real life, so they will now veer in the
play; those real-life counterparts are bound to make responses more
intense, and to inspire reflection on real life as well as on its theatrical
counterpart. For many, it would be as difficult to pin down their
reading of the politics as to pin down the *register* of the play, the sort
of tragedy this is: the difficulty of relating it to the *Eumenides*, and to
tragic tradition, has more facets than one.

So the portrait of democracy is unequivocally negative, but not
because that is the only response which remains possible in 408. It is
negative because it needs to be, so that the moral problematic will
centre on the behaviour of the aristocrats. This is not like *Suppliant
Women*, for in *Orestes* the strengths and weaknesses of democracy are
not what the audience are engaged to worry about. It is more like
*Hecuba*, where again there is a travesty of decision-making, this time
in the Greek camp; but this is not a focus of moral interest in itself,
but rather something taken for granted, an important ingredient in
our pity for Hecuba and our evaluation of her final violence.

In *Orestes*, some of our earlier moves are still legitimate. We can
still find it telling that the evaluation of democracy *can* be displaced
from centre stage, that the negative aspects can be so taken as read
that the issue need not be the most interesting. But we shall probably
find other aspects more interesting: the way that a popular audience
can be brought to enter into the psychology of an aristocratic faction
and to understand their motives; the way that élite friendship, *philia*,
can be presented to this audience as an immediately comprehensible
value. Several of these themes recall points which we earlier extracted
from Andocides' *On the Mysteries*. There too the values of aristocratic
*philia* could be presented as self-evident, and the speaker found it
rhetorically sensible to acknowledge behaviour and sentiment which
we would think anti-democratic.[79] This is a democracy which did not
find an aristocratic world as alienating and extraordinary as all that.

So tragedy is useful to the historian in illuminating the issues
which the audience would find absorbing. That is just as important
as isolating the views of any particular playwright, creatively quirky,
spiky, and atypical as he might be. Tragedy can help us to see what
moral issues the audience found most interestingly poised. We may
not infer that they all thought equally enthusiastically about
democracy or the law-courts; we should not assume that all would
equally have applauded Antigone or Neoptolemus for going against

authority. When the audience thought about Athenian institutions, most must have thought for most of the time that the systems could survive the reservations, but not all need have done. We can at least assume that the audience would have found these issues arguable, and that those would be the important factors in evaluating difficult cases.

We should also notice this readiness of Athenians to be self-critical, in this privileged setting of the tragic theatre: that remains a valuable corrective to the more trumpet-blowing praise of the Athenian way of life which we find in the *Epitaphioi*. Of course, an Athenian citizen was not wrestling with problems of civic self-definition in every moment of his waking life; but he was not always being as self-congratulatory as in the *Epitaphioi* either. Both are within the range of experience which can be expected of a citizen; both are ideologically authorised. Tragedy has its own register, more reflective and less topical than comedy, but we can recognise the same readiness to confront and acknowledge the deficiencies of the democratic institutions as we see in *Wasps* and *Knights*, just as we can recognise the same capacity for open-minded analysis as we find at the intellectual heights of Thucydides and Plato.

This allows a more profound insight into the 'disillusioned' public mood of the years after Sicily. Authorised self-criticism, rather like the authorised reversals of carnival,[80] works best when in normal circumstances the system can survive the attacks and the reservations, but also when the audience acknowledge that the criticisms have force, that the survival is not automatic, and that when the circumstances become abnormal the threat to the city's system, confidence, and identity may become real. When the crisis gets great, the criticisms will look more decisively destructive. The confidence of the masses in their own democratic ways can then be a very precarious thing. In the good times, the doubts could be limited to the tragic theatre, but even then the doubts were part of life just as the tragic theatre was part of life. We need not be surprised if, when disasters crowded in, those scales started tilting differently, and many Athenians' belief in themselves and their institutions did not survive.

# Chapter 10

# Lysistrata and others: constructing gender

## Sex in context

> If I must mention female excellence to those of you who will now be widows, a short word of advice will capture everything. It brings great repute if you are not worse than your underlying nature disposes you to be, and most especially to the woman who is least talked about, in praise or in blame, among males.
>
> ('Pericles' in Thucydides 2.45.2)

> We have courtesans (*hetairai*) for our pleasure, concubines (*pallakai*) for taking care of our bodies from day to day, and wives for having legitimate children and to have a reliable person to guard our household property.
>
> (Apollodorus in [Demosthenes] *Against Neaera* (59) 122)

> I aimed at good repute, and I gained it; yet I failed to acquire good fortune to accompany it. Whatever is wise for women, this I toiled at in Hector's house. First of all, whether or not women are blamed, it gives you a bad name if you do not remain at home: so I abandoned any desire to venture out, and stayed in the house. Within those walls I did not import any clever female talk; no, I had a natural teacher, my own good sense, and that was enough. I kept my tongue silent, I greeted my husband with a placid countenance; I knew where it was right for me to overcome my husband, and where it was right for me to yield victory to him.
>
> ('Andromache' in Euripides, *Trojan Women* 645–56)

These passages are all favourites of historians of Athenian social life. Taken together – and taken out of context[1] – they give a bleak

picture of female married life: all that quietness, with not a word to
the husband nor a word about you in public; all that remaining
indoors; all that placidity. And sex is for bearing children; the pleasure
part is taken with the *hetaira*, the sort of woman who might also even
dine and drink with the men. No wonder critics and novelists are
sometimes tempted to romanticise the life of the *hetaira* rather than
the married woman. Doubtless the *hetaira* had her legal and physical
insecurities, but at least she had a life.

Yet when their contexts are taken into account, all three passages
look a little different, and their reliability as a guide to real life looks
more questionable: certainly to real life as it was lived, possibly even
to the ideals of female behaviour which Athenians, even Athenian
males, applied to their everyday life. (Most of this chapter will be
concerned with male construction rather than with women
themselves: when males wrote the texts and males were the target
audiences, it is a valuable but much more speculative business to try
to do more.) Thucydides' Pericles has been urging a particular
ideology, pressing to the limit the convention that the public Funeral
Speech (*Epitaphios*) should concentrate on the city and minimise the
aspect of private grief. For him the individual is most fulfilled in the
service of the city; now, at the end of his speech, he does turn to
those bereaved, and his consolation strikes an expressively bleak note
– much bleaker than we find in the real-life public *Epitaphioi* which
survive.[2] You bereaved parents, console yourself with the thought of
having new children – except for those past childbearing age, in which
case reflect that the bigger part of your life has passed in good fortune,
and your remaining time will be short. You children and brothers of
the fallen, you will never be judged the equals of those who have
died, for such is the human envy felt by rivals towards those who
survive. And as for you widows, be as little talked about as possible
among men.

We should first note that he is addressing the war-widows:[3] the
extrapolation to *all* Athenian women is illegitimate. Secondly, the
rhetoric is not concealing the harshness of the life which awaits these
bereaved parents, brothers, and children, however alleviated by the
reflected glory from their dead menfolk. That suggests that the
harshness of the widows' lot is also felt: this is not straightforward
idealisation. A major Thucydidean theme is the demand which
Pericles makes on Athenians to submerge their individual concerns
within the state, and the Athenians' increasing incapacity to adapt
themselves to such an ideal.[4] Such resigned acceptance of individual

loss is asking a lot: within a few chapters, once the plague strikes, individual bereavements will shake the state's moral fabric. Thucydides' highlighting of Pericles' bleakness may already raise the question whether such demands for individual restraint are not unrealistic and unmeetable.

The *Against Neaera* passage, which dates from nearly a hundred years later,[5] poses a different problem. Some have taken the distinction between *hetaira*, concubine, and wedded wife very seriously; Pomeroy (1975: 8) even takes that 'we' as implying not just that 'we' males as a whole distinguish different types of partner, but that the same man might have three different women to serve each role (she concedes that only the wealthy might afford such a team).[6] Others more soberly comment that the categories must have been blurred in practice: for most Athenian males a wife rather than a *hetaira* would have been the main source of sexual 'pleasure', despite Apollodorus' categorisation.[7] (Otherwise the plot of *Lysistrata* would not make sense, and the end of Xenophon's *Symposium* famously describes a male audience's response to an erotic dance: 'the unmarried swore to marry, and the married leapt up on their horses and rode off to their own wives in order to obtain these things', 9.7.) So perhaps we should take Apollodorus' listing as cumulative rather than exclusive: *hetairai* give *only* pleasure, concubines give everyday care too, but only wives add the possibility of legitimate children?[8] That is better, but it still suggests firmer distinctions than can have operated in practice; the roles of a live-in *hetaira* and of a concubine must have been particularly similar (as with Pericles' renowned *hetaira* Aspasia, for instance); childbirth as well as 'daily care' could be envisaged as the role of concubines, not merely wives, and it may be (though it is hotly disputed) that a concubine's children could even be citizens provided that she was of citizen birth herself.[9] So even the cumulative approach does not quite work, as it imposes a more rigid scale of divisions than could have operated in reality.

So why does Apollodorus make so overstated a claim? It comes close to the end of the speech: Apollodorus has concluded his attack on Stephanus for representing Neaera's children (as Apollodorus claims them to be) as his own legitimate offspring, and therefore entitled to citizen-status. He has just acknowledged that Stephanus' line of defence will be to admit his relationship with Neaera, but to claim that she was living with him as his *hetaira* and that these children are not Neaera's but born legitimately of a previous marriage. This poses Apollodorus a rhetorical problem, as he has spent much of the speech attacking Neaera as, precisely, a *hetaira*, and a particularly travelled one. That, doubtless, is one reason why he delays till the end his acknowledgement of Stephanus' defence; had he mentioned earlier that Stephanus was not disputing that Neaera was a *hetaira*, the irrelevance of his attack would have been uncomfortably clear.[10] But he also claims that she was more, that she was living openly with Stephanus as his wife and was the mother of these children whom Stephanus had the effrontery to claim as legitimate. On the face of it, all this makes that strict distinction between *hetairai* and other sorts of sexual relationship even more surprising.

The key to it lies in the first person plural: *we* make that sort of distinction among our women, but Stephanus does not. All the categories are blurred in this unhealthy household: just as they were when (Apollodorus claims) Stephanus first set up house with her, thinking that he would 'both have a beautiful *hetaira* for free and someone to work and support the house' (§ 39) – 'support', rather than take care of its possessions as a good wife would; and just as when she charged extra on the grounds she was 'living with' a man – this is the regular term used throughout the speech for 'living with *as wife and husband*'[11] – and Stephanus sought to extract money from her clients on the grounds they were caught 'in adultery' (§ 41); and just as when Neaera's daughter Phano operated from the family home as if it were a brothel (§ 67).

*We* would never operate our households like that, implies Apollodorus: not families like Apollodorus' own, represented in Theomnestus' introduction as models of caring solidarity and propriety (§§ 1–2, 7–8); nor families like those of the jurors, such as Apollodorus has just been picturing. What will your wives, daughters, and mothers say when they cross-examine you on your day's work, if they discover you have acquitted Neaera? Will not the most proper among them be outraged that you have allowed her the same citizen-status[12] as themselves, whereas the foolish might be inspired to follow Neaera's pattern (they are evidently not following it yet, §§ 110–11)? Will not poor citizen families find it difficult to marry off their daughters, if they have to compete against prostitutes' children with the same citizen rights (§§ 112–14)? Notice this recurrent stress on the need to protect citizenship, that same citizenship which is the proud hallmark of the jurors' own families. This is a version of the rhetorical technique we noticed in Chapter 1, where the speaker establishes an us-and-them intimacy with the jury, assuming a set of values which the jurors share but his opponents do not; and where he posits a value-code which typifies a social class higher than that which his hearers possess, but which, during this exclusive citizen experience, they can appropriate (pp. 12–15). In reality the jurors might only aspire to a lifestyle which allowed such fine distinctions among their sexual partners – but they do not mind being addressed as if they already possess it.

The *Trojan Women* passage is tricky too. There are the usual problems of handling tragedy. This is set in a distant, mythical world. The issues are still real for an audience in 415, but they will be presented in a filtered and in some ways a simplified register: we should not expect a one-to-one equivalence with the modes in which a fifth-century wife, however proper, would see issues or express herself. We also need to feel the pathetic irony of the passage. Andromache's lament is that it is precisely these outstanding wifely qualities which have become known in the Greek camp, and have commended her to Neoptolemus, who has chosen her as his prize – his 'wife', and Andromache stresses the word (*damarta*, emphasised by metrical position at 660). She now must serve the son of Achilles, the man who slew her Hector: how can she transfer the same dutiful wifeliness to *him*, of all men? Now her submissiveness will be that of the true slave rather than the loving partner.[13] The etymological link of that *damarta*, 'wife', with *damazein*, to 'conquer' or 'tame', becomes pointed: a favourite (tellingly favourite, indeed[14]) image for marriage is that of the violent breaking in of a recalcitrant female, but that image is to have new, starker relevance to her servile future. The point would be lost if Andromache's marital behaviour and ideals were simply routine. She needs to be an extreme example of what she is.

All three of our passages now seem more problematic guides to real social life, but that does not terminate their value to the historian. What matters, as usual, is that such things are *sayable* in their contexts. In each case they can represent an ideological construct; in each case the point can partly be that they do *not* match neatly or comfortably against reality or normality – that this is asking too much of Athenian women, that Stephanus' family and even the jurors' are not so neatly organised, that most women are not like Andromache. It remains important that they can be presented in such an idealised setting; that the audience should not be impatient enough with Andromache to feel that such a doormat deserves all she gets. The marriage of Hector and Andromache was intertextually established from Homer as ideally happy: Andromache's code must be presented as something that fits comfortably within it. Equally, it matters that Apollodorus can present this as a categorisation which his audience might aspire to rather than ridicule, and that well-behaved males might be expected, not to avoid *hetairai* and concubines, but rather to keep them distinct from their wives.[15]

So ideological constructs matter. They matter in themselves, as part of Athenian mentality; they also matter because the relation of construct to reality may not be one-to-one, but it does exist. Cohen (1991a: especially chapters 2 and 6) uses comparative study of other 'Mediterranean cultures' (a deeply questionable term, but let it serve) to open our eyes to the gulf that can exist between an ideological construct of (say) proper maidenly activity and the real world; but he also brings out how deviants from the ideal, naughty girls, claim and even believe that others are conforming and they are the odd girls out – rather as contemporary advertising is predicated upon the viewer's readiness to believe that everyone has a tidier and better-equipped kitchen than we do ourselves, a more elegant car, a prettier garden, even a more fulfilling sex life. The advertisers would not do it unless we responded by buying the kitchen, the wheels, and the weedkiller, all doubtless in the happy belief that it would improve the romance. Deviant maidens too cannot remain unaffected even by unrealistic ideals, whether because they provide the frisson of enjoyment (naughtiness is much more fun when we know we are being naughty) or because they structure behaviour in ways more complex than simple compliance or deviation: people may deviate, but only in certain ways and within certain limits. And here it is not simply a question of literature *reflecting* the ideals, any more than contemporary television, including its advertising, simply reflects the societies it portrays. Literature also helped in *constituting* the ideals, as one of the vehicles by which society mediated its values to its impressionable members.

'Ideals', however, rather than 'ideal'. We saw enough in Chapter 9 to be suspicious of any view representing 'ideology' as a static and non-negotiable code, at least in fifth-century Athens. Ideologically charged literature provided a mode of measuring experience against ideals; it also allowed different ways of viewing (say) the law-courts to confront one another. Given the frequency with which gender issues surface in different genres, it would be odd if sexuality was any different. Consider Andromache's idealised submissiveness. The audience, we have seen, cannot sneer at that; the orators sometimes

give similar pictures of demure and non-combative women who are
outraged by the intrusion of men behaving badly (e.g. Lys. 3.6–7,
Dem. 21.79). But this is not the only picture of proper wifely or
womanly behaviour available, in the orators or in drama. Take
Apollodorus' picture of the jurors' womenfolk giving them a bad time
if they reach the wrong verdict on Neaera: that is not an Andromache-
like 'silent tongue and placid countenance', nor is it a sign of 'knowing
… where it was right for me to yield victory to him' – presumably
areas of public rather than household concern, yet those are precisely
where the women are now expected to show interest. Similar pictures
are found elsewhere (e.g. Lyc. *Leocr.* 141; Isae. 12.5), and are clearly
expected to strike jurors as a sign of a good citizen family, properly
ordered and commendably alert to public affairs. Doubtless, such
challenging women were not always so welcome. Aristophanes'
Lysistrata remembers times when she questioned her husband on
the wisdom of the day's decisions in the assembly, and was put in her
place (*Lys.* 510–20). Quite right too, thinks the Magistrate she is
addressing. But even here the scene will not work if the audience
think the same way as the Magistrate – indeed, his irrational and
short-sighted bluster has by then been made clear. We later sense
the contrast with her paternal home, where she learnt so much from
listening to sensible talk from her father and the elder generation
(*Lys.* 1126).

Such variation of available ideals need not surprise. Grave-
inscriptions reveal a host of different virtues, many of them identical
with male virtues, for which women can be praised: a woman may be
*sophron*, 'sensible', for instance, a prized male virtue, or 'pious'; or
hard-working or thrifty; or, once, 'intelligent', *eusunetos* (in an Attic
inscription of *c.* 380).[16]

Within tragedy too, ideals of female behaviour are not clear-cut.
Doubtless Antigone's aggressiveness to Ismene is unfeminine, and
doubtless the audience feels uneasy at her challenge to the authority
of the *polis* and of the male. We are unsurprised when Creon is
impatient at the notion of being worsted by a woman ('No woman
will rule over me while I live', *Ant.* 525; cf. 484–5, 678–80, 740–6, 756
'you slavething of a woman, don't split hairs with me' etc.). But we
should also note that this impatience emerges in tandem with other
signals which make his tyrannical temper increasingly clear. 'Is the
city to tell me what orders I should give?' (734); 'is not the city
considered the possession of the ruler?' (738). It is not or not only
Antigone's presumption, it is more Creon's refusal to listen, which
has to seem outrageous.

Nor, indeed, should we assume that even in the first scene the deferential Ismene strikes the audience as unambiguously right. Her case is stated in terms which are more extreme than they need be (notably more extreme than the language used by the closely similar Chrysothemis in *Electra*): 'we must remember that we are women, ... and that we are ruled by masters to obey these things and things more painful still' (*Ant.* 63–4). She refers to these masters as 'tyrants' (60), whereas Antigone called Creon 'general' (8): Antigone's term stresses the legality, Ismene's the absoluteness, of Creon's authority. Ismene also begins that speech by emphasising the history of the family, and the long catalogue of disasters. Such sisterly conflict is the next thing to expect in a house like this; such female assertiveness as Antigone's too; but perhaps also such unquestioning submissiveness as Ismene's. This is not a play, even at this early stage, which leaves the audience complacently clear on how a woman, faced with an outrage like this, ought to act.

## Gendering tragically

This has returned us to our principle of the preceding chapter (Chapter 9, pp. 182–4). Tragedy rarely illustrates *what* the audience thought, not least because it addresses issues which are difficult and belie such simple formulations of collective prejudice or response. But it does illustrate what seemed an interesting issue to the audience, and how the dice needed to be loaded for that issue to be interestingly poised. In a famous article Gomme (1925) used tragedy, sculpture, and art to question the more straightforward reconstructions of demure Athenian women: no author or audience used to such passivity would construct a tragic world populated by Clytemnestras, Antigones, or Medeas. In itself that argument gives insufficient weight to the demands of the mythical matrix. Tragedy has to transpose its issues to fit a world where, as the audience knew from Homer and myth, women like Arete, Penelope, Clytemnestra, even Helen were expected to assume some control over events. It does so, too, in the festival of Dionysus, and religion was the area of Athenian public life where women played their largest role. But a version of Gomme's point nevertheless holds. Tragedy deals with real issues, however much they are remoulded. It does not score cheap points against easy targets, cases where the audience have no doubts about rights and wrongs. And the frequency with which the tragic audience are invited to wonder about female behaviour, to agonise on the dilemmas faced by an Antigone, a Medea, or a Phaedra, is inexplicable if we posit an audience which does not regard such matters as interesting, whatever their initial prejudices might be. Tragedy itself will have contributed to ensuring that such interest continued to be felt, and that unthinking attitudes towards women could not remain unexamined – even if, in many masculine minds, the prejudices were strong enough to survive any testing.

'In masculine minds': that inevitably raises the thorny question of the composition of the theatre-audience. Were women present? Scholarly opinions differ, and will doubtless continue to do so; the direct evidence is inconclusive,[17] though the balance of probability tilts in favour of their presence. One recent investigation (Goldhill 1994) phrases the issue in terms of analogy: is the dramatic festival more like a meeting of the *demos*, in which case it would be a male-citizen affair? Or like the Panathenaea and other religious festivals, which would afford an important role for women? That way of putting the question is interesting, but it resists a straight answer: the Great Dionysia has elements in common with both, and where one puts the emphasis may vary with scholarly and critical fashion.[18]

We are on firmer ground if we talk, not of the 'audience', but of the 'constructed' audience – perhaps we can even say, the *target* audience.[19] Here comedy rather than tragedy is the more secure guide, as comedy is explicitly metatheatrical in audience-address; and it is clear there that the audience is figured as the citizen *demos* – in other words, male adults.[20] Whatever we say about the presence of women, the real and constructed audiences are anyway not identical, for the real audience would include metics, foreigners, and children. Sommerstein (1997) estimates that only about half of the audience would in fact be citizens. The rest are both 'there' and 'not there', present but ignored – rather as spouses are often rudely ignored in an after-dinner speech ('All of us will remember that happy day when Sarah first joined our organisation…'). That does not mean that we should ignore them too. We might find it interesting that tragedy finds such dramatic potential in women, central to a family or city and yet excluded from many of its processes, just as it finds potential in outsiders who turn out to be insiders after all (Orestes, Oedipus, Polynices, Theseus, the Erinyes in *Eumenides*) – all in front of an audience including metics and perhaps women too, groups which in this very festival are both insiders and outsiders, present but sidelined. And, of course, tragedy will still have influenced women's minds and affected their self-esteem, even if they were not the primary target. Still, it is reasonable at least to start by considering the constructed or target audience themselves, those citizen males; and, in analysing the literary sources, almost all written by and for males, we may not be able to get far beyond that start.

Nor is it straightforward to identify what the citizen male audience would find problematic; nor, doubtless, would every male think about the issues in the same way. Take *Medea*, and in particular Medea's great speech as she first appears. It follows an astonishing sequence in which we have heard her wails off-stage, within the *oikos* – the *oikos* that defines so much of her identity, and which Jason is now destroying.

*Medea:* Women of Corinth, I have come out of the house, so that you may not find fault with me. I know that many mortals give themselves airs, some out of sight and some in public; others tread quietly, and thus win themselves a bad reputation for idleness. There is no justice in the eyes of mortals; before knowing what a man is like inside, they hate on sight, even though no wrong is done them. A stranger in particular must fall in with a city's ways; but I do not approve the townsman either who is self-willed and treats his fellow-citizens badly through pure ignorance. As for me, I never expected this blow, and it has destroyed me. There is no pleasure in life. Dear friends, I want to die. He was everything to me, I know that well; and now he has turned out the worst of men, this man, my husband.

Of every creature that has life and wit, we women are the most miserable breed. First we must pay a fortune to buy a husband – and, even more painful evil, a master for our body. And that is the critical question, whether he is good or bad. For divorce is not respectable for women, and one cannot refuse a husband. If a woman has come to a new way of life and new customs, she needs divine guidance, not just native learning, to know what sort of man will share her bed. And if we do our tasks well and have a husband who does not struggle with the yoke, life is enviable. Otherwise, death is better. A man, when bored with life at home, goes out and refreshes himself elsewhere; but we must look to that one single soul. They tell us that we have a safe life there at home while they do the fighting in the battle-line. They are wrong: I would sooner stand three times in battle than bear one child.

But matters are different for you and for me. You have
your city here, your father's home, the enjoyment of life,
the company of friends. I have no-one and no city. My man
dishonours me. I was booty from a barbarian land; I have
no mother, no brother, no kinsman to offer a haven from
this catastrophe. I ask you just one thing. If I find a way, a
means, to punish my husband for these evils – be silent. A
woman is fearful in all else; she has no courage for fighting,
cannot bear the sight of steel. But wrong her once in her
bed, and there is no deadlier soul.

*Chorus:*   I shall do that. You will be right to take vengeance on your
husband, Medea. I do not wonder that you grieve at your
lot.

(Euripides, *Medea* 215–70)

The challenge to conventional male values is extreme, especially
that 'I would sooner stand three times in battle than bear one child':
that takes not merely fighting but *hoplite*-fighting, standing in the
front line man to man, and diminishes it. As so much in this play,
that is shocking.

But *how* it shocks is more difficult to say.[21] Let us take three
imaginary members of the audience. The first, A, thinks the ideas so
outlandish that they are automatically disqualified from serious
consideration: such a woman is evidently wrong-headed – and no
wonder Jason finds a new bride more comfortable. B is more
disquieted. He may not have thought quite like this before, and such
ideas are hard to accept out of the blue; yet childbirth *is* painful and
dangerous, he knows; and, now he comes to think of it, perhaps
standards *are* dual – though there must surely be another side to the
argument too: perhaps he will be able to remember later what it
must be. C reacts differently again. He will not be disquieted, but
delighted. (And if there were women in the audience he can see that
some of them are delighted too.) At last! Someone is finally seeing
the way things are, and it is about time all these other oafs are
reminded that childbirth takes valour too...

All these responses are possible: that brings out how difficult it
can be to infer audience mentality and prejudices, 'what' they think,
from a single text. For the play works well for all three, and even
with some similarity: A, B, and C can all leave the theatre at the end
not merely admiring the play's theatrical virtuosity, but also feeling
uncomfortable at what they have been brought to sympathise with

during the last three hours. With B and C that is straightforward: their degree of engaged approval (C), or at least disquieted understanding of Medea's viewpoint (B), is unlikely to have survived the children's killing. With A it is more complicated. He may have felt more initial understanding for Jason; yet Jason has been so bland and complacent, so clearly insensitive to the dangers Medea poses as well as to her reasonable expectations as a person – and this may be an uncomfortable version, even if overstated, of A's own complacencies. He may begin by thinking Jason is not behaving too irregularly, but that view will hardly withstand the relentlessness with which Jason's outrage is described: he has destroyed one to whom he owes his life (an extreme transgression of the creed of helping friends and harming enemies); he has broken the oaths he swore when he took her with him. The ensuing carnage will be Medea's fault, on A's view; but it is hard to escape the suspicion that it is Jason's fault too, for his failure to realise what a dangerous, as well as outrageously ungrateful, game he had chosen to play.

Not merely have our three imaginary viewers approached the play with different mindsets; they have also found different ways to become absorbed in the play and to pose the moral issue. No wonder that reconstruction of audience reception is such a precarious business. But there is no need to shrug and give up the enterprise. Some points, at least, can be extracted.

First, that initial broad point: the audience are *interested*, or at least Euripides expected them to be. The one audience for which Medea's speech will not work is the audience who regard it as all boring, and find their minds wandering to yesterday's exciting wrestling-bout in the gymnasium.

Secondly, the 'how' rather than the 'what' of the audience's construction of women. Just as *Wasps* and *Eumenides* allowed us to sense the agenda when one set out to criticise or defend the democratic courts (Chapters 7 and 9), so Medea's speech suggests what would spring to mind if 'the misery of women's life' was the subject. Some themes are conditioned by the plot (though even so they cannot strike the audience as far-fetched): no surprise that so much centres on the husband and his taste for finding 'refreshment' elsewhere, just as Jason has done; nor that Medea's role as mother as well as wife is critical at that most provocative moment, on battle-lines and births. We can still find illuminating the way she phrases this dual standard. She talks of the wealth it takes to buy a husband, but, even more 'painful', his role as *master* of her *body*; the impossibility of knowing his ways before marriage; the differing respectability of divorce for male and for female; the particular, violent passion aroused in a woman when the marriage-bed is wronged. She finds it natural to use the imagery of 'yoking' for both sides, with the husband too having to 'bear' its imposition. We might also notice the themes which do *not* occur: no resentment here at an *oikos*-based existence, for instance, when things are going well;[22] nor at any assumed male supremacy within that house (except, importantly, for that mastery of the body). It is Jason's betrayal of the *oikos*, not her own location within it, that Medea finds outrageous. When marriage goes well, 'life is enviable'. Without straining, all these points can be made expressive of fifth-century expectations.

It is interesting, too, how Medea contrasts her lot with that of the normal married women of Corinth. They have their 'friends', and can evidently see them and find them a valuable resource. It is important too that they have their 'father's houses', whereas Medea has no kinsman to turn to as a haven, and her isolation renders her easier to outrage. They were initially likely, though, to find 'fault', again an indication of a culture of group comment, even gossip; and it is thought of as natural that Medea should be concerned for what others might say about her.

Naturally, some of these points are also conditioned by plot: if married women could not gather and offer sympathy, tragedy would find itself short of sympathetic choruses, and the genre welcomed the audience's readiness to accept that as a feature of this constructed world. The association of ideas can still be revealing of fifth-century mentality, especially when combined with other genres. Take that stress on property, for instance (the dowry), and the continuing importance of the natal as well as the marital house, especially when things go wrong: both features show parallels with the propertied world of the orators, when a wife's relatives and their claim for a restoration of dowry can be important factors.[23] Naturally, neither Euripides nor his audience would assume a one-to-one equivalence of the mythical and the real worlds, and would probably not think about it at all. The points are fleeting and casual, but that makes them all the more revealing. They must still not grate or bemuse: the natural connection of ideas must be taken for granted.

Thirdly, we should widen our focus. We have so far been taking the speech largely out of context, as rhetoric aimed at the external theatre-audience; yet one of its points is its plot-function. It is Medea's rhetoric, not just Euripides': and it persuades – indeed, surely over-persuades, transforming Corinthian housewives into champions of something like militant feminism, rejoicing in their next ode that women too will now have songs sung of their great deeds (410–30: in this case, a deed of murderous revenge, as Medea has made clear). And this rhetoric is sinister and devious. 'I was booty from a barbarian land; I have no mother, no brother, no kinsman to offer a haven from this catastrophe.' That is a travesty: she was no booty, but a willing participant, giving (as she stresses elsewhere) the decisive help in return for Jason's oaths. And why does she have no brother? Because she killed him, scattering fragments of her brother Apsyrtus to delay her heartbroken father's pursuit – the first of the several times when she uses a father's love to murderous effect. The audience know it, too: there have already been moments in the play where their acquaintance with Medea's kin-slaying past has been taken for granted ('foully killing my own brother', 166–7: also 31–2 and probably 39, 93–5, 100–9).

Her whole rhetorical strategy is equally disquieting, with those first person plurals, 'we women…'. The insinuation is that, even though my situation is so much worse, I am an ordinary woman like you. The technique is not so different from what we saw with Apollodorus, establishing an us-and-them complicity against the dastardly enemy, there Stephanus, here Jason. Yet Medea is anything but ordinary. By the end of this scene she is praying to queen Hecate for vengeance – appropriately, for witchcraft will play a part in her method. 'I have many ways to kill them, but, dear friends, I do not know which to try first. Shall I burn down the nuptial house with fire, or thrust a whetted dagger through their livers, silently going into the house where the bed is prepared? … No, the best way is the most straightforward, the way for which we were born so gifted – to take them by poison' (376–85). The 'most straightforward' way, nothing subtle like burning the house down or running them through: no, poison – the most straightforward way *for her*. An ordinary woman? Hardly! And yet the chorus stay persuaded: it is just after this passage that they sing their ode in celebration of 'the honour that now comes to the female race' (416). It is part of Medea's *extra*ordinariness that she can carry along these ordinary women so far and so long. Even after the gruesome death of Jason's bride and her loving father Creon, they comment blandly that today is seeing many punishments for Jason, and they are just (*endikos*, 1231–2).

Our previous points about Medea's speech can still stand: the thought associations remain expressive. But now we can add a further association: Medea is clever, particularly with words; and, with sexual passion aroused, that cleverness can be deadly. Suspicion as well as appreciation of rhetoric was a fifth-century Athenian feature, as we saw in Chapter 1 (pp. 5–7, 10–12; see also below, p. 250). This audience can sense Medea's persuasive virtuosity, and are alert to its dangers.

Naturally, it is difficult to generalise from Medea's case: her extraordinariness makes that clear. Some stress her masculine characteristics[24] (by which they normally mean a version of 'heroism', her assertiveness and her insistence that her enemies shall not be able to mock or laugh at her); and by the end she is non-human and demonic. Yet her characteristics articulate a superhuman version of traits which are associated with human women:[25] the overwhelming passion, in particular when sexuality is concerned; the capacity for successful intrigue (plotting in tragedy is regularly more successful if a woman is involved[26]); and, in particular, the virtuoso control of manipulative language. Rationality, *logos*, is prized by Athenians and by males: so is mastery of one's own passions. But there are ways, very alarming ones, where *logos* is found in women too, and female *logos* tends not to confront and control emotion but to serve and advance it. There is a sequence here of paradoxical combinations: women are excluded from civic discourse but central to civic identity (they provide the stream of citizen blood); strangers to the house, yet vital to its perpetuation; dismissed from public debate yet alarmingly rational; mistresses of *logos* in ways which men find bewildering and extremely threatening. These paradoxes will be found in other genres too.

Let us return to that initial, broad point: audiences found such themes interesting. Can we define this interest more closely? In particular, true to this book's principles, can we say more about how it is exploited and developed in the dynamic of the theatrical occasion? In an influential paper Zeitlin argues:

> In the Greek theater ... the self that is really at stake is to be identified with the male, while the woman is assigned the role of the radical other. ... *Functionally* women are never an end in themselves, and nothing changes for them once they have lived out their drama onstage. Rather they play the role of catalysts, agents, instruments, blockers, spoilers, destroyers, and sometimes helpers or saviors for the male characters.[27]

At first sight this is a surprising claim. Many women have their lives changed by their actions while on stage, Medea prime among them: the miseries of her own future are not concealed (818, 1024–7, 1035–7, 1250, 1361–2). Even if we work Zeitlin's 'functionally' hard and stress the male lives changed by Medea, Antigone, or Phaedra, it is hard to think that the real significance of the Trojan women's suffering in *Hecuba*, *Trojan Women*, or even *Andromache* lies in its meaning for the males on stage.

There may be a broader sense, though, in which Zeitlin's remark has purchase, if we switch the focus on the 'self ... at stake' from male stage-figures to male audience. If we try to extract 'morals' in the most simple sense, it is striking how much easier it is to extract them for male behaviour than for female. What should Antigone do? Medea? Hecuba? Phaedra? The questions are real, but they belie simple answers, and it is hard to think that simple approval or disapproval is evinced.[28] It is much easier to be clear that Creon or Jason or Polymestor or Hippolytus was wrong, and there are indeed moral lessons to learn from this. It is not that the audience could apply such lessons in a one-to-one way to their real life experience: what *would* the everyday counterpart of Creon's dilemma be like? It is rather that viewers could enter empathetically into the stage situations, realise (perhaps gradually) that Jason's or Creon's priorities are misguided, and wonder whether there are any implications for their own priorities – and complacencies. Even the *Trojan Women*, with its sharp focus on female miseries, could respond to this type of analysis, if we remember its 415 dating. Whether or not we should think specifically of Athens' treatment of Melos the previous year, the Peloponnesian War is beginning again, and further brutalities are to be expected. Those in the audience who need to be aware what consequences their war-decisions can bring are, once again, the citizen males.

In other plays too the female choices are little more than data, however problematic they might potentially seem, and the issues are raised by the male dilemmas: *Alcestis*, where questions are raised about Admetus' and Pheres' choice to survive, but Alcestis' decision to die for her husband seems uncomplicatedly laudable; *Iphigeneia in Aulis* and *Heracleidae*, where again female self-sacrifice commendably cuts a knot after males have confronted agonising decisions; and the same was presumably true of the most famous Athenian female self-sacrifice of all, that of Praxithea in Euripides' *Erechtheus* (fr. 360 N[2]). That clearer-cut engagement with male choices is no more than we should expect if the target audience is male.

Still, we cannot push this far, for there is *involvement* with female choices too, even if the audience find it less straightforward to answer 'What should she do?' The thrust of so many plays, *Medea* again included, is to make the audience imagine what can drive a woman to kill her own children, what it must be like to face such defeat, desolation, and bereavement (*Hecuba*, *Trojan Women*), how concern for good repute or noble blood can drive a woman to devise her stepson's murder (Phaedra) or cease struggling to save her children's life (Megara in *Heracles*), how a woman can be persecuted (or construct her own persecution) to the brink of personal disintegration (Euripides' *Electra*), or how murderous vindictive rage can be (Hecuba again, Alcmene in *Heracleidae*, the deranged Agave in *Bacchae*).

That returns us to Zeitlin's argument.[29] She suggests that a central part of the tragic experience is 'playing the other', specifically a female 'other': for the audience, this involves empathy with female predicaments and passions, at least in this licensed setting of a Dionysiac festival. (And Dionysus, as a god who mediates between polarities like male/female, savagery/civilisation, old/young is an especially appropriate god to preside over such blurring and transgression of categories.)

> In the end, tragedy arrives at closures that generally reassert male, often paternal, structures of authority, but before that the work of the drama is to open up the masculine view of the universe. It typically does so … through energizing the theatrical resources of the female and concomitantly enervating the male as the price of initiating actor and spectator into new and unsettling modes of feeling, seeing and knowing.[30]

Others put the reassertion of male values more strongly. Hall, for instance, suggests that the terminating satyr-play, with its typical presentation of male satyrs behaving in lewd and uncouth masculine ways, reasserts male normality in a vigorous way 'in order to protect against the painful "feminine" emotions which tragedy has unleashed'.[31]

These are subtle and attractive views. If they are right, we should again resist the temptation to say that such 'playing the other' is not real life because of its distinctive festival setting: once again, this is part of real life along with all the others, and fills out the range of mental response of which a good, properly constituted male citizen should be capable on a distinctively citizen occasion. But it is natural to ask how limited to the festival such 'playing the other' really is, whether any final reassuring assertion of male values is enough to insulate female role-playing safely to this privileged occasion; and also to ponder whether the emotions and engagements encouraged are so distinctively 'female', and if such experiences are necessarily so unsettling.

First, the significance of the festival context. Hall may well be right about the terminating male uncouthness of the satyr-play; it remains a question how far such a conclusion to the day's festivities will offset the tragic experience of the other plays. The masculine reassurance can be real but inadequate, at least for some or even most spectators.[32] After all, the moral suggestions of the plays themselves are hard to confine to the tragic festival; and those suggestions also problematise any simple division into 'male' and 'female' concerns. We noticed that it was easier to debate what Jason or Creon *should* do, however much Medea's and Antigone's choices too engage us. What Jason and Creon get wrong is, arguably, their insensitivity to the proper demands of the *oikos*. And they are not alone: there is Heracles in *Trachiniae*, importing Iole to share the household; there is Agamemnon in the *Oresteia* – whatever we make of the complications at Aulis, his return with Cassandra is less than diplomatic; there is the absent Neoptolemus in *Andromache* (and it is striking, as Hall brings out elsewhere, that tragic females are often particularly transgressive when their *kurios*, their controlling male, is absent[33]). It may be natural that the females feel the needs of the *oikos* more completely, for that is their distinctive sphere; but males need to feel these things too, and it is catastrophic if they do not.

Compare too the *Bacchae*: once again it is the women whose irrationality eventually proves so menacing; but once again what initiates the catastrophe is Pentheus' refusal to accept the place of the Dionysiac in human experience. More particularly, he refuses to accept Dionysus himself, son of Semele, a member of his own *family*; and once again it is the family itself which is destroyed, with first the physical destruction of the house and then the final fragmentation, with Pentheus destroyed and Cadmus departing for exile with his wife Harmonia. Here, as in the other plays, what generates the catastrophe encompasses the females and their distinctive traits, especially their passion. But it was initially the males' fault for failing to take the whole range of legitimate responses, female and male, into account: in effect, for failing to respond to women as empathetically as the target male audience is encouraged to do. What is required is not a firm division designating the *oikos*, the 'within', as a female domain and the public *polis* as the male one, but a more productive and consistent sensitivity of *polis* to *oikos*, of male to female.[34] And the suggestions of *that* insight are not easy to limit to a moment of licensed transgression. That insight is for the whole of life.

There is no need to present all this as if the playwright was earnestly preaching a moral creed which his audience would find new and surprising, breaking down entrenched gender prejudices. We have seen before that moralising works best if it is not inculcating but reflecting, if it is working on and reinforcing the moral assumptions that the audience already have. That takes us to the question whether these empathetic 'modes of feeling, seeing and knowing' are really so distinctively associated with the feminine as Zeitlin suggests; and whether they really so 'enervate' the male, even transiently. For Zeitlin pity, for instance, is one of these softer 'female' traits commended to the males in the tragic experience.[35] Yet pity is found in oratory too as a distinctive part of the Athenian civic self-image:[36] this is not a momentary self-indulgence to be cast away or refined as the stronger male qualities reassert themselves, but a traditional claim of which citizens could always be proud.

At the other end of the moral scale from pity, is vindictive rage, for instance, felt as the preserve of the female? Thucydides' Cleon, defending such anger and vindictiveness as proper for an imperial city, gives one pause. Or grief? That *can* be figured as 'female', with restraint as correspondingly 'male': Plato, for instance, speaks in that way in his more repressive moods (e.g. *Republic* 387e–8a, 605c–d);[37] so does Euripides' *Medea*, in the course of hoodwinking Jason – 'a woman is a female thing, born for tears' (*Medea* 928). But Plato has to be repressive precisely because men too *do* go in for grief as well; Jason certainly will, later in the play. We also saw earlier that, even if Thucydides' 'Pericles' is (expressively) cold towards the bereaved, real Funeral Speeches were more ready to acknowledge those who grieved, males as well as females (above, p. 190). What, too, of trickery and deceit? Women may have a particular gift for that, as we saw; but the master of deviousness was already there in the *Odyssey*, and that master was male.

No doubt all these cases are more complex. The world of the *Odyssey* is one in which women play a large part, and it is telling that Odysseus has to behave in such irregular ways for a hero; it may be one of the disquieting things about Cleon that he commends what is so hard to defend in rational terms; it matters that the ideological construct of grieving as 'female' is available to Plato, even if it is not the only construct possible; and, even if males and females are both capable of empathy and pity, they may be figured as indulging this in different, more or less rational or emotional, idioms. Thus, famously, Aristotle: 'woman is more compassionate than man, more tearful, more given to envy and discontent with her lot, more likely to abuse and to strike out...' (*Hist. An.* 608b9–11). Still, even Aristotle is only talking about matters of degree ('more'), and in fact builds a zoological picture of the sexes which is subtler and admits exceptions.[38] The regularity with which gender categories are blurred remains striking; there must come a point where the transgression of expected boundaries becomes too familiar to shock or to challenge.

Perhaps, though, 'shocks' and 'challenges' are not the best way of putting it. If these modes of feeling are not quite so 'new and unsettling' as Zeitlin suggests, there is no need to deny the value, including the value to the historian, of much of her argument. Male spectators *are* invited to empathise with women, and this involvement with a female viewpoint may involve reassessment of their own responses to complicated issues: that much survives from our treatment of *Medea*. And, if clear-cut divisions of female and male characteristics have proved elusive, that does not mean that the distinctions are worthless. Fifth-century Greeks liked binary polarities, that is clear; but they also knew that a polarity does not need to be absolute to be useful – indeed, can be *more* heuristically valuable if boundaries blur and if there are marginal cases which invite further investigation (in Greek scientific terms, *epamphoterizonta*, cases which belong on both sides of a divide[39]). No scheme could be more natural than 'male'/'female': but, like other binary schemes such as 'Greek'/'barbarian', *oikos/polis*, even 'human'/ 'divine', it is a way of exploring, not a mental straitjacket.

So, if males are presented with aspects of the household which they need to respect, or are invited to identify with a female character's viewpoint, not all need have found this surprising or disconcerting; any more than Greek identity need be rocked by the insight that barbarians are often not too different, and Greeks can perpetrate the same sort of outrages. Such recognition had long been familiar, at least since the *Iliad* had brought out that the female voice of pitiable suffering captured something as important about war as the male preoccupation with glory.[40]

## Gendering comically

By the two goddesses, it is not ambition that has brought me to my feet to speak, ladies: but, for a long time now, I have been miserable and indignant to see how you are rubbished by Euripides, that son of a greengroceress, and having all sorts of dreadful things said about you. For what charge hasn't he rubbed off on to us? Where has he not attacked us, wherever there are spectators and tragic actors and choruses, calling us adulteresses, man-chasers, drunks, traitresses, chatterboxes, scabs, curses on men? So whenever they come back from the theatre, they give us a suspicious look, and hunt around to see whether there is a lover hidden anywhere in the house.

We can't do any of the things we used to: he's taught our men bad habits [or 'our bad ways']. A woman is weaving a garland: she must be in love. She is walking round the house and breaks something: her man asks, 'who is this pot broken for? It must be that stranger from Corinth'. A young girl is sick: her brother says straight off, 'I don't like the look of the girl's colour'. That's how it is. Then a woman, desperate for children, wants to pass off a baby on her husband – and she can't get away with that either, for the men are sitting there all the time. And what of the old men who used to marry young girls? He's put them off too: no old man these days wants to marry a woman, because of that line 'A woman is tyrant to a bridegroom who's old'. What's more, it's Euripides' fault that men are now putting up seals and bars to keep us in, and keeping Molossian dogs to put the scarers on our lovers.

All that we could forgive. But what of the things we used to take care of, and take some for ourselves – barley, olive-oil, wine? We can't do that any more either! For our husbands are now carrying keys around themselves, secret ones, dreadful, Spartan things, with three teeth. We used to be able to open the doors by having a ring made for three obols; now this curse on the house, this Euripides, has taught them to have seals made of worm-eaten wood, and carry them round hanging on their bodies.

Now, then, my proposal is to cook up some destruction or other for him, with poison or with some trick or other, to get rid of him. That is what I say publicly: the rest I shall get drafted with the secretary.

(Aristophanes, *Thesmophoriazusae* 383–432)

Thus the 'First Woman' – we later learn her name is Mica – in the assembly scene in *Thesmophoriazusae*. Comedy, as we have seen, typically relates to everyday life in more straightforward and direct ways than tragedy. What, if anything, can we learn from this about women's 'everyday life' – or, more accurately, about everyday male constructions of women and their life?

As with *Acharnians* (above, Chapter 8), we have first to be alert to parody, on several different levels. There is parody of a male assembly. Part of the point here is the fantastic reversal. The woman provides her own version of assembly-speak: she begins and ends with formal language, first the address to 'ladies' rather than 'gentlemen' (and with the feminine oath 'by the two goddesses' rather than, say, 'by Apollo' or just 'by the gods', cf. *Eccl.* 155–60, 171), then at the end talk of 'her proposal' and her intention to sort out the formalities with the 'secretary' afterwards. Like male speakers, she explains why she has had to overcome her previous diffidence, getting up to speak because of her indignation at what she 'sees'.[41] Then there is 'parody', though that may not be quite the word, of particular Euripidean originals: there seem to be recollections of a number of plays – most likely, *Stheneboea*, *Aeolus* or *Scyrians*, *Phoenix*, and *Danae*[42] – which had lovelorn women weaving crowns, breaking pots, losing colour, passing off suppositious children, lording it over old men, or being locked up. Some of these doubtless reflect real-life counterparts *as well*: it would be odd if losing colour had not figured in everyday love-affairs. But it would be rash to infer that passing off suppositious children, for instance, was a regular feature of real life (whatever the kinsman may say (502–17, 564–5) – that just takes the joke further, with reality and dramatic stereotype by now thoroughly jumbled[43]). It is a regular comic rhythm for a list to become more and more outlandish and fantastic as it goes on. What gives it point is the Euripidean original, not everyday life.

What about the keys? It requires faith to believe that husbands were really carrying three-toothed monstrosities on their belts. But, just as we saw earlier (Chapter 7, pp. 130–3), more telling than the fantasies themselves is what is taken for granted, what the audience must be assuming if they are not to be puzzled or distracted. In the good old days, it was still the case that men locked the store-rooms: in this comic world those locks were simply easier to pick, and a three-obol ring would do the job. Now naturally we need not strain the joke to infer that *all* real-life women regularly had *no* access to keys. Theophrastus' eighteenth character, the 'mistrustful man', asks his wife in bed if she has shut the chest and sealed the *kuliouchion* (perhaps 'money-box') and barred the door, and cannot stop himself getting up to check (18.4); but even he was evidently not so mistrustful as to insist on doing the initial locking-up himself. All that is necessary to make Aristophanes' joke intelligible is for some stores regularly to be locked,[44] so that 'keys' can be introduced without explanation (even so soon after a passage where other keys, those to the women's quarters, were in point); and, crucially, for overall male authority to be assumed, even here within the house. The woman was storekeeper, but under his authority.[45]

Earlier, it is taken for granted that the men will be returning from the theatre when the women have been at home: both points are required for the joke (the husbands need all that tragedy running through their heads to provide their instant quotes; the women need to have had a chance to entertain their lovers), and it does not follow that women never attended the theatre at all – but it would be distracting if husbands and wives regularly attended the theatre *together*. If that had been normal as it is today, the joke would have needed another step – an excuse, perhaps, why the wife was too unwell to go with the husband that morning.

Is there anything wider that is 'taken for granted'? The picture centres on the household, and at first glance that supports 'within' as the female domain; but second glance corrects or supplements that, for the next woman sells garlands in the market, and speaks of the damage to her business caused by Euripides and his new-fangled gods. True, she has her reasons for operating 'outside', and she finds it natural to give them: her husband died years ago on campaign, leaving her with five children (446–8).[46] But, in this more 'realistic' world than tragedy, women do operate in public, particularly when religion is involved.

Other 'taken-for-granted' elements concern male prejudice. A large part of the joke is that Mica keeps giving herself away, revealing that – in this comic world – all Euripides' slanders are true. There *are* lovers to be frightened off by the dogs; they *were* used to slipping the locks; the problem is that Euripides has blown their gaffe, and they cannot get away with it any more. This is the female stereotype so familiar from other comedies, the sexually ravenous and unfaithful woman: and the kinsman duly defends Euripides on the grounds that there are so many other things, especially sexual, that he might have revealed had he wished (466–520; cf. 'Euripides' himself at 1167–9). Other aspects soon recur. When the *Telephus* hostage scene (Chapter

8, pp. 141–145) is played out yet again, the hunted kinsman grabs a wine-skin which Mica has under her clothes as her 'baby' (688ff.): that is now the hostage, as dear to the women as the charcoal-burner was to the Acharnians. These women are as devoted to wine as to sex.

One cannot imagine Medea or Hecuba or Antigone as a bibulous lady of easy virtue, and we seem some distance from the seriousness with which women are treated in tragedy. Or are we? Tragedy and comedy have their own registers and idioms, but in each some of the same themes recur: the deceptive speech, the lack of self-control, the proneness to emotion, desire, and passion, the concern with the body and its gratification – and especially when the menfolk are away or when a woman is responding to a perceived male slighting of her concerns. And there are similar dangers too, even in the same way: Mica too thinks of poisons or drugs as her natural weapon (*pharmaka*, 430) – though this may also be part of the joke, with Euripides paid back in his own typical coin.[47] In Chapter 7 we noticed that even a comic conception can reveal a mental schema, and here again there seems some basic patterning of male prejudice. Once again, we cannot assume that its comic articulation maps in a one-to-one way on to the viewers' assumptions about their own womenfolk, any more than a *Carry On* film would be an accurate guide to the prejudices of 1970s Britain. But here as there, one cannot ignore these stereotypes as irrelevant, 'only' a joke. They remain one way of looking at women along with the others; and they will have played a part in constituting male perceptions as well as reflecting them. We can see oratory too adopting comic stereotyping when it suits a speaker's purpose:[48] so too does historiography, though rarely.[49] Once one genre has established the stereotype it is an available construction for others, and part of 'real life' mentality.

Mica is articulate, that is clear; so, in other plays, is Lysistrata, and so is the Praxagora of *Ecclesiazusae*. That too reflects in its own idiom a feature of tragedy, the female control of *logos*. But here there is a curious formal point. For its own reasons, Old Comedy often operated with some rather formal dramatic structures. In Chapters 7 and 8 we spent some time on various 'parabases', one of those structures; another is the 'epirrhematic agon', where two speakers join in debate, and in a reasonably strict format present first one side of the argument and then the other. The chorus encourage the first speaker; then that speaker presents, with interruptions, his point of view, normally in tetrameters and possibly chanted rather than spoken;[50] the chorus sing an ode in response, then encourage the other speaker; then that other speaker has his turn. That is how the two arguments fight it out in *Clouds* (889–1114), how Philocleon and Bdelycleon argue in *Wasps* (540–724), and how, in a complex elaboration, Aeschylus and Euripides confront one another in *Frogs*. But comedy's formal patterns are never indispensable, and Dicaeopolis did not confront the Acharnians or Lamachus in this form; nor do we find a regular epirrhematic agon in *Thesmophoriazusae*, and that in *Lysistrata* is also very odd, even though verbal confrontations are central to both plays. In *Thesmophoriazusae* there are three speakers, not two, and they use iambics; in *Lysistrata* the Magistrate uses his 'turn' (486–537) more for angry questions than for arguing his case, and here too Lysistrata herself does most of the talking (or chanting).

Why? The parallel with *Acharnians* gives a clue. It is essential for an epirrhematic agon that the two sides agree to debate: one side will go first, then the other. The Acharnians are too livid to agree to this: at first Dicaeopolis' case strikes them as too outlandish to deserve a reply. The same goes for *Lysistrata*. The Magistrate would never agree to hear Lysistrata out and engage in a formal debate, for it is simply monstrous that a woman should be speaking like this. And *Thesmophoriazusae* too can be treated similarly. The women engage in 'debate' assuming that they will all be arguing the same way. Had they known in advance that anyone would take Euripides' part, they would not calmly agree to listen: they would have been furious, just as they are once the kinsman's speech has taken them by surprise (520ff.).

Is this too a comic analogue to tragedy? Should we conclude that again women are virtuoso manipulators of words, but again those words subserve passion – too much passion for those words to be delivered in a properly calm and controlled way? In part, yes; but only in part. The *Lysistrata* scene gives one pause, for the loss of control is there on the side of the Magistrate. Lysistrata, we saw earlier (p. 195), has to be felt as talking sense, even if dangerous sense: she is the counterpart of Dicaeopolis, the Magistrate corresponds to the short-sighted and blustery Acharnians or Lamachus. It may be less the female speaker, more the nature of the issue in such battles of the sexes, that stands in the way of reasoned, formal debate.

If we seek a tragic analogy, it may rather be in that paradox of woman as evidently rational, insightful, and articulate, yet simultaneously marginalised and excluded from regular public discussion – a paradox which, as we hinted, is familiar from the *Iliad*, with those insights which women offer into a male world. A favourite ploy in modern mind-games is to ponder what a time-traveller or a visiting Martian would make of … the welfare state, the Christmas season, the Spice Girls, the World Cup, whatever it may be. (This book used it once: Chapter 7, pp. 123–4.) The time-traveller or a Martian is useful because she is assumed to be rational, yet without the cultural prejudices which our society has embedded in us. Fifth-century Athenian males found (the males' own version of) female perceptions useful for a similar strategy, looking at an issue with a rational but fresh viewpoint – and usually talking a sort of *sense*. (This may be one reason why there are so many female choruses in tragedy:[51] the audience do not of course simply appropriate choral views and frequently see their inadequacy – but there too the female viewpoint can open new perspectives on the action for the male spectators.)

The analogy cannot be pressed too far: indeed, when the plays use female viewpoints as eye-openers it is normally essential that the women are *not* unprejudiced, but retain their own cultural assumptions. Lysistrata and Praxagora may be 'masculine' in their assertiveness, and in the public roles they aspire to play; but, like the transgressively strong females of tragedy, they remain distinctively female in their approach and methods. This is an *alternative* viewpoint, not a wholly fresh one. The female viewpoint in the *Iliad* concentrated on war's devastating effect on the family, and Lysistrata does so too (*Lys.* 588–92). Just before, she has spoken of her new approach to politics and has carried with her all the mentality of the *oikos* and its female tasks:[52]

| | |
|---|---|
| *Magistrate:* | So how will you be able to put an end to all the confusion in the lands and clear it up? |
| *Lysistrata:* | Very easily. |
| *Magistrate:* | How? Tell me. |
| *Lysistrata:* | Just like a skein of wool when it gets tangled. We take it, we put it on our needles, we pull it gently first in one direction and then in another. That's the way we'll stop the war, if we're allowed; we'll use embassies, one to one place and one to another. |
| *Magistrate:* | You think wool and skeins and needles will help you to stop something serious? What morons! |
| *Lysistrata:* | You too, if you had had any sense, would have run things like our wool. |

| | |
|---|---|
| *Magistrate:* | How? I'd like to know. |
| *Lysistrata:* | It's just like a fleece in a bath. What you should have done first is to wash the dung out of the city, beating out the villains on a bed and picking out the caltrops; then take those who combine and press up together to get office, and card them out and knock their heads off; then mix everyone up together and comb them into a basket of general goodwill. You should mix in the metics and any foreigner who's our friend, and anyone too who's in debt to the treasury; and yes, you should also look at the cities who are the colonies of our land, and realise that these are like separate flocks of wool, each of them; so you should take all these flocks from each and bring them here and gather them into one, then make it all into a great ball, and use it to weave a cloak for the people. |

(Aristophanes, *Lysistrata* 565–86)

Margaret Thatcher, alert as ever to a populist line, once compared running the British economy to running the grocer's shop in which she was brought up: she always knew then that at the end of the week the books needed to balance. The experts could sneer; but many of the public felt uneasily that the domestic model might have something in it after all. Lysistrata too would not be too easy for even the most dismissive male to write off; and in her domestic, female idioms lies her strength. She provides a critique of contemporary politics which has its own logic, recognisable but different from the political logic which normally prevailed.

In *Ecclesiazusae* too (late 390s BC, perhaps 391[53]) Praxagora appeals to the women's expertise as storekeepers of the household as a reason for trusting them to run the city (211–12): *they* know you never make progress by chopping and changing (215ff.), and, once again, they know and they care about the city, as it is their sons who are at risk (233–4). Once again, too, they can see the idiocy of the men in failing to throw out what is rotten (176–208). Later, though, the women chop and change to a spectacular degree once in control, introducing a utopian form of communism, with predictable emphasis on the sexual aspects. It is no coincidence that it is women who find the communism so attractive. That is partly plot-directed, because of the sex. With women in charge, it allows all the jokes of the last part of the play, with the randy old women who cannot wait to get their hands on the attractive young man, a bizarre reversal of the regular closural male predations.[54] But women's other stereotypical concerns too, not just the sexual (224–8), go with the communist emphasis. In the household they provide food for all, and make sure there is enough money to go round (234–5, 442); women neighbours can share and borrow, without trying man-like to put one over on one another (446–50); as for the law-courts (the keynote of male Athenian democracy, as we saw in Chapters 7 and 9), women's co-operative natures will mean an end to all those prosecutions, sycophants, and false witnesses (452–3, 561–2, 676). No-one will be a thief, for everyone will have enough; no-one will go poor or naked (565–7, 604–5, cf. *Lys.* 1207–12) or hungry, for all the meals will be in common too. Just, indeed, like one big happy *family*, and Praxagora describes it as 'creating one big family house' (673–4).[55]

The communist programme is interesting in all sorts of ways. Once again the audience must be *interested*. Whether or not it is Plato who has already put such *Republic*-like ideas in the air around 391,[56] we can assume a public which will find, probably has already found, such ideas as intriguing as they are outlandish. But the unfamiliar logic again makes it appropriate that it is a woman's idea. The male audience can find the female viewpoint 'good to think with'. We seem to have a further counterpart to tragedy, this time to that empathetic 'playing the other' which Zeitlin found distinctive of the tragic viewing experience and which, with some reservations, we accepted.[57]

This is only one strand in the comic construction of women. A fuller treatment would stress the male acknowledgement of women's public role in the religious sphere: the female chorus of *Lysistrata* cite their involvement in festivals since childhood as a token of their involvement in the city (*Lys.* 636–47).[58] Here too there is a parallel with tragedy, in its different register. In Euripides' *Captive Melanippe*[59] a speaker claims that women are superior to men firstly because they preserve the *oikos*, and secondly because they play the most important part in religion – consider (she says) the Pythia, for instance, or the priestesses at Dodona. The claim of superiority is doubtless provocative, and for all we know the speaker may have paid for it later in the play;[60] still, the association of ideas must not have seemed ridiculous. Once again a woman speaks a sort of unsettling sense.

Much of the comic female, though, is less respected. Very often women serve not as filters for intrigued male involvement but as objectified targets for other forms of fantasy, especially sexual fantasy.

Once again, it is what is taken for granted that is most telling: the casualisation of rape, for instance, in passages like *Acharnians* 271–5, *Peace* 1337–40, and *Birds* 1252–6, as so often in New Comedy[61] (here tragedy can be similar, though it shows less relish for the prurient detail: *Ion* 545–54). In particular, the ends of comedies typically generate boisterous bonhomie, and the role envisaged for women tends to be simple and basic. When Philocleon steals the flute-girl (Chapter 7, p. 138), when the men in *Lysistrata* admire the geography of the naked female Reconciliation (Chapter 8, p. 160), when Dicaeopolis staggers off to his party with a girl on each arm, it is not a communion of true minds which the males have in prospect. And even this use of a female perceptual filter has more than one aspect. I have been presenting it as an enlightened form of mind-game, as if the audience would simply relish the fun of the fantasy and the excitement of intellectual experiment; but those spectators who chose (like our spectator A of *Medea*, p. 199) could equally seize on the femaleness of the viewpoint in order to disqualify it, to protect themselves from an alternative viewpoint which they found uncomfortable and would therefore discount as reassuringly ridiculous.[62] And nothing would prevent the different responses, the relish and the dismissiveness, from co-existing in the same spectator.

What is more, it is normally (male) political issues rather than the female condition itself which the audience are invited to think in new ways about. An important element in these fantasies is an affectation of despair about men, those men who have made such a dog's breakfast that even the women could do better. True, the use of a refreshing new filter for viewing old issues can hardly evade reflection on the filter as well as the issues; yet at the end of the plays the females usually (*Ecclesiazusae* is a partial exception) revert to their previous subordinate status, acquiescently at one with the males again in that closural mood of bonhomie. Even in *Thesmophoriazusae* the women finally, for reasons which are not explicit,[63] connive in the kinsman's escape rather than continuing to call for his blood; and after all 'Euripides'' subtle devices have failed, the simplest trick of all, a seductive dancing girl, turns out to work. That device exploits robust and crude masculine sexuality, the simplest gender categorisation of all, and here too normal service is being resumed. In tragedy too we noticed the argument for some final reassertion of male values; here too, even for the more sympathetic viewers, the female filtering need not last too long.

'Misogyny' is a word which often comes to scholars' and readers' minds when they reflect on fifth-century male perceptions, especially comic perceptions. It is easy to see why. Of course so much seems objectionable, and the more so because it echoes perceptions uncomfortably familiar from our own society: the objectification of women, the concentration on the body, the reductionist assumptions of what constitutes female concerns, the persistent emphasis on the emotional and the uncontrolled. But 'misogyny' is still too broad and culturally determined a word to be useful. If our time-travellers, male or female, came from fifth-century Athens, they would find our use of it more illuminating about our own cultural expectations than about theirs. It brings out only one side of the uneasy fascination with females, both empathetic and apprehensive, which typifies fifth-century drama; and the word suggests a closed-mindedness which renders incomprehensible many of the themes and theatrical strategies which the playwrights chose, both tragic and comic.

Even that reduction of the comic woman's preoccupations to the bodily, the sexual, and the vinous can be looked at in more than one way. The comic male's preoccupations are pretty bodily, sexual, and vinous too, and comedy celebrates them. Here, once again, the Other is not so Other as all that.

## Gendering forensically

The orators provide most of our information on the legal status of Athenian women; and to us that status seems extraordinary. A woman, it is often (misleadingly) said,[64] is a perpetual minor, needing a male *kurios* to act on her behalf, first her father, then her husband, then on her husband's death her son (or, if he is a minor, his own *kurios*); she is legally incapable of making any agreement involving more than a *medimnos* of barley (a few days' supply for a family – how interesting that it should be defined in this way!); her father can dissolve her marriage even against her will. Women are pervasively linked with property: the property which she comes with, bringing it into a house as a dowry; the property which passes to her new *kurios* if her husband dies, and reverts to her original *kurios* if she herself dies childless; or that other property, that of her husband, for which she through childbirth will provide an heir. To our minds, she seems a property herself: modern eyebrows rise when we notice how speakers designate respectable women not by their names but as the wife, daughter, or sister of a named male: not so much X, more the woman of Y.[65]

This conceptualisation is seen most sharply in those cases where a woman is an 'heiress', or more precisely an *epikleros* (for unlike an heiress she cannot legally control any inheritance[66]): that is, when her father dies without sons, so that she alone provides the conduit whereby the estate will pass on to a new generation.[67] In such cases the nearest available male relative of the deceased has the right to marry the *epikleros*, in some circumstances even if she is married already and a divorce is necessary. In property terms, it makes a sort of sense: thus, and only thus, can the estate stay within the man's natal family. 'Thus, and only thus' – provided, that is, society has accepted the initial assumptions that (a) a woman cannot herself own the property she inherits, (b) her children no longer belong to her own natal family but only to her husband's, and (c) it was not enough simply to leave the property to the nearest male relative, but it has to 'go with' her instead, eventually finding its way to her children. The reasons behind those assumptions doubtless repay exploration;[68] in a male-dominated society the last one in particular is not self-evident, for men without legitimate sons could legally leave their property as they chose. It doubtless has something to do with the male's desire to continue not merely collateral family but also something of blood-line, and that (whatever Aeschylus' Apollo might say[69]) would naturally be figured as a matter involving women as well as men. Nor is this simply a question of property. The notion of 'a deserted *oikos*' was emotionally as well as economically chilling: it was important to have a linear descendant to carry on the household cult, and the daughter could provide that line.[70] So once again the paradox recurs: women as both insiders and outsiders, central to the permanence of the *oikos* and its property, yet marginalised from the control of that same property.

We are used to litigious societies, and used too to the assumption that, if a status lacks legal underpinning, then it is unacceptably precarious. No wonder scholars have looked closely at women's legal position in Athens, and that so many of the best discussions at least begin with the legal material.[71] Perhaps this assumption of law's primacy should be questioned.[72] We can see that Athenian women sometimes managed sums of money and conducted transactions far greater than their legal capacity.[73] And there is a wider question of method: if, for instance, we were investigating the discovery and sentimentalisation of childhood in the last two centuries, legislation and court-cases about children's rights would give a part of the picture, but only a part. In particular, there are special reasons for that recurring emphasis on property in the orators. These are largely civil cases where property is at stake (hence the emphasis on the *epiklerate*); and not just any property, for these are cases involving the richest patrons, men who could afford to pay the best speech-writers.

There is still much to be said for this emphasis on the law, despite the atypicality of those involved. If our societies are litigious, then so was Athens; we have seen how 'the rule of law', particularly the authority of the law-courts, was central to Athenian identity (Chapters 1, 7, and 9). The litigants were rich but the jurors were often not: it would be odd if the ideals of women conveyed in court-speeches had no trickle-down effect on those who listened to them, just as middle-class television comedies of the 1950s and 1960s affected working-class domestic conceptions too.[74] That is especially true if we were right (Chapter 1) to think of jurors adopting a mindset more appropriate to their richer fellow-citizens. If Lysias can remind his listeners of the days when 'you had big houses', or Demosthenes can imply that property-taxes would be relevant to a sizeable number of his audience (Lys. 28.3; Dem. 1.6 etc.; Chapter 1, pp. 13–14), then it would hardly be surprising if the mentality implied in court con-structions of women came to be appropriated even by citizens whose circumstances were leaner; and we found some support for this in the thought-associations in Medea's speech (above, pp. 200–1), where the stress on dowries, for instance, and natal families maps closely on to the favourite themes of the courts.

We do, however, need to be on perpetual alert to the speakers' rhetorical strategies. That is evident when we are considering the facts of each case: we saw earlier (Chapter 2, p. 27) that Mandy Rice Davies' 'he *would* say that, wouldn't he?' is often called for when speakers make factual claims necessary to their case, and that is particularly so when they talk of their own or their opponents' womenfolk. Women, particularly rich women, often had little public visibility. It could even be a matter of dispute whether a man had had a woman living with him as his wife (Isaeus 6.13–16, Demosthenes 30.27), or a girl brought up in his house as his daughter (Isaeus 8.7–29). A person who is little seen is a person about whom almost anything can be claimed.

We also need to be vigilant about something more sophisticated which scholars use, what we may call the 'plausible might-have-been' argument. That usually runs something like this: we cannot know whether such or such a claim is factually true, but what matters is that it *might* have been true, that the jurors must find it a plausible picture; and that is just as valuable to the historian. That is a tempting step, and we used a version of it when discussing the evidence of Andocides' *On the Mysteries* for *hetaireiai* (Chapter 2, pp. 37–8). But that example suggests the limitations of this strategy as well as its possibilities. There, as often, the 'picture' painted was of a social class whose lifestyle was not too familiar to the jurors, and we found reason to suspect some fictitious colouring even of 'what might have been'. We cannot assume a one-to-one equivalence of the constructs the jurors can accept and the way things 'really' were: there is doubtless some relation of the two, but it may not be exact. We are sometimes on firmer ground when we consider, not how factually plausible a picture may be, but how attractive the jurors are expected to find it: after all, it is normally safe to expect a litigant's picture of himself or his family to be sympathetic, and that of the opponents to be hostile. But here too a simple categorisation as 'sympathetic' or 'unsympathetic' may be inadequate to the complexities of an argument.

Let us test all this in a particular case, Lysias' *On the Murder of Eratosthenes* (1). The speaker Euphiletus there admits the killing, but claims it was justified: he caught his wife in bed with Eratosthenes, and in such cases the law authorises the husband to inflict death on the adulterer.

The speech is a specially skilled production, with Lysias characterising the speaker in a subtle way; its vivid narrative also sketches a fascinating picture of Euphiletus' household and the course of his marriage. Euphiletus claims he kept a close eye on his wife in the early days, but once their child was born (notice the implicit claim that his child was legitimate)[75] he began to put greater trust in her. More's the pity. The trouble started on the day of his mother's funeral. His wife – typically, we never discover her name – left the house to go to the funeral; Eratosthenes spotted her, and later used her maid as a go-between to start the affair. We shall see more in a moment of the (beautifully told) way in which Euphiletus first discovered about the affair.

Then further information began to arrive. A discarded lover of Eratosthenes got her own back by sending to Euphiletus to tell him about the affair; eventually Euphiletus managed to extract the truth from his own household slave, the go-between, and this girl promised to let Euphiletus know the next time Eratosthenes visited. That duly happened, and Euphiletus gathered a posse of friends to act as witnesses; they burst in, and the first to arrive saw him still in bed with my wife, those who followed saw him standing up naked on the bed. Gentlemen, I hit him and knocked him down, then pinned his arms behind his back and tied him up. 'What is the meaning of this *hubris*,' I asked him, 'coming into my house like this?' He confessed he was in the wrong, but begged and pleaded with me not to kill him but to exact money instead. I said, 'It is not I who will be killing you, but the law of the city, which you have broken and regarded as less important than your own pleasures, preferring to commit such a wrong against my wife and my children than to obey the laws and behave decently'.

(Lysias 1.24–6)

The striking language here hides some equivocation, as various other courses of action were available to Euphiletus (that is why Eratosthenes can plead with him to 'exact money instead').[76] The law might permit killing, but it certainly did not 'order' it in the way he claims: this, we shall see, is most important to Euphiletus' defence strategy.

Thus the man died. His relatives were now prosecuting Euphiletus for homicide. They apparently acknowledged the sex (with so many witnesses it would have been hard to deny) but claimed that there was entrapment: as Lysias puts it, they claimed that Eratosthenes had been 'dragged in from the road' (§ 27). That would hardly explain everything. Those forcibly kidnapped do not normally end up naked in bed with their captor's wife, and Lysias is presumably picking those words to underline the implausibility (the prosecution, so it later seems, claimed that Eratosthenes was invited by a message, not really 'dragged in from the road': § 37). Still, it does seem that a husband's connivance offered a defence in adultery cases.[77] Eratosthenes' relatives could easily argue that Euphiletus knew what was going on (he almost admits as much) and was allowing the couple enough rope to hang themselves. He clearly needs to protect himself against that charge. At one point he seems to be building himself a second line of defence in case jurors disbelieve his simple denial of entrapment: even if he had sent the go-between himself that day to invite Eratosthenes, as the prosecution allege, that would surely be defensible when the man had so often done it before... (§§ 37–8).

We shall never know how far Euphiletus genuinely 'entrapped' Eratosthenes: certainly, there are suspicious features about his case.[78] There is anyway a blurred line between waiting to confirm a suspicion and 'connivance' in the naughtiness one suspects but cannot prove. Nor do we know if Euphiletus was acquitted. But, whatever his guilt or innocence, what can we infer from this speech about social life? First, the account of the early signs of the affair.

> In the first place, gentlemen (I do need to explain this) I have a little two-storeyed house, with the same dimensions on the two floors for men's quarters (*andronitis*) and for women's (*gunaikonitis*). When our child was born, the mother breast-fed the baby herself. To save her any risk in clambering down the staircase whenever the baby needed washing, I lived upstairs and the women down –
>
> (§ 9)

in other words, the opposite of the normal arrangement where the men's quarters would be nearer to the street and the house-door. For some time the arrangement worked well, and Euphiletus had no suspicions.

> Time went on, gentlemen, and on one occasion I returned unexpectedly from the country. After dinner the baby began to cry and grouse: the maid was deliberately hurting the child to make sure this happened, for the man was there. (I found all this out later.) I told my wife to go and feed the baby and stop the crying. At first she was reluctant. I had been away for a long time, and she was glad to have me back – that was the pretence. Then I grew cross and told her to go. 'Yes,' she said, 'it's so that you can have a go at the little slave-girl up here: you mauled her about before when you were drunk'. I laughed, and she got up, left, closed the door, pretending it was a joke, and took the key with her. I thought nothing of it, and had no suspicions. I slept deeply after my journey from the country.
>
> (§§ 11–13)

And even when he heard the doors banging in the night, he was fobbed off with an excuse that his wife had to get a light from a neighbour. It was odd, he thought: she seemed to be wearing make-up, even though her brother had died less than a month before (§ 14). But he still thought nothing of it. It was only the old servant from the rejected rival that roused his suspicions (§§ 15–17).

First, the arrangements of the house. It is natural to talk of this 'humble household':[79] that is the impression that Euphiletus himself gives, with this 'little house' (*oikidion*). In fact, the house was probably not as humble as all that. Euphiletus was wealthy enough to have a country property as well as a town-house,[80] and to hire Lysias' services; but there are advantages in making his circumstances not *too* different from those of the poorer jurors. There are several further reasons to dwell on these household arrangements. They cover an awkward point in the argument, explaining how Eratosthenes could have been a sexual visitor *without Euphiletus' knowledge* (for that would constitute connivance): he needs to make this clearly respectable. This desire for respectability is also reflected in Euphiletus' insistence on the way he kept men's and women's quarters separate, even though it led to an irregular arrangement. In many genuinely humble households that would not be possible; archaeology suggests that there was frequently no firm separation of female quarters, even if where possible a room was kept for the men.[81]

We cannot then infer the *normality* of seclusion, in a simple 'plausible might-have-been' way; but it does suggest that jurors again here accepted the practice of their richer fellow-citizens as *normative*, even if their own houses fell short of the ideal. Other speeches too are at pains to emphasise that the speaker kept his women as separate as possible, even when the house had fallen on hard times.[82]

So far Euphiletus' self-characterisation is simple, a conventional respectable man. The same is true in the way he emphasises that Eratosthenes needed a go-between, and it was only his wife's rare excursion to her mother-in-law's funeral which allowed him sight of her. Not every citizen woman would be so confined to indoors, including doubtless many of the jurors' wives; but this was a model household, again normative rather than normal.

Some of the self-characterisation is more individual. Euphiletus does *not* simply behave the way any good man would behave: he is too gullible. He is extraordinarily slow to suspect – and he stresses it, as we have seen. Once again, there are reasons. One is to stress the enormity of the outrage: why, his wife's affair was so blatant that she went with her lover's mother to the Thesmophoria, during one of Euphiletus' absences in the countryside (§ 20); Eratosthenes had been in the house 'often' before (§ 38, again in these frequent absences – no wonder this country-estate is so stressed). Clearly the lovers were taking it for granted that Euphiletus would not suspect a thing. Far more important, it provides an implicit defence against the charge of entrapment.[83] This is not the man who will skilfully and ruthlessly set about luring his victims: he is far too simple.

This affects the way we should read the bedroom scene with his wife (§§ 11–13). The teasing, though not necessarily the horseplay with the key, sounds surprisingly modern. It is most tempting to use it as a snapshot of – not a real marriage, as we cannot tell if the story is true – but of what a friendly partnership would be, a plausible and attractive might-have-been; just as it is tempting to stress the consideration shown by Euphiletus in his self-presentation, allowing his wife to sleep downstairs to make it easier to see to the baby, and even prepared to do without her on a night when sexual reacquaintance might have been expected.[84] Once again, though, Euphiletus has to tread carefully. He wants to stress that Eratosthenes has been in the house before, violating his domestic space in a way that would be outraging to Athenian sentiments. It is particularly shameless if he himself was at home at the time. But it is vital for him to avoid the suspicion of having connived. Being locked in is a very good explanation – *if* he can make it plausible. That again requires the gullibility. The characterisation is consistent, and essential.

Where does this leave the 'teasing' – especially the wife's broad jest, 'it's so that you can have a go at the little slave-girl up here: you mauled her about before when you were drunk'? It is rash to take this as a straightforward 'sympathetic' description of the marriage: Euphiletus' point may be implicitly that he was *too* put-upon, *too* indulgent by now (he was initially sterner, § 6) – even if his motives must be felt as basically good: so indulgent that he ends up in a bizarre sexual role-reversal, locked in the inside while his wife plays sexually downstairs.[85] There may also be concealed point in the slave-girl; it might allow Euphiletus to acknowledge a peccadillo himself (Carey 1989: 62, 70), though if so it is probably an attempt to retrieve some sympathy as a real man, not a riposte to a feeble accusation made by the prosecution; it might be a suggestion that his relationship with his wife was not specially prim, something which might deflect suspicions that he had not been able to satisfy her sexually (Herman 1993: 415). We cannot read off audience response, or audience prejudices, in a wholly straightforward way.

The same applies to more ambitious attempts to infer audience prejudices. Herman (1993) is here especially interesting. He argues that the speech provides evidence for a development in social and sexual assumptions: a more 'Mediterranean' (again a questionable category) ethic of honour, vengeance, and outrage at a *crime passionnel*, something which would have left Euphiletus' killing unproblematic, is in tension with, and partly giving way to, a more city-based view of the rule of law. Euphiletus 'implicitly rejects' (Herman 1993: 408, 419) the first code, and instead projects himself as an executioner rather than an avenger, acting on behalf of the city: hence the striking emphasis at § 26 (above, p. 222), 'It is not I who will be killing you, but the law of the city…'.

There is something of value in this, especially the emphasis on Euphiletus as 'executioner', acting for the city's laws. *Eumenides* naturally springs to mind as a parallel, where a simpler, vengeance-based model of justice gives way to a more complex rule of law. But the talk of a succession of 'codes' is more difficult. *Eumenides* suggests the problems as well: as we saw in Chapter 9, the new civic law is there seen as a way of guaranteeing honour and (where appropriate) vengeance, not of superseding it. Indeed, a law-case can itself be sensed as a way of vindicating a man's honour, winning a 'victory' over a humiliated opponent:[86] there too the rule of law provides a healthier counterpart of an older ethic, but the older values are not rejected but incorporated within the new. It is Herman's argument that Euphiletus 'implicitly rejects' the older code which is problematic; we should rather think of Euphiletus as justifying his honour and vengeance *at the same time* as championing the city's laws, thoroughly traditional as well as thoroughly civic.

One can put the point more simply. Let us again distinguish three spectators, this time jurors X, Y, and Z. Juror X is closer to Herman's 'Mediterranean' model: the picture, unchallenged by the prosecution, of Eratosthenes naked in the wife's bed is quite enough to justify Euphiletus. Just let X's own wife try anything! He would kill the man too. Juror Y is more disquieted: he knows of too many cases where men in Euphiletus' position have behaved differently, perhaps extracting a fine or a ransom, perhaps adopting the even more civilised technique of (say) inserting a radish or a particularly spiny fish in the adulterer's anus and exposing him to public ridicule.[87] Juror Z – and there are probably many more Zs than anything else – is torn: part of him ($Z_X$, shall we say) agrees with X, part ($Z_Y$) with Y.

Lysias knows his trade. With X, and indeed with $Z_X$, he is almost home and dry. He cannot neglect them: but the stylistic vigour of the descriptions, the recurrent stress both on the outrage to the women and on the trespass on the space of the *oikos*, will stop them from wavering.[88] The typical precedent argument – if you take the wrong view, adulterers will have a field day – is bound to strike a chord. It is Y, and $Z_Y$, who pose the problem. It is with the law and the *polis* institutions where Euphiletus has to work hardest, especially

given all those other options open to him which he had ignored. But
that need not imply an audience which has switched from one code
of values to another: the strategy works well with an audience
including people with time for both 'codes', people indeed who cannot
see why they should be any more incompatible now than they had
been in *Eumenides*.

With the 'laws' themselves, we might expect to be on firmer
ground: there are limits, surely, on how far these can be bent for
rhetorical purposes. Yes, there are: but these limits may be more
elastic than we would think. The wording of the laws is not included
in our text. Euphiletus evidently got the secretary to quote them in
performance.[89] All we have is the speaker's gloss on what has just
been read out: we saw earlier (Chapters 2 and 4, pp. 27 and 65–7)
that a speaker's paraphrase can throw sand into the audience's eyes,
persuading them that they have heard something different from what
was in fact said. Let us look at the passage closely:

First read out the law:

LAW

He did not dispute it, gentlemen; he confessed he was in the
wrong, he pleaded with me and supplicated me not to kill him,
he was ready to pay money. I did not go along with the payment
he suggested, but thought it right that the city's law should carry
more authority, and exacted that punishment which you thought
was most just and imposed on people who behave like that.
Witnesses, come and attest to this.

WITNESSES

Read me also that law which is on the pillar on the Acropolis.

LAW

You hear, gentlemen, that the Areopagus court itself, whose task,
both by tradition and in our own time, is to judge homicide cases,
has explicitly decreed that a man should not be condemned for
homicide who takes an adulterer with his own wife and exacts
that punishment. The law-giver was so convinced of the justice
of this in the case of married women that he imposed the same
penalty in the case of concubines, even though they are less
important. Evidently he would have imposed a harsher penalty
in the case of married women if he had had one to hand; as it
was, he could find nothing more severe, and had to define the
same as for concubines. Read me this law too:

LAW

You hear, gentlemen, that it [or 'he'] orders double recompense if someone rapes a free man or boy; if the victim is a woman of the categories where killing is legal, then the same penalties should apply. Thus, gentlemen, he thought rapists deserved a lesser punishment than seducers; for he fixed death as the penalty for seducers, but a double recompense for rapists. He thought that those who had their way by force would be hated by their victims, but those who used persuasion corrupted their victims' minds, making other men's wives fonder of them than of their husbands, bringing whole households into their own hands and making it uncertain whether children are fathered by husbands or to adulterers. That is why the law-giver imposed the death penalty.

(§§ 28–33)

And that final passage has found its way into many presentations of Attic social life: the claim that the Athenians regarded seduction as worse than rape was until recently canonical.[90]

Let us look first at the treatment of the laws. That welter of quotation is confusing, and in skilled rhetoric we should assume that confusing welters are deliberate. There are clearly three laws. We cannot be quite certain what the first one said,[91] but 'confession' seems to be important: hence Euphiletus goes on, 'he did not dispute it, gentlemen; he confessed he was in the wrong...'.[92] It also clearly envisaged the death penalty, but seems to have allowed an alternative of 'paying money' if both parties agreed. The second law relates to the Areopagus:[93] a man should not be condemned for homicide if he kills a lover discovered *in flagrante* with his wife or concubine. That is not quite the same as fixing death as 'punishment' or 'justice' for adultery, but it is natural that the speaker phrases it like that: this extension is important to his sleight-of-hand, for he wants to claim that the law *demands* summary execution, not simply allows or excuses it. The third law deals not in death penalties at all, but in material punishment: notice the way Euphiletus continues, '...you hear that it orders double recompense if someone rapes a free man or boy' or wife or concubine. 'Double' *what* recompense, we ask: presumably the wording of the law made that clear (the 'damages' payable in the case of a slave?[94]), and the language suggests that it assimilated such rape to damage to property, where some financial estimate of the damage might normally be possible.

Why mention this third law at all? Eratosthenes was not a rapist. But that presumably is Euphiletus' point: it is to intensify the jurors' distaste for seduction, even worse (so he claims) than rape. And that explains the emphasis on 'damages' too. Damages, he claims, are appropriate for rape *but not for seduction*. This is a way of justifying his insistence on not accepting damages from Eratosthenes – the weak point, we saw, in his case. So this contrast of rape and seduction, and the insistence that the jurors know seduction is worse, is an important part of his rhetorical strategy.

It requires some slipperiness, and extreme oversimplification. First, the contrast between the penalties was not so clear. As we have seen, seduction was often punished less drastically; the second law about 'catching an adulterer with his wife' seems itself to extend to rape as well as seduction;[95] and – at least in some circumstances, and with women of a certain status – a rapist might possibly be charged with *hubris*, and the penalties for that went well beyond monetary fines, perhaps even as far as death.[96]

There is further slipperiness too. In earlier chapters (Chapters 2, 8, and 9, pp. 31, 136, and 175) we noted the ploy whereby jurors can be envisaged as acting on behalf of the *demos*, forming a continuous stream with past assemblies and courts where other citizens have been similarly functioning as 'the city'. The same is true here with the first law: Euphiletus 'exacted that punishment which you thought was most just and imposed on people who behave like that...', when in fact the legislation presumably dates from generations earlier. That continuity is then extended to the second and third laws too: the argument works on the assumption that all the laws embody a single mentality, though this time (given that the second law moves us to the Areopagus) it can no longer be 'you' who enacted it. Instead we have 'the law-giver', who 'was so convinced of the justice' of death for adulterers that he imposed the same penalty for concubines; and then, with the third law, Euphiletus speaks as if it is the same imaginary legislator who evidently 'thought rapists deserved a lesser punishment than seducers...'.

The notion that the same person is behind both the second and the third law is a fiction: they may date from different periods, and the mentality embodied in the two measures is different too. The second law deals with homicide, and included *in flagrante* detection as one among several legitimate excuses or justifications (Dem. 23.53); the third is concerned with damage to property, and assimilates women to other forms of 'goods' – a conceptual mode which classical Athens (we saw) would not have found alien. That fiction of a single 'law-giver' is aided by other Athenian habits of thought: the 'law' (as at the end of the passage we quoted) or 'laws' of the city can be envisaged as a collective unity, too; and there was a habit of attributing 'laws' to Solon anyway, whatever their real provenance.[97] Yet Euphiletus' single rationale for the differing penalties – rape produces only hatred, whereas seduction undermines the fabric of the whole house – is dependent on that fiction. In fact, we do not need to look for any such single rationale. It was typical of Athenian law to have a number of courses of action available for a litigant or prosecutor, each carrying different penalties for the accused and different risks for the prosecutor,[98] and there is no reason why the same way of looking at an offence should be embedded in all the procedures. When property is in point, one thinks of recompense; when homicide is in point, one thinks of acceptable justifications; they are simply different mindcasts.

Even slippery rhetoric can still be useful to the historian. What Euphiletus says cannot seem stupid or unreasonable; the points he makes about seduction undermining the household will certainly have struck a chord.[99] But that is a long way short of claiming that the audience regularly assumed seduction to be worse than rape. Had this been a rape-case, the speaker would have found something to say for the exactly opposite viewpoint. If we are to debate whether the Athenians 'really' thought rape was better or worse than seduction, we would have to do it in a quite different way, examining a whole web of social attitudes and not limiting ourselves to the law or to oratory.[100] We should not be surprised if no clear answer emerges.

A lot looks more problematic for the social historian than we at first thought. It is not straightforward to extract a view of friendly, teasing, genial married behaviour; nor to assume how genuinely 'humble households' might regularly have separated men's and women's quarters; nor to isolate a new, *polis*-based conception of law in the jurors' collective mindset; nor to extract what those jurors really thought about the relative outrageousness of seduction and rape. Yet something remains from the discussion in all of these points. It is still important that these pictures could be painted and these viewpoints expressed without *damaging* the case. Euphiletus can be concerned to represent himself as gullible as much as sympathetic; it is still important that he thought he would not alienate the audience by presenting himself as so indulgent to his wife's affected playfulness. It is still important that the jurors, whatever the set-up of their own houses, could nod approvingly at such separate quarters as the ideal. It was still important for Euphiletus to concentrate on the *polis*-based conception of law: that need not be the only code in his audience's minds, but he clearly thought that this was where he was most vulnerable. And the greater outrageousness of seduction could not have seemed a preposterous argument to that audience even though it may not have been self-evident, and whether or not everyone would automatically have accepted it. As usual, what was sayable and arguable has its own historical importance, even if what was arguable may also have been questionable.

## Gendering prescriptively

First there must be a union of those who cannot exist without one another, such as (a) male and female, for the sake of procreation (and this is not a matter of rational choice, but it is natural, as with other living beings and plants, to want to leave behind one a replica of oneself), and (b) natural ruler and natural subject, to ensure survival.

Moreover the relation of male to female is one of superior to inferior, with one ruling and one being ruled.

There are three parts of household management, one the rule of the master [or 'despot'] which I have already discussed, one that of the father, and the third that of the husband. For a man rules over his wife and his children too, but both as free people, and in different ways: he rules his wife in a way suited to the *polis* (*politikos*) but his children as a king: for the male is naturally more suited to leadership than the female (unless occasionally things come together unnaturally) and the senior and full-grown more suited to leadership than the younger and immature.

There are differences in the way the free rules the slave, the male rules the female, and an adult rules a child, and all have the parts of the soul within them, but differently. The slave has no deliberative capacity; the female has it, but without the capacity to carry through (*akuron*); the child has it, but immature.
(Aristotle, *Politics* 1.1252a26–31,
1254b13–14, 1259a36–b4, 1260a9–14)

The trouble with philosophers is that they have minds of their own.

These formulations, all from the first book of the *Politics*, are irresistibly quotable, but how much do they show of the mindset of the society as a whole? Some of those remarks sound familiar from other genres, like the claim of male superiority and the choice of the word *akuron*, 'unable to carry through' (for does not a woman need a *kurios* to act for her?). Others, especially the dismissal of female deliberative power, sound more extreme: elsewhere we have often found men granting that women are uncomfortably adept at *logos* and command a type of rational cogency. What about that 'urge to leave a replica of oneself'? Elsewhere too reproduction is central to marriage, as in that initial threefold distinction in *Against Neaera* (above, p. 189); to give one's daughter 'for the ploughing of legitimate children' seems to have been a regular, blunt formulation used in a betrothal ceremony.[101] But even in *Against Neaera* there is more to marriage than this (remember that role of the wife to shame their husbands into voting correctly), and anyone reared on Hector and Andromache would be taken aback by Aristotle's *reduction* of the marital impulse to a reproductive urge. We would not quote Plato's picture of utopian sexual communism as typical of fourth-century thought. Need Aristotle tell us any more about his own society than that it could produce a quirky male who could think so strangely? Can we possibly tell how far the ordinary Crito in the street, and still more the ordinary Critylla, would agree?

We may make some progress by developing the principles outlined earlier, and concentrating on what is *most* problematic, what needs to be argued fiercely because it will be disputed, and on what is *least* problematic, what can be taken for granted. The first of those approaches is tantamount to what has been called 'reading a text upside down', looking at the one side of the argument to reconstruct the dialectic to which it is contributing: that can illuminate what the audience found difficult. The second is rather concerned with the assumptions that seem so obvious that they underlie everything else, the unconscious rather than conscious mindset. Both approaches have much in common with the approach of Foucault in the second and third volumes of his *History of Sexuality* (1985, 1986), which were heavily concerned with homiletic texts, and concentrated on tracing the changing problematic issues and 'anxieties' as well as the underlying axioms.

To take the second approach first: what does not need arguing at all? It does not seem to be disputed that, even if woman is inferior, that does not equate marriage to slavery: the different hierarchies do not merge (e.g. 1253b9–10), and it is indeed a mark of barbarians that female and slave should blur into one another (1252b5–6). The distinction between husband–wife authority and father–child authority again seems self-evident in our fourth passage, as before at 1253b7–11 (and so the easy modern formulation 'a woman is a perpetual minor'[102] requires challenging): what Aristotle elaborates in that paragraph is not the distinction itself, but the analogy of the two relationships to '*polis*-like' and 'kingly' authority. It also seems that our second 'man is naturally superior to female' comment falls within this category, for it is thrown off as self-evident – possibly in itself a rhetorical ploy, but it does not look like that. It is not this thesis which gets the space, it is rather that *slavery* is a matter of natural hierarchy: this genuinely seems to be an interesting question, a matter expected to be in dispute (1253b21–2, 1254a17–55b4).

What about the first question: can we tell anything of the dialectic to which the book is contributing?

The *Politics* is a theoretical work, but much of it will be very empirical theorising. Aristotle will form general principles of statecraft on the basis of perceived reality within particular states. He begins, though, with a more abstract type of abstraction. He tries to establish the 'naturalness' of the city (thus 'the human is a civic animal', 1253a2–3 and elsewhere), and of a hierarchy of authority within it. This builds on analogies with other dominant relationships taken as natural, especially soul and body, master and slave, husband and wife, adult and child. It also brings out how those other hierarchies are themselves embraced within the city, for he is keen to make the city a community but not a unity: if one abandons lesser units such as that of the *oikos*, one is left with no city at all (especially 1261b6–15, 1263a40–b5, 1263b32–5).

There is engagement with Plato here, and that is the first debate to which the argument is contributing. The *Politics* will not itself be a utopian work, but it will be less vulnerable if it can first protect itself against the utopianism of the *Republic*. Aristotle does this by playing Plato at his own game. He accepts the *Republic*'s picture of an ideal state where different people have different roles, but prefers a very un-Platonic picture of how that state should work – and in particular an un-Platonic picture of how women fit into it, that most striking feature of Plato's utopia and the one from which Aristotle will begin in the second book. The argument requires him not merely to re-establish the *oikos* as an important component of the community; he also extracts from his analogies a thesis about ethical virtue. 'Thus it is clear that all these have ethical virtue, and self-control is not the same in the case of a woman and of a man, as Socrates thought, nor bravery, nor justice, but the one sort of bravery is that of the ruler and the other of the ruled, and the same applies with the other virtues' (1260a20–4). Hence women and children must be *educated* with an eye to the state, but also to their differences[103] (1260b13–20, the note on which the book ends); that strange Platonic sex-mingling can be avoided (the theme of the early second book); and the traditionally minded can heave a sigh of relief.

Women and the *oikos*, then, are not merely components in the state, they also give an analogy to it. That emerges most clearly in the third passage cited above, with the master's rule assimilated to the despot's, the father's to a king's, and a husband's to 'ruling in a way suited to the *polis*'. This analogy is important to Aristotle, so important that he presses it despite immediately emphasising that a central aspect of *polis*-rule does *not* apply within marriage: in a *polis* there is typically an alternation of ruling and being ruled, whereas in a family the husband is always the ruler (1259b4–10). Not much of the analogy seems left by now, a mere six lines after introducing it. So why does Aristotle bother? Presumably because it prepares for an essential ingredient in his analysis of the ideal state, the notion of proportional equality (especially 1282b14–83a3, 1301b26–02a8). If people are not equal, they should not be treated equally or have the same power or rewards, but that does not mean that the rule need degenerate to despotism, with all ruled like slaves, any more than to oligarchy, with wealth rather than virtue as its criterion of worth. For the analogy to work, the woman *needs* to be neither equal nor servile, to have virtue but not the same virtue – an icon for the free, full, but still inferior participant in the community. And, if the analogy does not fit the *polis* alternation of 'ruling and being ruled', that too prepares for a later equivocation; for Aristotle has sympathy for the view that, if some people are simply better than others, proportionality implies that they *should* rule all the time (especially 1261a37–b2, 1284b25–34, 1332b12–23), and the analogy between house and state should be even closer.

Aristotle has an agenda, and a rhetoric. The remarks about female capacity are anything but casual: we are close to a refined, intellectualised version of 'he would say that, wouldn't he?'

So what? The fact that an assertion fits into an argument does not make it a lie or disingenuous; it must be something Aristotle felt his audience would accept, and there is no need to doubt that this is

what he really thought. Some aspects, especially the assumption of
male superiority, are recurrent in his thought, extending to the view
that the female is a natural deformity: he is accordingly convinced
that the male is hotter, longer-lived, has harder bones, a bigger brain,
and even a larger number of teeth.[104]

Still, the aspects stressed in the *Politics* are not the *only* things he
thought; he selects and presents in the ways which best fit the
argument. Take our fourth passage, on intelligence. When talking
about slaves' intelligence, he used the general words *episteme*,
'knowledge' (1255b20–40) and *logos*, 'rationality' (1254b22–4,
1259b27–8); but now the emphasis has shifted to 'deliberative power',
*to bouleutikon* – a word more geared to political activity, thinking and
debating in public council, and one which goes well with 'not able to
carry through' (*akuron*). For an audience used to male-only
deliberations and women incapable of public action without a *kurios*,
the phraseology would not seem absurd. Aristotle's project in this
book is to present such hierarchies as 'natural'; we might wonder if
his nimble footwork here has not moved us into 'convention',[105] those
limitations on female action imposed by a particular culture. At least
he has deftly sidestepped other aspects of female *logos* which, in a
different frame of mind or chain of argument, he acknowledges: for
instance, the female's greater swiftness to learn, retentiveness of
memory, and capacity for mischievous scheming, all of which are
stressed in his systematic contrast of male and female in *Hist. An.*
608a21–b18.[106]

The same goes for that reduction of the marital instinct to the
urge to reproduce. Notice that the passage links this with a similar
'union' of ruler and ruled *for survival*. That is a key emphasis: survival
is vital, not merely nourishment and protection but also the survival
into future generations (e.g. 1260b19–20, 1308a23–32, 1313a30–3,
1319a33–20a3; 1307b26ff., 1313a18ff.). Procreation is central to that
picture; affection (on which the text has notably little to say[107]) is
not.

So we may continue to quote these passages, and take them as
insights which Aristotle regarded as true and expected his audience
to find plausible; but we may not take this as the *whole* truth of the
matter for Aristotle, and certainly not for his audience. It is a selection
from a wider repertoire of gender ideas, and the principles of selection
are argumentative and rhetorical.

And the 'dialectic' to which this contributes? One element is the
engagement with Plato. Even for the great practical thinker and

systematiser Aristotle such utopianism is the place to start, and its most arresting feature is its thinking about women. That illuminates the agenda for debate, if not for the Critylla in the street then at least for the Crito in the *peripatos*. Another is the relationship between house and city. Aristotle begins the *Politics* by confronting the views of those who make the analogy too simple, who think that there is a single sort of authority defined by the number of subjects – 'master's' authority if over a few, 'household' if over more, 'statesman's' or 'king's' if over a whole state (1252a7–16). As we saw in our third passage, Aristotle makes it more complex: control varies in its style as well as in its subjects.[108] But to complicate the analogy is not to dismiss it, and we noticed Aristotle straining to keep the analogy in working order. Despite the elements which do not fit, the household still provides a useful way in to exploring equality, justice, and authority within the state.

This ingrained taste for analogy itself illuminates Aristotle's and his audience's argumentative reflexes. The household is also more than an interesting comparison: Aristotle insists that households constitute nuclear unities within the community, for otherwise a city will cease to be a city. Yet all this is indeed one side of the argument, and clearly expected to be controversial. The *oikos–polis* antithesis and relation is anything but simple. The polarity was a useful strategy of thought and exploration; it was also a subject for intense contestation.

The date of the *Politics* is the subject of more polite scholarly contestation, but it is clearly later than most of the material handled in this book – perhaps the 330s or even the 320s. Let us return to an earlier 'prescriptive' text, profitably treated by Foucault (1985: 152–65; 1986: 160–1): Xenophon's *Oeconomicus*, especially the section on Ischomachus' wife (7–10). It is tempting to contrast Xenophon's treatment with Aristotle's, and to stress Xenophon's greater concern for companionship and for 'educating' the female, as well as his greater emphasis on the wife's role in managing the house.[109]

Structurally, the *Oeconomicus* is complex, with dialogue embedded within dialogue in Chinese-box fashion. It opens in the narrator's own voice: 'I once heard Socrates discussing household-management, too, in the following way'. Then we have the report of Socrates' conversation with Critobulus, an extremely rich figure who finds his resources under constant demands. The last two-thirds of the dialogue is given to Socrates' account of an earlier conversation with an Athenian 'gentleman' (*kalos kagathos*) Ischomachus. In that exchange Ischomachus told Socrates of his own earlier instructional conversations, first with his wife, who – tellingly but unsurprisingly[110] – remains unnamed, and then with his stewards; finally Ischomachus instructs Socrates himself on farming technique, and Socrates is cast in the role of the admiring but uninformed interlocutor which so often falls to others.[111]

So the conversation between Ischomachus and his wife is triply embedded, recounted as it is by Ischomachus to Socrates, by Socrates to Critobulus, and by Xenophon to the external audience. The nearest parallel to such conversational embedding is Plato's *Symposium*, which may well be an intertextual presence here.[112] Plato there has Apollodorus telling a friend what Aristodemus had told him of that symposium long ago. The speeches include Socrates' account of his own earlier conversation with Diotima, in which Socrates had similarly been cast as interlocutor rather than intellectual leader. So the Diotima–Socrates conversation is again triply or even quadruply embedded: it is what Socrates told the symposiasts, what Aristodemus told Apollodorus, what Apollodorus told his friend, and what Plato tells us.

That embedding ensures that several distinct audiences for the original conversation are sensed, and the relation of those audiences to the advice is thought-provoking. In Plato's case, at least on a straightforward reading, the audience may simply be persuaded by Diotima's insights: Socrates was persuaded, and that was why he felt the need to pass on such insight to others (212b1–4); Apollodorus was persuaded (173b9–e2); and we might be persuaded too – though even here there may be a hint that not every Athenian was so persuaded, at least about the educational role that Socrates saw for himself, and that is why he was killed. With the *Oeconomicus*, the audiences' relation to Ischomachus' advice is more quizzical. His young wife herself seems persuaded; though here too there may be a more complex perspective to which we will return. There is also Critobulus, a rich man like Ischomachus and one who like him had married a young wife who needed to be educated (3.13, cf. 7.4–6). But Critobulus talked much less to his wife than Ischomachus did:

| | |
|---|---|
| *Socrates:* | Is there anyone to whom you entrust a larger number of serious matters than to your wife? |
| *Critobulus:* | No-one. |
| *Socrates:* | Is there anyone with whom you have fewer conversations than with your wife? |

*Critobulus:*    If so, there are not many.

(*Oeconomicus* 3.12)

(It should go without saying that we cannot cite Critobulus as *typical* here, any more than Ischomachus: both men are being characterised, and the contrast works best if both are taken as extreme.) Perhaps Critobulus will take the hint from Socrates, and talk to his wife more: here and elsewhere, his demeanour suggests that he could do with some enlightenment – unless of course it is already too late, and his wife is beyond training.

Critobulus is not the only internal audience for Ischomachus' husbandly wisdom; nor is Ischomachus' wife. There is also Socrates himself, who is audience to Ischomachus as well as informant to Critobulus. Socrates is there throughout the work as the perpetual alternative: the man who has no wealth and does not know how to get any, but also needs none, yet has a lifestyle which is less financially pressed than Critobulus' own (2.1–8; 11.1–6 goes on to contrast that poor lifestyle with that of Ischomachus too). Is he to be taken as simply endorsing all Ischomachus' style and values? If we recall his own marriage with Xanthippe, then we might also wonder if all wives might be so easy to instruct as Ischomachus found (or thought he found) his own.

'Instruction' is indeed the keynote, particularly of the section on wifeliness; and this contrasts with Aristotle's *Politics*, which had something to say about female education but nothing about the husband's role in wife-training.[113] Critobulus finds the notion odd:

*Critobulus:*    These men, Socrates, who you say have good wives – did
                they educate them themselves?
*Socrates:*      We had better look at that. I'll arrange you a meeting
                with Aspasia too, who will explain everything to you
                more knowledgeably than I can. I think that a woman
                who is a good partner in the house is just as important
                as her husband in her contribution towards the good...
                (*Oec.* 3.14–15)

There is obviously some sort of joke here, and part of it will bite on Socrates' own professed ignorance of household management – particularly of wife-training (remember Xanthippe). Part of it may also recall Plato's *Symposium*: Aspasia might fulfill the role of Diotima, that other Socratic instructress in 'erotics'. But there must also be an irony in Aspasia, of all women, being cited as an example of training a demure wife. 'It is quite remarkable,' says Pomeroy (1994: 232), to pick as a potential mentor the most renowned, not of wives, but of *hetairai* – particularly as Socrates has already warned Critobulus of the dangers of *hetairai* (1.13). A joke is a joke, and we should not press it: this need not completely destabilise the later presentation. Still, if Socrates is one perpetual alternative to Ischomachus' wisdom, this is also a pointer to other sorts of 'partnership in the house', and less trainable women who are matches for their men in different ways from those which Socrates here, and Ischomachus later, envisage.

Critobulus finds the 'training' image strange: whether or not Xenophon's text problematises that further (and I shall suggest that it does), it is clear that this is not a familiar, uncontested picture of the husband–wife relationship. In part it is a literary device. Once Xenophon is committed to a Socratic dialogue form for presenting management principles, then he needs to find a natural context for these to be enunciated: a didactic setting is the obvious answer, and the wife, basic as she is to the household, is the natural recipient for the fundamental lessons. As matters become more specific – running the estate, planting the trees – then the stewards or Socrates will be more suitable interlocutors. That may explain some artificiality, for instance when Ischomachus 'conducts his wife on a tour of the house in which she has evidently been living for some time' (9.2–5).[114] Or there is the occasion when she could not find something, and her husband treats her to a 'place for everything and everything in its place' sermon (8.1–23, picking up the theme from 3.2–3). Ischomachus dwells on the subject far longer than the needs of the moment or of her education require, elaborating the comparison with generalship, with farming, with keeping things ship-shape at sea, and (once again as in the *Politics*) with the *polis* itself.[115] The comparison with other spheres is important to Xenophon (the parallel between generalship and farming recurs at 5.14–20, 20.6–9, and 21.4–7, and the ship-imagery at 20.27–8 and 21.3). This is the logical place for the theme to be treated, and so the material is hung on this handle. But Xenophon is too good a writer to do this at the expense of plot plausibility. What makes it credible is the characterisation of Ischomachus himself, thorough and meticulous (and to our minds complacent and long-winded[116]) as he is.

Immediately we become interested in Ischomachus as a character, other aspects become interesting too: in particular, his rhetoric.

'Training' requires psychology, knowing the sorts of argument which will not merely make the point clear but also make the pupil receptive; and Ischomachus is more skilful than is sometimes realised. At the end of a long list of his wife's responsibilities, Ischomachus concludes:

> 'One thing,' I said to her, 'that you ought to do may be a little unwelcome, taking care of the treatment of any of the slaves who fall sick.'
> 'Not at all,' my wife replied; 'that is the most welcome thing in the world, if after good treatment they will be grateful and show more goodwill than in the past...'
>
> (*Oec.* 7.37)

She is getting the idea: her insight echoes several earlier themes, touching the need for a general to gain the goodwill of his troops and a master that of his subordinates (3.4, 4.18–19, 5.16; later 9.11–13, 12.5–6, 21.2–12). But we should also notice the blatant pedagogic ploy. It is not likely that she will find this duty any more irksome than the rest: it maps closely on to traditional female roles. But it does give a two-way texture to the exchanges, giving her a cue for making her own engagement clear: a good way, in fact, for both marking and encouraging her own 'goodwill'.

Other parts too can be read as illuminating Ischomachus' rhetorical strategy as much as Xenophon's convictions: the long analysis of the way the gods ordain the differences and similarities between male and female, and the consequences for their partnership roles (7.18–29); the flattering (even if hackneyed) comparison with the queen-bee, who controls from within and is respected for it (7.32–4); the paradoxical claim that, in certain circumstances, the wife could even be superior to the husband in her contribution:

> I am putting in all my possessions for us to share, and you have also put in everything which you brought [as your dowry]. And we must not consider which of us has contributed the greater amount, but we should be clear that whichever of us is the better partner, that is the person who makes the more valuable contribution.
>
> (*Oec.* 7.13)

That again seems paradoxical, even to his wife. That is not to say

Xenophon did not himself subscribe to it, or regard his Socrates as
subscribing to it. We have already seen Socrates himself saying
something similar to shock Critobulus (3.15, quoted on p. 238). But
it is also a useful protreptic device to encourage the wife along her
path, setting out a high target and a high reward; just as Ischomachus
later allows the possibility that either the man or the woman might
be the better at self-control, and have the 'greater part of this good'
(7.27); or that, if she does well, she might

> turn out better than me and make me into your attendant. Then
> you would not need to fear that you might grow less honoured in
> the house with your increasing years; you could be confident
> that as you grow older, the better partner you become and the
> better guardian of the house for the children, and the greater
> will be your honour in the house. For what is fine and good is
> increased for humans not by youthful beauty, but by the virtues
> by which one lives...
>
> (*Oec.* 7.42–3)

One notices not merely the target ('turn out better than me...',
'become more honoured') but the hint of the alternative. Respect in
the house does not come or stay automatically, and the reminder
that beauty fades suggests ways in which a wife's position may be
vulnerable to rivals, a dreadful prospect[117] – and a theme which we
will find recurring. It is not too cynical to read the *Oeconomicus* as
investigating not only household management but also the rhetoric
of masculine control, exploring the strategies whereby a male can
induce an impressionable wife to acquiesce in her role.

There is another point at which the wife gets her cue right.
Ischomachus has been explaining that a particular responsibility falls
on his wife because of her stake in the household:

| | |
|---|---|
| *Socrates:* | How did your wife respond to that instruction? |
| *Ischomachus:* | It's extraordinary, but she told me, Socrates, that I was wrong if I thought I was telling her anything hard when I was teaching her to take care of her own possessions. It would be harder, she said, if her instructions had been to neglect them, rather than that she would have to take care of goods which were her own. For just as it seems natural, she went on, for a sensible woman to take care of her own |

children rather than to neglect them, thus she
thought it more pleasurable for the sensible woman
to take care of, rather than neglect, those
possessions which belong to her and give joy.

*Socrates:*   By Hera, Ischomachus, what a man-like intelligence
your wife evidently has.

(*Oec.* 9.17–10.1)

A 'man-like intelligence'? It is not hard to sense Socratic irony here,[118] especially after Ischomachus has been so amazed at the not-very-profound remarks of his wife – and after she has expressed her acquiescence with the most female comparison of all, with childcare. Management of the household is being figured as an extension of her traditional role. But irony is not sarcasm, and as usual Socrates is pointing a paradoxical truth. This *is* a man-like vision, the vision of the household that Ischomachus shares and which assimilates it closely to the world of the camp or the *agora*;[119] that analogy between *oikos* and *polis* is not nuanced or problematic as in Aristotle, but clear-cut and thorough; his wife has been brought to acquiesce with a will, and the training has worked (or so Ischomachus is convinced). She will supervise the household, but with the insight given her by her husband. This is not so different a picture from the one we found in Aristophanes, with the woman managing the household under her husband's overall authority (above, p. 211); or indeed from the inferior but free role within the house envisaged by Aristotle.[120]

If we revert to our strategy of investigating the most and the least problematic strands, Chapter 10 of the *Oeconomicus* is particularly suggestive.[121] One day, Ischomachus tells Socrates, he found his wife wearing cosmetics and high heels. Unsurprisingly, he turned didactic (this was a favourite topic for moralists). It would be wrong for a husband to deceive his wife about the household income, and wrong for a wife to deceive her husband about how she looks. Anyway, it does not work: a husband sees his wife as she is getting up in the morning, or leaving her bath, or perspiring or in tears. But there is no need to fear losing her beauty: the exercise of household supervision will keep her trim and attractive, especially if she cultivates the art of standing at the loom like a mistress instead of always sitting down like a slave-girl.

And as for appearance, whenever it is a competition with a slave,[122] the mistress is cleaner [or 'purer', i.e. more free of cosmetics, cf. §§ 7, 9] and more appropriately dressed, that is more arousing – particularly whenever there is the additional bonus of a woman giving pleasure to the man willingly rather than being forced to service him.

(*Oec.* 10.12)

And since that moment she has carried on in the way her husband instructed. Or so Ischomachus tells Socrates, twice (10.9, 13). Socrates hastens on to other topics (11.1), and the wife disappears from the text, re-emerging only to act as judge for Ischomachus' declamatory exercises and the mock-trials of their servants (11.25, cf. above, p. 5) – another moment when he is hardly typical but rather an extreme.

What is taken for granted here, and what are the points of problematisation and anxiety? It is taken for granted that the cosmetics are a sign of the *wife*'s anxiety – her nervousness that the slave-girls may be more attractive to Ischomachus. This is a 'competition' with her husband to judge, elegantly mirrored by the rhetorical competition where it will be her turn to judge her husband. It also seems implied that Ischomachus will not award her a sexual monopoly, only a pre-eminent position within the house:[123] the language ('whenever there is the additional bonus...') might imply that she is not always so willing or that his sexual activity does not always involve her – very likely both. It also seems assumed, more comfortably for modern tastes, that a good husband should give his wife full knowledge of the household income, and that there should be no deceit between them.

The wife is assumed to be anxious about her slave-girl rivals; is Ischomachus anxious about anything? It requires an excess of goodwill to assume he is anxious about the slave's lack of sexual satisfaction: his point is simply that it is more arousing for him when the woman enjoys it too.[124] Perhaps the twofold stress on his wife's continued good behaviour evinces unease, but that is probably too psychological an interpretation: repetitiveness is no surprise in Ischomachus, and we should infer complacency rather than anxiety.

Perhaps, though, he had more ground for anxiety than he saw: perhaps the 'anxiety' about reliable wifeliness is pointed, not by Ischomachus' own insight, but by the lack of it – and by the greater insight possessed by the text's external audience. For there is more to this wife than we have so far seen. Ischomachus was a real person, active in the last quarter of the fifth century (the dramatic date of the dialogue is perhaps in the 410s[125]). As usual in prosopography, there are problems in identification;[126] but it is at least very likely that he is the same as an Ischomachus who was said to have left little money when he died (Lys. 19.46): so perhaps his – or his wife's – household management was not so wonderful after all. Far more significantly, he is also likely to be the Ischomachus whose wife and daughter crop up in Andocides' *On the Mysteries* (400 or 399: above, Chapter 2).

Ischomachus is by then dead, and his daughter has married the rich aristocrat Callias. Within a year her mother – presumably if not certainly[127] this same demure wife of Ischomachus – moves in too. This is the point at which she acquires a name, Chrysilla: and, as we might expect, she acquires it because she is a Bad Woman. According to Andocides, she has an affair with her son-in-law Callias, and becomes pregnant by him. Her daughter is so horrified that she tries to hang herself: Chrysilla drives her out of the house. Callias soon tires of Chrysilla, and drives her out too, denying that the child is his own; later he takes her back, and admits paternity (Andoc. 1.124–9). Andocides has a case to plead, and we should by now know better than to believe him implicitly. But at least we can infer that these things were said: Andocides said them. There was scandal. And Xenophon must have known it.[128] He did not have to choose Ischomachus, for there were other 'gentlemen' in Athens. As Goldhill (1995: 141–2) insists, that choice brought with it a whole set of extratextual suggestions of how Ischomachus' wife really turned out – or at least of how some people said she had.

We cannot know what Xenophon intended his audience to make of this. Perhaps the irony is just 'hilariously funny', debunking Ischomachus' pomposity.[129] Perhaps it is a text of nostalgia, looking back to the time when Ischomachus' house, like Athens itself, was more fortunate.[130] Some might take it as a defence of the woman, based on the conviction that so fine a tutor as Ischomachus could not have had so bad a pupil.[131] Some could rather see it as a defence of Ischomachus himself: in a rather laboured passage, Socrates suggests a distinction between the 'wife who is taught well by her husband but behaves [or 'manages'] badly', and the wife who is never taught at all; the first might be blamed, but if the second goes wrong it is her husband's fault (3.11) – and by the end of the *Oeconomicus* there could be no doubt that Chrysilla fell into the first category. Or perhaps we should think more of the difficulties of persuasion, for we saw that the technique of embedded dialogue drew attention to those multiple audiences. However impeccable the insights conveyed (and none of these interpretations need make Ischomachus talk anything but total sense[132]), will the recipient listen, especially if she is a woman?[133] Was it any wiser to trust his wife to manage the house than it would have been to trust Socrates to do his farming? And what of the other audiences, internal and external? Ischomachus imparted all this managerial knowledge to Socrates, and sent him off to teach others if he wished (20.24), just like the Socrates of Plato's *Symposium* who was persuaded by Diotima and so tried to persuade others (212b1–4; above p. 237). But Ischomachus' insights into marital training did not save his house from scandal. Will they be any more effective with Critobulus, or with us? Perhaps we can simply find this a thought-provoking and multivalent text, with no single interpretation imposed on the reader. Xenophon can be subtle too.

The historian should not ignore the interpretative difficulties, but equally need not decide which view to take. What is important is that the future scandal *matters*. That suggests that there is indeed 'anxiety' here, centring not on the adequacy of the advice but on the capacity of the authoritative male to inculcate such lasting propriety. Will the woman be so trainable? Might she escape from the guidelines which her sober-minded males established, and become more like an Aspasia – or a Chrysilla? (That too is not absent from Aristotle, who fears that women who marry too young may grow wanton: eighteen is the ideal age (*Pol.* 1335a25–29). Chrysilla married at fourteen.) This, rather than the danger that she may wear too much rouge or forget the right place to put the spatula, is the real worry in the *Oeconomicus*. And we moderns should think the worse of Xenophon, as we do of Ischomachus, if he was not worried at all.

# Chapter 11

# Conclusions: texts, audiences, truth

Texts have audiences, and our texts were performed for real people. Much of our project has been to see what we may detect about those people from the texts themselves; in the terms of reader-response theory, to investigate the audience 'inscribed in the text', and infer what we can about the real audience.

That is not easy, and some think it impossible. It depends what questions we ask. In some cases we are on fairly secure ground, most clearly when asking what the audience must be taking for granted if they are not going to be bewildered. That may be facts of everyday life, like vermilion ropes herding people into the assembly (Chapter 7, p. 131), or keys to a store-room under the husband's ultimate control (Chapter 10, p. 210–11); or, more sinisterly, 'pledges', bonding associates by shared complicity in an outrage or crime (Chapter 2, p. 39). Or it may be particular events which the audience must know about: *something* public must have happened between Cleon and Aristophanes/Callistratus, otherwise the audience of *Acharnians* will be bemused (Chapter 8, pp. 145–50). The difficulty is to know exactly what this something was. Several reconstructions are possible, and we cannot be sure that the simplest, most literal interpretation of Dicaeopolis' words is the right one.

As the questions get deeper, the difficulties multiply. That is particularly so when we probe audience attitudes, what they must think and feel rather than what they know. We can make some progress, certainly. We can infer what an author expected to be sayable and performable without alienating the audience (though even here different occasions and genres can impose different norms and allow different licences). Andocides felt he could appeal to a code in which comradeship counted most, even if the city suffered (Chapter 2, pp. 40–2); Euripides' *Orestes* works best if we assume a similar engagement, even if provisional, with the aristocratic solidarity of Orestes, Electra, and Pylades (Chapter 9, pp. 184–8); Aristophanes thought that it would not damage his chances of success if he harped on the attractions of peace (Chapter 8, pp. 158–63).

More ambitious attempts to detect audience attitudes tend to collapse. Different viewers of *Medea* could have different reactions to the heroine's assertiveness, and still find the play absorbing and rewarding (Chapter 10, pp. 199–200); the final scenes of *Wasps* work well both for those who would love to get into aristocratic symposia and for those who felt they were an undemocratic disgrace (Chapter 7, pp. 136–40); Aeschylus' *Eumenides* and Euripides' *Suppliant Women* would strike a chord both with those who despaired of democracy and with those who thought it could withstand the criticisms (Chapter 9, pp. 180–2); Lysias' first speech can play both to jurors who felt the civilised cuckold should reach for the radish and to those who felt he should kill (Chapter 10, pp. 225–7). All this is no surprise. Crowds do behave as crowds, and are not simply a composite of the disparate individuals who constitute them; but collective attitudes remain complex things, and resist reduction to a single 'the audience think that…'. If a playwright or orator was to be successful, he had to mix his ingredients in ways which would work with a range of audience responses and prejudices, and the ones whose works have survived were good at what they did.

We have found it better to concentrate on *how*, rather than what, the audience thought. That may be a question of thought-association, the items which figure on the agenda when the subject is, say, the deficiencies of the law-courts (self-interest of those judging, misleading rhetoric, avoidance of real issues: Chapters 7 and 9, pp. 139 and 182), or what women are like (emotional, uncontrolled, but also disconcertingly rational; Chapter 10), or how wars start (and then… and then… and then…; Chapter 8, p. 155). Or it may be the adoption of particular expectations for a particular occasion: the assumption that comedy will air uncomfortable truths in one register, tragedy in another (Chapters 7–10); that sitting on a jury is a citizen experience, and hence one aligns oneself and one's prejudices with those higher up the social scale more than with those lower down (Chapter 1, pp. 12–16; Chapter 10, pp. 191–3, 220–4).

That is already following the example set by Herodotus and Thucydides, who knew how rhetorical dynamic could be made historically illuminating (Chapter 1, pp. 9–12); and we have seen ways of examining 'dynamic' in other genres too. We explored the mindset which male spectators might adopt in watching tragedy and comedy, adopting different filters for exploring familiar issues: this might involve a certain amount of 'playing the other' and adopting a female viewpoint, especially in comedy's fantasies about how women would set about running the state (Chapter 10, pp. 213–18) – but we also found reasons to hesitate about categorising compassionate reactions to tragedy in firmly gendered terms (Chapter 10, pp. 203–8).

Tragedy proves particularly helpful in categorising what the audience find interesting issues: here we took a hint from Foucault's strategy of tracing what a culture finds problematic. Tragedy does not take easy targets. At the end of plays we may develop a firm view about who was right or (much more) about who was wrong, but during most of the plays we can assume that the moral issues are in some balance. Should Theseus or Pelasgus accept the suppliants in Euripides' and Aeschylus' *Suppliant Women*, despite the risk to the state and the moral ambivalence of the women's case? Should Antigone confront state and family authority, even in so extreme a case? Should Euripides' Orestes and Electra accept the verdict passively, or take extreme measures to fight for vengeance and safety? Should Neoptolemus obey orders which he finds appalling? Or, rather differently (because this is more a question of dispensing emotion rather than passing moral verdicts) should we feel sympathy for Medea, or Xerxes, or Pentheus, or Eurystheus in *Heracleidae*, or Helen in *Trojan Women*? We can continue to debate the answers. Members of the audience probably debated them too as they left the theatre. But the more illuminating point is that they were good *questions*: good, because the issues were interesting; good, because the scales were sufficiently balanced for there to be arguments on both sides – even if they finally tilt one way. New historicists pride themselves on oblique approaches to old problems: the poised dilemmas of tragedy provide a promising oblique approach to investigate moral sensibilities, if only we assume the playwrights knew their trade well enough to mix their ingredients in the most interesting proportions.

In tragedies the problematising is generally within the text itself, with both sides of issues aired. But Foucault's notion of 'problematising' should itself be problematised: quite often, the problem a text suggests is not so much in the issues it explicitly addresses, more in the relation that its content bears to reality. (This point has some contact with the critique of Foucault in Goldhill (1995), who brings out that the novels of the Second Sophistic explore moralistic platitudes with wry humour, suggesting that erotic life is too complicated and labyrinthine to allow easy answers.) One example was Xenophon's *Oeconomicus*, where the later adventurousness of Ischomachus' wife adds an extratextual perspective to his advice: *will* she, in fact, be so easy to train? Another example, not discussed in this book, would be the pseudo-Demosthenic *Erotikos* ([Dem.] 61), with its long and rosy description of the boy whom the speaker is pursuing. Foucault (1985: 204–14) discusses this at length, emphasising that its problematisation centres on the behaviour of the boy (when should he feel shame about yielding?) rather than the pursuing adult. But a further dimension is given if we remember that the speech is *persuasive*: this is seduction rhetoric. Is, for instance, the high-minded praise of philosophy (§§ 36–50) what the lover really thinks? Or is this simply the line most calculated to outflank the less high-minded rivals (cf. §§ 56–7)? Is the pursuer out to play Socrates to the beloved's Alcibiades, despite the disclaimer of § 48? Will it work? The speech purports to praise the love-object, rather than debate what love is like (to use a distinction later exploited by Foucault himself, 237–8); but its choice of themes is itself a way of commending the lover, as well as ironically displacing attention from his self-interest – so the strategy implies a view of what love-behaviour is like too. Whether we take this as a real erotic speech or as a playful exercise, the text is too complicated to allow the concentration to fall wholly on the boy's role. Those are questions raised about the adult lover and his ploys, and they are raised by the gap between what he says and what we can detect behind it.

The gulf between a text and reality can 'problematise' in other ways too. Take that claim in *Against Neaera* that 'we have courtesans for our pleasure, concubines for taking care of our bodies from day to day, and wives for having legitimate children and to have a reliable person to guard our household property' ([Dem.] 59.122: Chapter 10, p. 189). Foucault finds it significant that this and similar formulations were not explicitly problematised, unlike (say) the place of pleasure in Christian constructions of marriage (1985: 143–51). That again is too simple. True, it is significant that Apollodorus can present the distinction as self-evidently ideal: that could not be bewildering. Still, in its rhetorical context what makes the ideal worth articulating is precisely its problematic relation to reality. The whole point is that Stephanus' household is *not* like that, though (the audience are invited to agree) in a proper world it ought to have been: nor need it follow that the audience themselves would have been able to apply such strict divisions to their own extra-court-room existence (Chapter 10, pp. 191–3): this is a normative construct, not something which necessarily maps simply on to real life.[1]

The highlighting of 'problematisation' remains a healthy approach, and that lesson from Foucault is well-taken. Even in the *Against Neaera* passage some of the moves remain possible: it is still important that the mismatch between this norm and this reality can be made so central to the rhetorical strategy, that it all matters so much. But the approach does need to be made more capacious: more capacious in interpreting problematisation, more capacious in the problems it identifies, more capacious in the genres it considers, more capacious in its reading strategies.[2]

One problematisation we have not yet considered: the problematisation of rhetoric itself, and in particular the ways in which rhetoric *fails*. In genre after genre we find concerns and reservations. In drama, the most skilful speakers are treated with suspicion: perhaps their argument is sinister or off-key in one way or another ('Wrong' in *Clouds*, Polynices in *Phoenissae*, the Nurse in *Hippolytus*, Medea, Apollo in *Eumenides*); perhaps they simply fail to persuade, like Hippolytus defending himself before Theseus, or Hecuba pleading with Odysseus in *Hecuba*. Thucydides' speakers frequently misrepresent reality, or contradict their own moral stances; often (but not always[3]) they make no difference, and the decision is taken that was always going to be taken. *Logos* can be perverted or distorted in Herodotus too, as we saw in Chapter 1 (pp. 10–11). And Plato's reserves about rhetoric are famous. There is constant anxiety, then, that rhetoric somehow misses the mark. The problematisation of rhetoric is interesting as a piece of intellectual history; does it also problematise the approach taken in this book? For the argument here has often been predicated on the presumption that rhetoric is well-judged, that authors knew what they were about and gauged the right stratagems to approach, interest, and persuade an audience.

Yes, a problem perhaps; but not an insuperable one. We should distinguish different types of failure. One, certainly, is the failure to persuade: Hecuba, Hippolytus, Thucydides' Plataeans, his Nicias, and others. Even here it need not follow that the rhetoric was ill-judged: there are always good reasons why the decision will go the other way – overwhelming non-rhetorical considerations predetermining the judgement, or reasons why the speaker cannot use the strongest argument (Hippolytus will *not* break his oath and tell the truth about Phaedra – not that it would necessarily do much good if he did). The choice of arguments can still, normally, be a reasonable one, and the best they can do: that is all the strategy of this book demands. But sometimes the best is not good enough.

More often, though, the failure of rhetoric is not so much a failure to persuade, but more a failure to hit the factual mark, a misrepresentation of reality. In such cases the suspicion can rather rest on its tendency to *over*-persuade: that is the point with most of our 'off-key' instances, and the focus of Plato's concern. That need not invalidate our attempt to derive historical insight from those choices of rhetorical strategies; if anything, it confirms that the speakers knew their trade all too well.

What it does complicate is the attempt to see through the rhetoric and get at the truth, at what really happened. Here too we have seen how important it is to explore rhetorical strategies; several times we have recalled Mandy Rice Davies' 'he would say that, wouldn't he', and been appropriately suspicious (especially Chapter 2, pp. 27–8; Chapter 10, pp. 220, 233–5). We have seen, too, how easy it is for scholars to tell a plausible story to explain why the textual evidence looks the way it does, and how difficult it is to be sure that the story is the only or best one (all those 'Poirots', especially Chapter 2, p. 34, where the term was explained; then Chapters 4 and 8, pp. 75–7 and 149).

Here, though, there may be limits on how far literary approaches can take us. When material looks suspect, normally I have said something like 'we should be suspicious', or 'our nose should twitch': for instance, with Apollodorus' and Euphiletus' mis-summarising of laws which have just been read out; with Plutarch's statement that Alcibiades went off to Caria to raise money, and his ordering of events before the war; with Aristophanes' Simaetha (respectively Chapters 4, pp. 65–7; 10, pp. 227–30; 3, p. 56; 5, pp. 106–11; 8, pp. 151–5). In each case we found reasons why the texts would say that, wouldn't they; in each case it fits the author's narrative or persuasive strategy to manipulate and remould what really happened. Yet, in each case, is this not itself a sort of 'Poirot', a story which I am telling (in this case, a story about the text and the way it functions) to explain why the evidence looks the way it does? Historians and classicists like to use court-room models.[4] If these texts are the 'witnesses' and we demand proof beyond all doubt that they are 'lying', then we have not yet got it. If the events happened exactly as Apollodorus, Euphiletus, Plutarch, or Aristophanes say and they happened to know it, the evidence would look exactly as it now looks. So have we been wasting our time?

Not at all. To give alternative explanations of the evidence is one thing; it need not follow that the explanations are of equal plausibility. In one case (the terms of the Plataean decree; Chapter 4, pp. 74–7) we toyed with two explanations and found one more powerful than the other. In a second (the possible identification of the Megarian exclusion decree and the Charinus decree; Chapter 5, pp. 109–11) we found the arguments more poised. When we identify a strategy which explains why a text should have remoulded material, we have at least altered that balance of probabilities: if there were no clear reason why the sources should misrepresent, if (particularly) a statement even *harmed* their argument, we should be more likely to believe it. In fact, we have done more than that. If we keep our court-room analogy, these are not cases when we should believe every statement in a source 'innocent', i.e. true, until we have proved it guilty – not, for instance, when we can so often trace Plutarch's readiness to rewrite his material elsewhere. The 'burden of proof' might rest on the other side; in an extreme case a source no longer affords 'evidence' at all if it makes statements which it would be making *in any case*, whether they are true or false. But even these phrasings accept the court-room analogy too readily. We are weighing likelihoods, not trying to convict, and we can be pretty sure in those cases where the balance of likelihood falls.

Jane Austen's Catherine Morland did not like reading history.

> 'I can read poetry and plays, and things of that sort, and do not dislike travels. But history, real solemn history, I cannot be interested in. Can you?'
> 'Yes, I am fond of history.'
> 'I wish I were too. I read it a little as a duty, but it tells me nothing that does not either vex or weary me. The quarrels of popes and kings, with wars or pestilences, in every page; the men all so good for nothing, and hardly any women at all – it is very tiresome: and yet I often think it odd that it should be so dull, for a great deal of it must be invention.'
>
> (*Northanger Abbey*, Chapter 14)

It has not been the purpose of this book to put back into history all the themes, including the women, which Miss Morland's men left out. These have been prolegomena, no more. I have often been concerned with the techniques men used to make history look the way they wanted, how (Miss Morland would say) they made it so tiresome. But those methods of 'invention' – at least in the Latin sense of finding and choosing what to say, not necessarily of making it all up – are part of history too. If we look at them carefully, then perhaps we can make it all a little less solemn and a little less dull.

# Notes

## 1 A culture of rhetoric

1 See especially Thomas 1989 and 1991, and on literacy levels also Harris 1989: chapter 4.

2 Thomas 1991: 103–4, 123–6 and Thomas 1993. Even private study of a text would often mean listening to a slave read the text aloud; or even listening to oneself, for silent reading was rare. – True, the evidence for oral performance is late and anecdotal even for Herodotus; it becomes stronger for writers of the third century and later (Momigliano 1978). But there is little evidence of *any* sort for fifth-century reception of the historians. The neighbouring genre of sophistic prose was certainly recited, and the burden of proof is on anyone who would posit a different form of reception for the historians, then a change two centuries later. See also [ch. 8] p. 154.

3 See especially Bers 1985; Ober 1989: 104, 138, 147. On the theatre, *DFA* 272–3 and Csapo and Slater 1995: 290 collect the evidence.

4 Thus for example Gomme, *HCT* iii: 525 and Hornblower 1996: 227, emphasising *Knights* 1303ff. (on which see p. 125).

5 See recently for example Papke 1991; Weisberg 1992; R. West 1993; LaRue 1995; Brooks and Gewirtz 1996.

6 Dershowitz 1996; cf. Pelling 1999b: 343–4.

7 See pp. 101–3; and on the patterning of the Sicily narrative, Rood 1999. Herodotus could suggest the recurrent features of human nature by his own narrative patterning, as tyrant after tyrant launches on self-destructive expansionism. Thucydides confines his attention to the single paradigmatic case of the Peloponnesian War. His readers could best sense what was recurrent by noticing parallels outside rather than within his text: by looking back to Herodotus (Homer too), and forward to their experience of their own time: Pelling 1999b, and p. 102.

8 On tragic suspicion of rhetoric see Halliwell 1997, in particular pp. 137–40 on rhetorical narratives; on tragic rhetoric more generally see Bers 1994.

9 'I am still the same man', 3.38.1 ~ 2.61.2; 'your empire is a tyranny', 3.37.2 ~ 'like a tyranny', 2.63.2; the alternative is 'to play the gentleman in safety', 3.40.4 ~ 2.63.2. These echoes have been widely discussed:

see Hornblower 1991: 334, 337–8 and for example Cairns 1982; Andrews 1994.

10  Gomme, *HCT* ii: 315.

11  Thus at 3.40 'justice' (*ta dikaia*) ends by being dissociated from 'decency' (*epieikeia*) and 'what is proper' (*to prosekon*) and 'reasonable' (*eikos*), and aligned closely with 'expediency' (*to xumpheron*). The language is unnatural; we already see the transvaluation of moral language which will be emphasised at 3.82.4.

12  I have said more about it in Pelling 1991 and 1999a, and more about the Themistoclean example in Pelling 1997d: those articles give further references.

13  See also p. 122.

14  Modern legal theorists similarly warn against taking unquestioned premises or common ground as a pointer to incontestable assumptions, for instance in establishing precedent. Advocates or judges may decide that the best strategy is to abandon some possible lines and concentrate their argumentative fire. See Posner 1988: 4–5.

15  Ober 1989 is the outstanding example of this approach.

16  On this and what follows see especially Jones 1957: 35–7; Dover 1974: 34–5; Markle 1985; Todd 1990b; and especially Ober 1989: chapters V–VI.

17  Cohen 1995.

18  This is well brought out by Ober 1989: 272–7, 324.

19  *Clouds* 521, 526, 527, 535. Cf. Hubbard 1991: 94–5, 102, drawing the parallel with the orators' technique at pp. 94–5 note 20. Markle 1985: 281 similarly speaks of 'flattery'.

20  Geertz 1973: 208–33 is particularly interesting on the complex way imagistic tropes map on to, and can be used to explore, a society's ideology; Kurke 1991 is a fascinating study of Pindaric imagery and the societal constructs it implies. We shall understand much more about this issue in tragedy when the exhaustive and illuminating study of Roger Brock is published.

## 2  Rhetoric and history (415 BC)

1  The precise dating of these events is much discussed: cf. in particular MacDowell 1962: 181–90; Dover, *HCT* iv: 264–76; Aurenche 1974: 156–8; Furley 1996: 119–30.

2  This ugly word is appropriate for the Greek *paranomia* (6.15.4, 28.2). To be *paranomos* is to go against, transgress, human *nomos*; and *nomos*, any convention which normalises human behaviour, embraces both 'law' and 'custom'. Alcibiades shocked.

3  On the timing cf. Dover, *HCT* iv: 276, but the details are very uncertain.

4  Why not? Furley 1996: 52 assumes that Thucydides is 'covering' for Andocides, but the narrative's sympathy is clearly with denounced rather than denouncers. Thucydides' naming habits are generally interesting: see especially Hornblower 1996: 134–7. In ancient literature naming often suggests an alertness to the individual, non-naming focusses more on a figure's type, role, or status (cf. for example Goldhill

1984 on Aeschylus, index s.v. 'naming'; Schaps 1977: 330): but that works less well in Thucydides, where figures are often introduced only to fill a single predictable role. Elsewhere naming can confer a compliment, while non-naming is a gesture of contempt: it is noticeable, for instance, how often Cicero names his friends and allies, but dismisses the likes of Clodius and Antony with a contemptuous 'that robber' or 'that gladiator'. The same may be true here. Andocides did not deserve the respect – even the literary immortality – which naming him would have conferred. – Such habits die hard. In delivering judicial decisions, a style-conscious modern judge tends to give names and personalities to figures favoured in the verdict, while finding against a depersonalised 'plaintiff' or 'defendant': Weisberg 1992: 16–31.

5  On the date of the trial cf. MacDowell 1962: 204–5.

6  For elaborate discussions of the contact between the two sequences, cf. Rawlings 1981: 100–17, Vickers 1995a, and Rood 1998: 180–1. The subtlest treatment is that of Stahl 1966: 1–11, though he is over-sceptical.

7  *Alc.* 18.4–8, *Nic.* 13; cf. Pelling 1992: 24.

8  On this and what follows see the sophisticated discussion of Osborne 1985b.

9  Furley 1996: 21–8.

10  Andocides, *On the Mysteries* (1) 137–9 and other passages quoted by Dover, *HCT* iv: 284, especially Antiphon 5.82–4; Parker 1983: 9 and note 39.

11  On this see especially Sourvinou-Inwood 1990: especially 305.

12  Xen. *Hell.* 1.4.20, Plut. *Alc.* 34: cf. Lewis 1966: 177–8; Murray 1990: 156; and on the seriousness of such profanation Parker 1983: 168–70, 178.

13  I am grateful to Judith Mossman and Christiane Sourvinou-Inwood here.

14  Vernant in Vernant and Vidal-Naquet (1988), 113–40; cf. p. 261, n. 18.

15  Well analysed by Hornblower 1992: see also Powell 1979, especially 21–5 on these events.

16  On this technique in Thucydides see now Rood 1998: 21–3, 109–30.

17  For example MacDowell 1962: 184; more tentatively, Dover, *HCT* iv: 272 and Edwards 1995: 172. *Contra*, Furley 1996: 127–8.

18  At the time of Diocleides' revelations, he has the Boeotians already campaigning 'after hearing about what was happening': but the Boeotians would have had to get wind of Diocleides' revelations a day or so in advance for this to be plausible. Then the troops only slept 'in arms' for one night, so we would also have to posit a very swift Boeotian demobilisation and an unbelievably swift reception of the news of that demobilisation at Athens, convincing them that the external threat was over.

19  Philochorus *FGrH* 328 F 133 (Σ Ar. *Lys.* 1096); cf. Cratippus *FGrH* 64 F 3.

20  Above, note 5.

21  Though Andocides could probably have saved his life by returning into exile. There are some indications that this was what the prosecution wanted (cf. MacDowell 1962: 13, 63).

22  Though here too there may be some disingenuousness: Boegehold 1990.
23  See especially Cohen 1995: 107–12, and his good remarks on several fourth-century cases, 129–30, 137–9, 165–74; Calhoun 1913: 77–85; Humphreys 1985; Todd 1990a and 1993: 96–7.
24  Stadter 1989: lxix–lxxi; for Plutarch's penchant for documentary evidence see also Theander 1951: 78–83, Pelling 1990b: 25–6, and p. 260, n. 6.
25  MacDowell 1962: 167–71, 179; Marr 1971: 326–9, and Edwards 1995: 19–21 are more sceptical.
26  On Lydus, pp. 34–5; on Thessalus, it may be that this denunciation belongs at a later stage of the process, once Alcibiades has fled to Sparta; a new indictment may then be needed to reopen the trial and secure a condemnation in absence. (Thus Marr 1971: 328; Murray 1990: 154 note 17; Furley 1996: 32, 129.) If so, Andocides may have omitted it either as irrelevant, or because of his desire to play down Alcibiades (p. 42).
27  [Dem.] 40.53, cf. MacDowell 1962: 79–80 and the other instances cited by Ober 1989: 149–50 (with some good remarks), 180.
28  As Aristotle knew (*Rhet.* 1408a32–6): cf. Ober 1989: 149.
29  Cf. Xen. *Hell.* 1.2.13; MacDowell 1962: 104; Davies 1971: 17.
30  MacDowell 1962: 88: at least, the *boule* finally 'went out in secret and arrested us' (45).
31  Todd 1990a: 29–30; 1993: 96 note 20.
32  In every 100 citizens 63 might be over 30 (Todd 1990b: 168 note 190), 29 over 45 (Hansen 1985: 12; Todd and Hansen are using the same tables). If the population is constant at year $x$ and at year $x + 15$, as it might well be in normal circumstances, 34 will have died. Some of the rest may also have emigrated. (415–400 were not normal circumstances and the population will have dwindled, but that is taken into account in the text.)
33  Apparently the normal figure: Todd 1993: 83 and note 9.
34  This will only affect matters if the same group is over-represented both on the 415 *boule* and on the 400 jury. The rich may well have been over-represented in the *boule*, but not necessarily on a jury, perhaps indeed the opposite (that issue is hotly disputed); those living locally might well be over-represented on a jury, but the *boule* was constituted by quota from the demes, and these remained population-centres as well as administrative units (Osborne 1985a: 42–3, 47–63, 225 note 90). But there will be subtler slantings, for example under-representation in both groups of the apathetic or the incapable.
35  Cf. MacDowell 1962: 66. This will become important in several later connections, for instance with Aristophanes and Aeschylus: see pp. 136 and 175. This point tells against the suggestion (Bers 1985: 10, cf. Worthington 1992: 199 on Dein. 1.42) that the address may also be aimed at the surrounding crowd (in Roman terms the *corona*). They are not acting as 'the state' in the same sense, and the Deinarchus passage is anyway an invitation to men 'in the court' to tell those 'close to you'. On the Deinarchus passage see Markle 1985: 288–9.
36  Cf. especially Edwards 1995: 21–4.

37 At 22 Leogoras is said to have produced slaves for torture during his prosecution of Speusippus (a spin-off case from Lydus' denunciation of Leogoras), arguing that it was illogical not to accept slave-testimony when offered 'while also forcing to produce their slaves those who refused to do so'. This last 'compulsion' of those who refused most naturally refers to Andocides' own actions.

38 Todd 1990a: 33–5; Gagarin 1996 (preferable to Mirhady 1996). The standard treatment is Thür 1977.

39 That is what happened in the two clearest parallel cases, Dem. 37.40–2 and Isoc. 17.15–17. Cf. also Furley 1996: 66, explaining it all differently.

40 Which may not be much, for Plutarch may well depend on Thucydides here. Plutarch adds that Andocides included some of his own servants among those denounced: not in Thucydides, but perhaps a misinterpretation of Andoc. *Myst.* 64, the prytaneis 'took some slave-girls' – in fact as witnesses, but Plutarch could easily have misunderstood. Cf. Marr 1971: 331; Edwards 1995: 24 note 59.

41 Cf. Ginzburg 1989: 96–125, who engagingly links Freud and the art critic Morelli with Poirot's predecessor Sherlock Holmes: in the late nineteenth century spectacular inferences from minute clues became the hallmark of all three. I owe the Ginzburg reference to Don Fowler, and it was a conversation with him which first suggested the form the argument takes here. Richard Rutherford points out to me that the illogicality of such arguments was already familiar to Aristotle (*Poetics* 1460a18–26: cf. Rutherford's note on *Od.* 19.218). He also reminds me that Michael Innes' *Hamlet, Revenge!* plays wittily on the multiplicity of possible solutions: the detective's sidekick produces a complex scenario which seems to be the solution, but the detective then puts him right with a different, equally contorted story.

42 Thus Marr 1971: 327; Edwards 1995: 19.

43 On this tendency cf. Dover, *HCT* iv: 280–1 note 2; Furley 1996: 44.

44 So Todd 1990c: 171–2.

45 The outstanding example of this aproach is Murray 1990, to which this section is heavily indebted. Osborne 1996 applies similar techniques in discussing earlier Greek history: for instance, he uses Herodotus' account of Salamis to illustrate the post-war political exchanges, thus switching the focus from 480 to the 470s and 460s (Osborne 1996: 339–42).

46 See especially Ostwald 1986: 328–33, 537–50, refining Aurenche 1974; the catalogue of Dover, *HCT* iv: 277–80 is also useful. Their wealth is confirmed by the so-called 'Attic stelai', recording the subsequent sale of their property, *IG* i³: 421–30 (extracts in ML 79 = Fornara 147): on these see especially Lewis 1966 and briefly Osborne 1987: 21–3.

47 On *hetaireiai* see especially Calhoun 1913; Connor 1971: 25–32; Aurenche 1974; Andrewes, *HCT* v: 128–31; Murray 1990.

48 Thus Murray 1990: 151 suggests that real sympotic groups would be less kin-based than Andocides' Diocleides here suggests (42), but that this picture reflects a popular misconception, an 'outsider's view'.

49 Cf. MacDowell 1962: 91; Edwards 1995: 41.

50 As Marr 1971: 328 note 2 ('a clear enough admission of responsibility'), Ostwald 1986: 549, Edwards 1995: 20, and Furley 1996: 62 infer. Furley puts weight on the presence of this Alcibiades' name on the 'Attic stelai' (note 46, above), but that shows only that he was taken to be guilty, not that he was. MacDowell 1962: 104 and Murray 1990: 152 are more cautious.

51 Cf. Marr 1971: 337.

52 Cf. *On his Return* (2) 7, where it is hard to choose between betraying his friends and causing his father's death: Murray 1990: 153. On such a sensitive issue one would not expect audience views to be clear-cut, and in a different context a speaker could present the issue differently. Dem. 54.35 is scathing about Conon's circle, who (he claims) tell lies to support one another in court, then ask 'isn't this what friends and *hetairoi* are for?' Cf. Ober 1989: 258; Calhoun 1913: 77–82.

53 Furley 1996: 103–18.

54 At 4, where he pictures his enemies as convinced that he will not stay in Athens: when he can go safely into exile, 'Will he want to risk his life here? What could lead him to do that? Does he not see the state of the city?' This is not just a matter of adverse conditions for 'a prosperous merchant' (MacDowell 1962: 65). Notice, though, that here as at 36 (below) the delicate point is distanced by being put in the mouth of an enemy. He goes on more cautiously: 'even if the city is as bad as my enemies say…' (5): he avoids making the criticism of the democracy his own. On Andocides as an oligarchic sympathiser cf. (despite frequent overstatements) Missiou 1992.

55 Especially Lysias 14–15, Isocrates 16, [Andocides] 4 (whatever its date), and Demosthenes 21. Cf. now Gribble 1999.

56 Thus, rightly, Murray 1990: 151: otherwise the allegation would not be worth making or the item worth mentioning.

57 We should not try to reduce these varied divisions into one. Alcibiades' enemies would not all be democrats or all oligarchs (cf. Dover, *HCT* iv: 283–4); the pro- or anti-Sicilian debate must have split both the élite (Alcibiades would not have been the only one to hope for glory) and the *demos* (too many ordinary people had seen too much of the war to be sanguine about the risks); not all symposia would be oligarchic, at least not all the time (cf. Aurenche 1974: 26; Ar. *Wasps* 1219–64, with pp. 127–8).

### 3 How far would they go? Plutarch on Nicias and Alcibiades

1 The concept of genre in fifth- and fourth-century historiography is complicated: I discuss some of the issues in Pelling 1999b.

2 Momigliano 1985 and 1993 suggested that biography operated with different truth-standards from historiography, but this is too crude: cf. Pelling 1990b.

3 With four exceptions, *Galba* and *Otho* which formed part of his earlier series of *Lives of the Caesars*, and the free-standing *Aratus* and *Artaxerxes*.

Among the *Parallels* there is also one double pairing, in which the
Spartan kings Agis and Cleomenes are paired with the Gracchi.

4  On this pairing see Stadter 1975, and on comparison in general
especially Erbse 1956, Pelling 1986a, and Larmour 1992.

5  I borrow some material here and in the next few paragraphs from the
fuller discussions in Pelling 1992 and 1997g, and Albini and Pelling
1996.

6  Cf. for example 3.3, 3.7–8 (inscriptions, probably drawn from Craterus'
?early third-century collection of Athenian decrees); 4.5–8, 8.3–4, 11.7
(comic poets); 4.2 (dialogue of Pasiphon); 10.1, 11.10 (Theophrastus);
17.4 (Euripides); 23.8 (Philochorus); 28.5 (Timaeus). Contrast 6.4,
where he might have extracted more from Thucydides about both
Mende and Cythera.

7  On these see pp. 106–11.

8  See the chastening study of Saller 1980, who traces the variations in
detail among imperial anecdotes, and concludes that 'the presumption
must lie against the anecdote's accuracy with regard to facts in the
narrow sense' (81) – and even in some ways the broader sense, for
anecdotes can misrepresent even the structure of institutions and social
practices; their value lies rather in illuminating 'attitudes and
ideologies', provided they are used discriminatingly. Cf. Dover 1988.

9  The further qualification is necessary, for some of the anecdotes may
have originated, and many were doubtless improved, after Alcibiades'
death: still, the idiom of the earliest strata of anecdotes is not noticeably
different from that of the later. – The value of anecdotes has become a
central tenet of 'New Historicism' (cf. for example Fineman 1989 and
several other papers in that volume, Veeser 1989), though it can be
overdone: we cannot *ignore* problems of provenance and historicity, as
many new historicists do in practice.

10  Cf. Pelling 1988a, index s.v. 'characterisation by reaction', and for
example Russell 1963: 23, 25 (= Scardigli 1995: 362, 365); Moles 1988:
38; Duff 1997: 180 and 185 note 45.

11  On that rewriting of *Aratus*, Pelling 1988b: 264–7.

12  For example at 16.2, where Nicias sends the man from Catana on his
missions, and at 19.4, where he makes no response to Gylippus' peace-
offer; at Thuc. 6.64.1–2 it was 'the generals', at 7.3.1–2 'the Athenians'.
At 18.7 Nicias transiently turns to hope; at Thuc. 6.103.3 it was the
Athenians. For similar techniques in other *Lives* cf. Stadter 1989: xlix;
Gomme, *HCT* i: 62–3; Russell 1963: 25 (= Scardigli 1995: 366); Moles
1988: 37; Pelling 1980: 129, 139–40 (= Scardigli 1995: 129–30, 151–4).

13  Pelling 1997f.

14  Stadter 1989: xlix–li compares *Cimon* and *Pericles* along these lines. In
Pelling 1980 I applied this methodology to six Roman *Lives* which seem
to have been prepared simultaneously: they have many divergences of
report and interpretation.

15  Thus for example Russell 1966: 43 (= Scardigli 1995: 201), thinking
that Plutarch discovered more information between *Nicias* and
*Alcibiades*; Camon 1963: 145; Marasco 1976: 114–15. Raubitschek 1948:
208–10 and 1955: 123 (= 1991: 129–31, 321) has a more complicated
picture.

16 What those reasons were may partly depend on the dating, which is disputed. Bianchetti 1979 and Lehmann 1987: 42–5 still prefer the older date of 417, despite epigraphic evidence which suggests that Hyperbolus was active in Athens later in that year (Woodhead 1949); many, for example Kagan 1981: 144–7, Andrewes, *HCT* v: 261 and *CAH* v$^2$: 442, Furley 1989: 140, Mattingly 1991: 23–4, and Harding 1994a: 156–7, now opt for 416; Raubitschek 1948, 1955, and 1958 and tentatively Rhodes 1994, prefer 415, and so on balance do I. Especially if 415 is right, Thucydides' suppression focusses attention more starkly on the Sicilian issue, the sole filter through which we see the Nicias–Alcibiades dispute. That is perfectly possible: on Thucydides' silences see l Chapter 5; and compare how the rift between Pericles and his opponents is filtered through the war-debates of 431–29. It is unsafe to argue in generalities about the political situation, guessing when the ostracism fits best (so especially Lehmann 1987: 43–5). Many events do not happen when they fit best. It is even rash to assume that the issue primarily concerned Nicias and Alcibiades; ostraka reveal votes against several other men, including Cleophon. Cf. Harding 1994a: 158.

17 Especially Camon 1963: 149–50; Kagan 1981: 144–5; Rhodes 1994: 94–6.

18 On the institution cf. especially Vernant in Vernant and Vidal-Naquet (1988), 133–5, making the crucial connection with the scapegoat schema: it targets less 'men of distinction' than 'men who are successful enough' (or 'threaten enough success') 'to risk divine envy', or simply 'men one can blame'. On the reasons for its abandonment, the *graphe paranomon* became a more favoured way of dealing with those held responsible for disasters: the first datable *graphe* comes precisely from 415. Cf. the judicious remarks of Hansen 1991: 205; Harding 1994a: 154–5; Rhodes 1994: 97–8.

19 Connor 1971: 81–4 has some good remarks here.

20 For example Connor 1971: 83–4; Rhodes 1986: 139 and 1994: 93. Hansen 1983: 220–2 is sceptical.

21 The next few paragraphs abbreviate a longer discussion in Pelling 1992.

22 p. 22.

23 Plutarch found this thought-provoking for *Nicias* too, where he extends the generation-gap analysis to Nicias' earlier career (Pelling 1992: 20–1); Andrewes, *CAH* v$^2$: 442 may be wrong to assume he has source-authority.

24 p. 23.

25 p. 23.

26 This is not the place to argue this in detail, but for *Antony* cf. Pelling 1988a: 261–3; for *Caesar* Pelling 1997e; for *Coriolanus* Albini and Pelling 1996 and Pelling 1997g.

27 *Hell. Oxy.* III (p. 3 1.4 Bartoletti): cf. Andrewes 1982: 17. Ephorus' Cymocentricity was acknowledged in antiquity, as Richard Rutherford reminds me: cf. Strabo 13.3.6 = Ephorus *FGrH* 70 F 236 with Barber 1935: 86–7.

28 As does Ellis 1989: 91, seeking to find some truth in all the versions. However, it may also be dangerous to write off Plutarch's version as

'an aberration' or 'a muddled recollection' of *Hell.* 1.4.8–9 (Andrewes 1982: 18): Plutarch may have known what he was doing.

29   As Kagan 1987: 322; cf. Ellis 1989: 93 and even Andrewes, *CAH* v²: 490.

30   Pelling 1988b: 268–74, and more generally on *Lysander* Stadter 1992 and Duff 1997.

31   Ameling 1985; Fuscagni 1989; Hornblower 1983: 120; cf. Gomme, *HCT* i: 72 note 1.

32   I have argued this in Pelling 1995: 208–13; on the few and the many, see also Pelling 1986b and de Blois 1992. An extreme elaboration of 'the few' and 'the many' is found in *Per.* 11, which again has figured too large in discussions of the texture of Athenian politics: Plutarch has reasons for developing the few–many antinomy particularly sharply in this part of *Pericles*. Cf. Pelling 1992: 26–7 and, for scepticism about the political picture implied, Andrewes 1978, and Hansen 1983: 220–2 and 1991: 280–7.

33   Cf. pp. 42, 53; Gribble 1999.

## 4   Rhetoric and history II: Plataea (431–27 BC)

1   The details of the oath are disputed: the version of Plut. *Arist.* 21.1–2 presents various difficulties (though it is less problematic than the discussion at *ATL* iii: 101–4 suggests). On one question, see pp. 73–4.

2   Cf. Isoc. 12.93–4, 14.13, 62; Arrian, *Anab.* 1.9.7; Ael. Arist. 32.402, 35.449, 456, 37.470, 54.112. The emblematic qualities of Plataea were felt as early as 421, when the Athenians treated their disloyal allies at Scione in a way which matched the Spartan treatment of Plataea, then gave their territory to the surviving Plataeans (Thuc. 5.32.1). They were making a point.

3   For the echoes cf. Nouhaud 1982: 263 and especially Trevett 1990: 412–13.

4   So Trevett 1990, suggesting the fourth-century historian Daimachus of Plataea, and Hornblower 1995: 52. Carey 1992: 133 prefers to assume Apollodorus' alterations are his own invention: that, it will become clear, is also my view.

5   As Hornblower 1991: 240 ad loc. suggests, Thucydides may here be tacitly correcting Herodotus 7.233.2, who digresses on the family and puts Eurymachus in command of the Theban assault-force.

6   'King' (in fact, regent): 97. On this Plataean prosecution, cf. p. 262 and note 11 below.

7   Palmer emended the manuscripts' 'ten' to 'two' at 101: Trevett 1990: 413 and Carey 1992: 137–8 ad loc. defend 'ten'. A 'ten-year siege' was a suggestive notion to audiences brought up on the Trojan War (below, note 24).

8   Unless they are the same as the 'most useless males and the women and children' mentioned at 2.6.4 (cf. 78.3): these came to Athens in 431, a full two years before 'the Spartans came to attack', but Apollodorus has already elided that two-year interval at 101.

9   See pp. 74–7.

10  As do the preceding distortions of Plataea's history in the Persian Wars, especially 480–79, at §§ 93–6: Trevett 1990: 408–9.

11  The story may be essentially accurate: so Trevett 1990: 410–11 and Hornblower 1991: 218–19 on Thuc. 1.132.3; *contra*, Fornara 1967 and Carey 1992: 134–5 ad loc. The possibility of oral tradition, Delphian or Athenian and reliable or not, should not be discounted, though Trevett prefers to posit a literary source.

12  As emerges from Thuc. 3.92 and 5.51: cf. Trevett 1990: 416 and Carey 1992: 137 on § 101.

13  Trevett 1992: 190–1 convincingly defends the authenticity of the documents of this speech. This one cannot have been reconstructed later from the surrounding text, for in that case we should not have the mismatches with Apollodorus' glosses (Gawantka 1975: 177–8 note 31); and its detail can be defended as plausible for a 427 decree (pp. 75–6).

14  Grammatically the decree's contrast between first-generation Plataeans and 'their descendants' could refer either (a) to both hereditary priesthoods and archonship or (b) to archonship alone; but later generations would no more have the requisite (presumably patrilinear) ancestry for the priesthoods than their fathers, so (b) must be right.

15  Cf. Osborne 1983: 13–14; Trevett 1990: 189.

16  p. 27.

17  Compare *GHI* ii: 100, the Phyle-fighters of 401–0.

18  For fourth-century ignorance of even the main lines of fifth-century history cf. especially Thomas 1989: 118–23, 201–6.

19  Connor 1985: 10 here has some good remarks, though Robinson 1985: 20 reasonably objects that so peculiarly visual a register is not wholly typical.

20  Cf. Rusten 1989 on 2.4.4.

21  On Thucydides' subtle variations in focalisation see now Rood 1998: *passim*.

22  Notoriously, there is still some awkwardness here. At 5.20.1, if the text is sound, Thucydides seems to look back to the invasion of Attica as the beginning of the war; but the time-period specified in 5.20.1 points rather to Plataea. Cf. especially Rawlings 1979; 1981: 19–25; Hornblower 1991: 236–7 on 2.2–6; Gomme, *HCT* ii: 70 on 2.19.1 and iii: 683–5 on 5.20.1. I agree with Hornblower that Thucydides might think differently about this in different frames of mind – rather as Cassius Dio gives three different dates, 31, 29, and 27, for the beginning of the principate (51.1.1, 52.1.1, and 53.17.1).

23  Contrast Hornblower 1991: 236 on 2.2–6: 'It was arbitrary of Th. to treat an unsupported attack by Thebes as initiating the war when he had refused to do the same for comparable actions by Corinth'; so also Rawlings 1981: 24–5; Smart 1986: 22. But those Corinthian actions preceded the critical decisions by the principals.

24  So, rightly, Stahl 1966: 73–4. There were also attractions in a ten-year war to rival Troy: so Rawlings 1981: 10–12, 24–5, 43–4. Most writers could have found that point suggestive even with a war a little less

than ten years, beginning a few weeks later with the invasion of Attica; but Thucydides, at least when in the mood for chronological precision, is not 'most writers'.

25 p. 72.

26 On this cf. Rood 1998, index s.v. 'delay, narrative', and pp. 89–93.

27 Badian 1993: 112–13. He, like Connor 1984: 52 note 1, sees the importance of the literary technique here.

28 Hence the preoccupation with the unprecedented sufferings, παθήματα, of the war in 1.23: cf. especially Macleod 1983: 105, 140.

29 Macleod 1983: 123–31.

30 See especially Macleod 1983: 103–22, especially 106–7, 113–16, 120–1.

31 There may be some misrepresentation here, though the truth about the Theban constitution in 480 is elusive: cf. Hornblower 1991: 455–7 on 3.62.3 and Macleod 1983: 238–9. Still, such misrepresentation is not Thucydides' point: if it had been, he would have given us the material to identify it. The text focusses the point of principle concerning evasion of responsibility, not the historical reality of 480.

32 A conventional rhetorical protest, but here it is tellingly accurate: Macleod 1983: 113.

33 At 3.36.1 Salaethus, the captured Spartan commander at Mytilene, begs for his life and includes among his offers a promise to get the Spartans to withdraw from Plataea. He may have been lying, or overconfident of his capacity to deliver (Hornblower 1991: 418 ad loc.); but the Athenians never gave themselves the chance to find out, as they executed him straight away. Cf. Rood 1998: 121.

34 The language is ambiguous, with τὰ μὲν κατὰ Πλάταιαν both 'the Plataean affair' in the war, as in the corresponding τὰ κατὰ Λέσβον at 3.50.3, and 'Plataea's history' or at least that of her relationship with Athens: Fowler 1989: 90.

35 Thus, rightly, Hornblower 1987: 35 and 1991: 465–6 ad loc.

36 p. 75.

37 As Fowler (note 34) assumes.

38 See Mossman 1995: 63 on the suggestive exploitation here of formal features and stagecraft; and for a more elaborate comparison of Hecuba with the Plataean debate, Hogan 1972.

39 So also Kagan 1974: 104: 'This offer [of temporary migration], like the others, was a charade': better his p. 174, where the Spartan terms of 429 are 'reasonable'.

40 Gomme, *HCT* ii: 206 on 2.72.3: 'Thucydides himself did not believe in the honesty of the Spartan proposals', cross-referring to 3.68.1. In the latter passage, a complex and probably corrupt sentence, the Spartan justification for their procedure includes the point that 'the Plataeans had rejected the Spartan offer of neutrality'. It is the ironic particle δῆθεν – 'in general terms, conveying that the words used are untrue' (Denniston 1954: 265) – which there suggests Spartan disingenuousness. Yet it need not follow that the offer of neutrality was not 'sincere'. Later in 3.68 Thucydides makes the nature of this disingenuousness clearer: whatever the Spartans said in justification, their true motive was now to gratify the Thebans (§ 4: pp. 77–81).

That need not imply that, whatever their motives, the Spartans would not have honoured the offer made at 2.72.1.

41 Badian makes too much of the Plataeans' failure to respond directly. For all we know, they did protest, but Thucydides felt it too uninteresting to mention: he was clearly less interested in the precise terms of the 479 oath than in the differing ways of arguing its moral implications, for otherwise he would have told us exactly what was sworn. If they did not protest, that may be as much an awareness that the Spartan mind was made up; or an acknowledgement that Archidamus' terms were not ungenerous, and it might be counterproductive to nitpick.

42 Cf. p. 24; pp. 79–80.

43 At 2.11, his encouraging and warning speech to his army before he begins his ravaging: but we know from 1.80–5 that he thinks both encouragement and warning ill-placed, for ravaging will not succeed, and the Athenians need not come out to fight. See Pelling 1991.

44 Badian 1993: 143 comments on 7.18 that 'we are meant to see the Spartans as developing a conscience only when things begin to go wrong'; Hornblower 1994: 148 note 45 agrees. This, I think, overstates. The Spartan religious conscience certainly becomes most relevant in retrospect: the Spartans in 414–13 felt that their moral and religious position was stronger, and were hence more confident. That is why the point is made there rather than earlier, and the language makes it clear that it was later events, Pylos in particular, which brought the point home to the Spartans. But that need not mean that there were no scruples at all earlier. As we are seeing, the narrative itself suggests that Archidamus' reasoning seemed sound to him and his countrymen, and I am unconvinced that Thucydides was so insensitive to his own narrative suggestions as Badian's view implies.

45 For a sensible brief discussion see Hornblower 1991: 449–50 on 3.55.2, refining Amit 1973: 75–8. Similar lines are taken by MacDowell 1985: 319 and Trevett 1990: 188–9. Less plausibly, Hammond 1992: 145–7 makes both Thucydides and Apollodorus refer to the same grant to the refugees, made (he assumes) in 428; that causes problems with the logic of Thuc. 3.55.3, where the Plataeans adduce the grant as a reason for remaining loyal to Athens in (apparently) 431. The speakers might admittedly be fudging; but in that case Thucydides would naturally have given us the information we need to identify the fudge (cf. the argument on pp. 76–7).

46 For speculation on the relationship between Plataeans and Athenians before 479 cf. Badian 1993: 116–22, qualified by Hammond 1992: 143–5: unsurprisingly, in no way an equal relationship.

47 So, rightly, Hornblower 1987: 35 and 1991: 466 on 3.68.5.

48 'Includes' need not imply that Thucydides is necessarily fabricating or reconstructing here (though he may be): see p. 76.

49 3.56.7 has something in common. The Plataeans are pleading with the Spartans to keep faith with good allies, i.e. themselves for their services in 480–79, and to define expediency accordingly: yet this very phrasing accentuates the hopelessness of their cause, for the Spartans' 'good allies' now are the Thebans, and expediency demands that the Spartans favour them rather than the Plataeans. There too, then, a good moral

argument is counterproductive. Cf. Macleod 1983: 110, though he puts it differently.

50  p. 34.

51  The mover is Hippocrates, who – if the 427 dating is allowed – may well be Pericles' nephew, the general of Delium (Davies 1971: 456): so Kagan 1974: 174. But that is not certain enough to count as an argument for 427. The name is not uncommon.

52  Osborne 1983: 13–14, comparing the grant to the Samians (ML 94 = Osborne I.D4).

53  At *Frogs* 694 the chorus of initiates refer to the slaves enfranchised after Arginusae as 'those who fought one sea-battle, and are immediately Plataeans and masters instead of slaves'. This cannot be a reference to anything like 'Plataean rights', a second-class citizenship status like 'Latin rights' at Rome: any suggestion of second-best would be damaging to the rhetoric. Nor is it likely that 'Plataean citizenship' rather than Athenian is in point (Hammond 1992: 147). But it does suggest that the Plataean grant was *the* paradigmatic block-grant in people's minds in 405.

54  On this crucial point see pp. 118–19.

55  Cf. Hornblower 1996: 122–37, especially 131; 142.

56  Note the similar 'alone' exaggeration of [Dem.] 59.94, 95, and Isoc. 12.93, 14.57; Lys. 2.46 is similar. Cf. Hornblower 1996: 131.

57  The same point of principle arises with the Thebans' claim to have been ruled in 480 by a closed regime (*dunasteia*) of a few men (3.62.2), an assertion which is similarly uncontrollable by Thucydides' own narrative, though in that case one we cannot be certain is false: cf. above, note 31.

58  For example Hornblower 1987: 78–80, though I am in sympathy with his criticisms of Schneider and Hunter (see note 59), and Westlake 1973: 106. See also Hornblower's later discussion of such 'privileged access' at 1994: 136–7.

59  For this process cf. especially Schneider 1974 and Hunter 1973; both may overstress this. For criticism of Hunter in a particular instance, cf. Pelling 1991: 128. As Hornblower 1991: 442–3 suggests, there may be such hindsight here at 3.52.2, where the Spartans manipulate the Plataeans into voluntary surrender because they are already thinking forward to the peace terms. What the Spartans foresee is what eventually happens (5.17.2): see note 62. But hindsight is not necessarily wrong: we do need an explanation for the Spartan preference for voluntary surrender, and Thucydides' explanation may be right.

60  Cf. Vidal-Naquet 1986: 64, 70; Edmunds 1984.

61  Fr. 530 N²: Euripides is taken to task by Aristotle fr. 74 Rose, who himself argues in a similarly rationalist way. Cf. Edmunds 1984: 73.

62  The 'almost' needs to be stressed. There remain some uncertainties here. It is unlikely that the neutrality offer of 429 was done for Thebes: that can be excluded under 'almost'. But what of the Spartan scheme at 3.52.2 to secure the surrender of Plataea on terms, 'so that, if it came to peace with the Athenians on the basis that each side should restore the places captured in war, they might retain Plataea on the grounds that it had come over voluntarily'? We are not told that this

too was done 'for the Thebans': should we assume that there too Theban interests are in the Spartans' minds, or is this another exception covered by 'almost'? At 5.17.2 it is the Thebans who argue in 421 against the surrender of Plataea on precisely the grounds given here (cf. above, note 59), which may suggest the first of those alternatives: in that case this is further progressive redefinition, as we come to understand the motives more clearly as we go on.

63    Thebes gained practically from Plataea's destruction, for it gained another two votes in the Boeotian federal constitution, giving them now four out of eleven: cf. *Hell. Oxy.* 11.3 with Bruce 1967: 105–6 ad loc. But Thucydides does not tell us that. The only Theban interest in Plataea he has so far specified is the desire to occupy it, and the long-standing hatred.

64    See note 62.

65    See note 40.

66    And even if the Thebans now represent that offer as 'ours' rather than the Spartans' (3.64.3, if the reading ἡμῶν is right: Gomme prefers ὑμῶν with AEM¹): whether that 'we' is to be taken as 'we Thebans' or 'we of the Peloponnesian alliance', it is in any case a natural rhetorical ploy, assimilating the Spartan actions to their own in order to strengthen the identification with the Spartan audience.

67    On the strategic importance of Plataea cf. for example Kagan 1974: 44. Gomme puts the point rather better at *HCT* iii: 539 on 4.76.5 than at ii: 354.

68    A phrase of Epaminondas: Plut. *Marc.* 21.2, cf. *Mor.* 193e.

69    pp. 90–4.

## 5  Explaining the war

1    It may be a little, but only a little, less presumptuous than it seems. The text may mean 'no-one may be at a loss for *an* answer (Hornblower 1991: 64 ad loc.); and Thucydides is anyway here referring to the 'grounds and elements of rift', i.e. the less contentious narrative of Corcyra and Potidaea, not the 'truest explanation', which he introduces with a more subjective 'I regard as…' – though by then Thucydides' 'I' has acquired a great deal of confidence and authority (cf. Loraux 1986b). Yet those 'grounds and elements of rift' have an explanatory character too, as we shall see; and he does not envisage a future audience which needs or chooses to cast around for alternative explanatory 'grounds and elements of rift', for instance the Megarian decree.

2    Bakhtin 1981 collects important essays on this theme: especially important is his 'Discourse in the Novel' (1981: 259–422), first published in 1934–5.

3    pp. 71–2.

4    Lloyd 1979: 234.

5    This is a very complex area. I hope to return to it in a projected book on fifth-century ideas of historical explanation, and their relation to explanation in other fields.

6  It may not be coincidence that so clear a distinction is made there: there is a good deal of dissembling in the air in that stretch of narrative (note 27).

7  Cf. Hornblower 1991: 31 on 1.9.1, a further instance of this, and 348 on 2.65.11; 1994: 157; Westlake 1969: 161–7.

8  Thus, rightly, von Fritz 1967: i: 624, 629; Heath 1986.

9  A point which some have found so bemusing that two separate words have been posited, (a) πρόφασις from πρό-φημι = 'proffered explanation' and (b) πρόφασις from προ-φαίνω = 'a preceding phenomenon': so Rawlings 1975: especially 36–60; the possibility was already aired by Weidauer 1954: 14. That is impossible; at one point (*On the Sacred Disease* 2 II p. 142 J. = 1 VI p. 356 L.) it requires taking πρόφασις in two different senses within the same sentence; and no linguistic community could continue to distinguish two phonologically identical words, operating in a closely similar semantic range. As for Thucydides, he has no rigorous and systematic causal vocabulary (de Ste Croix 1972: 53–4); it may still be true that at 1.23.6 he deliberately challenges linguistic conventions by using the less expected πρόφασις for his 'truest explanation'. Thus Sealey 1957: 4 ('a suggestion of oxymoron', as more definitely at Dem. 18.225); von Fritz 1967: i: 623–4; Heubeck 1980.

10  pp. 112–13.

11  Fraenkel 1950: 805. Stadter 1993: 43 and Hornblower 1994: 142 stress the importance of this technique in Thucydides. It is a major theme of Rood 1998.

12  An impression which some historians find confirmed in the Callias decrees (ML 58 = Fornara 119), if rightly dated to 434–3: the Athenians are prudently concentrating their treasures on the Acropolis. Cf. the commentary in ML p. 158, and Lewis, *CAH* v²: 373. But the date is very uncertain: see Kallet-Marx 1989 (arguing for 431).

13  Cf. especially Walker 1957: 30–1. The connection of 1.89–118 to the 'truest cause' is already recognised by Dionysius of Halicarnassus: that must be the point of his 'not only is it a natural requirement to set out earlier things before later *and true things before false...*' (p. 82), though 'false' is a misunderstanding of Thucydides' attitude to his *aitiai*.

14  Stadter 1993: 45. In the Archaeology too fortification and maritime power had been emphasised (McNeal 1970: 312–13). We already know that this is how nations become great, and fight great wars.

15  I have said more about this in Pelling 1991: especially 125, 129.

16  Cf. especially Walker 1957; Stadter 1993; Rood 1998: 205–48.

17  So Rood 1998: 217–19, with some further good points.

18  In indirect speech: why? Perhaps because here it is the substance, not the style in which Pericles put it over, which affected planning. When Pericles' own inspiring presentation is what matters, we have full-dress orations in direct speech.

19  So Stadter 1993: 61–2.

20  Kitto 1966: 271, cited by Hornblower 1991: 166 ad loc. Andrewes, *HCT* v: 380 singles out the scale of Chapter 106 as particularly bewildering.

21  The fundamental treatment is now that of Andrewes, *HCT* v: 361–83

and Dover, *HCT* v: 384–444: not all their points convince, but many do. Among the many who have thought the Pentekontaetia unfinished note especially Gomme, *HCT* i: 362–3; Meiggs 1972: 444–6; Connor 1984: 43 note 48; Hornblower 1991: 195; Lewis, *CAH* v²: 372.

22  Though the finishing at the Hellespont, just as Herodotus had finished at the Hellespont, remains intriguing.

23  Thus for example Kagan 1969: 271, 372 and Meiggs 1972: 431 on the Megarian decree; Richardson 1990, arguing more generally that Thucydides was contributing to a continuing debate.

24  p. 82.

25  Not all the points raised by these scholars can be addressed here. Their interpretations, especially those of Badian, are countered in more detail in two outstanding chapters of Rood (1998: 205–48). Dr Rood and I have discussed these issues many times; in this chapter as elsewhere I have indicated where I am aware I am indebted to him, but there may be more besides.

26  That is already true in the first few chapters: Paris' abduction of Helen is not inspired by a desire to get even with the blameworthy Greeks, but a feeling that, now that the mutual recriminations are so strong and so unproductive, he will certainly get away with it (1.3.1).

27  For an especially clear case see the narrative of Cyrene, 4.145–205: the Persians' desire for vengeance may be bogus (4.167.3: p. 86), but Pheretime's certainly is not (4.165.3, 202), and that draws the Persians in. Cf. Sealey 1957: 5–6. The contrast of the two may indeed explain Herodotus' unusual interest in discriminating true and false Persian motives at 4.167.3, and various other disingenuous motives which the sequence subtly explores. I hope to discuss these and other explanatory techniques of Herodotus in my longer work on historical explanation (above, note 5).

28  pp. 10–11. I discuss various aspects of Xerxes' limited freedom of action in Pelling 1996 and 1999a.

29  I have had my say about this in Pelling 1997d.

30  For 'atticising', perhaps a bold neologism, cf. the Thebans at 3.62.2 with Macleod 1983: 116 (though cf. too Hornblower 1991: 455 ad loc.); for Athens as Persia's successor, especially 1.69.5, 77.4, 6.76.4; Stahl 1966: 49–50. For Athens like a tyrant city, Pericles at 2.63.2; the 'like' is dropped by Cleon, 3.37.2; thus, already, the Corinthians at 1.122.3, 124.3. The language of 'empire', 'enslavement', and 'revolt' in the Pentekontaetia pulls no punches: notice especially 1.93.4, 98.4, 99.2–3.

31  Badian 1993: 133–4 is here trenchant and right.

32  Badian 1993: 132 here (as elsewhere in his article) explains such points by saying that the 'enslavement' was too clear to be denied; it could only be palliated. Such an approach is not nonsensical, but it also cannot lose: pro-Athenian points are tendentious, anti-Athenian ones were just impossible for Thucydides to sidestep. Here this is most doubtful. Even the language of 'subjects' could have been presented in a much sunnier way, as for instance by 'Pericles' at 2.41.3.

33  See pp. 119–20, for discussion on whether the Athenians could really have argued in this way.

34  Badian 1993 presents us with a Thucydides who makes Spartans into systematic oath-breakers, and who has Pericles a 'liar' on the terms of the truce. But 'oaths' are mentioned more rarely in a Spartan context than Badian's language suggests; and Pericles' 'lie' concerns an assumed general clause guaranteeing autonomy to the Greeks, which Pericles (he claims) misrepresents at 1.144.2. Badian may be right to posit such a general autonomy clause, but here as elsewhere he represents the moral issues as too clear-cut. 'Autonomy', like freedom and independence today, is a matter of interpretation: it would be no easy matter to define which states were really autonomous in 446, and we need not assume the terms made everything clear. Pericles' 'we will release our cities as autonomous if they were autonomous when we made the truce' need not be an impossible interpretation of those terms, even though it was doubtless tendentious, and presented here in a pointed rhetorical mode. Alternatively, it may be that there was no such clause, and 'Pericles' is simply exposing the Spartan hypocrisy in agreeing terms without demur in 446, and only now turning autonomy into an issue: cf. Rood 1998: 216–17.

35  1.78.4, 85.2, 140.2, 144.2; then 145 includes the item in the Athenian reply to Spartan demands – there too, then, a matter of diplomatic rhetoric.

36  Badian 1993: 151. Moles 1995: 214 points out the importance of Sthenelaidas here.

37  As it is, for instance, in the narrative of Kagan 1969: 170–2. Notice that Plutarch mentions an Athenian offer of truce and arbitration (*Per.* 25.1); Thucydides does not.

38  So, in particular, de Ste Croix 1972: 200–3, following Jones 1952–3 and followed by Cartledge 1982: 262–3 and Badian 1993: 138. I prefer Meiggs 1972: 190 note 3: 'There is no need to infer more than that Sparta thought the subject deserved consideration'. Cf. Rood 1998: 218. The 'Peloponnesians' seem to have been taken into account in the post-war Samian settlement (ML 56 = Fornara 115 line 7), but we cannot tell how.

39  Whether or not we count that a real League 'congress': on that issue, cf. de Ste Croix 1972: 201 and Hornblower 1991: 108–9. The important point here is that Thucydides' text does not encourage us to distinguish that summons from that in 440: so few details are given of each that confusion of the two processes is easy (as the scholarly literature amply demonstrates).

40  So Rhodes 1987: 162–3. Rood 1998: 214–15 reasonably objects that we do not know enough of these issues, especially the Aeginetan affair, to be sure that Athens' case was so weak.

41  pp. 108–11; cf. Connor 1962: 233–4, followed by de Ste Croix 1972: 251.

42  To use the term introduced on p. 34.

43  Thus Gomme, *HCT* i: 466 and Sealey 1991: 156–7; de Ste Croix 1972: 244–5 is rightly more sceptical.

44  To judge from Diodorus 12.38–40, where we see a careful supplementation of a Thucydidean framework from other sources; some may be owed to Diodorus himself, but probably not all.

45 p. 46.

46 That is, 'the agora of the Athenians' (de Ste Croix 1972: 396–8). The interpretation of 'agora' is hotly disputed: de Ste Croix 1972: 267–84 argued for the demarcated Agora proper, rather than the wider commercial area or a less physically conceived Athenian 'market'; Gauthier 1975 has some good arguments for a more traditional, commercial interpretation.

47 Thus Brunt 1993: 1–16 (first published 1951) was wrong to use Thucydides' silence to argue for a date well before 433 (though it is true that nothing *precludes* an early date: cf. below, note 67); Gomme, *HCT* i: 450 note 3 was wrong to wonder whether Thucydides' silence should exclude a 432–1 dating for the Charinus decree; and Connor 1962 and 1970 was wrong to use Thucydides' silence as an argument (admittedly only a supporting argument) for dating the Anthemocritus and Charinus sequence to 350–49, and inferring that Plutarch or a source had wrongly attached it to events a century earlier.

48 Thucydides' Corinthians in 433 mysteriously urge the Athenians to 'do something to diminish the previously existing suspicion over Megara' (1.42.2). That may have something to do with the Megarian decree (Tuplin 1979 demolishes linguistic arguments against this interpretation), but even if it does it need not mean the decree has already been passed (there was doubtless some build-up); and other interpretations are anyway possible, though less likely. No inferences can be based on it.

49 Badian 1993: 156 finds this too simple a view, with some reason: usually the best thing to do with an insincere proposal is to accept it, and expose the insincerity. Matters might however be different in this case. An acceptance, even a provisional acceptance, of Sparta's demand would damage Athenian prestige before the other Greeks; if Pericles opposed the proposal (as was particularly likely, given his association with the Megarian decree), then the divisiveness would be more damaging still. If war came anyway, both aspects would give an unfortunate impression of weakness of resolve.

50 Dover, *HCT* v: 421–2 finds 'a certain lack of balance' between the rest of Book 1, emphasising Corinth, and the demands made in 1.139: but any imbalance merely suggests that Sparta's stance in 1.139 is disingenuous.

51 Badian 1993: 155–6 prefers to assume that, had the Athenians repealed the decree, that would be the end of it and Sparta would be content, though her allies would most certainly not be. On that view, the risk Sparta was taking with her alliance was very great: cf. Cawkwell 1997: 36–7. Sparta would also be inept in making the one demand which made it a trial of Pericles' personal strength, and phrasing it in terms which allowed him no room for manoeuvre.

52 p. 151.

53 On this, and on much of what follows, see Fornara 1975, Stadter 1984 and especially 1989: 263–305.

54 Historians here tend to pick and choose among Plutarch's items, and to assume they had source-authority accordingly. Badian 1993: 160 and

235–6 note 62 accepts Pericles' responsibility for changing the mind of the assembly, but not for the original ten-ship decision; he regards the charge of pettiness against Lacedaemonius as absurd, but assumes Plutarch found it in a source. So does de Ste Croix 1972: 76–7, though he doubts Pericles' responsibility for either decision, and suggests that Cimon's son was chosen as the man least likely to break the treaty if he could avoid it. Kagan 1969: 238–9 accepts Pericles' responsibility for both decisions, and thinks he implicated Lacedaemonius as a ploy against Thucydides son of Melesias. Kagan is less likely to be right than Badian or de Ste Croix, but all three underplay the possibility of Plutarch's own guesswork and expansion.

55 pp. 47 and 48–9.

56 Thus Stadter 1983: 135 note 7 and 1989: 265, suggesting that Plutarch has transferred to Pericles a decision attributed to 'the Athenians'.

57 De Ste Croix 1972: 231, 388–91 is surely right to assume that this 'every' (πάσης μὲν ἀγορᾶς) is simply Plutarch's rhetorical elaboration of Thucydides' wording; he might have added that the double hiatus in Thucydides' μηδὲ τῇ Ἀττικῇ ἀγορᾷ (1.139.1, the passage presumably before Plutarch's eyes) would be unacceptable to Plutarch. But such elaboration makes it less likely that, as de Ste Croix also thinks, the phrase 'under Athenian control' is authentic, and taken by Plutarch from Craterus.

58 The imperfect ἐδόκει has equal manuscript support to the present δοκεῖ, and is probably right: it was the perception of Pericles' contemporaries (something easy to infer from Thuc. 1.139.4, 140.4) which explains why he opposed the repeal so vehemently, and goes on to explain the hostility he incurred.

59 Stadter 1989: 272 ad loc. concedes that this translation is possible, but prefers 'was responsible' for ἔσχε... τὴν αἰτίαν. But aitia strongly suggests 'blaming', the charges made at the time, and that suits the context's stress on Pericles' unpopularity.

60 Dover 1966 makes a lot of these 'Megarians', taking them to be written sources, but we need not take them very seriously. It is characteristic of Plutarch to construct how audiences respond (p. 47); here he can be reporting or constructing how his contemporary Megarians would respond to the charges (notice the present 'turn' and 'quote', which could refer to earlier written sources but could equally mean a current oral tradition: cf. Connor 1970, de Ste Croix 1972: 387, Stadter 1989: 282, and for contemporary sensitivity to the issue Paus. 1.36.3).

61 Thus Stadter 1984 and 1989: 276. Plutarch's phrasing at *Advice on Public Life* 812d confirms that he identified the two decrees: Pericles 'carried the decree against the Megarians through Charinus'. The same assumption seems to be made by Σ Arist. *Peace* 246 (as emended).

62 There was evidently some: at *Arist.* 26.2–5 (= *FGrH* 342 fr. 12) Plutarch criticises Craterus for his claim that Aristides was convicted of corruption, and says that it would normally be in Craterus' manner to cite his evidence, epigraphic or literary, for such a claim. Other fragments also look like commentary (e.g. frs. 1, 17, 19, 21). Cf. Jacoby, *FGrH* III.b Komm. 96, and for Plutarch's use of Craterus Stadter 1989: lxix–lxxi.

63  The exception is Stadter 1984, building on a suggestion made by Holzapfel 1879 and rejected ever since.

64  Though perhaps not inevitably: see below.

65  Not very, according to de Ste Croix 1972, supported for example by MacDonald 1983; more substantially, according to most who have responded to de Ste Croix, for example Gauthier 1975; Fornara 1975: 223; Legon 1981: 213–23; Hornblower 1991: 111; Sealey 1991 (stressing particularly exclusion from harbour and agora *courts*). We shall return to this when discussing *Acharnians* (p. 156).

66  Stadter 1984: 364–5, 367–9. (Stadter's other arguments, dismissing further objections to the identification, seem to me well-founded.)

67  Fornara 1975: 226–7 argues against Brunt (above, note 47) that, if the decree were much before 432, Thucydides would have had more, not less, reason to mention it, as it would have exposed Sparta's negotiating position as a diplomatic ploy. Perhaps; but Thucydides' narrative has unmasked the Spartan tactics in other ways (by including their prior decision to fight, by stressing their fear, by including the Megarian demand in a sequence of pose-striking demands). His disposition of detailed narrative is more concerned to highlight the matters of substance. A full Megarian section would have given the impression that it all mattered.

68  So Brunt 1993: 15. It is probably after the 1.139 diplomatic exchanges too. Connor 1962 feels that there is no room for Anthemocritus' gentle message after Pericles' strong stance there, and certainly the response of 1.144.2 is not at all courteous. But reasonableness of tone need not exclude firmness of substance; and it is possible that 1.144.2 is combining material from several different contexts, including later, more uncompromising responses: see p. 117.

69  For instance Cawkwell 1969: 333–4 and 1997: 111–14 places Anthemocritus' mission in spring 431: at that point heralds would regularly have toured Greece offering truces for the Eleusinian mysteries, and this time the herald to Megara and Sparta might reasonably denounce the affront to the goddesses instead. Connor 1970: 307–8 finds this harder to believe at Sparta than at Megara; but 'remonstrance', lit. 'speaking in the language of right and wrong' (*dikaiologia*), need not represent an attempt to justify themselves to the Spartans (hard to believe after Thuc. 1.145.1) as much as a propaganda display before the Greek world.

70  I resist the temptation less well on p. 156.

## 6  Thucydides' speeches

1  Cf. de Ste Croix 1972: 62, Dover, *HCT* v: 417–18, Ostwald 1988: 2–3, Hornblower 1991: 66 on Thuc. 1.23.6, all emphasising the 'fear'.

2  See especially Ostwald 1988: 5.25.3 is particularly revealing (Ostwald 47–8, Dover, *HCT* v: 419–20).

3  On this aspect of the Corcyra and Corinth narrative, see Rood 1998: 210–13; on the 470s as prefiguring 432, Pelling 1991: 124. Ostwald 1988: 25–32 collects and illuminatingly treats these *ananke* passages.

4  Cf. Stahl 1966: 39–40 on the Corcyrean debate; Kagan 1969: 242.

5  The sort of retrospect that enabled Thucydides not merely to write 1.23.6, but also at 1.118.2 to talk of the Spartans as 'in the past, too, slow to go to war *unless forced to do so*', and to imply that their 432 decision was a further instance of this (note that 'too').

6  Grant 1965, arguing that the Athenian speech at Sparta is no more provocative than we should expect.

7  Gomme, *HCT* i: 139.

8  For Dover, *HCT* v: 394, the significant problems are posed not by the statement of principle but by its relation to the speeches; in itself, it would have been 'obvious' that he was aiming for maximum accuracy. That is over-bland.

9  Thus, effectively, de Ste Croix 1972: 8 note 9.

10  I have translated 'sense' despite the arguments of Badian 1992, quoting with approval 'Willensrichtung' (Schwartz) and arguing for 'intention'. True, a spoken *gnome* is a rendering into words of what one thinks (*gignoskei*), which, like the Latin *sententia*, can range from a specific 'proposal' to a wider 'thesis' about an issue or a state of affairs. But 'intention' ties it too closely to the mental preliminaries rather than the speech-act itself (Thucydides speaks of 'the general *gnome* of what was really said', not 'of those who really said it'). At 6.21–3 the *gnome* in Nicias' mind may be 'let's put the Athenians off', but the *gnome* of what he says is 'if we do it, let's do it on a large scale'.

11  De Ste Croix 1972: 8–10.

12  Cf. Dover, *HCT* v: 394–5.

13  Thus, correctly, Wilson 1982: 98–9.

14  One cannot put it stronger than that: the possibility of 'Poirots' (p. 34) is clear, and other explanations might also work, for example the suggestion of Dover, *HCT* v: 396–8 and others that Thucydides' technique altered linearly over time, with an increasing proportion of free composition. But little supports that suggestion (for even before his exile Thucydides would not have heard many of the speeches he relays), whereas the possibility aired here is both powerful, in that it explains the phrasing well, and plausible, in that we might not be surprised if Thucydides followed different procedures with different source-material.

15  Or expected to compose: but the methodological introduction, like most prefaces, was probably written when much of the work was already complete, as the tenses suggest – 'it was difficult', 'I have put things', 'I have thought it right', 'as it seemed to me', 'at which I was present', 'of which I heard from others'. Thus for example de Ste Croix 1972: 10–11.

16  So Meyer 1899: 385 and others; Dover, *HCT* v: 398 note 1 is too harsh on this suggestion.

17  Cole 1991: 104–11. Badian 1992 takes *gnome* as 'intention' (above, note 10), and thinks Thucydides is promising to allow his speakers the most rhetorically effective way of producing their intended effect on their audience. That is vulnerable to the same objection.

18  Egermann 1972: especially 580–5. For Archidamus at 2.11 cf. Pelling 1991.

19  Including, interestingly, a contrast between the speeches 'either before the war or after its outbreak' and the actions 'done in the war': he does not seem to be extending the same principles to the actions he has collected in Book 1 (particularly, I suppose, the Pentekontaetia). It is uncertain how much we should make of this.

20  On the verbal echoing cf. especially Wille 1965: 61–9 = Herter 1968: 700–16. Dover, *HCT* v: 395 infers from it that Thucydides' procedures with speeches and actions would be closely parallel: that is too simple, for the verbal patterning suggests points both of parallel and of contrast. Here the echoed key-word 'precision' contrasts what was feasible and attained in each case, despite Gomme, *HCT* i: 143: so, rightly, Wille 1965: 64 = Herter 1968: 705.

21  The previous day Cleon had 'won' (3.36.6) which does suggest that he was the most effective advocate of harshness; Diodotus had 'particularly opposed him' (3.41), which again says nothing of effectiveness.

22  Cf. Gomme, *HCT* i: 141 and especially Dover, *HCT* v: 397–8. As Dover recommends, the sceptical might try condensing a fourth-century symbouleutic speech into Thucydidean form, a most revealing experiment.

23  Which is not to exclude a degree of characterisation by style: cf. Hornblower 1987: 57; Pelling 1991: 133; Francis 1991–3; and especially Tompkins 1972 and 1993.

24  On this progressive redefinition see especially Connor 1984: 36–47 and index s.v. '*tropoi*'. Rood 1998: 225–48 brings out the ways in which the Pentecontaetia both confirms and (especially on the Spartan side) refines the initial categories.

25  On this cf. especially Raubitschek 1973: 36–8, bringing out the expressive contrast with Euphemus at Camarina (6.82–7).

26  On this fundamental principle I agree with Kagan 1975: 77–9, though his general standpoint is more one-sidedly 'accurist' than mine.

27  As de Ste Croix 1972: 261 and Brunt 1951: 271 = 1993: 3 base arguments on the Corinthians' silence about the Megarian decree in 1.68–71. But 1.67.4 has already made it clear that the Megarian decree was in the air; nothing would be gained by going over the same ground in the speech.

28  Most famously by Gomme, *HCT* i: 252–4; also by Westlake 1973: 101–2, who argues that preambles and speeches are often imperfectly integrated and date from different strata of composition. Cf. also Raubitschek 1973, especially 34–6, 39, 48, and particularly Stahl 1966: 43–54. – Richard Rutherford points out to me that *Iliad* 24.649 may be a partial parallel for the procedure I here suggest, if ἐπικερτομέων there introduces an element not apparent in the speech itself.

29  This preamble is particularly elaborate, and labours the speakers' pacific intent; was Thucydides aware that the tone of his direct speech would be particularly difficult to judge, and concerned to protect his readers from misunderstanding (a suggestion made in passing by Stahl 1966: 46)?

30  p. 11.
31  On the interesting focalisation here (is it Thucydides or the sailors who think the task horrible?) cf. the good remarks of Hornblower 1994: 135. The sailors at least must *share* that view, otherwise there was no reason for the ship to be going slowly. – Philip Stadter puts to me that *allokotos* is a fascinating word to use: it means more 'strange' or 'striking the wrong note' than, in itself, 'horrid'. 'The horrid aspect', he suggests, 'is not in the word, but in our own reactions, which is very nice on Thucydides' part: is the focalisation that of the sailors, the Athenians, Thucydides, or us his readers?'


## 7  'You cannot be serious': approaching Aristophanes

1  *Life of Aristophanes* (*Proleg.* XXVIII 46–9, p. 135 Koster); Riginos 1976: 176–8.
2  The text of the *Life* has Plato sending 'the poetry of Aristophanes, the accusation of Socrates in *Clouds*'. Some have deleted the reference to Socrates and *Clouds*; van Leeuwen suggested that the word 'removing' had fallen out of the text before 'the accusation', and in the standard edition Koster comments that something like van Leeuwen's suggestion 'is what you might expect from Plato'. That is naïve. Athens' treatment of Socrates was, for Plato, the most telling indictment of the city's political culture.
3  Though we sometimes make them a little too ordinary. Strepsiades in *Clouds* has married a rich woman, and Philocleon in *Wasps* has a son more than ready to support him in comfort. This alignment with the slightly better off reminds one of the way in which rhetorical audiences aligned themselves with those better off (Chapter 1, pp. 13–16): it may be relevant that theatre-going too was a citizen experience (pp. 134–5), and citizens were alert to their privileged status.
4  Respectively, *The Brittas Empire*; *Waiting for God*; *Absolutely Fabulous*; and several shows, in particular *One Foot in the Grave*. I am grateful to my teenage daughter Sally for invaluable help with this paragraph.
5  As my daughter puts it: see last note. *Saved by the Bell, Boyz Unlimited, Friends*, and *California Dreams* are the telling evidence in this sentence.
6  This has something in common with what Barthes called 'reality effects': cf. Goldhill 1991: 188.
7  So fine that an item can cross it within a few years. In the 1980s the notions of privatising prisons, of a standardised Eurosausage, and of calling hospital patients 'customers' all appeared in satirical burlesques; by the 1990s all had happened.
8  This insight draws on Bakhtin's work on Rabelais (1968), but is easy to misuse. For sensitive modern treatments, with very different emphases, cf. Henderson 1990 and Goldhill 1991: 176–88. A further point is the way in which the diction of comedy contrasts with more elevated norms, rather as Bakhtin stressed the prevalence of the lewd, vulgar, excretory, and corporeal as features of carnival: but the parallel is complicated by the importance of *tragedy*, not just the norms of establishment

institutional language, as a distinctive elevated pole which is inverted, and against which comedy defines itself. See also p. 164.

9  As Henderson 1990: especially 274, emphasises: he distinguishes the carnival festival as more 'autonomous' than the Athenian equivalent. This, I think, is misleading: carnivals are typically sited firmly in the life of the community and in the rhythm of the agricultural year. Any 'autonomy' is societally authorised.

10  An important qualification, for the challenge to norms can, in unusual and tense circumstances, become very dangerous (cf. Stallybrass and White 1986: especially 14–16 and 42–3, and for a brilliant analysis of a particular instance Le Roy Ladurie 1979); and it is arguably central to carnival's ordered function that potential danger is sensed and overcome. Goldhill 1991: 176–88 has some good remarks here.

11  As both Goldhill 1991: 184 and Henderson 1990: 274 stress.

12  Cf. especially Jackson 1981.

13  Which is not to say that patterns of structure and predictability in fantasy always map in a one-to-one way on to those of real life. Any *Star Trek* addict develops a nose for the five or so recurrent story patterns – will Commander Data or the holographic doctor be taken over by an alien force yet again? Will there be a problem with the prime directive not to interfere with other cultures? – without knowing any one-to-one counterparts. But even these map in a subtler way on to obsessive fears and moral problems familiar in real life, and in some ways articulate them in a particularly clear way: it is revealing of our real-life codes that a prime directive would make moral sense, and would cause problems of this sort. And as usual the ideological patterns of literature interact with and become part of life. Once one has learnt to characterise rude hotel-keepers as Basil Fawlties, that pattern is infected by and infects our categorisation of its real-life counterpart, just as the Athenians might categorise their Sicilian experiences in modes parallel to those of *Birds*.

14  On Sicily as a step into the unknown cf. 6.1.1, subtly reinforced within 6.1–5: cf. Connor 1984: 158–61, and on the likely exaggeration of Athenian ignorance, Hornblower 1987: 147–8 and 1994: 146–7 note 43. On Syracuse and Athens as 'of the same character', especially Thuc. 6.20.3, 7.55.2, 8.96.5 with Avery 1973. Thucydides' narrative accordingly leaves the impression that Syracuse was more clear-cut a democracy than seems to have been the case. Aristotle *Politics* 1304a27 talks of Syracuse as becoming 'a democracy instead of a *politeia*' (whatever that may mean) *after* the Athenian defeat, and Diod. 13.34.6 points to some democratic reforms in or after 412. Cf. Dover, *HCT* iv: 430–1, unduly minimising the non-Thucydidean indications. On the Athenian flavour of the Hermocrates–Athenagoras debate (6.32.3–41) cf. especially Connor 1984: 168–76.

15  Cf. especially Bowie 1993a: 166–77; Konstan 1995: 42–3.

16  We might also, for instance, find it indicative of deeply structured assumptions that the new ordering which they bring to the birds' society involves the demarcating of space, defending their air and refusing to allow others to transgress it: see Konstan 1995: 29–44.

17 Bowie 1993a is the outstanding example of this approach. The schemata need not always be as conscious, either in author or in audience, as Bowie's own treatment implies: we do not, for instance, have to assume a skit on or parody of ephebic transitions or religious initiations to find the categories useful for interpreting *Wasps*, *Clouds*, or *Frogs*.

18 Cf. Stallybrass and White 1986: 56–8, to whom the term is owed.

19 p. 108.

20 p. 108, and note 60.

21 Philochorus: *FGrH* 328 fr. 121 = Σ Arist. *Peace* 605. Ephorus: *FGrH* 70 fr. 196 = Diod. 12.39.1–2 (though Jacoby in *FGrH* assumes too readily that all the Diodorus passage is Ephoran).

22 *Per.* 31.5: cf. Stadter 1989: 285–7, 296: see also p. 152. The source is probably Craterus' collection of Athenian decrees (pp. 45 and 109).

23 *FGrH* 115 fr. 93: 'Theopompus in *Philippica* 10 says that the knights hated Cleon: for he was humiliated and angered by them, and so set upon the constitution [? – or 'state', or 'political line': the Greek is *politeia*] and continued to work against them: for he attacked them for desertion (*leipostratia*)'. Fornara 1973 argues that 'set upon the constitution' is a misunderstanding of an attack on the cavalry's equipment loan (he suggested that the underlying word might be *katastasis*, 'set-up', which could be used of either constitution or loan). It is more likely that the scholiast is simplifying some Theopompan suggestion that hostility to the knights launched Cleon on his public career: so Connor 1968: 50–3.

24 As they later came to be, with a strong oligarchic tinge, especially in 411 and 404/3: cf. Bugh 1988: 114–18, 120–53, Spence 1993: 215–17 and for example Hornblower 1991: 89 on Thuc. 1.45.2, Ober 1989: 204, Siewert 1979: 285–7. Lys. 20.24–5 suggests that the knights' oligarchic flavouring was as early as Sicily ('although I served in the cavalry' I was an impeccable democrat...). Bugh 1988: 80–1, 107–14 and Spence 1993: 211–15 make a good deal of the assumed hostility between 'the knights' and Cleon in the Archidamian War.

25 Cf. Gomme, *HCT* ii: 278–9 on Thuc. 3.19.1; Sommerstein 1981 on *Knights* 924. At *Knights* 773–6 and 923–6 the Paphlagonian's taste for *eisphorai* might well be a general feature of the demagogue rather than a personal feature of Cleon, but it is unlikely that Theopompus would have read it that way. The wording of fr. 93 (above, note 23) suggests that Theopompus had some specific attack of Cleon's in mind. We should not make much of that. How would one best attack cavalry? By claiming that they were shirking the hard work of the hoplite infantry or of the ordinary rowers – so (*pace* Carawan 1990) even the 'desertion' charge can be imaginative inference, Theopompus' or his source's and correct or not. Alternatively, Theopompus may be inferring from a scene in a lost comedy: so Reckford 1987: 512 note 13.

26 Which is not to say that they could not co-operate in other ways, conscious of their *military* unity: in the mid fifth-century they dedicated a monument commemorating a cavalry victory (*IG* i²: 400 = Fornara 83). For discussion cf. Bugh 1988: 45–52.

27 Cf. Dover 1968a: l–li, lxvii, and note on *Clouds* 331; Wilson 1977: 282–3.

28 'Probably', because our source ($\Sigma$ *Ach.* 6 = *FGrH* 115 fr. 94) simply tells the story and adds a note that 'Theopompus tells of this': a manuscript problem means that we cannot even tell whether this note came at the end or in the middle (Connor 1968: 54–5). Most scholars (including Connor 53–9 and Flower 1994: 172) assume that Theopompus told the whole story, and that may be right; it is possible however that he only mentioned the 'demanding back'. But even that is surely no more than extrapolation from Aristophanes.

29 An allusion to Euripides' *Telephus* (fr. 720 N$^2$), the first of many: see pp. 141–5.

30 Connor 1968: 56–7 and Bugh 1988: 109–11 doubt that there was any trial (and Theopompus' words do not have to be taken that way); but they accept that the knights demanded the return of five talents which Cleon had allegedly received. Spence 1993: 212–13 is more non-committal. Reckford 1987: 512 note 13 prefers, as I do, to assume a reference to a comic rather than real-life scene. Carawan 1990 defends the Theopompus material, and thinks that Cleon was prosecuted by *probole* for misdemeanours involving Miletus and settled expensively out of court.

31 One again needs to point to the Poirot-dangers (p. 34) of a 'natural reading'. This is not the only way of explaining the phenomena; if there had been a real trial, that is how the spectators would take it, and they would not be bemused. But the point is that Aristophanes' words are not evidence for such a trial, even if Theopompus took them as such.

32 As for example Carawan 1990 assumes: this then causes difficulties, as the fragments of *Babylonians* do not lend themselves to such a scene (p. 141) – though they hardly exclude it either.

33 If indeed these islanders do come from Theopompus: above, note 28.

34 Cf. Sommerstein 1980: 158 ad loc.

35 Above, note 25.

36 Despite the massive fifty-talent fine on Miltiades at Hdt. 6.136.2, where the sum may paradoxically have been set so large to encourage an acquittal. The half-talent proposed for Socrates at *Apol.* 38b is presumably closer to the going rate. On 'fines' cf. Todd 1973: 143–4; MacDowell 1978: 257–8; Harrison 1968–71: ii: 179–85, 209. We should not confuse a fine payable to the state with compensation or reimbursement payable to the wronged party, and the latter is more likely to be (or to have been taken by Theopompus to be) in point here – if indeed we are talking of a trial at all.

37 pp. 145–50. The identification of the 'I' of the clash with Cleon is very difficult, as we shall then see: but it is again unlikely that Theopompus or his source would have found it so.

38 For 'Poirots' cf. p. 34.

39 Or, as Dover 1987: 281 puts it, 'the tacit assumptions without which the joke is not a joke'.

40 Sommerstein 1980: 159 on *Ach.* 22.

41 Sommerstein 1980: 159 on *Ach.* 43.

42 Todd 1990b: 155–6.

43 The parabasis is a section found in many, though not all, the plays,

when the chorus address the audience directly and discuss issues –
sometimes the poet's work, sometimes the chorus' own identity or
experience, sometimes some other political topic – in a register less
tied to the plot.

44  It is disputed whether this refers to *Knights* or *Wasps* itself: I prefer the
first alternative, but it makes no difference to the argument here.
Aristophanes was proud enough of the lines to reuse some of them in
the parabasis of *Peace* 752–9 a year later.

45  Mastromarco 1993: 347–54 thinks that the trick was played not on Cleon
but on the 'some who said I'd made my peace'. He identifies these with
some rival comic poets; the 'trick' will be something extradramatic
and now unidentifiable. That is less likely: any such 'trick' on dramatic
rivals would surely be something dramatic itself (what other setting
did comic dramatists have for making statements to one another?),
presumably some less anti-Cleon play – yet there is no room for any
such play between *Clouds*, with its anti-Cleon digs at 575–94, and *Wasps*
itself.

46  Thus MacDowell 1971: 299 ad loc. and 1995: 176. Sommerstein 1980:
2–3 and 1983: 234 thinks that it happened in court, and Cleon dropped
a prosecution in return for Aristophanes' promise. He suggests that
the prosecution was for exercising citizen rights illegally: this is based
on $\Sigma$ *Ach*. 378 and the ancient *Lives* of Aristophanes (*Proleg.* XXVIII 20,
XXIXa 14–15, pp. 134, 137 Koster). But those passages look like
scholiastic guesswork based on the assumption that Aristophanes was
an Aeginetan (which may itself be largely or wholly inferred from *Ach*.
653–4): cf. Lefkowitz 1981: 109; Rosen 1988: 63–4. And, for what it is
worth, the more detailed *Life* puts the prosecution before *Acharnians*.

47  This qualification is required. One fantasy which lasted was the
cartoonist Steve Bell's creation of a John Major who wore Superman Y-
fronts outside his trousers. Another is the story of David Mellor (a
disgraced Cabinet minister and football fanatic) having sex with his
girlfriend in a Chelsea football shirt, which found a relishing tabloid
audience and remained a standing joke long after it was revealed as a
complete fabrication. But the notion of Cleon attacking Aristophanes,
if false, is not so funny as either.

48  Thus Halliwell 1991, analysing the evidence for restrictions with a
scepticism which is largely justified. He does accept the evidence of $\Sigma$
*Ach*. 67 that a decree 'about not *komoidein*' was passed in 440–39 and
repealed three years later. That decree is normally taken as restricting
attacks on individuals (*onomasti komoidein*). Halliwell 58–9 prefers to
think that the restriction applied to the Dionysia and topics of central
civic importance, but that draws on what may be an over-literal
reconstruction of the dispute over *Babylonians* (pp. 145–50). Halliwell
accepts that the restriction was inspired by the crisis of the Samian
revolt, and that itself suggests that the assembly felt comedy could be
a seriously destabilising influence. In 415, so $\Sigma$ *Birds* 1297 reports, one
Syracosius 'seems to have proposed a decree prohibiting named ridicule
in comedy'. The scholiast is only guessing ('seems'). If there is substance
in the notice (and Halliwell 59–63 again has some good grounds for

scepticism), the 415 dating points to another national crisis. Cf. also Sommerstein 1986.

49  Cf. for example Sommerstein 1980: 16; Heath 1987b: 12–13.

50  Cf. Carey 1993a.

51  Reckford 1987: 189–93, who usually exploits modern parallels with insight and dexterity, I think goes astray in his parallels to the *Acharnians* scene (a Chaplin film and a Trudeau cartoon-series). The effect of domesticating the scene to modern sensibility is to render the humour more bittersweet and tragicomic than it is safe to assume.

52  p. 197.

53  So Wilson 1997. The introduction of the *theorikon* is admittedly of very uncertain date.

54  pp. 13–16.

55  Most famously in Eupolis fr. 384 K-A, looking back to the days when all was well, generals came from the best families, and 'we treated them like gods' – though we cannot know how the play as a whole treated the speaker. Cf. for example Dover 1974: 35–7 and 1993: 69–70; Carey 1994: 73–7. The nostalgia is often tongue-in-cheek, as Heath 1987b: 23–4 emphasises, but not unaffectionately so. Attacks on 'demagogues' seem to have become hackneyed comic fare, as Aristophanes himself scathingly points out in Hyperbolus' case (*Clouds* 551–9): cf. Mastromarco 1993: 347 and note 14; Storey 1993: 377–8.

56  As Carey 1994: 76–7 reasonably emphasises.

57  Richard Rutherford reminds me of the scene in *Airplane* (1980) in which a singing flight attendant wields her guitar so enthusiastically that she disconnects a child's life support system, and the child goes into spasms. The scene is significantly cut from the version sold on video.

58  Whatever exactly the 'attack' may have been: cf. pp. 145–50.

59  Nock 1972: 543, a reference I again owe (like the previous two examples) to Richard Rutherford.

60  p. 31.

61  Cf. Bowie 1993a: 89–90.

62  Konstan 1995: 27.

63  Which is not to deny that, in more domestic, less public contexts, a retiring modesty could be seen as a virtue: Konstan 1995: 24 and especially Carter 1986. Ideology can be flexible enough to accommodate both viewpoints in different settings.

64  In fact the play only came second, but we should not use that as an indication that Aristophanes somehow misjudged his audience (so for example Cartledge 1990: 53 and Hubbard 1991: 136–7). We cannot know the qualities of the play which came first, nor the reasons why the judges preferred it. The important point is that Aristophanes knew his audience better than we do, and thought that the humour of *Wasps* would work.

65  Cf. the good remarks of Henderson 1993: 308 on Aristophanes' general 'attacks' on the people's institutions: 'Comedy does criticize the demos; but never for the reason ... that the demos is unfit to hold sovereignty and ought to surrender power to its élite betters. The standard position is rather that the demos is unhappy and frustrated because it has chosen

bad leaders; that it has done so because these leaders have deceived, flattered, and bullied the demos; and that the demos has forgotten that they, not the leaders, are sovereign.'

66  Cf. Bowie 1993a: 98–100; Konstan 1995: 23; Hubbard 1991: 133.

67  Cf. Cartledge 1990: 43–53, especially 46, 50–3. This has something in common with Foley's reading of *Acharnians* (Foley 1988): see p. 288, n. 66.

68  Bowie 1997b: 11.

69  The pinning down of the symposiasts' names raises difficult problems: cf. MacDowell 1971 and Sommerstein 1983 on *Wasps* 1301–2; Storey 1985; Carter 1986: 65–70. Such discussions are bedevilled by the assumption that the original audience could pin down exactly which 'Antiphon' or 'Phrynichus' is meant; but they doubtless knew even more of them than we do. The 'flavour' of the names, rather than exact identification, is all we should talk about.

70  Storey 1985: 325–7.

71  Bowie 1993a: 101.

72  Though not for Foley 1988: p. 288, n. 66.

73  I owe the formulation of this question to a tutorial essay by my pupil Miranda Bevan. The question is good; I do not presume here to answer it.

74  p. 124.

75  Henderson 1987: xxx–xxxi, 1990, and 1993: 314–19, and Carey 1994: especially 76–7 have some very good remarks.

76  Ps.-Xen. *Ath. Pol.*, especially 1.14–18; Thuc. for example 1.76.2–3 (and the general unquestioned assumption of *opheleia*, 'advantage', as an imperialist motive in that speech), 3.37.2, and especially Euphemus at Camarina, 6.82–7; Xen. *Poroi* (*Ways and Means*).

## 8  Aristophanes' *Acharnians* (425 BC)

1  This is much more likely than the alternative view (Rau 1967: 23 and Sansone 1985) that Telephus defended only his own people, the Mysians. Cf. Heath 1987a: 272–3.

2  The Telephan origin is deduced partly from scholiast references and partly from overlap with Kinsman's speech at *Thesmo.* 468–519. For detailed argumentation see Handley and Rea 1957: especially 34; Rau 1967: 38–40; Heath 1987a: 278.

3  That is, 'comedy': *truges* were wine-lees, and this seems a comic formation – perhaps Aristophanes' own – to give a pun on 'tragedy'. The Greek could also mean '*even* trugody knows what is just': the ambiguity may be intentional, but the *Telephus* parallel confirms that the 'trugody *too*' suggestions are important – you don't have to be in the Euripidean original to know about right and wrong. See Taplin 1983.

4  That is, the earlier of the two main dramatic festivals, held in late January; the Great Dionysia followed two months later, when the allied representatives were in town.

5  For the metaphor in 507–8, cf. Sommerstein 1980 ad loc.

6  Kottabos, a game in which drinkers sat around a disk or a basin and tossed wine-lees at it. With *hetairai* present, the game could turn erotic: Scaife 1992: 27–30.

7  Silk 1993, especially 479, distinguishes paratragedy and tragic parody: 'parody is essentially negative: it works by recalling a more or less specific original and subverting it. Non-parodic paratragedy is not necessarily subversive or negative at all' (480). (For a similar distinction cf. Foley 1988: 35 note 14, following Pucci.) This is an undernuanced view of parody, for 'subversion' or 'negation' are too broad terms for the complex renuancing and destabilising of voice which parody typically generates, just as they are inadequate for the revaluation of an original model which parody inspires: Goldhill 1991 is good on this, especially 206–11; so is Zeitlin 1981: especially 181–3. Silk is certainly right in saying that *Telephus* affords 'a tragic co-presence', ensuring 'that the situation of the *Telephus* is available as a parallel to enrich the given action' (496); and that this bifocal effect is enhanced by what he calls 'collision' with the suggestions of the original (something which, he acknowledges, typifies 'parody' too).

8  Cf. especially Handley and Rea 1957, Rau 1967: 19–42, Heath 1987a, and Collard, Cropp, and Lee 1995: 17–52. Several points are dubious.

9  Thus Collard, Cropp, and Lee 1995: 24–5: cf. for example Heath 1987a: 275, Rau 1967: 25 note 21, and Taplin 1977: 35 note 2. Harriott 1962: 5 comments more generally that 'again and again it is visual effects which Aristophanes recalls, knowing that for an audience a play is a thing done in their presence'.

10  There are other ways in which plays or passages could have become more familiar to an audience after their first performance, for instance by re-production around the demes (what were actors supposed to do for the rest of the year, during all those days when not required for the two urban festivals?), or by recitation of speeches or singing of songs at symposia: see especially Harriott 1962. But we still need to explain why *Telephus* was such a special case.

11  On this see the exchange of Halliwell 1980 and MacDowell 1982 and 1995: 34–41. The problem is difficult, but MacDowell may be right in thinking of Callistratus as the subject of the parabasis, and – it presumably follows – as the man whose unfortunate experiences with Cleon showed some parallel with those of Dicaeopolis (below). This, it should be stressed, would not be a problem for the original audience: they would *know* who had been attacked the previous year and in what way (below), and our problem is to reconstruct this extradramatic knowledge which they would feed into their interpretation. Callistratus acted as producer of Aristophanes' first three plays, *Banqueters* (427), *Babylonians* (426), and *Acharnians* (425). The *Acharnians* parabasis uses both *didaskalos* (producer) and *poietes* (poet, or 'maker') as the chorus praise the man responsible for *Babylonians* (p. 146). It is marginally harder to think that Aristophanes could be described as 'producer' than that Callistratus could be described as 'maker', given the importance of staging, rehearsal, music, etc. (so MacDowell 1982: 25 = 1995: 40). That does imply that there was more interest in the producer, or at

least in this producer (for all we know he may have been particularly experienced or charismatic), than in the young writer; but it need not follow that Aristophanes' role in this was really secret (for *Wasps* 1016–22 can be jokey overstatement). His role as writer was known by the time of *Knights* (424), where 512–16 and 541–4 would be incomprehensibly bemusing if the audience did not know that he had written but not produced his earlier plays (also *Clouds* 528–33; cf. Halliwell 1980: 35–6). We do not need to posit an earlier phase when Aristophanes contributed in genuine 'secrecy' to other writers' plays (thus Halliwell, Mastromarco 1979; against, MacDowell, Gilula 1989).

12  On this see especially Bowie 1982: 29–32.

13  For recent discussion cf. especially Lefkowitz 1991, a series of studies which argue that reference to the poet, 'in his most professional persona', is an irreducible element in most (or even all) cases of 'I'; Goldhill 1991: especially 142–5, arguing for complexity, with a multiplicity of poetic voices reflected in the range of possible applications – not necessarily mutually exclusive – to performers, to audience, or to a paradigmatic human who transcends any single reference.

14  Biographical sketches: for example Sommerstein 1980: 2; T. Gelzer, *R-E* Spb. xii (1970): 1398–9; cf. also Henderson 1990: 288, 304, and Cartledge 1990: 44–5. Athenian law or constitution: for example Rhodes 1985: 4, 189.

15  Goldhill 1991: 167–222 argues this elaborately and convincingly.

16  Antimachus' refusal of a meal need be taken no more literally than (I will argue here) Cleon's denunciation in the *boule*: if Antimachus had been *choregos* and had a reputation for stinginess, that is quite enough to make the lines funny.

17  Halliwell 1980: 44–5 argues that the 'me' there must refer to another chorus *of Aristophanes*, and infers that Aristophanes put on a play at the Lenaea of 426. It is unclear to me why we must assume that a chorus could identify itself as 'Aristophanic chorus' but not as 'comic chorus' in general. Here I follow Dover 1963: 23 = 1987: 303.

18  Thus Dover 1963: 15 = 1987: 296: 'Aristophanes treats Dikaiopolis as if he were an annual visitor to Athens who got into trouble on the last occasion on which he attempted to δίκαια λέγειν (i.e. 'tell what was just')'.

19  Parker 1991: 203–4 rightly insists on this.

20  It begs the question still more to assume that Dicaeopolis is played by Aristophanes *as actor*, an old suggestion which is coming back into fashion: cf. Bailey 1936, Sutton 1988, and Slater 1989; endorsed by Halliwell 1989: 527 note 23, by Ghiron-Bistagne 1976: 148, with some not very convincing parallel suggestions for other plays, and tentatively by Reckford 1987: 179 and 516–17 note 76 and by Cartledge 1990: 44–5. Even in a play as metatheatrical as this, and even when identities are so shifting (Dicaeopolis getting dressed up as Telephus, pretending to be a Greek beggar, to speak in the voice of Aristophanes/Callistratus; cf. Reckford 1987: 179 and Goldhill 1991: 193), it is hard to believe that identity can penetrate the mask in this way. For all Aristophanes'

taste for metatheatricality, we do not find clear references to the extradramatic identities of the plays' actors. There are no jokes about the speakers' famous past roles: contrast for instance John Cleese, who in *Fawlty Towers* intertextually mimicked a Monty Python silly walk, and as Petruchio in a Stratford *Taming of the Shrew* threatened his servant with a Basil-gesture from *Fawlty Towers*. Indeed, in Aristophanes references to *any* actors are rare (the clearest cases are *Frogs* 303, *Wasps* 579, 1279, *Peace* 804, and fr. 490 K-A): it is in the fourth century that actors become greater celebrities (see the evidence collected by Ghiron-Bistagne 1976: 135–61). The only point to lend the suggestion credibility here is the assumed identity of experience between Aristophanes/Callistratus and Dicaeopolis, but that is what needs to be demonstrated, not assumed. The same objections apply to the idea that Aristophanes was personally coryphaeus for *Acharnians*: Russo 1994: 26–32.

21  On the investigative and punitive functions of the *boule* see Harrison 1968–71: ii: 55–9 on *eisangelia* and especially Rhodes 1985: 179–207. In the case of serious crimes and penalties the *boule* seems to have handed victims over to the courts or the assembly, but initial denunciations in the *boule* were regular. There is disagreement over details: see the debate of Hansen 1975: 21–8 and 1980 with Rhodes 1979.

22  It need not follow from that passage that the real Cleon was a member of the *boule* at any time, as assumed for example by Hignett 1952: 262 note 3 and (more cautiously) Gomme, *HCT* ii: 278. This 'Paphlagonian' is not Cleon, but a blurred mixture of traits of the real Cleon with those of a stereotypical demagogue (p. 129).

23  The *Telephus* origin there is deduced from the similarity with *Thesmo.* 469–72, the other parody of the same *Telephus* speech, where the kinsman begins his defence of Euripides with the same disarming device: 'Now I hate that man myself, I'd be mad not to – but still we ought to talk it out among ourselves: we're on our own, and what we say will be secret'.

24  On this cf. West 1968: 6 note 5, discussing *Ach.* 100 and 104. Conte 1986: 35, 70–87 stresses the similar tendency of 'poetic memory' to focus on first lines.

25  p. 34.

26  Especially Russo 1994.

27  Cf. Sommerstein 1980 on *Ach.* 505. It is true that in principle these differences might have had an emblematic significance which goes beyond pure numbers.

28  I owe this point to Christiane Sourvinou-Inwood.

29  Notice that aliens could sing in the chorus, and resident aliens could be *choregoi*, at the Lenaea but not at the Dionysia (*DFA* 41: I owe this point to Edith Hall). That may well reflect the lower prestige of the Lenaea (thus *DFA*); but it is not what one would expect if the Lenaea were ideologically fixed as a citizen-only festival, or a site for citizen-only discourse.

30  This is the best argument against the suggestion (Rosen 1988: 63–4) that the whole thing was fictional: cf. the similar arguments about the later brush after *Knights*, pp. 132–3.

31 'Wealth, you are blind: it would have been good if you had never appeared on earth or on the sea or on the continent, but had lived in Tartarus and Hades: for all human evils are your fault' (Timocreon fr. 5 Page). That is why Dicaeopolis talks of 'laws worded like drinking-songs'.

32 Though this possibly only reflects further terms of the main exclusion decree: see pp. 109–11.

33 As assumed, for instance, by Fornara 1971: 28; MacDowell 1983: 153–4 and 1995: 65–6; Hornblower 1987: 15 and 1991: 111.

34 This parodies a line of Archilochus, 'oh, you needy citizens, attend to my words…' (fr. 109 W), sufficiently well-known for Cratinus (fr. 211 K-A) and Eupolis (fr. 392 K-A) too to get jokes out of it.

35 We cannot quite exclude the notion of heavy irony here, if the story were really old hat; but in that case two speakers agreeing that it is 'news' would seem to be overdoing a weak joke.

36 See pp. 128–30, and on the *Pericles* passage p. 108. Notice that Plutarch does not commit himself to accepting the allegations but Diodorus does, at least in general terms. It may of course be that Ephorus was more circumspect.

37 For discussion of what sort of trouble and when, see especially Stadter 1989: 284–6, 291–6.

38 We must not here base anything on Simaetha's absence from the *Peace* passage. The strategy in *Peace* is to present the war as having served the interests of everyone except the poor suffering farmers, the *georgoi*, who by this stage of that play are emerging as the distinctive identity of the chorus, and an easy focus for audience engagement. Pheidias, Pericles, the allies, the bigwigs at Sparta, the Athenian demagogues: all have used the war to ward off threats or to line their own pockets. In such a context Pericles' self-*protection* might figure more naturally than any self-*indulgence* in a private quarrel of Aspasia, and the Pheidias allegation is exactly what we need. On the coherence of the speech within *Peace* see especially Cassio 1982; Olson 1998: xli–ii, 196.

39 Cf. MacDowell 1983: 149–50 and 1995: 61–2.

40 If the hypothesis (from which the quotations are taken: *P. Oxy.* 663) can be trusted: Dover 1972: 218 is cautious. The play's date is uncertain. It is usually put in 430–29, when Pericles was still alive, because the hypothesis has 'Pericles is comically ridiculed for bringing on the war…': but *Acharnians* of 425 could have been described in precisely those terms. It may even be that Cratinus was responding to *Acharnians*' lead – or the other way round. Eupolis too called Aspasia 'Helen' (fr. 267 K-A, cf. Storey 1993: 395–6): the theme may have been even more hackneyed.

41 p. 70.

42 Already in Aeschylus (*Agam.* 62, 448–9, 681–7, 800, etc.). Several plays of Euripides – *Trojan Women, Helen, Orestes* – depend for their impact on this tradition.

43 In that case, the contact between *Telephus* and Herodotus' proem (below) becomes most interesting: perhaps both were picking up something similar in the sophistic air, for it does seem that the Trojan War had by now become a test-case for questions of guilt and responsibility (as it

was in Gorgias' *Helen*); or for that matter *Telephus* might even have influenced Herodotus. Cf. Heath 1987a: 272–3.

44  It need not follow that these real-life runaway slaves included women, as Pomeroy 1994: 64 assumes: they may have done, but the femaleness is owed to the *Telephus* rather than real life.

45  On these see especially Plut. *Per.* 32, with Stadter 1989: 297–305. It makes no difference here whether these were real legal charges or attacks in comedy: their familiarity is all that matters.

46  See especially Fornara 1971. The relevant Herodotus passages are 6.98.2 (Artaxerxes' death was in 424), 7.235.2–3 (Cythera became crucial in 424), and 9.73.3 (taken to suggest that the Archidamian War is over): on all three passages cf. Fornara 32–4, together with the counter of Cobet 1977. None of the passages is decisive, cumulatively they impress.

47  p. 2 and note 2. The later stories are collected, and treated with due scepticism, by Podlecki 1977. For Herodotus' orality see now the fascinating comparative study of Stadter 1997; for suggestions of both performance-text and reading-text, Flory 1980.

48  Flory 1980: 24–6 and MacDowell 1983: 151 and 1995: 62–3 are here convincing; cf. Fornara 1971: 25–8 and on the other side Cobet 1977: 9–12.

49  As here with the introduction of *Telephus*: pp. 141–2.

50  Griffin 1995: 6; cf. Griffin 1977.

51  'Close to', but not exactly, retaliation: even in those initial exchanges the rhetoric of revenge becomes a matter of excuse and opportunity as much as motivation. Cf. p. 96 and note 26.

52  Especially pp. 86, 95–6.

53  Especially p. 111.

54  Cf. Fornara 1975: 226 note 53. This may also help to explain another feature of that later scene, the sycophant's denunciation of the goods as contraband rather than hauling the Megarians off for execution. Scholars sometimes infer that the Charinus decree was not then in force. That need not follow. Within Aristophanes' text the contraband-emphasis aids the continuity: it is indeed 'the same old story', this is how it all started. It remains important that the audience should not find this contraband-declaration bewildering; but it was a feature of Athenian law to leave complainants several options (Osborne 1985c). A sycophant might get more out of a contraband-declaration – probably half the value of the goods involved (cf. Harrison 1968–71: ii: 218–21, Todd 1993: 119) – than from a hauling off to death.

55  Thus for example de Ste Croix 1972: 383–6, MacDowell 1995: 64–5 (though neither makes the mistake of assuming that this is a *necessary* implication of Aristophanes' language).

56  As assumed for example by Kagan 1969: 255–6.

57  So Legon 1981: 206.

58  Cf. Sommerstein 1980: 182 on 519–21; E. Meyer, *R-E* xv (1932): 172–3.

59  Thus for example Legon 1981: 205–6. If that is so, then the remark at Thuc. 1.42.2 to 'the previously existing suspicion concerning Megara' might refer to the same incident; but that passage is too vague and ambiguous to serve as the basis for any argument (cf. p. 271, n. 48).

60  On the implications of the Old Oligarch's analysis see also especially Halliwell 1991; Henderson 1990 and 1993.
61  p. 134.
62  MacDowell 1983: 148–55 and 1995: 59–67.
63  De Ste Croix 1972: 368 (his italics), countered by Heath 1987b: 15.
64  Especially de Ste Croix 1972: 363–4.
65  p. 146: cf. especially Bowie 1982.
66  This tells against the interpretation of Foley 1988, arguing that the discerning audience is supposed to see through Dicaeopolis' rhetoric and regard the Acharnian chorus as too easily persuaded (cf. also Reckford 1987: 179–86). Foley therefore stresses the parallels between Aristophanes himself and Telephus (37), and suggests that the wiser viewer realises Dicaeopolis is disingenuously assimilating himself to this model of 'just speaker'. Some viewers may indeed have reacted like that; but for most it is probably one mental gyration too many. It also runs the same aesthetic danger as noted for parallel interpretations of *Wasps* (p. 140), with the audience having no sympathetic focus during the play's final scenes.
67  Foley 1988: 39–40.
68  Though, for the parody to work, it does need to follow that *this is the way people might argue*, just as Telephus had argued, if they were keen on peace.
69  p. 153 and note 40.
70  Carey 1993a: 261–3 and 1994: 75 has some good remarks.
71  Yet Forrest 1963: 10 emphasised that, if one went by Second World War experience, peace-suggestions might particularly count as 'treachery' when times were bad: it is only when times improved that an audience might be prepared to toy with magnanimity. We again notice the limits of the modern parallel as much as its illumination. See also de Ste Croix 1972: 370 against Forrest's description of Athens' position in 425.
72  Recent work on Augustan 'propaganda' at Rome has found this insight helpful: Kennedy 1984 and Zanker 1988 have been most influential. I have tried elsewhere to extend this approach to Plutarch (Pelling 1995) and to Aeschylus' *Persians* (Pelling 1997b): see also pp. 207–8.
73  Especially de Ste Croix 1972: 361–2; Henderson 1990: 284; Carey 1994: 79; and on Alcibiades' surprising lack of prominence, Halliwell 1991: 61. (This statement assumes what I cannot argue here, that Alcibiades is not so recurrent an *allegorically* represented figure as Vickers 1989a, 1989b, 1993, and 1995b suggests.)

## 9  Tragedy and ideology

1  pp. 141–5.
2  Easterling 1997; cf. Easterling 1985: especially 7; Bers 1994: 180–2.
3  Easterling 1985: 2–3.
4  Vidal-Naquet 1997. Thus Herman 1987: 34–5 goes astray when he tries to use tragic evidence to illuminate the possibility of women acquiring *xenoi*, something which happens in the distanced world of tragedy but

is hard to trace in real life; and Ogden 1996: 155–6 in basing an argument for the non-citizenship of bastards on a phrase in Euripides' *Ion* (592–3).

5  Sommerstein 1989: 16–17 makes this important point clear.

6  This is the view strongly argued by Zuntz 1955, and it is now close to orthodoxy. Cf. especially Bowie 1997a.

7  A democratic court, set up on a hill to judge a visiting suppliant, in the Danaids' case for husband-killing, in Orestes' for matricide: given the intertextual ubiquity of *Eumenides*, the audience may well contrast this Argive court with its Athenian equivalent on 'the hill of Ares'.

8  Cf. for example Rawson 1972: 160; Euben 1986: 222; Vidal-Naquet 1988: 335. Courts and assemblies were not always easy to keep apart in real life, as the 'trial' of the generals after Arginusae shows. On the formal background of that debate see the discussions of Hansen 1975 and 1980 and Rhodes 1979.

9  Here and on the other *Orestes* passages see Willink 1986 ad loc.

10  Euripides' *Suppliant Women* 439–40 is here exactly similar: below, note 65. Cf. Bers 1985: 3–4.

11  The Cleophon identification is already found in the scholiast. For Antiphon, cf. Hall 1993: 267.

12  At least in his own mind. True, the audience, rather like Orestes himself (1668–9), may come to wonder if this coercion was only a psychological figment: cf. Euben 1986: 242–4; but at the end of the play Apollo himself talks of compulsion (1665).

13  All the early characters except Tyndareus say something along those lines: 28–32, 75–6, 121, 160–5, 191–5, 268–76, 285–7, 327–31, 416–20, 591–9, cf. 955–6. Not that Apollo's role is clear-cut; in particular, the recurrent Tantalus paradigm encourages the reflection that humans bring disasters on themselves and then blame the gods. Cf. especially Sourvinou-Inwood, forthcoming. It is still disquieting that the court ignores the issue.

14  The cinematic analogy is developed by Sourvinou-Inwood 1989. Cf. pp. 170–1, 173, 182.

15  Thus the exchange of Orestes and Pylades at 772–3. But Pylades' 'when they get good leaders, they always reach good decisions' seems naïve when measured against the realities of the assembly itself (cf. Euben 1986: 228, 241); and it uneasily recalls the clichés of Menelaus a few minutes earlier (696–703).

16  Cf. especially Zeitlin 1980 and Euben 1986.

17  But here the audience may have some doubts, given the mythical flexibility of Helen stories, and Euripides employs skilful *suggestio falsi* to make them think Helen might really have been killed: cf. Willink 1986: xxxvii–viii, 312–13 on 1395–9, 327 on 1491, 328 on 1494–7. Euripides surely can't go that far – but he just might.

18  *Iphigeneia in Aulis*, a year or so later, affords a parallel: time and again Menelaus and Agamemnon change their minds, try to rewrite the myth of Iphigeneia before it happens; but we always know they will fail, for the myth is fixed. I have benefitted from discussions of this with David Mumford.

19  pp. 71–2.
20  The latter is the version of Plut. *Cim.* 15.2–3, followed for example by Rhodes, *CAH* v²: 69. But Plutarch may, as often, be imposing his own chronological smoothing on events: it suits his general pattern of Cimon's vulnerability when away on campaign (15.1), and that fits a wider theme of *Cimon–Lucullus*.
21  That may have changed a little in the previous generation, as from 487/6 archons were not elected but chosen by lot from a list of 100. We should therefore expect them to be both more representative and less prestigious. But they still needed to come from the top two property-classes, and in fact archons after 487/6 are not noticeably different in texture from those a generation before that date: cf. Hignett 1952: 195, Badian 1971, and Cawkwell 1988. It seems likely that they were still sufficient of an élite to be a worthy target, that Ephialtes was a genuine 'giant-killer' rather than 'a woodman cutting down a rotten tree' (the terms are those of Cawkwell 1988: 3).
22  The bibliography is large: cf. especially Hignett 1952: 193–213, Sealey 1964 and 1983, Rhodes 1981: 309–22 on *Ath. Pol.* 25, Wallace 1985: 77–93, and Cawkwell 1988.
23  This is controversial. Cawkwell 1988: 2 objects that the powers stripped away in 462/1 would be regarded as 'traditional', *patria*, for they had been exercised for generations, and the Athenian public would not have so keen a sense of the origins as to regard them as 'additional'; but Ephialtes could still have made the claim, and the respect for origins was strong enough to make the rhetorical strategy a sensible one. Sealey 1964: 13 sees these *epitheta* as certain functions lost under Ephialtes' attack but restored (and therefore 'additional') in the Demosthenic period; Cawkwell thinks of the guardianship of the laws as restored in 403/2, and therefore 'additional' to the pre-403/2 powers in a similar sense. Both those interpretations seem forced (and see *contra* Rhodes 1981: 314), though the implied telegraphic style is not impossible in *Ath. Pol.*
24  Also certain religious offences (Lys. 7 shows that they were responsible for the sacred olives), and some cases of poisoning, wounding, and arson; there may have been more, but the evidence is very slight. Cf. Hignett 1952: 199; Rhodes 1981: 315–16 on *Ath. Pol.* 25.2; Sealey 1983: 275–96.
25  Cf. Sommerstein 1989: 215–6 ad loc. for the ambiguity here.
26  So Antiphon *On the Murder of Herodes* 68; cf. also Diod. 11.77.6. *Ath. Pol.* 25.4 says he was murdered 'through' one Aristodicus of Tanagra, presumably an agent (so Rhodes 1981: 322 ad loc.). Malicious rumours naturally abounded: one had Ephialtes murdered by a jealous Pericles (Idomeneus ap. Plut. *Per.* 10.7–8).
27  For the cinematic analogy cf. Sourvinou-Inwood 1989 and p. 166.
28  I have discussed this in more detail in Pelling 1997b.
29  De Ste Croix 1972: 183–4. Cf. the similar remarks of Quincey 1964: 190; Podlecki 1966: 94 ('such repeated and dramatically unnecessary prominence ... [of] the Argive alliance').
30  Macleod 1983: 20–40 = 1982. Cf. also Goldhill 1984: 254: '...the search for the origin of this speech of Athene in the political views of Aeschylus

is insufficient to control the play of signifiers within the discourse of the work'.

31 This aspect helps to explain the setting in Argos. The brothers, Agamemnon and Menelaus, and the sisters, Clytemnestra and Helen, did share a house: that would be implausible if the setting were either Mycenae or Sparta, but the vaguer 'Argos' makes it more comfortable. It also helps the contemporary resonance of an Argive alliance; but there is more to it than simply that topicality. Cf. Macleod 1983: 22–3 = 1982: 126–7.

32 Still most profitably, perhaps, in the classic articles by Dover 1957 and Dodds 1960. Cf. the surveys of Bowie 1993b: 10–12, and (of older work) Podlecki 1966: 80–94.

33 The text is uncertain, but something like this must be the sense.

34 This 'honour' theme is especially clear at *Eum.* 807, 824, 833–6, 854–69, 881–4: cf. Macleod 1983: 34–40 = 1982: 138–44.

35 Cf. especially Dover 1987: 170–1 = 1957: 235–6; Sommerstein 1989: 31. But the thematic importance of Athens to Argos is as important as that of Argos to Athens, as the linkage emblematises the righting of past Argive disorder.

36 As is increasingly recognised: cf. Sommerstein 1989: 32; Bowie 1993b: 11. Dover 1957: 235 = 1987: 169 rightly concluded that in this respect 'the political language of *Eumenides* is neutral...', but went on to argue that Aeschylus supported the democratic reforms.

37 So Sommerstein 1989: 218.

38 Σ *O.C.* 92: this should not be doubted in view of Xen. *Hell.* 1.1.33, *Mem.* 3.5.4, and Diod. 13.72.

39 This is even truer if we accept recent attempts to trace analogies between the mythic and cultic codes of the *Oresteia* and the ideology of Ephialtes' reforms: cf. especially Meier 1993: Chapter 5, and Bowie 1993b.

40 *HCT* i: 302.

41 So Heath 1987c: 64–71; the phrase is from p. 69.

42 The qualification needs to be stressed. Cohen 1995: chapter 3 has some good remarks on the different ways in which this idea could be appropriated by different interpreters.

43 Compare Orestes' claim that 'Loxias Apollo is *jointly* responsible, pronouncing pains to prick the heart if I do not punish those responsible for these things' (465–8). Earlier the Furies attacked Apollo as *not* 'jointly responsible', but 'you did everything as wholly responsible' (*panaitios*, 199–200) – but as justification for their pursuing Orestes, not a reason to relent. The distance from modern assumptions is plain.

44 Anaxagoras DK[12] A 107, cit. Aristotle, *De Generatione Animalium* 763b31–3: cf. Sommerstein 1989: 206–8 on 657–66. But this is only one view among several found in the pre-Socratics and medical writers: see especially Lloyd 1983: 86–94.

45 The phrase of Vickers 1973: 394: cf. 425, 'Aeschylus' progressive demolition of her case'.

46 The phrase of Lebeck 1971: 135.

47 Notice especially the parody at *Clouds* 904–7, in the mouth of 'the Worse

Argument'; similar rhetorical strategies are followed by the Nurse in
*Hippolytus* (especially at 451–8), in another speech which has
transparent holes in its specious rhetoric.

48  For example Conacher 1987: 161 talks of a 'patent suggestion of
bribery': quoted with approval by Sommerstein 1989: 184.

49  Cf. p. 31. But 'modern equivalent' courts may be changing, at least in
the United States. Gewirtz 1996: 153 comments on the increase in
'jury-nullification', juries today thinking they are 'the people', who
therefore – disconcertingly to legal tastes – have the right to remake
the law. – The issue of 'identification' of Athenian *demos* and courts has
aroused controversy: cf. Hansen 1978 and 1990: 216–22; Rhodes 1981:
318 on *Ath. Pol.* 25.2; Ostwald 1986: 10–11, 34–5; Ober 1989: 145–7;
but the formulation in the text would be acceptable to both sides in
that dispute.

50  For example Lys. 21.13–14. Cf. Reinhardt 1949: 145–6; Cohen 1995:
112–15, 171–2, 184–5.

51  Though the issue is difficult and controversial: cf. for example Sealey
1983: 284.

52  *Pace* Sommerstein 1989: 264–5 (note on lines 934–7). Cf. Dodds 1973:
51, 55 = 1960: 23, 26; Goldhill 1990b: 120–2.

53  The episode is doubted by Badian 1993: 213 note 50, I think (with
Hornblower 1991: 171 on Thuc. 1.107.4) on insufficient grounds; but
even if Badian is right, the *suspicions* of such treachery are likely to go
back to the time (otherwise this would be an odd context for later
writers or speakers to anchor them), and that is itself telling for the
audience's response to *Eumenides*. The date is disputed: most put those
events in 457, Lewis in 458 itself (*CAH* v$^2$: 114, 501).

54  Cf. Geuss 1981: 4–22 for an analysis of the various pejorative uses of
'ideology'.

55  I elaborate the grammatical analogy in Pelling 1997c: 225–6.

56  I argue this more fully, and in different ways, in Pelling 1997c.

57  For example Althusser 1965: 232–4.

58  Cf. Eagleton's attack (1994: 10; cf. 1991: 57–61) on 'the dubious
assumption that ideology is never able to reflect upon itself – that, as
Louis Althusser observes, it is never able to announce "I am
ideological" '. We should distinguish this question of self-awareness
from that of universalisation. As a western liberal or a new man I *may*
think that my views would be right for everyone everywhere, if only
people were not so benighted as to fail to see their wisdom; the more
ideologically committed I am the more likely I am to think in these
terms; but it need not follow that I am unaware of the ideological nature
of my commitment.

59  Cf. especially Lloyd 1966.

60  'Comparatively' straightforward, but not totally: cf. for example Pelling
1997c: 232 and pp. 190–1.

61  Thus Goldhill 1990a draws attention to the preplay of the festival itself,
a glorifying projection of civic power and duty – the libations poured
by the generals, the display of the allied tribute, the naming of state
benefactors, the march of war-orphans – and posits a 'sense of tension

between the texts of tragedy and the ideology of the city' and 'a questioning of the terms of that civic discourse' (115, 126).

62  For a fuller statement of this approach cf. Pelling 1997c and bibliography there cited.

63  For example Isoc. 4.112, Lys. 2.14, Dem. 24.170–1, 25.81: other passages are collected by Stevens 1944: 15–19, Dover 1974: 200–1, Mills 1997: 105–6. The motif duly figures in Plato's parody of Athenian self-praise, *Menex.* 244e. Cf. p. 207.

64  Probably potential rather than real, if the conventional dating of the play around 430 is correct.

65  Again a version of 'who wants to speak?', the herald's opening words in an assembly; and again an *imprecise* version, in keeping with tragic vagueness. Cf. above, note 10.

66  2.8.1 (with 1.140.1): 19–21, 4.21.2 (with 4.17.4: 41.4, 6.12, 19, 24, 30–1). Cf. Macleod 1983: 147–9, and works cited in Pelling 1997c: 233 note 81.

67  Especially Ps.-Xen. 1.13, 16, 18; Plato, for example *Tht.* 172c–6a, *Gorgias* 521c–2c, *Rpb.* 405b, 492b; Thuc. 6.29.3, 7.48.3, and especially 6.91.7, where 'Alcibiades' refers to the profits 'from the courts' as important to Athenian purses: that plays to the Spartan stereotype of their enemy (Dover, *HCT* iv: 365 ad loc.).

68  For this reading of Aeschylus' *Suppliant Women* see Sommerstein 1997: especially 76: 'What we see is a democratic state, very like Athens itself, deceived with 'tricks of oratory' (623, δημηγόρους ... στροφάς) into voting for a war that was to prove disastrous – a war which, to judge from Pelasgus' tactics, they never would have accepted if the issue had been put to them honestly.'

69  Not that Apollo's settlement need be felt as wholly inadequate (cf. Burkert 1974, Dunn 1996: 159–61): the audience might well find comforting the divine reassertion of mythical order. Cf. especially Sourvinou-Inwood, forthcoming. But the audience would grimly know that Apollo was not so straightforwardly available to correct mortal politics when they went so awry.

70  Longo 1975: 286–7 concludes a sensitive reading in such terms.

71  Hostility to Orestes and Electra has been almost universal; it begins with a note in the ancient hypothesis, 'all the characters are bad except for Pylades' (a somewhat illogical exclusion).

72  Chapter 2.

73  On this see especially Rawson 1972, Longo 1975, and Willink 1986: xliv and 211 on 804–6.

74  West 1987: 32–7 makes this point well, in the course of a spirited defence of the plotters. Contrast Zeitlin 1980: 67: '...Orestes' negative intentions in this play – to settle private scores, and by further violence to another female, to do patriotic service to his country'. Would the contemporary audience find such intentions straightforwardly 'negative'?

75  Contrast Aristotle's criticism that Menelaus is *needlessly* bad (*Poetics* 1454a29, 1461b21) – a comment of peculiar critical insensitivity.

76  On this aspect see especially Boulter 1962 and Longo 1975: 283–5. The imagery is reinforced by echoes of the *Oresteia*, this time largely

*Agamemnon*, in the Phrygian slave's monody: this becomes a parodic version of the Trojan War over again, with Pylades and Orestes as two new lion-men hunting down Helen (1401–2), but this time against pathetically feeble adversaries.

77 Cf. especially Dunn 1996: 159–60. On *Medea* see also pp. 198–208.

78 The speakers of Lysias 20.7 and 25.26–7 stress the string of corrupt prosecutions, though admittedly the first speaker is defending one of those accused in such a trial, and the second defending himself against oligarchic suspicions: so they would say that, wouldn't they (cf. p. 27)? But, as usual, the sayability and thinkability of the viewpoint remain important.

79 pp. 40–1.

80 p. 125 and note 10.

## 10 Lysistrata and others

1 So much out of context that the first is frequently attributed to Pericles himself, rather than to Thucydides' constructed Pericles: so for example Pomeroy 1975: 74 and 1994: 262–3; Foley 1981b: 130; Keuls 1985: 88; Murnaghan 1988: 20 note 22. Here I assume the view sketched in Chapter 6: that Thucydides may have taken over content from the real Pericles and would not ascribe to Pericles' sentiments he thought inappropriate to the historical figure; but that the emphasis and selectivity is Thucydides' own, so that questions must be asked about the sentence's role in Thucydides' text as well as in Pericles' ideology.

2 'Bleakness' is Gomme's word, *HCT* ii: 143; cf. Schaps 1977: 323, the advice to widows as 'cold comfort'; Rusten 1989: 173, 175: the 'words become ever more austere and develop into admonition rather than sympathy' ... 'the language of the two items of "advice" [to widows] is unrelievedly harsh, even cruel' (176 goes on to argue, I think unnecessarily, that Thucydides subscribes to this repressive ideology himself). Contrast Hyperides *Epitaphios* (6) 29ff. and 41ff.; Lysias *Epitaphios* (2) 71–6, calling for pity for the surviving relatives – 'For what pleasure is left for them as these men are buried... I envy their children for being too young to know how great were their fathers, I pity their parents for being too old to forget their misery... The better their menfolk were, the greater grief for those who survive...'; then § 75 discusses what each of us can do to help them in their suffering. Contrast also Pericles' own remark in a Funeral Speech (probably for those who fell at Samos in 440–39, cf. Plut. *Per.* 8.9, 28.4–8) that the death of the young men was 'as if the spring had gone out of the year' (Arist. *Rhet.* 1.7.34 (1365a31–3), 3.10.7 (1411a2–4)): that too is much warmer, and suggests the intensity of personal grieving.

3 Kallet-Marx 1993 rightly emphasises this. Cf. Sourvinou-Inwood 1995: 117–18, arguing from grave-inscriptions that it was commendable in women to be 'praised', both in life and after death.

4 pp. 22 and 52–3. It is tempting here to accept the further twist suggested by Cartledge 1993b. The most 'talked about' woman in Athens was surely Aspasia. Thucydides himself keeps an 'earsplitting silence'

(Cartledge) about her: Pericles' private life did not affect his public statesmanship, and Thucydides' narrative emphasis itself chimes in with 'Pericles'' ideology. The text will not be so silent about Alcibiades' private excesses, once individual interests have come to impinge more destructively on the public process.

5  On the circumstances of the speech, pp. 61–2.

6  Others who assume that the passage gives a good guide to real life include Keuls 1985: 99, 267; Pomeroy 1994: 35. Foucault 1985: 143–51 sees that the distinctions are rhetorically adapted to the case in hand: on his treatment cf. Chapter 11, pp. 249–50.

7  Carey 1992: 148, quoting Vernant 1980: 48 and Just 1989: 137: cf. especially Cohen 1991a: 167–70.

8  Lacey 1968: 113, followed by Foucault 1985: 149 and rejected by Just 1989: 151.

9  An archaic homicide law (Demosthenes 23.53, Lysias 1.31 [quoted on pp. 227–8]) put in the same category the *in flagrante* killing of wives and of concubines 'kept for the production of free children': see Carey 1989: 78–9 and Ogden 1996: 33. Citizenship for the bastard children of citizen parents: see recently Ogden 1996: 152–65, coming down against the possibility of bastard citizenship. On the other side, Carey 1995: 416–17 note 38. This old issue cannot be regarded as closed.

10  Contrast Trevett 1992: 102, who finds it 'a definite fault' that Apollodorus addresses Stephanus' defence only at this late stage.

11  *Sunoikein*: cf. Just 1989: 43, 62–4.

12  That is, their status as wives and daughters of citizens who would in turn transmit citizenship to their sons, and who (importantly) fulfilled a distinctive role in the city's religious life (cf. note 34). The words normally used for this status are *Attike*, 'woman of Attica', or *aste*, 'townswoman', rather than *politis*, 'citizeness': cf. Gould 1980: 46, Just 1989: 21; Cartledge 1993a: 73–4. It is normally assumed that only males were 'citizens'; it is possible, though, that women too were figured as citizens, and it is our definition of citizenship which requires revision (so J. Blok, in a paper given in Oxford in 1998).

13  Croally 1994: especially 90, 99, 217–18. Mossman 1995: 71.

14  Cf. p. 16, for the value of imagery in illuminating thought-patterns and assumptions. On the elements of violence embedded in marriage conceptualisation cf. especially Sourvinou-Inwood 1987 = 1991: 58–98 (stressing also some consensual elements); Robson 1997; King 1983: 111; Keuls 1985: 33–64; Just 1989: 231–2.

15  Thus § 22 stresses that Lysias (the orator) did not introduce *hetairai* into his own house 'in respect for his wife … and his mother, who was already elderly and lived with them', but lodged them with Philostratus: that, evidently, is the way to behave.

16  Sourvinou-Inwood 1995: 117. 'Intelligent' and 'sensible': *CEG* 2.516.

17  Thus Goldhill 1994, with a good discussion of the direct evidence and its difficulties; his analogic argument eventually leads him to decide that women were probably not present. On the other side, see especially Henderson 1991. The evidence is conveniently collected in *DFA* 264–5 and Csapo and Slater 1995: 286–305: at 286–7 Csapo and Slater argue reasonably for female attendance.

18  Thus Schnurr-Redford 1996: 225–40, writing independently of Goldhill and in a different scholarly climate, used the same analogic argument as one of the strongest supports for female presence: she privileged the religious, Goldhill the political.

19  'Target' and 'constructed' audience *need* not be identical. Speakers in the British House of Commons frequently purport to be addressing the House, when clearly aiming more at the wider public which will catch the soundbites later. But it is hard to see why there should be any similar distinction here. True, Plato speaks of tragedy as demagogic rhetoric aimed at (*pros*) 'a demos such as is composed of children together with women and men, slave and free' (*Gorg.* 502d): not at all the 'constructed' audience of citizen *demos*. But Plato is being provocative, and 'a *demos* such as is composed… (τοιοῦτον οἷον)' marks his paradox – not a regular *demos* at all (as, he may imply, one would expect?). A more particular 'target' audience might be the judges, but these too will be male, and as with the juries (Chapters 2 and 9) the judging activity is constructed as civic: judges were selected from a list nominated by the tribes and approved by the *boule* (Csapo and Slater 1995: 157–8).

20  See Sommerstein 1997 and 1998a.

21  For a similar analysis cf. Sourvinou-Inwood 1997: 257–8.

22  It is misleading, I think, to include Medea among those who 'resist marriage and confinement to the *oikos*': Foley 1981b: 142, cf. 152.

23  Cf. especially Schaps 1979: 74–88; Just 1989: 49–50, 70–5, 82–3.

24  For example Foley 1981b: 151–2: on Medea as 'hero' and (eventually) as something more than human, cf. especially Knox 1977.

25  This is rightly emphasised by Shaw 1975 and Just 1989: 269.

26  Zeitlin 1990: 81–3.

27  Zeitlin 1990: 63–96 (quotation from 68–9).

28  Pomeroy 1975: 109 writes: 'I prefer' Medea and Hecuba to Deianira and Antigone 'because they are successful'. The personal voice hints that Pomeroy is consciously adopting subjective and contemporary criteria: there is nothing wrong with that, but it reflects how difficult it is to apply any counterpart fifth-century BC categories. For the immediate audience, the female characters would have resisted categorising in such simple terms.

29  Zeitlin 1990.

30  Zeitlin 1990: 86–7.

31  Hall 1998: the quotation is from p. 37.

32  As for instance the posthumous cults at the end of tragedies themselves may offer some form of 'moral redress' (the term of Stinton 1975), reassuring the audience that a destroyed hero has some form of posthumous compensation; but the compensation of a cult to Hippolytus, for instance – hair-cuttings offered by virgins as they are about to marry, giving up the chastity that Hippolytus cherished and articulating a more multifaceted sensitivity to Artemis than Hippolytus himself achieved (*Hipp.* 1422–30) – may be ironically off-key, a real but cold comfort for his annihilation.

33  Hall 1997, especially 106–10.

34  Foley 1981b: 153–4 has some good remarks on this: '…the simple equation female:*oikos* as male:*polis* does not hold fully even at the level of an ideal'; the complexities are also brought out by Humphreys 1983: 1–21. Since then a number of works have further deconstructed the absolute nature of this polarity: in particular, Sourvinou-Inwood 1995 brings out that it is wholly inadequate to capture the gendering of religious roles. Cf. also Schnurr-Redford 1996: 202–12.

35  Zeitlin 1990: 85.

36  p. 293, n. 63.

37  Both passages are quoted by Hall 1998: 32–3. Compare also Sophocles, *Ajax* 580, 'a woman is indeed a thing which loves pity' – but this is *expressively* dismissive of Tecmessa's feeling: it contrasts with Hector's loving words to Andromache in *Iliad* 6, a strong intertextual presence in that scene. Ajax then is himself 'womanised *in his speech*' when he 'pities Tecmessa' in the next scene (651–2) – too problematic for easy interpretation (cf. for example Gill 1996: 204–16), but anyway an indication that even with Ajax the stereotyping breaks down.

38  Lloyd 1983: 98–100.

39  See especially Lloyd 1983: 44–53 and more fully Lloyd 1966.

40  Cf. also Griffin 1998: 45–6 on the degree to which these 'new and unsettling' ways of approaching human experience, especially pity, are already prominent in Homer.

41  Cf. Sommerstein 1994 ad loc.: Isoc. 6.1–2 is a particularly close parallel, again with 'seeing' (ὁρῶν). The parody of the trope undermines Henderson's inference (1991: 142–3) that women were physically 'visible' at the festival. His other arguments are stronger (above, note 17).

42  For the details, and for other points of interpretation, cf. Sommerstein 1994 ad loc.; Schnurr-Redford 1996: 83–4.

43  On this see especially Zeitlin 1981; Taaffe 1993: 89–91.

44  Cf. Plato, *Laws* 954a–b. At Aesch. *Eum.* 828 Athena claims that she alone knows where the keys are kept to Zeus' sealed store of thunderbolts: an interesting tragic moulding and distancing of familiar human reality. Cf. Arist. *Birds* 1538; Fraenkel 1950: ii: 302–3 on *Agam.* 609.

45  Sourvinou-Inwood 1995: 113.

46  Cf. Dem. 57.45, where the speaker explains that 'poverty forces free people to do many things which are servile and humble … I gather that many women of citizen status [*astai*; above, note 12] were forced to become nurses, wool-workers, and grape-pickers in those times *because of the city's misfortunes*, and many have since become rich instead of poor': cf. Just 1989: 113. But in that passage it seems an equal humiliation whether one becomes an indoors-worker or a grape-picker: it does not seem a crucial criterion whether one is seen *in public* as a worker.

47  Cf. 561, 'nor [has Euripides revealed] how one woman drove her husband mad with *pharmaka*', where again (cf. pp. 407–9 and note 43) the kinsman's presentation of 'reality' is given a distinctively Euripidean tinge.

48  Harding 1994b.

49  Pelling 1999b: 338. The rarity, I there suggest, is because of historiography's elevated themes and register.
50  Thus Csapo and Slater 1995: 332, 335–6: *DFA* 164 is more cautious. The standard work on the epirrhematic agon is Gelzer 1960. Händel 1963 has some good remarks on why epirrhematic form should be especially appropriate to the dramatic configurations of comedy.
51  Choruses indeed which are often marginalised in ways beyond their femaleness – foreign or enslaved or otherwise rootless: on this see especially Gould 1996 with Goldhill 1996. I am grateful to Carolyn Dewald for this point.
52  See more fully the commentaries of Henderson 1987 and Sommerstein 1990 ad loc., and on the general domestic figuring especially Vaio 1973, Foley 1982, and Konstan 1993.
53  Thus Sommerstein 1998b: 1–8.
54  See especially McLeish 1980: 99; Taaffe 1993: 123–9.
55  On this theme cf. especially Saïd 1979 and Foley 1982.
56  On this cf. Ussher 1973: xvi–xx, though his search for a shared 'source' puts too much weight on written texts rather than oral discussion; Sommerstein 1998b: 13–17, preferring the view that Plato is influenced by, and providing a serious counterpart to, Aristophanes' comedy (at *Rep.* 452a–d Plato acknowledges that some find such ideas 'comical'). In so oral a society, the influence may be two-way, with Plato and similar circles airing ideas, Aristophanes exploiting them, and Plato then responding to Aristophanes in the written *Republic* some years later. See also Halliwell 1993: 224–5, who is more sceptical of any link.
57  This point would be still stronger if the audience was alert to the maleness of the actors, rather than taking for granted male impersonation of females as convention or 'illusion'. That critical assumption is fashionable: it is developed thoughtfully by Taaffe 1993, who builds a wider thesis about the association of the female with theatricality and artificiality. I remain sceptical about the premiss. In a genre as metatheatrical and crude as comedy, alertness to the actor's maleness offers immense potential for humour; yet the attempts to find such humour in particular passages are strained (e.g. Taaffe 1993: 33, 41, 56–9, 68–9, 82–6, 91, 96–8, 111–18, 122–3). We should expect at least some jokes to be less subtle and more funny. Here again (cf. Chapter 8 note 20) metatheatricality seems not to penetrate the mask.
58  The details of this passage are difficult: cf. Henderson 1987 and Sommerstein 1990 ad loc., and especially Sourvinou(-Inwood) 1971 and 1988: 136–48. This point would have special bite if, as many suspect, the name Lysistrata would suggest to the audience Lysimache, the current priestess of Athena Polias: thus Lewis 1955: 1–12. See Henderson 1987: xxxviii–xli for discussion of this, and of the less likely possibility that Myrrhine too suggests a priestess of Athena Nike.
59  660 Mette, accessible in Collard, Cropp, and Lee 1995: 254–7.
60  Cf. Collard, Cropp, and Lee 1995: 242–4 for what we know of the plot. It involved suffering for both the Queen and Melanippe, either of whom may have delivered this speech (Melanippe is the likelier of the two). Compare the nice anecdote at Sen. *Ep.* 115.15: when the audience voiced their outrage at a Euripidean character who praised 'Wealth, the great

boon of human kind...', Euripides himself came forward, begging them to wait and see what happened to the man before the end of the play.

61 On New Comedy cf. especially Pierce 1997.

62 Notice such formulations as Saïd 1979 on *Eccl.*, '...the city of Athens ... is now only a kitchen since the women have come to power'; 'making sex democratic only serves to worsen the woes it was supposed to alleviate...' (305, 312 of the 1996 reprint); or Taaffe 1993: 39–41, 44–7 on *Peace* and *Birds*, 'with femininity present, Aristophanes suggests that any utopia may not be as ideal as it seems' (47; cf. also 109, 128–9, 132–3 on *Eccl.*). Those are *possible* responses, especially for our imaginary intemperate male; but not the only ones (here I agree with Bowie 1993a: 266, discussing *Eccl.*).

63 Zeitlin 1981 sees 'Euripides'' success as largely consequent on his increasingly total mimesis of the female and feminine roles. There is something in this, but the play's movement is less linear than this, and she is over-hasty in appropriating 'mimesis' itself as distinctively female.

64 For example Gould 1980: 43; Foley 1981b: 129; Just 1989: 32. But parent–child and husband–wife tutelage were figured differently, despite the legal similarity: p. 233 and Foxhall 1998: 125.

65 Schaps 1977. (Other genres name women more freely, as do grave-inscriptions: Schnurr-Redford 1996: 127–8, 144.) Compare the central female figure in Hitchcock's *Rebecca* (and in Daphne du Maurier's original), so subdued a person that we never discover her own name.

66 Schaps 1979: 20–4: a woman can technically 'inherit', but the property immediately comes under her new *kurios* (though it seems that the *kurios* of an *epikleros* has less control than most *kurioi*, and is figured more as the trustee of the estate during her children's minority: Schaps 1979: 27–8).

67 On the legal position cf. especially Harrison 1968–71: i: 9–12, 132–8, and especially Schaps 1979: 25–47.

68 See especially Schaps 1979: 32–3, 39–42, bringing out the inherent paradoxes. He concludes that it was *not* the 'function' of the Athenian *epiklerate* to preserve the *oikos*: the *epikleros'* marriage to (say) an uncle would keep the property not in her father's *oikos* but in her grandfather's, which would not lack for heirs in any case. He puts more weight on the *epikleros'* protection: the man who would anyway be her *kurios* now has to marry her, rather than allowing her to age unmarried while he controls her property. There is something in this, but 'function' is a slippery concept: the reasons for an institution's survival can be different from those for its origin, and tend to be multiple. Schaps still seems to me to understate the importance of the father's blood-line.

69 *Eum.* 658–61: see Chapter 9, p. 174.

70 This emotional and religious aspect is rightly emphasised by Just 1989: 84, 89–90, 97–8.

71 Especially Lacey 1968; Schaps 1979; Gould 1980: 43–6; Foley 1981b: 129–30; Just 1989; Cohen 1991a. Path-breakers were Pomeroy 1975 and in a different way Harrison 1968–71.

72 It *is* questioned by Gomme 1925: 2–3, with typical vigour and style but a little simplistically. Cf. Gould 1980: 43 – though Gould's own counter

is itself dangerously simple, appealing to our contemporary alertness to the interconnection of legal and social issues. Cohen 1991a is especially good on the law as only one form of social control; Schaps 1979 on the way that society can countenance certain 'illegal' everyday transactions without implying that the law is a totally dead letter (cf. also Just 1989: 105).

73   Schaps 1979: 14–15, 52–6, quoting Lys. 31, Dem. 27.53–5, 36.14–16, 41.8–11, and *IG* ii²: 1672.64.

74   Cf. Humphreys 1983: 7: the courts 'did provide the Athenian public with a lively presentation of models of correct behaviour and examples of moral delinquency. It was the Athenian equivalent of the television soap opera'.

75   Pomeroy 1975: 82; Carey 1989: 67.

76   Cf. for example Carey 1989: 60–1, 75; Cohen 1991a: 129–32; Herman 1993: 412.

77   This is suggested by [Dem.] 59.67: thus Carey 1989: 60, 81–2 and 1992: 119–20. 'Knowledge of what was going on' may be a better formulation than 'connivance' or 'collusion', English words which naturally suggest agency rather than simple awareness: in [Dem.] 59 it is the mother who is said to 'be aware' (*suneidenai*). That makes Euphiletus' position even more difficult.

78   Carey 1989: 62–4.

79   Walker 1993: 81.

80   Carey 1989: 68–9.

81   Jameson 1990, though the point is controversial; cf. Pomeroy 1994: 295–7 and the full discussion of Schnurr-Redford 1996: 89–98. Walker 1993 brings out the parallel with modern purdah-cultures, where seclusion can be accepted as an ideal even though the poorer classes often cannot afford to achieve it in practice. See also Cohen 1991a: 133–70.

82   For instance [Dem.] 47.56; cf. § 54 for the diminished circumstances of the speaker there.

83   On this point see especially Carey 1989: 61–2, 66, with a very good treatment of the self-characterisation; Herman 1993: 414–15.

84   Gould 1980: 50, cf. 47–8; Lacey 1968: 170; Just 1989: 142–3.

85   On the sexual role-reversal cf. especially Porter 1997: 430–1.

86   On this see the interesting and largely cogent analysis of Cohen 1995. Cohen may put too much weight on the notion of litigation as a mode of pursuing rather than replacing an agonistic concern for honour; we can reasonably see it as both, a healthier counterpart.

87   For these and other modes of humiliation, for instance plucking out the adulterer's pubic hair or singeing with hot ash, see the differing views of Cohen 1985; Roy 1991; Ogden 1997: 37 note 23; Carey 1989: 86 and especially 1993b. For the appearance of the anal radish in a later epigram, Pelling 1997h: 321.

88   Herman 1993: 415–16 is right to stress the recurrent emphasis on Eratosthenes' violation of the *oikos* (particularly striking in Euphiletus' indignant question at § 25; below, note 92); but Herman dissociates this too much from 'honour'. The trespass too is an act of dishonouring *hubris* against Euphiletus (e.g. § 4: cf. Cohen 1991a: 143–4, 147, Gould 1980: 47–8). The insult embodied in the adultery is anyway more

stressed than Herman allows: the proem's 'acts like this' which every Greek city condemns must refer primarily to adultery rather than trespass; the conclusion too emphasises the outrage against wives rather than houses (§§ 48–9).

89 This glosses over a substantial methodological issue. I have been writing as if the speech was delivered in the form we have it, with such obvious changes as the suppression of the laws' wording. Some argue for wider alteration before publication. Thus Dover 1968b: 188 wonders why Euphiletus did not offer the slave-girl go-between to give evidence under torture, and thinks that the original speech must have dealt with the issue; Porter 1997 goes further, arguing that the speech is 'a particularly sophisticated form of practical rhetorical exercise – a fictional speech based upon a fictional case, designed not only to instruct and delight but quite probably to advertise the logographer's skill' (441). Even if that is right (and the cases do not seem to me made out), it remains important that the texts *purport* to be delivered and deliverable. The only usable method is to assume, at least provisionally, that they are geared to work as real speeches would work; in other words, that they can serve as a guide to the dynamic of court-cases, whether or not they authentically preserve the words and arguments used on the real occasion itself.

90 For example Harrison 1968–71: i: 34; Pomeroy 1975: 86; Foucault 1985: 146; other scholars cited by Harris 1990: 370–1 note 2. Harris challenges that consensus for reasons similar to those given here; he is countered by Carey 1995, but Carey acknowledges that the Lysias passage is inadequate in itself to support that view.

91 I follow Cohen 1991a: 110–18 (despite the arguments of Carey 1995: 411–12) in suspecting that this first law concerned *kakourgia*, and that 'confession' was important to justify the summary execution of such 'wrongdoers'. But Cohen 111–12 simplifies in inferring from Aeschines 1.91 that adulterers (*moichoi*, however exactly that term was defined) were 'included' in this class of offenders. Aeschines is mounting a precedent argument: if you do not convict, 'what cloak-snatcher or thief or adulterer or murderer, or anyone else who falls into the class of those who commit the worst crimes and do so secretly, will ever be punished?' (Cohen's quotation misleadingly suppresses the 'murderers'.) The extension of the *kakourgia* statute to murderers was arguable but contentious, as Antiphon 5.9–10 makes clear; the same was presumably true of *moichoi*. Hansen 1976: 44–8 reasonably concludes that murderers and adulterers were not explicitly listed in the statute but that in an individual case the court might extend the scope of *kakourgia* to include them. That possibility of extension is enough to allow Aeschines his precedent argument. The vagueness of this provision made it desirable for Euphiletus to quote his second law as well, where adultery ('...who takes an adulterer with his own wife...') was clearly specified, but the need for 'confession' probably was not. See also Harris 1990: 376–7 against Cohen.

92 Exactly what he 'confessed' is another question: just 'he was in the wrong', and the same vague word is used twice (*adikein*, §§ 25, 29). This

is an answer to Euphiletus' indignant question, 'What is the meaning of this *hubris*, coming into my house like this?' (§ 25; quoted on p. 222). Eratosthenes could hardly deny all 'wrongdoing', but it need not follow that he confessed to everything Euphiletus now implies, particularly the intrusion into the household space. If there *had* been some 'entrapment' and Eratosthenes had been invited into the house (if not into his wife's bed) by Euphiletus himself, his confession of 'doing wrong' could be limited to the sexual shenanigans.

93  It is quoted at Dem. 23.53: see above, note 9. Cf. Cohen 1991a: 99–109.

94  Carey 1989: 79.

95  Thus Harris 1990: 373–4; Carey 1995: 409–10; Ogden 1996: 142–3 = 1997: 30; cf. Cole 1984: 100–3. In the case of *in flagrante* detection, it would anyway often be unclear to the outraged husband how much persuasion and how much coercion there had been.

96  So Cole 1984: 99; Harris 1990: 373–4; Cohen 1991b; Fisher 1992: 41–2; Todd 1993: 277 (tentatively); Carey 1995: 410; Omitowoju 1997 (rightly stressing the importance of status).

97  Carey 1996: 37. As it happens, the homicide law (i.e. the second of Euphiletus' three) was a rare exception, and was attributed to Draco (Plut. *Sol.* 23.1 says that 'Solon allowed anyone who took an adulterer to kill him', but may be misled by Lysias' language here: so Harris 1990: 371 note 2, Ogden 1996: 149 = 1997: 34). Lysias naturally keeps quiet about this, as it would suggest a plurality of law-givers which would compromise the argument.

98  Osborne 1985c; Todd 1993: especially 64–7, 122, 160–3; Carey 1996: 38.

99  See for example Cohen 1991a: 107; Carey 1995: 415–17; on the importance of blood-line, Ogden 1996: 136–50 = 1997. Notice Xen. *Hiero* 3.6: 'Cities too realise that friendship is the greatest and most delightful good for mankind: at least, they define adulterers as the only class who can be killed with impunity, evidently because they regard them as the destroyers of the affection which exists between husband and wife'. Xenophon too is overarguing to make his point: the pattern was not so standard throughout Greece (Carey 1995: 415). But he too cannot be talking what would strike his audience as nonsense.

100 For instance, Brown 1991 points out that the young farmer Gorgias in Menander's *Dyskolos* (316 BC) mentions both rape and seduction, and describes rape allusively as the one which 'deserves a thousand deaths' (ll. 289–93). That too cannot be so outlandish a view as to distract or confuse the audience (though it is true that Gorgias may be speaking 'in character', either as a prig or as someone concerned with the implications for his property: Pierce 1997: 170). For attempts to ask the question in broader terms, cf. especially Carey 1995 (concentrating on law and arguing that seduction *did* seem worse); and the various viewpoints explored in Deacy and Pierce 1997.

101 For example Menander, *Perikeiromene* 1013–14 with Gomme and Sandbach 1973: 531 ad loc.; Gould 1980: 53 and note 112; Just 1989: 47–50, 231.

102 p. 218.

103  ἀναγκαῖον δὲ διαφέρειν at *Politics* 1260b18 is deliciously ambiguous.
 The text has treated the need for education of children and women –
 'there must be a difference' – because women are half of the free, and
 from children there grow participants in the state. Does that mean
 'they must make a difference' (Jowett), or 'there must be a difference
 in their education'?

104  See especially Lloyd 1983: 94–105, and the passages he collects and
 discusses.

105  Not that this antithesis is straightforward for Aristotle, for whom
 'nature' sanctions certain 'conventional' developments such as society
 itself: see especially 1252b30ff. But within this same book Aristotle
 himself uses the antithesis as a heuristic device when it suits him,
 especially at 1253b20ff. but also at 1255a5–7, 1257a3–5, 1257b10–11.

106  Lloyd 1983: 98–9; cf. p. 208, on the greater capacity for pity there also
 assigned to the female.

107  The most substantial passages are 1280b38–40, 1295b21–5, and
 1327b39–28a5; elsewhere 'friends' emerge mainly in discussion of Plato
 (1262b7–14, picked up at 1330a1–2), or as an unattractive feature
 ('croneyism') or a threat: for example 1287b30–5, 1308b18, 1311b28,
 1312a6–8, 1313b29–32. See Price 1989: 195–200: in the *Eudemian* and
 *Nicomachean Ethics* the city subserves utility more than pleasure. Price
 suggests that the argument of the *Politics* implies a larger place for
 goodwill, but stresses (195 note 21) that this is not made explicit.

108  The point recurs towards the end of the work: 1325a27–31, 1333a3–11.
 Cf. also *Nicomachean Ethics* 1160b22–61a6, with Price 1989: 193.

109  The contrast is helpfully elaborated by Pomeroy 1994: 34–5 and
 Cartledge 1993a: 86–8.

110  Cf. p. 218 and note 65.

111  On this theme see the good remarks of Giny 1993: 486.

112  The date of neither *Symposium* nor the *Oeconomicus* is secure. *Symposium*
 must be later than 385 BC (182b6–7, 193a2): Dover 1980: 10 dates it to
 384–79. The *Oeconomicus* is tentatively dated after 362 by Pomeroy 1994:
 8, but the evidence is very slight.

113  Female education: pp. 233–4. Husband's role, and the contrast between
 Aristotle and Xenophon: Pomeroy 1994: 34–5.

114  Murnaghan 1988: 10.

115  On this see especially Murnaghan 1988 and below, note 119.

116  'Paternalistic, pompous, and priggish', Harvey 1984: 69–70; 'a pompous
 fool', MacKenzie 1985: 95.

117  Cf. Foucault 1985: 163.

118  Goldhill 1995: 139–41, following Murnaghan 1988 but making more of
 the irony. Giny 1993 takes it more literally, arguing that several of the
 wife's replies show bite and intelligence; if so, that would support an
 interpretation allowing more independent qualities to the wife than
 Ischomachus realises (pp. 243–5).

119  On this see especially Murnaghan 1988, who suggests that Ischomachus,
 by making his wife as 'man-like' as possible, is trying to suppress and
 control her female potential for disorder and passion: household order
 becomes a symbol for female virtue, especially female chastity.

Murnaghan, like Humphreys 1983: 13, assumes that Xenophon is fully supporting this assimilation of the household to other, manly spheres. Yet the text may be more ironic if the wife's later career (below) is brought into the picture, reminding us that Ischomachus' repressive technique was not an unqualified success: cf. Goldhill 1995: 140–1.

120 For the emphasis on the wife managing the outgoings as the husband manages the income, cf. Xen. *Oec.* 3.15, 7.35–41. Schaps 1979: 15, Henderson 1987: 132–3 on Arist. *Lys.* 495, and Pomeroy 1994: 281–2 collect evidence for women handling household finances.

121 See Foucault 1985: 160–4.

122 Pomeroy 1994: 308 points out that this might include 'slave-boy' as well as 'slave-girl'; but the feminine ἀναγκαζομένην later in the sentence ('a woman ... being forced') shows that heterosexual intercourse is more in point.

123 Thus, rightly, Foucault 1985: 163–4, Just 1989: 138, and Pomeroy 1994: 297–8.

124 A point already made by Aristophanes' Lysistrata (163–7). 'The master hesitates to make sexual advances to an unwilling slave' (Pomeroy 1994: 65, cf. 39) is a misreading, but her note on the passage itself (pp. 308–9) is very helpful.

125 Thus Pomeroy 1994: 18–19.

126 On these cf. MacDowell 1962: 151–2, 207; Davies 1971: 264–9; Pomeroy 1994: 259–64. The case for the identification of the crucial Ischomachi is stronger than that for the identification of the wife: see next note.

127 MacDowell 1962: 152 sensibly notes that Ischomachus may have married more than once, a point too quickly dismissed by Harvey 1984: 69 note 2 and Goldhill 1995: 177 note 68: both confuse Davies' 'wealth of documentation' (Harvey) for identifying Ischomachus with the much sparser evidence for identifying the two 'wives'. That case comes down to a similarity of age at marriage of Andocides' and Xenophon's 'wives' (Davies 1971: 267): but Ischomachus could easily have married successively two fourteen-year-olds. There is a stronger point. Andocides' 'wife of Ischomachus' was surely the famous one; she was also presumably the one married to Ischomachus at the dramatic date of the *Oeconomicus* (their daughter was born *c.* 430). If Xenophon intended a different, earlier wife, how could his audience possibly have told? There are no clear pointers to suggest one wife rather than another (e.g. on date of marriage or the wife's parentage).

128 *Pace* Anderson 1974: 174 note 1 and (tentatively) Pomeroy 1994: 263–4. Apart from anything else, that overlooks the nature of performance and 'publication': texts would receive continuous feedback from friends who heard and read them. Had Xenophon's choice of Ischomachus been an ill-informed blunder, someone would have told him.

129 MacKenzie 1985.

130 Thus Pomeroy 1994: 264. Goldhill 1995: 178 note 72 is sceptical, and so am I.

131 This formulation (adapting the suggestion of Harvey 1984) meets the objection of Pomeroy 1994: 263 – that this could not be a defence, for if Xenophon knew Chrysilla well enough to defend her that would itself

be evidence of her improperly close acquaintance with an outsider. But propriety could be inferred from acquaintance with husband-tutor rather than with wife-pupil.

132 Pomeroy 1994: 263 thinks that it would 'undermine his entire treatise' to introduce such ideas of how it later went wrong: in that case 'there would be little point in his writing the *Oeconomicus*'. That simplifies. The perspective would not 'undermine' the advice, but point the difficulty of transmitting it.

133 Nails 1985, pointing to the 'atmosphere of shared misogyny', with Xenophon 'reminding his listeners that any woman, no matter how well trained, will go wild if the harness is removed': cf. Goldhill 1995: 141.

## 11 Conclusions: texts, audiences, truth

1 Cohen and Saller 1994 bring out Foucault's failure to pay sufficient attention to normative structures.

2 The last three points in particular are made by many of his critics, who often stress that his choice of genres and 'problems' is uncomfortably androcentric: see especially the collections of Goldstein 1994 and Larmour, Miller, and Platter 1998.

3 Alcibiades at Sparta is one speech which makes a difference; Thuc. 6.93.1–2 makes that plain. Hermocrates at Gela is another clear case (4.65.1).

4 I discussed this model, and different sorts of 'evidence', in Pelling 1997c: 213–14.

# Bibliography

Albini, F. and Pelling, C.B.R. (1996) *Plutarco: Vita di Coriolano, Vita di Alcibiade*. Firenze.

Althusser, L. (1965) *For Marx*. London.

Ameling, W. (1985) 'Plutarch, Perikles 12, 14', *Historia* 34: 47–63.

Amit, A. (1973) *Great and Small Poleis*. Brussels.

Anderson, J.K. (1974) *Xenophon*. Oxford.

Andrewes, A. (1978) 'The opposition to Perikles', *JHS* 98: 1–8.

Andrewes, A. (1982) 'Notion and Kyzikos: the sources compared', *JHS* 102: 15–25.

Andrews, J.A. (1994) 'Cleon's ethopoetics', *CQ* 44: 26–39.

*ANRW: Aufstieg und Niedergang der römischen Welts*, Berlin and New York (1972–).

*ATL: The Athenian Tribute Lists*, eds B.D. Meritt, H.T. Wade-Grey, and M.F. McGregor, i–iv, Princeton (1939–53).

Aurenche, O. (1974) *Les Groupes d'Alcibiade, de Léogoras et de Teucros*. Paris.

Avery, H.C. (1973) 'Themes in Thucydides' account of the Sicilian expedition', *Hermes* 101: 1–13.

Badian, E. (1971) 'Archons and *Strategoi*', *Antichthon* 5, 1–34.

Badian, E. (1992) 'Thucydides on rendering speeches', *Ath.* 80: 187–90.

Badian, E. (1993) *From Plataea to Potidaea: Studies in the History and Historiography of the Pentecontaetia*. Baltimore and London.

Bailey, C. (1936) 'Who played Dicaeopolis?', in *Greek Poetry and Life*, pp. 231–40. Oxford.

Bakhtin, M.M. (1968) *Rabelais and his World* (tr. H. Iswolsky: Russian original 1965). Bloomington.

Bakhtin, M.M. (1981) *The Dialogic Imagination* (ed. M. Holquist, tr. C. Emerson and M. Holquist). Austin.

Barber, G.L. (1935) *The Historian Ephorus*. Cambridge.

Bers, V. (1985) 'Dikastic *thorubos*', in Cartledge and Harvey 1985: 1–15.

Bers, V. (1994) 'Tragedy and rhetoric', in Worthington 1994: 176–95.

Bianchetti, S. (1979) 'L'ostracismo di Iperbolo e le "Nuvole" di Aristofane', *SIFC* 51: 221–48.

Boegehold, A.L. (1990) 'Andokides and the decree of Patrokleides', *Historia* 39: 149–62.

Boulter, P.N. (1962) 'The theme of ἀγρία in Euripides' *Orestes*', *Phoenix* 16: 102–6.

Bowie, A.M. (1982) 'The parabasis in Aristophanes: prolegomena, *Acharnians*', *CQ* 32: 27–40.

Bowie, A.M. (1993a) *Aristophanes: Myth, Ritual, and Comedy*. Cambridge.

Bowie, A.M. (1993b) 'Religion and politics in Aeschylus's *Oresteia*', *CQ* 43, 10–31.

Bowie, A.M. (1997a) 'Tragic filters for history: Euripides' *Supplices* and Sophocles' *Philoctetes*', in Pelling 1997a: 39–62.

Bowie, A.M. (1997b) 'Thinking with drinking: wine and the symposium in Aristophanes', *JHS* 117: 1–21.

Brooks, P. and Gewirtz, P. (eds) (1996) *Law's Stories: Narrative and Rhetoric in the Law*. New Haven and London.

Brown, P.G. McC. (1991) 'Athenian attitudes to rape and seduction: the evidence of Menander, *Dyskolos* 289–93', *CQ* 41: 533–4.

Bruce, I.A.F. (1967) *An Historical Commentary on the Hellenica Oxyrhynchia*. Cambridge.

Brunt, P.A. (1951) 'The Megarian Decree', *AJP* 72: 269–82, reprinted with a postscript in Brunt 1993: 1–16.

Brunt, P.A. (1993) *Studies in Greek History and Thought*. Oxford.

Bugh, G.R. (1988) *The Horsemen of Athens*. Princeton.

Burkert, W. (1974) 'Die Absurdität der Gewalt und das Ende der Tragödie: Euripides' Orestes', *AuA* 20: 97–109.

*CAH*: *Cambridge Ancient History*, Cambridge (2nd ed. 1961–; 1st ed. 1923–39).

Cairns, F. (1982) 'Cleon and Pericles: a suggestion', *JHS* 102: 203–4.

Calhoun, G.M. (1913) *Athenian Clubs in Politics and Litigation*. Austin.

Cameron, A. and Kuhrt, A. (eds) (1983) *Images of Women in Antiquity*. London.

Camon, F. (1963) 'L'ostracismo di Iperbolo', *Giornale Italiano di Filologia* 16: 142–62.

Carawan, E.M. (1990) 'The five talents Cleon coughed up (Schol. Ar. *Ach.* 6)', *CQ* 40: 137–47.

Carey, C. (1989) *Lysias: Selected Speeches*. Cambridge.

Carey, C. (1992) *Greek Orators VI: Apollodoros, Against Neaira [Demosthenes] 59*. Warminster.

Carey, C. (1993a) 'The purpose of Aristophanes' *Acharnians*', *RhM* 136: 245–63.

Carey, C. (1993b) 'The return of the radish or Just when you thought it was safe to go into the kitchen', *LCM* 18.4: 53–5.

Carey, C. (1994) 'Comic ridicule and democracy', in Osborne and Hornblower 1994: 69–83.

Carey, C. (1995) 'Rape and adultery in Athenian law', *CQ* 45: 407–17.

Carey, C. (1996) '*Nomos* in Attic rhetoric and oratory', *JHS* 116: 33–46.

Carter, L.B. (1986) *The Quiet Athenian*. Oxford.

Cartledge, P. (1982) 'Sparta and Samos: a special relationship?', *CQ* 32: 243–65.

Cartledge, P. (1990) *Aristophanes and his Theatre of the Absurd*. Bristol.

Cartledge, P. (1993a) *The Greeks*. Oxford.

Cartledge, P. (1993b) 'The silent women of Thucydides: 2.45.2 re-viewed', in Rosen and Farrell 1993: 125–32.

Cartledge, P., Millett, P., and Todd, S. (eds) (1990) *Nomos: Essays in Athenian Law, Politics, and Society*. Cambridge.

Cartledge, P. and Harvey, F.D. (eds) (1985) *Crux: Essays in Greek History presented to G.E.M. de Ste Croix*. London.

Cassio, A.C. (1982) 'Arte compositiva e politica in Aristofane: il discorso di Ermete nella *Pace*', *RFIC* 110: 22–44.

Cawkwell, G.L. (1969) 'Anthemocritus and the Megarians and the decree of Charinus', *REG* 82: 327–35.

Cawkwell, G.L. (1988) '*Nomophulakia* and the Areopagus', *JHS* 108: 1–12.

Cawkwell, G.L. (1997) *Thucydides and the Peloponnesian War*. London.

*CEG*: *Carmina Epigraphica Graeca*, ed. P.A. Hansen, Berlin and New York (1983, 1989).

Cobet, J. (1977) 'Wann wurde Herodots Darstellung der Perserkriege publiziert?', *Hermes* 105: 2–27.

Cohen, D. (1985) 'A note on Aristophanes and the punishment of adultery in Athenian law', *ZSS* 102: 385–7.

Cohen, D. (1991a) *Law, Sexuality, and Society: the Enforcement of Morals in Classical Athens*. Cambridge.

Cohen, D. (1991b) 'Sexuality, violence, and the Athenian law of *hubris*', *G&R* 38: 171–88.

Cohen, D. (1995) *Law, Violence, and Community in Classical Athens*. Cambridge.

Cohen, D. and Saller, R. (1994) 'Foucault on sexuality in Greco-Roman antiquity', in Goldstein 1994: 35–59.

Cole, S.G. (1984) 'Greek sanctions against sexual assault', *CP* 79: 97–113.

Cole, T. (1991) *The Origins of Rhetoric in Ancient Greece*. Baltimore and London.

Collard, C., Cropp, M.J., and Lee, K.H. (1995) *Euripides: Selected Fragmentary Plays* i. Warminster.

Conacher, D.J. (1987) *Aeschylus' Oresteia: a Literary Commentary*. Toronto.

Connor, W.R. (1962) 'Charinus' Megarean decree', *AJP* 83: 225–46.

Connor, W.R. (1968) *Theopompus and Fifth-century Athens*. Washington, DC.

Connor, W.R. (1970) 'Charinus' Megarean decree again', *REG* 83: 305–8.

Connor, W.R. (1971) *The New Politicians of Fifth-century Athens*. Princeton.

Connor, W.R. (1984) *Thucydides*. Princeton.

Connor, W.R. (1985) 'Narrative discourse in Thucydides', in *The Greek Historians: Literature and History: Papers presented to A.E. Raubitschek*, pp. 1–17. Stanford.

Conte, G.B. (1986) *The Rhetoric of Imitation: Genre and Poetic Memory in Virgil and other Latin Poets*. Cornell.

Croally, N. (1994) *Euripidean Polemic: the* Trojan Women *and the Function of Tragedy*. Cambridge.

Csapo, E. and Slater, W.J. (1995) *The Context of Ancient Drama*. Michigan.

Davies, J.K. (1971) *Athenian Propertied Families*. Oxford.

De Blois, L. (1992) 'The perception of politics in Plutarch's *Lives*', *ANRW* ii.33.6: 4568–615.

De Ste Croix, G.E.M. (1972) *The Origins of the Peloponnesian War*. London.

Deacy, S. and Pierce, K.F. (eds) (1997) *Rape in Antiquity*. London.

Denniston, J.D. (1954) *The Greek Particles* (2nd ed., rev. K.J. Dover: first ed. 1934). Oxford.

Dershowitz, A. (1996) 'Life is not a dramatic narrative', in Brooks and Gewirtz 1996: 99–105.

*DFA*: *The Dramatic Festivals of Athens*, ed. A.W. Pickard-Cambridge, Oxford (1953); 2nd ed. by J. Gould and D.M. Lewis, Oxford (1968).

Dodds, E.R. (1960) 'Morals and politics in the *Oresteia*', *PCPS* 186: 19–31, reprinted in Dodds 1973: 45–63.

Dodds, E.R. (1973) *The Ancient Concept of Progress, and Other Essays on Greek Literature and Belief*. Oxford.

Dover, K.J. (1957) 'The political aspect of Aeschylus' *Eumenides*', *JHS* 77: 230–7, reprinted in Dover 1987: 161–75.

Dover, K.J. (1963) 'Notes on Aristophanes' *Acharnians*', *Maia* 15: 6–21, reprinted in Dover 1987: 288–306.

Dover, K.J. (1966) 'Anthemocritus and the Megarians', *AJP* 87: 203–9, reprinted in *The Greeks and their Legacy: Collected Papers II* 1988: 181–6.

Dover, K.J. (1968a) *Aristophanes: Clouds*. Oxford.

Dover, K.J. (1968b) *Lysias and the Corpus Lysiacum*. Berkeley and Los Angeles.

Dover, K.J. (1972) *Aristophanic Comedy*. London.

Dover, K.J. (1974) *Greek Popular Morality in the time of Plato and Aristotle*. Oxford.

Dover, K.J. (1980) *Plato: Symposium*. Cambridge.

Dover, K.J. (1987) *Greek and the Greeks*. Oxford.

Dover, K.J. (1988) 'Anecdotes, gossip, and scandal', in *The Greeks and their Legacy: Collected Papers II*, pp. 45–52. Oxford.

Dover, K.J. (1993) *Aristophanes: Frogs*. Oxford.

Duff, T. (1997) 'Moral ambiguity in Plutarch's *Lysander–Sulla*', in Mossman 1997: 169–87.

Dunn, F.M. (1996) *Tragedy's End*. New York and Oxford.

Eagleton, T. (1991) *Ideology: an Introduction*. London and New York.

Eagleton, T. (1994) 'Introduction', in *Ideology* (ed. T. Eagleton), pp. 1–20. London.

Easterling, P.E. (1985) 'Anachronism in Greek Tragedy', *JHS* 105: 1–10.

Easterling, P.E. (1997) 'Constructing the heroic', in Pelling 1997a: 21–37.

Edmunds, L. (1984) 'Thucydides on monosandalism (3.22.2)', in *Studies presented to Sterling Dow on his eightieth birthday* (eds A.L. Boegehold *et al.*), pp. 71–5. North Carolina.

Edwards, M. (1995) *Greek Orators – IV: Andocides*. Warminster.

Egermann, F. (1972) 'Thukydides über die Art seiner Reden und Darstellung der Kriegsgeschehnisse', *Historia* 21: 575–602.

Ellis, W.M. (1989) *Alcibiades*. London.

Erbse, H. (1956) 'Die Bedeutung der Synkrisis in den Parallelbiographien Plutarchs', *Hermes* 84: 398–424.

Euben, J.P. (1986) 'Political corruption in Euripides' *Orestes*', in *Greek Tragedy and Political Theory* (ed. J.P. Euben), pp. 222–51. Berkeley and Los Angeles.

Fineman, J. (1989) 'The history of the anecdote: fiction and faction', in Veeser 1989: 49–76.

Finley, M.I. (1982) *Authority and Legitimacy in the Classical City-state*. Copenhagen.

Finley, M.I. (1985) *Ancient History: Evidence and Models*. London.

Fisher, N.R.E. (1992) *Hybris: a Study in the Values of Honour and Shame in Ancient Greece*. Warminster.

Flory, S. (1980) 'Who read Herodotus' history?', *AJP* 101: 12–28.

Flower, M.A. (1994) *Theopompus of Chios: History and Rhetoric in the Fourth Century B.C.* Oxford.

Flower, M.A. and Toher, M. (eds) (1991) *Georgica: Greek Studies in Honour of George Cawkwell* (*BICS* Suppl. 38). London.

Foley, H.P. (ed.) (1981a) *Reflections of Women in Antiquity*. Philadelphia.

Foley, H.P. (1981b) 'The conception of women in Athenian drama', in Foley 1981a: 127–68.

Foley, H.P. (1982) 'The "female intruder" reconsidered: women in Aristophanes' *Lysistrata* and *Ecclesiazusae*', *CP* 77: 1–21.

Foley, H.P. (1988) 'Tragedy and politics in Aristophanes' *Acharnians*', *JHS* 108: 33–47.

Fornara, C. (1967) 'Two notes on Thucydides', *Phil.* 111: 291–5.

Fornara, C. (1971) 'The date of Herodotus' publication', *JHS* 91: 25–34.

Fornara, C. (1973) 'Cleon's attack against the cavalry', *CQ* 23: 24.

Fornara, C. (1975) 'Plutarch and the Megarian decree', *YCS* 24: 213–28.

Forrest, W.G. (1963) 'Aristophanes' *Acharnians*', *Phoenix* 17: 1–12.

Foucault, M. (1985) *The Use of Pleasure* (*The History of Sexuality* ii, tr. R. Hurley: French original 1984). Page references are to the Penguin edition (Harmondsworth 1987).

Foucault, M. (1986) *The Care of the Self* (*The History of Sexuality* ii, tr. R. Hurley: French original 1984). Page references are to the Penguin edition (Harmondsworth 1990).

Fowler, D.P. (1989) 'First thoughts on closure: problems and prospects', *MD* 22: 75–122.

Foxhall, L. (1998) 'Pandora unbound: a feminist critique of Foucault's *History of Sexuality*', in Larmour, Miller, and Platter 1998: 122–37.

Fraenkel, E. (1950) *Aeschylus: Agamemnon* i–iii. Oxford.

Francis, D. (1991–3) 'Brachylogia Laconica', *BICS* 38: 198–212.

Furley, W.D. (1989) 'Andokides IV ("Against Alkibiades"): fact or fiction?', *Hermes* 117: 138–56.

Furley, W.D. (1996) *Andokides and the Hermes: a Study of Crisis in Fifth-century Athenian Religion* (*BICS* Suppl. 65). London.

Fuscagni, S. (1989) *Plutarco: Cimone e Lucullo* (with B. Scardigli). Milan.

Gagarin, M. (1996) 'The torture of slaves in Athenian law', *CP* 91: 1–18.

Gauthier, P. (1975) 'Les ports de l'empire et l'*agora* Athénienne: a propos du "décret Mégarien" ', *Historia* 24: 498–503.

Gawantka, W. (1975) *Isopolitie: ein Beitrag zur Geschichte der zwischenstaatlichen Beziehungen in der griechischen Antike*. München.

Geertz, C. (1973) *The Interpretation of Cultures*. London.

Gelzer, T. (1960) *Der epirrhematische Agon bei Aristophanes*. München.

Geuss, R. (1981) *The Idea of a Critical Theory*. Cambridge.

Gewirtz, P. (1996) 'Victims and voyeurs: two narrative problems at the criminal trial', in Brooks and Gewirtz 1996: 135–61.

*GHI*: *Greek Historical Inscriptions*, ed. M.N. Tod, Oxford (vol. i, 2nd ed. 1946 [1st ed. 1933]; vol. ii, 1948).

Ghiron-Bistagne, P. (1976) *Recherches sur les Acteurs dans la Grèce Antique*. Paris.

Gill, C. (1996) *Personality in Greek Epic, Tragedy, and Philosophy: the Self in Dialogue*. Oxford.

Gilula, D. (1989) 'A career in the navy (Arist. *Knights* 541–4)', *CQ* 39: 259–61.

Giny, A. (1993) 'The manly intellect of his wife: Xenophon, *Oeconomicus* ch. 7', *CW* 86: 483–6.

Ginzburg, C. (1989) *Clues, Myths, and the Historical Method* (tr. J. and A.C. Tedeschi: Italian original 1986). Baltimore and London.

Goldhill, S. (1984) *Language, Sexuality, Narrative: the* Oresteia. Cambridge.

Goldhill, S. (1990a) 'The Great Dionysia and civic ideology', in Winkler and Zeitlin 1990: 97–129; original version in *JHS* 107: 58–76 (1987).

Goldhill, S. (1990b) 'Character and action, representation and reading', in Pelling 1990a: 100–27.

Goldhill, S. (1991) *The Poet's Voice*. Cambridge.

Goldhill, S. (1994) 'Representing democracy: women at the Great Dionysia', in Osborne and Hornblower 1994: 347–69.

Goldhill, S. (1995) *Foucault's Virginity*. Cambridge.

Goldhill, S. (1996) 'Collectivity and otherness: the authority of the tragic chorus: response to Gould', in Silk 1996: 244–56.

Goldstein, J. (ed). (1994) *Foucault and the Writing of History*. Oxford.

Gomme, A.W. (1925) 'The position of women in Athens in the fifth and fourth centuries B.C.', *CP* 20: 1–25, reprinted in Gomme 1937: 89–115.

Gomme, A.W. (1937) *Essays in Greek History and Literature*. Oxford.

Gomme, A.W. and Sandbach, F.H. (1973) *Menander: a Commentary*. Oxford.

Gould, J.P. (1980) 'Law, custom, and myth: aspects of the social position of women in classical Athens', *JHS* 100: 38–59.

Gould, J.P. (1996) 'Tragedy and collective experience', in Silk 1996: 217–43.

Grant, J.R. (1965) 'A note on the tone of Greek diplomacy', *CQ* 15: 261–6.

Gribble, D. (1999) *Alcibiades and Athens*. Oxford.

Griffin, J. (1977) 'The epic cycle and the uniqueness of Homer', *JHS* 97: 39–53.

Griffin, J. (1995) *Homer: Iliad IX*. Oxford.

Griffin, J. (1998) 'The social function of Greek tragedy', *CQ* 48: 39–61.

Hall, E.M. (1993) 'Political and cosmic turbulence in Euripides' *Orestes*', in Sommerstein, Halliwell, Henderson, and Zimmermann 1993: 263–86.

Hall, E.M. (1997) 'The sociology of Athenian tragedy', in *The Cambridge Companion to Greek Tragedy* (ed. P.E. Easterling), pp. 93–126. Cambridge.

Hall, E.M. (1998) 'Ithyphallic males behaving badly; or, satyr drama as gendered tragic ending', in *Parchments of Gender: Deciphering the Bodies of Antiquity* (ed. M. Wyke), pp. 13–37. Oxford.

Halliwell, S. (1980) 'Aristophanes' apprenticeship', *CQ* 30: 33–45.

Halliwell, S. (1989) 'Authorial collaboration in the Athenian comic theatre', *GRBS* 30: 515–28.

Halliwell, S. (1991) 'Comic satire and freedom of speech in classical Athens', *JHS* 111: 48–70.

Halliwell, S. (1993) *Plato: Republic 5*. Warminster.

Halliwell, S. (1997) 'Between public and private: tragedy and Athenian experience of rhetoric', in Pelling 1997a: 121–41.

Hammond, N.G.L. (1992) 'Plataea's relations with Thebes, Sparta and Athens', *JHS* 112: 143–50.

Händel, P. (1963) *Formen und Darstellungsweisen in der aristophanischen Komödie*. Heidelberg.

Handley, E.W. and Rea, J. (1957) *The Telephus of Euripides* (*BICS* Suppl. 5). London.

Hansen, M.H. (1975) *Eisangelia*. Oxford.

Hansen, M.H. (1976) *Apagoge, Endeixis, and Ephegesis against Kakourgoi, Atimoi, and Pheugontes*. Odense.

Hansen, M.H. (1978) '*Demos*, *Ekklesia*, and *Dikasteria* in classical Athens', *GRBS* 19: 127–46.

Hansen, M.H. (1980) 'Eisangelia in Athens: a reply', *JHS* 100: 89–95.

Hansen, M.H. (1983) *The Athenian Ekklesia: a Collection of Articles 1976–83*. Copenhagen.

Hansen, M.H. (1985) *Demography and Democracy*. Herning.

Hansen, M.H. (1990) 'The political powers of the people's court in fourth-century Athens', in Murray and Price 1990: 215–43.

Hansen, M.H. (1991) *The Athenian Democracy in the Age of Demosthenes*. Oxford and Cambridge, Mass.

Harding, P. (1994a) *Androtion and the Atthis*. Oxford.

Harding, P. (1994b) 'Comedy and rhetoric', in *Persuasion: Greek Rhetoric in Action* (ed. I. Worthington), pp. 196–221. London.

Harriott, R. (1962) 'Aristophanes' audience and the plays of Euripides', *BICS* 9: 1–8.

Harris, E.M. (1990) 'Did the Athenians regard seduction as a worse crime than rape?', *CQ* 40: 370–7.

Harris, W.V. (1989) *Ancient Literacy*. Cambridge, Mass.

Harrison, A.R.W. (1968–71) *The Law of Athens* i–ii. Oxford.

Harvey, F.D. (1984) 'The wicked wife of Ischomachos', *EMC/CV* 28: 68–70.

*HCT*: *A Historical Commentary on Thucydides*, eds A.W. Gomme, A. Andrewes, and K.J. Dover, Oxford (1945–81).

Heath, M. (1986) 'Thucydides 1.23.5–6', *LCM* 11.7: 104–5.

Heath, M. (1987a) 'Euripides' *Telephus*', *CQ* 37: 272–80.

Heath, M. (1987b) *Political Comedy in Aristophanes* (*Hypomnemata* 87). Göttingen.

Heath, M. (1987c) *The Poetics of Greek Tragedy*. London.

Henderson, J. (1987) *Aristophanes: Lysistrata*. Oxford.

Henderson, J. (1990) 'The Demos and the comic competition', in Winkler and Zeitlin 1990: 271–313.

Henderson, J. (1991) 'Women and the Athenian dramatic festivals', *TAPA* 121: 133–47.

Henderson, J. (1993) 'Comic hero versus political élite', in Sommerstein, Halliwell, Henderson, and Zimmermann 1993: 307–19.

Herman, G. (1987) *Ritualised Friendship and the Greek City*. Cambridge.

Herman, G. (1993) 'Tribal and civic codes of behaviour in Lysias I', *CQ* 43: 406–19.

Herter, H. (1968) *Thukydides* (Wege der Forschung xcviii). Darmstadt.

Heubeck, A. (1980) 'πρόφασις und keine Ende (zu Thuk. 1.23)', *Glotta* 58: 222–36.

Hignett, C. (1952) *A History of the Athenian Constitution to the End of the Fifth Century B.C.* Oxford.

Hogan, J.C. (1972) 'Thucydides 3.52–68 and Euripides' Hecuba', *Phoenix* 26: 241–57.

Holzapfel, L. (1879) *Untersuchungen über die Darstellung der griechischen Geschichte bei Ephoros*. Leipzig.

Hornblower, S. (1983) *The Greek World 479–323 B.C.* London and New York.

Hornblower, S. (1987) *Thucydides*. London.

Hornblower, S. (1991) *A Commentary on Thucydides. Volume I: Books I–III*. Oxford.

Hornblower, S. (1992) 'The religious dimension to the Peloponnesian War, or, what Thucydides does not tell us', *HSCP* 94: 169–97.

Hornblower, S. (1994) 'Narratology and narrative techniques in Thucydides', in *Greek Historiography* (ed. S. Hornblower), pp. 131–66. Oxford.

Hornblower, S. (1995) 'The fourth-century and Hellenistic reception of Thucydides', *JHS* 115: 47–68.

Hornblower, S. (1996) *A Commentary on Thucydides ii: Books IV–V.24*. Oxford.

Hubbard, T.K. (1991) *The Mask of Comedy: Aristophanes and the Intertextual Parabasis*. Ithaca and London.

Humphreys, S.C. (1983) *The Family, Women, and Death*. London.

Humphreys, S.C. (1985) 'Social relations on stage: witnesses in classical Athens', in *The Discourse of Law* (*History and Anthropology* 1.2) (ed. S.C. Humphreys), pp. 313–69. London.

Hunter, V. (1973) *Thucydides: the Artful Reporter*. Toronto.

*IG*: *Inscriptiones Graecae*, Berlin (1873–)

Jackson, R. (1981) *Fantasy: the Literature of Subversion*. London and New York.

Jameson, M. (1990) 'Private space and the Greek city', in Murray and Price 1990: 171–95.

Jones, A.H.M. (1952–3) 'Two synods of the Delian and Peloponnesian Leagues', *PCPS* 2: 43–6.

Jones, A.H.M. (1957) *Athenian Democracy*. Oxford.

Just, R. (1989) *Women in Athenian Law and Life*. London.

Kagan, D. (1969) *The Outbreak of the Peloponnesian War*. Ithaca and London.

Kagan, D. (1974) *The Archidamian War*. Ithaca and London.

Kagan, D. (1975) 'The speeches in Thucydides and the Mytilene debate', *YCS* 24: 71–94.

Kagan, D. (1981) *The Peace of Nicias and the Sicilian Expedition*. Ithaca and London.

Kagan, D. (1987) *The Fall of the Athenian Empire*. Ithaca and London.

Kallet-Marx, L. (1989) 'The Kallias decree', Thucydides, and the outbreak of the Pelopennesian War', *CQ* 39: 94–113.

Kallet-Marx, L. (1993) 'Thucydides 2.45.2 and the status of war widows in Periclean Athens', in Rosen and Farrell 1993: 133–43.

Kennedy, D.F. (1984) Review of T. Woodman and D. West (eds), *Poetry and Politics in the Age of Augustus* in *LCM* 9.10: 157–60.

Keuls, E.C. (1985) *The Reign of the Phallus*. Berkeley, Los Angeles, and London.

King, H. (1983) 'Bound to bleed: Artemis and Greek women', in Cameron and Kuhrt 1983: 109–27. Revised version in King 1998: 75–98.

King, H. (1998) *Hippocrates' Woman: Reading the Female Body in Ancient Greece*. London.

Kitto, H.D.F. (1966) *Poiesis*. Berkeley and Los Angeles.

Knox, B.M.W. (1977) 'The *Medea* of Euripides', *YCS* 25: 193–225.

Konstan, D. (1993) 'Aristophanes' *Lysistrata*: women and the body politic', in Sommerstein, Halliwell, Henderson, and Zimmermann 1993: 431–44.

Konstan, D. (1995) *Greek Comedy and Ideology*. New York and Oxford.

Kraus, C.S. (ed.) (1999) *The Limits of Historiography: Genre and Narrative in Ancient Historical Texts*. Leiden.

Kurke, L. (1991) *The Traffic in Praise: Pindar and the Poetics of Social Economy*. Ithaca and London.

Lacey, W.K. (1968) *The Family in Classical Greece*. London.

Larmour, D.H.J. (1992) 'Making parallels: *Synkrisis* and Plutarch's *Themistocles and Camillus*', *ANRW* ii.33.6: 4154–200.

Larmour, D.H.J., Miller, P.A., and Platter, C. (eds) (1998) *Rethinking sexuality: Foucault and Classical Antiquity*. Princeton.

LaRue, L.H. (1995) *Constitutional Law as Fiction*. Pennsylvania.

Le Roy Ladurie, E. (1979) *Carnival in Romans* (tr. M. Feeney). Harmondsworth.

Lebeck, A. (1971) *The Oresteia: a Study in Language and Structure*. Cambridge, Mass.

Lefkowitz, M.R. (1981) *The Lives of the Greek Poets*. London.

Lefkowitz, M.R. (1991) *First-person Fictions: Pindar's Poetic 'I'*. Oxford.

Legon, R.P. (1981) *Megara: the Political History of a Greek City-state to 336 B.C.* Ithaca and London.

Lehmann, G.A. (1987) 'Überlegungen zur Krise der attischen Demokratie im Peloponnesischen Krieg: Vom Ostrakismos des Hyperbolos zum Thargelion 411 v.Chr.', *ZPE* 69: 33–73.

Lewis, D.M. (1955) 'Notes on Attic inscriptions (II)', *ABSA* 50: 1–36.

Lewis, D.M. (1966) 'After the profanation of the Mysteries', in *Ancient Societies and Institutions (Studies presented to Victor Ehrenberg)*, pp. 177–91. Oxford.

Lloyd, G.E.R. (1966) *Polarity and Analogy*. Cambridge.

Lloyd, G.E.R. (1979) *Magic, Reason, and Experience*. Cambridge.

Lloyd, G.E.R. (1983) *Science, Folklore, and Ideology*. Cambridge.

Longo, O. (1975) 'Proposte di lettura per l'Oreste di Euripide', *Maia* 27: 265–87.

Loraux, N. (1986a) *The Invention of Athens* (tr. A. Sheridan: French original 1981). Cambridge, Mass. and London.

Loraux, N. (1986b) 'Thucydide a écrit la Guerre du Péloponnèse', *Métis* 1.1: 139–61.

MacDonald, B.R. (1983) 'The Megarian Decree', *Historia* 32: 385–410.

MacDowell, D.M. (1962) *Andokides: On the Mysteries*. Oxford.

MacDowell, D.M. (1971) *Aristophanes: Wasps*. Oxford.

MacDowell, D.M. (1978) *The Law in Classical Athens*. London.

MacDowell, D.M. (1982) 'Aristophanes and Kallistratos', *CQ* 32: 21–6.

MacDowell, D.M. (1983) 'The nature of Aristophanes' *Akharnians*', *GR* 30: 143–62.

MacDowell, D.M. (1985) Review of Osborne 1983 in *CR* 35: 317–20.

MacDowell, D.M. (1995) *Aristophanes and Athens*. Oxford.

MacKenzie, D.C. (1985) 'The wicked wife of Ischomachus again', *EMC/CV* 29: 95–6.

Macleod, C.W. (1982) 'Politics and the *Oresteia*', *JHS* 102: 124–44, reprinted in Macleod 1983: 20–40.

Macleod, C.W. (1983) *Collected Essays*. Oxford.

Marasco, G. (1976) *Plutarco: Vita di Nicia*. Rome.

Markle, M. (1985) 'Jury pay and assembly pay in Athens', in Cartledge and Harvey 1985: 265–97.

Marr, J.L. (1971) 'Andocides' part in the Mysteries and Hermae affairs 415 B.C.', *CQ* 21: 326–38.

Mastromarco, G. (1979) 'L'esordi "segreto" di Aristofane', *Quaderni di Storia* 10: 153–96.

Mastromarco, G. (1993) 'Il commediografo e il demagogo', in Sommerstein, Halliwell, Henderson, and Zimmermann 1993: 341–57.

Mattingly, H.B. (1991) 'The practice of ostracism in Athens', *Antichthon* 25: 1–26.

McLeish, K. (1980) *The Theater of Aristophanes*. New York.

McNeal, R.A. (1970) 'Historical methods and Thucydides 1.103.1', *Historia* 19: 306–25.

Meier, C. (1993) *The Political Art of Greek Tragedy* (tr. D. McLintock: German original 1990). Cambridge, Mass. and London.

Meiggs, R. (1972) *The Athenian Empire*. Oxford.

Meyer, E. (1899) *Forschungen zur alten Geschichte* ii. Halle.

Mills, S. (1997) *Theseus, Tragedy, and the Athenian Empire*. Oxford.

Mirhady, D.C. (1996) 'Torture and rhetoric in Athens', *JHS* 116: 119–31.

Missiou, A. (1992) *The Subversive Oratory of Andocides: Politics, Ideology, and Decision-making in Democratic Athens*. Cambridge.

*ML: A Selection of Greek Historical Inscriptions*, eds R. Meiggs and D.M. Lewis, Oxford (revised ed. 1988; 1st ed. 1969).

Moles, J.L. (1988) *Plutarch: Cicero*. Warminster.

Moles, J.L. (1995) Review of Badian 1993 in *JHS* 115: 213–15.

Momigliano, A.D. (1978) 'The historians of the classical world and their audiences: some suggestions', *ASNSP* iii.8: 59–75, reprinted in *Sesto Contributo alla Storia degli Studi Classici e del Mondo Antico* 1980: 361–76.

Momigliano, A.D. (1985) 'Marcel Mauss and the quest for the person in Greek biography and autobiography', in *Category of the Person* (eds M. Carrithers, S. Collins, and S. Lukes), pp. 83–92. Cambridge.

Momigliano, A.D. (1993) *The Development of Greek Biography* (expanded ed.: original ed. 1971). Cambridge, Mass.

Mossman, J.M. (1995) *Wild Justice: a Study of Euripides'* Hecuba. Oxford.

Mossman, J.M. (ed.) (1997) *Plutarch and his Intellectual World*. London and Swansea.

Murnaghan, S. (1988) 'How a woman can be more like a man: the dialogue between Ischomachus and his wife in Xenophon's *Oeconomicus*', *Helios* 15: 19–22.

Murray, O. (1990) 'The affair of the Mysteries: democracy and the drinking group', in *Sympotica, a Symposium on the Symposium* (ed. O. Murray), pp. 149–61. Oxford.

Murray, O. and Price, S. (eds) (1990) *The Greek City from Homer to Alexander*. Oxford.

Nails, D. (1985) 'The shrewish wife of Socrates', *EMC/CV* 29: 97–9.

Nock, A.D. (1972) *Essays on Religion and the Ancient World* (ed. Z. Stewart). Oxford.

Nouhaud, M. (1982) *L'utilisation de l'Histoire par les Orateurs Attiques*. Paris.

Ober, J. (1989) *Mass and Elite in Democratic Athens: Rhetoric, Ideology, and the Power of the People*. Princeton.

Ogden, D. (1996) *Greek Bastardy in the Classical and Hellenistic Periods*. Oxford.

Ogden, D. (1997) 'Rape, adultery, and the protection of bloodlines in classical Athens', in Deacy and Pierce 1997: 25–41.

Olson, S.D. (1998) *Aristophanes: Peace*. Oxford.

Omitowoju, R. (1997) 'Regulating rape: soap operas and self-interest in the Athenian courts', in Deacy and Pierce 1997: 1–24.

Osborne, M.J. (1983) *Naturalization in Athens* i, ii, and iii/iv. Brussels.

Osborne, R. (1985a) *Demos: the Discovery of Classical Attika*. Cambridge.

Osborne, R. (1985b) 'The erection and mutilation of the Hermae', *PCPS* n.s. 31: 47–73.

Osborne, R. (1985c) 'Law in action in classical Athens', *JHS* 105: 40–58.

Osborne, R. (1987) *Classical Landscape with Figures: the Ancient Greek City and its Countryside*. London.

Osborne, R. (1996) *Greece in the Making, 1200–479 B.C.* London.

Osborne, R. and Hornblower, S. (eds) (1994) *Ritual, Finance, Politics; Athenian Democratic Accounts presented to David Lewis*. Oxford.

Ostwald, M. (1986) *From Popular Sovereignty to the Sovereignty of Law: Law, Society, and Politics in Fifth-century Athens*. California.

Ostwald, M. (1988) Ἀνάγκη *in Thucydides* (American Classical Studies 18). Atlanta.

Papke, D. (ed.) (1991) *Narrative and the Legal Discourse: a Reader in Storytelling and the Law*. Liverpool.

Parker, L.P.E. (1991) 'Eupolis or Dicaeopolis?', *JHS* 111: 203–8.

Parker, R. (1983) *Miasma: Pollution and Purification in Early Greek Religion*. Oxford.

Parker, R. (1997) 'Gods cruel and kind', in Pelling 1997a: 143–60.

Pelling, C.B.R. (1980) 'Plutarch's adaptation of his source-material', *JHS* 100: 127–41, reprinted in Scardigli 1995: 125–54.

Pelling, C.B.R. (1986a) 'Synkrisis in Plutarch's *Lives*', in *Miscellanea Plutarchea, Quad. Giorn. Fil. Ferr.* 8: 83–96.

Pelling, C.B.R. (1986b) 'Plutarch and Roman politics', in *Past Perspectives: Studies in Greek and Roman Historical Writing* (eds I.S. Moxon, J.D. Smart, and A.J. Woodman), pp. 159–87. Cambridge. Reprinted in Scardigli 1995: 319–56.

Pelling, C.B.R. (1988a) *Plutarch: Life of Antony*. Cambridge.

Pelling, C.B.R. (1988b) 'Aspects of Plutarch's characterisation', *ICS* 13.2: 257–74.

Pelling, C.B.R. (ed.) (1990a) *Characterization and Individuality in Greek Literature*. Oxford.

Pelling, C.B.R. (1990b) 'Truth and fiction in Plutarch's *Lives*', in *Antonine Literature* (ed. D.A. Russell), pp. 19–52. Oxford.

Pelling, C.B.R. (1991) 'Thucydides' Archidamus and Herodotus' Artabanus', in Flower and Toher 1991: 120–42.

Pelling, C.B.R. (1992) 'Plutarch and Thucydides', in *Plutarch and the Historical Tradition* (ed. P.A. Stadter), pp. 10–40. London and New York.

Pelling, C.B.R. (1995) 'The moralism of Plutarch's *Lives*', in *Ethics and Rhetoric: Classical Essays for Donald Russell on his seventy-fifth birthday* (eds D. Innes, H. Hine, and C. Pelling), pp. 205–20. Oxford.

Pelling, C.B.R. (1996) 'The urine and the vine: Astyages' dreams (Herodotus 1.107–8)', *CQ* 46: 68–77.

Pelling, C.B.R. (ed.) (1997a) *Greek Tragedy and the Historian*. Oxford.

Pelling, C.B.R. (1997b) 'Aeschylus' *Persae* and history', in Pelling 1997a: 1–19.

Pelling, C.B.R. (1997c) 'Conclusion: Tragedy as evidence' and 'Tragedy and ideology', in Pelling 1997a: 213–35.

Pelling, C.B.R. (1997d) 'East is East and West is West – or are they? National characteristics in Herodotus', *Histos* 1, posted on World Wide Web March 1997.

Pelling, C.B.R. (1997e) 'Plutarch on Caesar's fall', in Mossman 1997: 215–32.

Pelling, C.B.R. (1997f) 'Is death the end? Closure in Plutarch's *Lives*', in *Classical Closure: Endings in Ancient Literature* (eds F. Dunn, D. Fowler, and D. Roberts), pp. 228–50. Princeton.

Pelling, C.B.R. (1997g) 'The shaping of *Coriolanus*: Dionysius, Plutarch, and Shakespeare', in *Shakespeare's Plutarch* (ed. M.A. McGrail), *Poetica* 48: 3–32.

Pelling, C.B.R. (1997h) *Plutarco: Filopemene e Tito Flaminino* (with Italian translation of text by E. Melandri). Firenze.

Pelling, C.B.R. (1999a) 'Modern fantasy and ancient dreams', in Sullivan and White 1999: 15–31.

Pelling, C.B.R. (1999b) 'Epilogue', in Kraus 1999: 325–60.

Pierce, K.F. (1997) 'The portrayal of rape in New Comedy', in Deacy and Pierce 1997: 163–84.

Podlecki, A.J. (1966) *The Political Background of Aeschylean Tragedy*. Ann Arbor.

Podlecki, A.J. (1977) 'Herodotus in Athens?', in *Greece and the Eastern Mediterranean in Ancient History and Prehistory* (*Studies presented to Fritz Schachermeyr...*) (ed. K. Kinzl), pp. 246–65. Berlin and New York.

Pomeroy, S.B. (1975) *Goddesses, Whores, Wives, and Slaves: Women in Classical Antiquity*. New York.

Pomeroy, S.B. (1994) *Xenophon, Oeconomicus: a Social and Historical Commentary*. Oxford.

Porter, J.M. (1997) 'Adultery by the book: Lysias 1 (*On the Murder of Eratosthenes*) and comic *diegesis*', *EMC/CV* 41: 421–53.

Posner, R.A. (1988) *Law and Literature: a Misunderstood Relation*. Cambridge, Mass. and London.

Powell, C.A. (1979) 'Religion and the Sicilian expedition', *Historia* 28: 15–31.

Price, A.W. (1989) *Love and Friendship in Plato and Aristotle*. Oxford.

Quincey, J.H. (1964) 'Orestes and the Argive alliance', *CQ* 14: 190–206.

Rau, P. (1967) *Paratragodia: Untersuchungen einer komischen Form des Aristophanes* (*Zetemata* 45). München.

Raubitschek, A.E. (1948) 'The case against Alcibiades (Andokides IV)', *TAPA* 79: 191–210, reprinted in Raubitschek 1991: 116–31.

Raubitschek, A.E. (1955) 'Theopompus on Hyperbolos', *Phoenix* 9: 122–6, reprinted in Raubitschek 1991: 320–4.

Raubitschek, A.E. (1958) 'Theophrastus on ostracism', *C&M* 19: 78–109, reprinted in Raubitschek 1991: 81–107.

Raubitschek, A.E. (1973) 'The speech of the Athenians at Sparta', in Stadter 1973: 32–48.

Raubitschek, A.E. (1991) *The School of Hellas*. New York.

Rawlings, H.R. III (1975) *A Semantic Study of PROPHASIS to 400 B.C. (Hermes* Einselschriften 33). Wiesbaden.

Rawlings, H.R. III (1979) 'The *Arche* of Thucydides' War', in *Arktouros: Hellenic Studies presented to B.M.W. Knox on … his 65th birthday* (eds G. Bowersock, W. Burkert, and M.C.J. Putnam), pp. 272–9. Berlin.

Rawlings, H.R. III (1981) *The Structure of Thucydides' History*. Princeton.

Rawson, E. (1972) 'Aspects of Euripides' *Orestes*', *Arethusa* 5: 155–67.

Reckford, K. (1987) *Aristophanes' Old-and-New Comedy*. Chapel Hill.

Reinhardt, K. (1949) *Aischylos als Regisseur und Theologe*. Berne.

Rhodes, P.J. (1979) 'Εἰσαγγελία in Athens', *JHS* 99: 103–14.

Rhodes, P.J. (1981) *A Commentary on the Aristotelian Athenaion Politeia*. Oxford.

Rhodes, P.J. (1985) *The Athenian Boule* (2nd ed.: first ed. 1972). Oxford.

Rhodes, P.J. (1986) 'Political activity in classical Athens', *JHS* 106: 132–44.

Rhodes, P.J. (1987) 'Thucydides on the causes of the Peloponnesian War', *Hermes* 115: 154–65.

Rhodes, P.J. (1994) 'The ostracism of Hyperbolus', in Osborne and Hornblower 1994: 85–98.

Richardson, J. (1990) 'Thucydides 1.23.6 and the debate about the Peloponnesian War', in *Owls to Athens: Essays on Classical Subjects presented to Sir Kenneth Dover* (ed. E.M. Craik), pp. 155–61. Oxford.

Riginos, A. (1976) *Platonica*. Leiden.

Robinson, P. (1985) 'Why do we believe Thucydides? A comment on W.R. Connor's "Narrative discourse in Thucydides" ', in *The Greek Historians: Literature and History: Papers presented to A.E. Raubitschek*, pp. 19–23. Stanford.

Robson, J.E. (1997) 'Bestiality and bestial rape in Greek myth', in Deacy and Pierce 1997: 65–96.

Rood, T.C.B. (1998) *Thucydides: Narrative and Explanation*. Oxford.

Rood, T.C.B. (1999) 'Thucydides' Persian Wars', in Kraus 1999: 141–68.

Rosen, R.M. (1988) *Old Comedy and the Iambographic Tradition*. Atlanta.

Rosen, R.M. and Farrell, J. (eds) (1993) *Nomodeiktes: Greek Studies in honor of Martin Ostwald*. Michigan.

Roy, J. (1991) 'Traditional jokes about the punishment of adulterers in ancient Greek literature', *LCM* 16.5: 73–6.

Russell, D.A. (1963) 'Plutarch's *Life* of Coriolanus', *JRS* 53: 21–8, reprinted in Scardigli 1995: 357–72.

Russell, D.A. (1966) 'Plutarch, *Alcibiades* 1–16', *PCPS* 12: 37–47, reprinted in Scardigli 1995: 191–205.

Russo, C.F. (1994) *Aristophanes, an Author for the Stage* (tr. K. Wren: Italian original 1962). London.

Rusten, J.S. (1989) *Thucydides: the Peloponnesian War, Book II*. Cambridge.

Saïd, S. (1979) 'L'assemblée des femmes: les femmes, l'économie et la politique', in *Aristophane, les Femmes et la Cité*, Les Cahiers de Fontenay, Fontenay-aux-Roses École Normale Supérieure 17: 33–69, reprinted and translated as '*The assemblywomen*: women, economy, and politics' in Segal 1996: 282–313.

Saller, R. (1980) 'Anecdotes as historical evidence for the principate', *G&R* 27: 69–83.

Sansone, D. (1985) 'The date of Herodotus' publication', *ICS* 10: 1–9.

Scaife, R. (1992) 'From kottabos to war in Aristophanes' *Acharnians*', *GRBS* 33: 25–35.

Scardigli, B. (ed.) (1995) *Essays on Plutarch's Lives*. Oxford.

Schaps, D.M. (1977) 'The woman least mentioned: etiquette and women's names', *CQ* 27: 323–30.

Schaps, D.M. (1979) *Economic Rights of Women in Ancient Greece*. Edinburgh.

Schneider, C. (1974) *Information und Absicht bei Thukydides*. Göttingen.

Schnurr-Redford, C. (1996) *Frauen im klassischen Athen: Sozialer Raum und reale Bewegungsfreiheit*. Berlin.

Sealey, R. (1957) 'Thucydides, Herodotus, and the causes of war', *CQ* 7: 1–12.

Sealey, R. (1964) 'Ephialtes', *CP* 59: 11–22.

Sealey, R. (1983) 'The Athenian courts for homicide', *CP* 78: 275–96.

Sealey, R. (1991) 'An Athenian decree about the Megarians', in Flower and Toher 1991: 152–8.

Segal, E. (ed.) (1968) *Euripides: a Collection of Critical Essays*. Englewood Cliffs.

Segal, E. (ed.) (1996) *Oxford Readings in Greek Tragedy*. Oxford.

Shaw, M. (1975) 'The female intruder: women in fifth-century drama', *CP* 70: 255–66.

Siewert, P. (1979) 'Poseidon Hippios am Kolonos und die athenischen Hippeis', in *Arktouros: Hellenic Studies presented to Bernard M.W. Knox...* (eds G.W. Bowersock, W. Burkert, and M.C.J. Putnam), pp. 280–9. Berlin and New York.

Silk, M.S. (1993) 'Aristophanic paratragedy', in Sommerstein, Halliwell, Henderson, and Zimmermann 1993: 477–504.

Silk, M.S. (ed.) (1996) *Tragedy and the Tragic: Greek Tragedy and Beyond*. Oxford.

Slater, N.W. (1989) 'Aristophanes' apprenticeship again', *GRBS* 30: 67–82.

Smart, J.D. (1986) 'Thucydides and Hellanicus', in *Past Perspectives: Studies in Greek and Roman Historical Writing* (eds I.S. Moxon, J.D. Smart, and A.J. Woodman), pp. 19–35. Cambridge.

Sommerstein, A.H. (1980) *Aristophanes: Acharnians*. Warminster.

Sommerstein, A.H. (1981) *Aristophanes: Knights*. Warminster.

Sommerstein, A.H. (1983) *Aristophanes: Wasps*. Warminster.

Sommerstein, A.H. (1986) 'The decree of Syrakosios', *CQ* 36: 101–8.

Sommerstein, A.H. (1989) *Aeschylus, Eumenides*. Cambridge.

Sommerstein, A.H. (1990) *Aristophanes: Lysistrata*. Warminster.

Sommerstein, A.H. (1994) *Aristophanes: Thesmophoriazusae*. Warminster.

Sommerstein, A.H. (1997) 'The theatre audience, the *Demos*, and the *Suppliants* of Aeschylus', in Pelling 1997a: 63–79.

Sommerstein, A.H. (1998a) 'The theatre audience and the demos', in *La Comedie Griega y su Influenca en la Literature Española* (ed. J.A. López Férez), pp. 43–62. Madrid.

Sommerstein, A.H. (1998b) *Aristophanes: Ecclesiazusae*. Warminster.

Sommerstein, A.H., Halliwell, S., Henderson, J., and Zimmermann, B. (eds) (1993) *Tragedy, Comedy, and the Polis: Papers from the Greek Drama Conference, Nottingham, 18–20 July 1990* (Bari).

Sourvinou, C. (1971) 'Aristophanes, *Lysistrata*, 641–7', *CQ* 21: 339–42.

Sourvinou-Inwood, C. (1987) 'A series of erotic pursuits: images and meanings', *JHS* 107: 131–53, reprinted in Sourvinou-Inwood 1991: 58–98.

Sourvinou-Inwood, C. (1988) *Studies in Girls' Transitions: Aspects of the Arkteia and Age Representation in Attic Iconography*. Athens.

Sourvinou-Inwood, C. (1989) 'Assumptions and the creation of meaning: reading Sophocles' *Antigone*', *JHS* 109: 134–48.

Sourvinou-Inwood, C. (1990) 'What is polis religion?', in Murray and Price 1990: 295–322.

Sourvinou-Inwood, C. (1991) *'Reading' Greek Culture*. Oxford.

Sourvinou-Inwood, C. (1995) 'Male and female, public and private, ancient and modern', in *Pandora* (ed. E.D. Reeder), pp. 111–20. Baltimore.

Sourvinou-Inwood, C. (1997) 'Medea at a shifting distance: images and Euripidean tragedy', in *Medea: Essays on Medea in Myth, Literature, Philosophy, and Art* (eds J.J. Clauss and S.I. Johnston), pp. 253–96. Princeton.

Sourvinou-Inwood, C. (forthcoming) *Women, Religion, and Tragedy: Readings in Drama and the Polis Discourse*.

Spence, I.G. (1993) *The Cavalry of Classical Greece*. Oxford.

Stadter, P.A. (ed.) (1973) *The Speeches in Thucydides*. Chapel Hill.

Stadter, P.A. (1975) 'Plutarch's comparison of Pericles and Fabius Maximus', *GRBS* 16: 77–85, reprinted in Scardigli 1995: 155–64.

Stadter, P.A. (1983) 'The motives for Athens' alliance with Corcyra', *GRBS* 24: 131–6.

Stadter, P.A. (1984) 'Plutarch, Charinus and the Megarian Decree', *GRBS* 25: 351–72.

Stadter, P.A. (1989) *A Commentary on Plutarch's* Pericles. London and Chapel Hill.

Stadter, P.A. (1992) 'Paradoxical paradigms: *Lysander* and *Sulla*', in *Plutarch and the Historical Tradition* (ed. P. Stadter), pp. 41–55. London and New York.

Stadter, P.A. (1993) 'The form and content of Thucydides' Pentecontaetia', *GRBS* 34: 35–72.

Stadter, P.A. (1997) 'Herodotus and the North Carolina oral narrative tradition', *Histos* 1, posted on World Wide Web January 1997.

Stahl, H.-P. (1966) *Thukydides: die Stellung des Menschen im geschichtlichen Prozeß* (Zetemata 40). München.

Stallybrass, P. and White, A. (1986) *The Politics and Poetics of Transgression*. London.

Stevens, E.B. (1944) 'Some Attic commonplaces of pity', *AJP* 65: 1–25.

Stinton, T.C.W. (1975) '*Hamartia* in Aristotle and Greek tragedy', *CQ* 25: 221–54, reprinted in Stinton 1990: 143–85.

Stinton, T.C.W. (1990) *Collected Papers on Greek Tragedy*. Oxford.

Storey, I.C. (1985) 'The symposium at *Wasps* 1299 ff.', *Phoenix* 39: 317–33.

Storey, I.C. (1993) 'Notus est omnibus Eupolis?', in Sommerstein, Halliwell, Henderson, and Zimmermann 1993: 373–96.

Sullivan, C. and White, B. (eds) (1999) *Writing and Fantasy*. London.

Sutton, D.F. (1988) 'Dicaeopolis as Aristophanes, Aristophanes as Dicaeopolis', *LCM* 13.7: 105–8.

Taaffe, L.K. (1993) *Aristophanes and Women*. London.

Taplin, O.P. (1977) *The Stagecraft of Aeschylus*. Oxford.

Taplin, O.P. (1983) 'Tragedy and trugedy', *CQ* 33: 331–3.

Taplin, O.P. (1986) 'Fifth-century Tragedy and Comedy: a Synkrisis', *JHS* 106, 163–74, reprinted in Segal 1996: 9–28.

Theander, C. (1951) *Plutarch und die Geschichte*. Lund.

Thomas, R. (1989) *Oral Tradition and Written Record in Classical Athens*. Cambridge.

Thomas, R. (1991) *Literacy and Orality in Ancient Greece*. Cambridge.

Thomas, R. (1993) 'Performance and written publication in Herodotus and the sophisticated generation', in *Vermittlung und Tradierung von Wissen in der griechischen Kultur* (eds W. Kullmann and J. Althoff), pp. 225–44. Tübingen.

Thür, G. (1977) *Beweisführung vor den Schwurgerichtshöfen Athens. Die Proklesis zur Basanos*. Vienna.

Todd, S. (1990a) 'The purpose of evidence in Athenian courts', in Cartledge, Millett, and Todd 1990: 19–38.

Todd, S. (1990b) '*Lady Chatterley's Lover* and the Attic orators: the social composition of the Athenian jury', *JHS* 110: 146–73.

Todd, S. (1990c) 'The use and abuse of the Attic orators', *G&R* 37: 159–78.

Todd, S. (1993) *The Shape of Athenian Law*. Oxford.

Tompkins, D.P. (1972) 'Stylistic characterization in Thucydides: Nicias and Alcibiades', *YCS* 22: 181–214.

Tompkins, D.P. (1993) 'Archidamus and the question of characterization in Thucydides', in Rosen and Farrell 1993: 99–111.

Trevett, J. (1990) 'History in [Demosthenes] 59', *CQ* 40: 407–20.

Trevett, J. (1992) *Apollodorus the Son of Pasion*. Oxford.

Tuplin, C.J. (1979) 'Thucydides 1.42.2 and the Megarian Decree', *CQ* 29: 301–7.

Ussher, R.G. (1973) *Aristophanes: Ecclesiazusae*. Oxford.

Vaio, J. (1973) 'The manipulation of theme and action in Aristophanes' *Lysistrata*', *GRBS* 14: 369–80.

Veeser, H.A. (ed.) (1989) *The New Historicism*. London and New York.

Vernant, J.P. (1980) *Myth and Society in Ancient Greece* (French original 1974). London.

Vernant, J.P. and Vidal-Naquet, P. (1988) *Myth and Tragedy in Ancient Greece* (tr. J. Lloyd: French originals 1972 and 1986). New York.

Vickers, B. (1973) *Towards Greek Tragedy*. London.

Vickers, M. (1989a) 'Alcibiades on stage: *Thesmophoriazusae* and *Helen*', *Historia* 38: 41–65.

Vickers, M. (1989b) 'Alcibiades on stage: Aristophanes' *Birds*', *Historia* 38: 246–65.

Vickers, M. (1993) 'Alcibiades in Cloudedoverland', in Rosen and Farrell 1993: 603–18.

Vickers, M. (1995a) 'Alcibiades at Sparta: Aristophanes' *Birds*', *CQ* 45: 339–54.

Vickers, M. (1995b) 'Thucydides 6.53.3–59: not a "digression" ', *Dialogues d'Histoire Ancienne* 21.1: 193–200.

Vidal-Naquet, P. (1986) *The Black Hunter* (tr. A. Szegedy-Maszak: French original 1981). Baltimore and London.

Vidal-Naquet, P. (1988) 'Oedipus between two cities: an essay on *Oedipus at Colonus*', in Vernant and Vidal-Naquet 1988: 329–59.

Vidal-Naquet, P. (1997) 'The place and status of foreigners in Athenian tragedy', in Pelling 1997a: 109–19 (French original 1992: *L'étranger dans le monde grec*, pp. 297–313, Nancy).

Von Fritz, K. (1967) *Die griechische Geschichtsschreibung* i–ii. Berlin.

Walker, P.K. (1957) 'The purpose and method of "the Pentekontaetia" in Thucydides, Book I', *CQ* 7: 27–37.

Walker, S. (1993) 'Women and housing in classical Greece: the archaeological evidence', in *Images of Women in Antiquity* (eds A. Cameron and A. Kuhrt), pp. 81–91. London.

Wallace, R.W. (1985) *The Areopagos Council, to 307 B.C.* Baltimore and London.

Weidauer, K. (1954) *Thukydides und die Hippokratischen Schriften*. Heidelberg.

Weisberg, R. (1992) *Poethics and other Strategies of Law and Literature*. New York.

West, M.L. (1968) 'Two passages of Aristophanes', *CR* 18: 5–8.

West, M.L. (1987) *Euripides, Orestes*. Warminster.

West, R. (1993) *Narrative, Authority, and Law*. Michigan.

Westlake, H.D. (1969) *Essays on the Greek Historians and Greek History*. Manchester.

Westlake, H.D. (1973) 'The settings of Thucydidean speeches', in Stadter 1973: 90–108.

Wille, G. (1965) 'Zu Stil und Methode des Thukydides', in *Synusia, Festgabe für Wolfgang Schadewaldt* (eds H. Flashar and K. Gaiser), pp. 57–77. Pfullingen. Reprinted in Herter 1968: 700–16.

Willink, C.W. (1986) *Euripides: Orestes*. Oxford.

Wilson, A.M. (1977) 'The individualized chorus in Old Comedy', *CQ* 27: 278–83.

Wilson, J. (1982) 'What does Thucydides claim for his speeches?', *Phoenix* 36: 95–103.

Wilson, P.J. (1997) 'Leading the tragic *khoros*: tragic prestige in the democratic city', in Pelling 1997a: 81–108.

Winkler, J.J. and Zeitlin, F.I. (eds) (1990) *Nothing to do with Dionysos? Athenian Drama in its Social Context*. Princeton.

Woodhead, A.G. (1949) '*IG* I².95 and the ostracism of Hyperbolus', *Hesperia* 18: 78–83.

Worthington, I. (1992) *A Historical Commentary on Dinarchus*. Michigan.

Worthington, I. (ed.) (1994) *Persuasion: Greek Rhetoric in Action*. London and New York.

Zanker, P. (1988) *The Power of Images in the Age of Augustus* (German original 1987). Michigan.

Zeitlin, F.I. (1980) 'The closet of masks: role-playing and myth-making in the *Orestes* of Euripides', *Ramus* 9: 51–77.

Zeitlin, F.I. (1981) 'Travesties of gender and genre in Aristophanes' *Thesmophoriazusae*', in Foley 1981a: 169–217.

Zeitlin, F.I. (1990) 'Playing the Other: theater, theatricality, and the feminine in Greek drama', in Winkler and Zeitlin 1990: 63–96.

Zuntz, G. (1955) *The Political Plays of Euripides*. Manchester.

# General index

Phaeax 49–51, 57
Phano 66, 192
Pharnabazus 57
Pheidias 128, 151–2, 286 n. 32
Phocaea 56
Phocis 63–4
Phoenicia and Phoenicians 86, 154, 169
Phorbanteion 31, 37
Phrynichus 57, 59, 186
Piraeus 91
Pity 11–12, 122, 180, 207–8, 248, 293 n. 63, 297 n. 40
Plataea 62–81, 86, 94–5, 117, 252
Pledges 39–40
Poirot, Hercule, and 'Poirots' 34–5, 75–7, 101, 130, 149, 251, 274 n. 14, 279 n. 31
Poland 95, 103
Pomeroy, Sarah B. 191, 239
Potidaea 82, 88–90, 100–1, 104–5, 107, 114, 119, 267 n. 1
Profumo, Sir John 27
*prophasis* 85–8, 93, 112, 268 n. 9
*prytaneis* 131, 165
Pylos 265 n. 44
Pythia 216
Pythonicus 27, 35

Rabelais, François 277 n. 8
Radishes 226, 247
Rape 134, 217, 227–31
Reagan, Ronald 134
Reception-criticism 58–9
Revision before publication 301 n. 89
Rhodes, P.J. 95
Rigg, Dame Diana 144
Russia 102–3

Saddam Hussein 95
Salaethus 264 n. 31
Salaminia 21
Salamis 258 n. 45
Samos 39, 53, 92, 98–9, 281 n. 48
Satyr-plays 205–6
Scione 262 n. 2
Scythians 84, 169
Seclusion 223–4, 230–1, 301 n. 81

Seduction 227–31
Selymbria 46
Seriphus 143
Sicily 18–19, 22–4, 40, 43, 45, 47, 50, 82, 87, 95, 126–7, 184, 188, 260 n. 61, 277–8 n. 14
Sicinnus 11
Simaetha 142, 151–5, 158, 159, 251, 286 n. 38
Simpson, O.J. 36
Slaves 193, 232–4, 242–3, 304 nn. 122–4
Socrates 7, 123, 138, 236–45, 279 n. 36
Solon 230, 302–3 n. 97
Sommerstein, A.H. 131, 197
Sparta 3, 8, 19–21, 24–5, 54, 57, 59, 61–122, 142–3, 151–2, 156, 168, 171, 180
Spercheius 64
*Star Trek* 277 n. 13
Stephanus 61, 66, 191–2, 249–50
Sthenelaidas 92, 98, 113
Sycophants 126, 156, 216
*symposia* 21, 37–8, 128, 136–40
Syracosius 281 n. 48
Syracuse 25, 47–52, 126–7

Taplin, Oliver 164
Teucrus 27, 33, 35, 39
Thatcher, Baroness (Margaret) 123, 134, 148, 160, 215
Theagenes 66
Thebes 62–81, 159, 165, 173, 180–2
Themistocles 8, 11, 38, 82, 90–1
Theognis 130
Theomnestus 192
*theorikon* 135
Theramenes 54, 166, 186
Theseion 21, 24
Thesmophoria 224; *see also* Aristophanes: *Thesmophoriazusae*
Thespiae 77
Thessalus 27–8
Thirty Years' Peace 97–8, 100–1, 104, 270 n. 34
Tholos 29
Thrace and Thracians 67, 82, 141
Thrasybulus son of Lycus 56

# Index of authors and texts